10-17   1277.2   -   13.3 gals

SPORTSMANLIKE DRIVING

SPORTSMANLIKE

Third, Revised Edition

DRIVING

Published by

AMERICAN AUTOMOBILE ASSOCIATION

WASHINGTON, D.C.

FOREWORD

I T I S M Y belief that a program of high school Driver Education is the most effective, long range means of reducing traffic accidents. By having professionally trained educators apply to a program of Driver Education those techniques and methods that they have so successfully developed and used in other areas of instruction assures maximum results. Such instruction conducted in the high schools of the nation has the added advantage of reaching practically all future drivers.

Thomas D. Bailey
President, National Council of Chief State School Officers; and Superintendent of Public Instruction, Florida State Department of Education.

A S W E C O N T I N U E together in what may be termed the Atomic Age, we may forget that, however interesting a challenge the Atomic Age may become, we shall not live to see what happens if we do not understand and practice sportsmanlike driving.

As one interested in safety education for many years, it is my sincere hope that every high school in America will undertake regular and systematic courses in Driver Education—a necessity of our modern industrial age. Only in such a manner can we rear a new generation of competent drivers. Today, only drivers who are competent can be good citizens.

Henry H. Hill
President, George Peabody College for Teachers; formerly President of the American Association of School Administrators of the National Education Association; and formerly Chairman of the "Commission on Safety Education" which produced the 1940 AASA Yearbook, "Safety Education."

D R I V E R E D U C A T I O N is functional education at its best. The business of schools and colleges is to make successes—not failures. This principle has never been, and I venture to say never will be, more true than when applied to the educational task of preparing safe drivers. In our complex traffic society, people must be taught safe habits and practices. Through quality Driver Education programs, youths learn self-discipline, self-guidance, and self-protection. They develop social-consciousness and concern for the rights and safety of others. This life-centered learning is not an end in itself. Rather, it is a means to that greater end—a good life.

Norman Key
Executive Secretary, National Commission on Safety Education, National Education Association.

TWO PRACTICAL outcomes of high school Driver Education have special appeal to women—the safeguarding of life and the development of self-reliance. Traditionally, women are deeply concerned with the well-being of youth. So they naturally welcome the offering of Driver Education courses by an increasing number of high schools.

There was a day when young people spent more time in the close protection of the home. Now, with the new freedom to come and go in cars, new kinds of youth education are required. As a part of their school education, our young people need to develop the skills and attitudes that will make them self-reliant, responsible citizens of the world in which they live.

Mrs. Raymond Sayre
Member of The President's Action Committee for Traffic Safety, representing national women's organizations.

THE VALUE of any community to the human beings of which it is composed depends almost entirely upon the attitudes and habits of cooperation exercised by its members for the achievement of their common purposes. The growth and effectiveness of any group, whether it be a club, a church, a town, a state, a nation, or a world, is dependent upon the exercise of these attitudes and habits of cooperating intelligently for the common welfare of all members. No other subject taught in our schools is more highly motivated than learning to drive a car, and no other subject provides the learner greater satisfactions than learning, as a member of the traffic pattern, to exercise effectively the basic attitudes and habits of a good citizen.

M. R. Trabue
Dean, College of Education, The Pennsylvania State University; former Chairman of the National Commission on Safety Education, National Education Association; and Past President of the American Association of Colleges for Teacher Education.

INTRODUCTION

In the decades ahead, highway transportation is destined to occupy an increasingly significant place in the life and development of our country. It therefore will become even more important that every young person develop the fundamental understandings necessary for assuming his responsibilities as a Motor Age Citizen. Great emphasis is placed on these concepts in this new edition of "Sportsmanlike Driving."

In its two previous editions, "Sportsmanlike Driving" has been the most widely-used textbook in Driver Education in the high schools of the United States. According to a recent, country-wide study, made by the leading national organization of educators, more than four-fifths of the schools offering up-to-standard courses in the subject use "Sportsmanlike Driving" as their text. This attests to its educational soundness and acceptance.

The rapidly growing numbers of school administrators, college professors, classroom teachers, and high school students experienced in Driver Education constituted an important resource used for guidance in revising this text. They have advised on selection and reorganization of content, relative emphasis on particular subjects, and on the grade leveling of the material.

The revised book is set up in five Parts, offering five units of instruction which can be used flexibly. The unit treating of practice driving is placed second, following advice of the majority of Driver Education teachers responding to a prerevision questionnaire.

In addition to being rewritten, reorganized, and brought up-to-date, this edition contains two new chapters: "Learning to Drive Cars with Automatic Transmissions" and "Driving Under Unfavorable and Special Conditions." The artwork, new throughout, has been carefully developed for technical accuracy, instructional clarity, appeal to youth, and functional use of a second color.

Part i, The Driver, orients the student in the Motor Age. It also analyzes physical, mental, and emotional characteristics as they affect driving, and is topped off by an analysis of driver psychology which young drivers are not likely to forget.

Part ii, Learning How to Drive, covers basic information on the car and how it runs. It provides practical, detailed, step-by-step procedure for use in practice driving in both gearshift and automatic transmission cars.

Part iii, Traffic Laws, treats those natural laws that should be understood by every driver for driving efficiency and safety. It develops the subject of traffic laws and regulations, emphasizing the responsibility of every driver to give voluntary observance to such regulations. It develops also the principles of modern, selective, traffic law enforcement.

Part IV, SOUND TRAFFIC PRACTICES, presents sound driving suggestions for the open road, for urban areas, and under driving conditions that are unfavorable or demand special knowledge because of topographical or other special features. It develops the need for safe maintenance of the car, and presents information that every driver should have concerning pedestrian traffic.

Part V, YOU AND THE MOTOR AGE, enriches the course with background material important in producing good traffic citizens. It is invaluable in helping build sound, mature, traffic attitudes. It discusses car economy, occupational possibilities in commercial driving, and the demands of the Motor Age in automobile production, highway construction, and traffic engineering.

All five Parts of the book emphasize the building, in young drivers, of the sound attitudes essential to sportsmanlike driving.

The principal writing and reorganizing of this book was done by my associate, Helen K. Knandel, Educational Consultant, American Automobile Association, and formerly of the School of Education of The Pennsylvania State University, chosen for this writing because of much work on earlier editions and because of her background of training and experience in Educational Psychology. Principal editing of the manuscript was done by Mrs. Knandel, W. L. Robinson, Associate Director of the Department, and by the writer. Mr. Robinson and Mrs. Knandel were responsible for guiding the artwork and assisting the book designer, Andor Braun of the Kingsport Press, Inc., in creating the styling and preparing the material for the printer.

For critical review of the entire manuscript and for valuable contributions, acknowledgment is made to associates on the Department staff: Earl Allgaier, Charles N. Brady, Harold O. Carlton, and Amos E. Neyhart.

The steps developed in Part II for use in practice driving are an outgrowth of original outlines on the subject by Amos E. Neyhart, Administrative Head, Institute of Public Safety, The Pennsylvania State University, and Consultant on Road Training, American Automobile Association, and of his later experiences, and those of Harold O. Carlton, Educational Consultant in teacher preparation, American Automobile Association.

The McCoy Art Studio did most of the illustrations. Louis H. Calnek produced many of the cartoons, and Spencer Hart a number of drawings. Edward C. Michener, of Michener and O'Connor, created the cover design.

Burton W. Marsh,
Director, Traffic Engineering and Safety Department
American Automobile Association

ACKNOWLEDGMENTS

FOR REVIEWING special chapters of this edition in manuscript, and for professional and technical suggestions, grateful acknowledgment is made to:
Donald Blanchard, Secretary, Technical Board, Society of Automotive
Engineers
J. Allen Davis, General Counsel, Automobile Club of Southern California
Howard K. Gandelot, General Motors Engineering Staff, General Motors
Corporation
Hal H. Hale, Assistant to the Vice President—Highway Transportation,
Association of American Railroads.
Carl F. Hansson, Chief of Police, Dallas, Texas
Joseph E. Havenner, Manager, Public Safety Department, Automobile
Club of Southern California
George E. Keneipp, Director of Vehicles and Traffic, Washington, D.C.
Norman Key, Secretary, National Commission on Safety Education, National Education Association
John H. King, Automobile Manufacturers Association
Col. Franklin M. Kreml, Director, Northwestern University Traffic Institute
Alvhh R. Lauer, Professor of Psychology, Iowa State College
Miss Jean McGregor, Physics Instructor, McKinley Tech High School,
Washington, D.C.
W. F. Sherman, Manager, Engineering and Technical Department, Automobile Manufacturers Association
C. W. Stark, Consultant, National Committee on Uniform Traffic Laws
and Ordinances
Robert J. Test, then of American Trucking Associations, Inc.
Marion R. Trabue, Dean, School of Education, The Pennsylvania State
University
John S. Urlaub, Director of Driver Education, Berkeley, California, High
School
Cecil Zaun, Supervisor, Health and Safety Education, Los Angeles City
Schools, Los Angeles, California
We wish to express appreciation also to associates in other Departments of
the American Automobile Association: Charles C. Collins, LeVerne Johnson,
J. H. Lamb, A. J. Montgomery, Ross D. Netherton, James L. Reardon, and
K. B. Rykken, as well as to additional associates on the staff of this Department: William L. Carson, J. E. Johnston, and Claud R. McCamment.
In connection with previous editions, we acknowledge the assistance of:
W. Roy Breg, then Executive Secretary, Allied Youth, Inc.
William J. Cox, then of Yale University
Roy W. Crum, then Director, Highway Research Board
Maurice R. Davie, then of Yale University
R. J. Devereaux, The B. F. Goodrich Company

Dr. H. C. Dickinson, then with the National Bureau of Standards

Robert W. Eaves, now Executive Secretary, Department of Elementary School Principals, National Education Association

John W. Gibbons, Director, Public Relations, Automotive Safety Foundation

William M. Greene, Director, Connecticut Highway Safety Commission

Harold F. Hammond, now Executive Vice President, Transportation Association of America

John E. Kane, American Petroleum Industries Committee

G. Donald Kennedy, President, Portland Cement Association

J. Willard Lord, now Fleet Safety and Motor Maintenance Consultant

D. Grant Mickle, Director, Traffic Engineering Division, Automotive Safety Foundation

Ralph A. Moyer, Institute of Transportation and Traffic Engineering, University of California

H. G. Odgers, Director of Safety Education, Dearborn, Michigan, Public Schools

R. E. Royall, Chief, Division of Research Reports and Statistics, U.S. Bureau of Public Roads

Edwin H. Silver, then Chairman, Motor Vision Commission, American Optometric Association

Peter J. Stupka, then with the American Automobile Association

George R. Wellington, then Chief, Section of Safety, Interstate Commerce Commission

Sidney J. Williams, Assistant to the President, National Safety Council

For reviewing the manuscript of "Learning to Drive Cars with Automatic Transmissions," adapted for use in this book, we acknowledge the generous help of the following men whose industry connections then were:

C. F. Arnold, Chief Engineer, Cadillac Motor Car Division, General Motors Corporation

Frank R. Austermann, Department of Technical Data and Information, Chrysler Corporation

Ralph F. Beck, Staff Engineer, Detroit Transmission Division, General Motors Corporation

N. L. Blume, Lincoln-Mercury Car Engineer, Ford Motor Company

B. W. Bogan, Chief Engineer, Dodge Division, Chrysler Corporation

G. A. Delaney, Chief Engineer, Pontiac Motor Division, General Motors Corporation

J. R. Ferguson, Chief Engineer, Automotive Division, Packard Motor Car Company

George A. Hirshman, Administrative Engineer, Oldsmobile Division, General Motors Corporation

Ralph H. Houghton, Administrative Services Department, Ford Motor Company

R. F. Kohr, Executive Engineer, General Engineering Office, Ford Motor Company

A. G. Laas, Chief Product Engineer, The Studebaker Corporation

G. C. Lind, Engineering Department, Technical Data Group, Chevrolet Division, General Motors Corporation

V. P. Mathews, Chief Engineer, Buick Motor Division, General Motors Corporation

M. E. St. Aubin, Director, Service Section, General Motors Corporation

M. H. Toncray, Chief Engineer, Hudson Motor Car Company

CONTENTS

PART ONE
THE DRIVER

PART TWO

LEARNING HOW TO DRIVE

PART THREE

TRAFFIC LAWS

xiii

PART FIVE

YOU AND THE MOTOR AGE

SPORTSMANLIKE DRIVING

A POWER AGE

WE LIVE in a Power Age.

We still find ourselves speaking of power in terms of the horse. For not so long ago the power of a horse to do man's work was top-ranking power, and we accepted it as an easy unit of power measurement.

But the power of a single horse now seems puny indeed. For, in our day, man has learned to produce and harness power almost beyond his own measurement and comprehension.

The *rate* at which man is multiplying the power at his command has increased amazingly in the lifetime of each of us. Man required centuries to learn to increase his own manpower by making good use of such simple mechanical principles as the wheel, the lever, and the wedge. Over long periods of time and only gradually, he learned to look to the elemental forces of water, wind, and fire for new sources of power to harness and make do his work.

As the history of mankind goes, it was only yesterday that man tremendously stepped up his available power by inventing the mechanical and electrical machines that introduce the Power Age. Now man has turned for new power to the mighty forces within the atom. He releases the terrible energy of nuclear fission, and thermonuclear energy many times as great. For miraculous new power, he now anticipates harnessing the unfathomable energy forces of the sun. Yes, ours is a Power Age!

THE DRIVER

The forces that give us a Power Age unequaled in history challenge man's control. For the scientific contraptions of man, whether developed through combustion, electricity, or atomic energy, carry out man's will, never any will of their own. The machines themselves cannot learn from experience or act with conscience. They produce results that are destructive or wholesome depending on the understanding and conscience of the men in control. No machine is good or bad. Man behind the machine is wholly responsible for whatever the machine is made to do.

The important question of our age is not how to produce more power but whether or not man's purposes in life are worthy of the power he can now summon to make his wishes and purposes come true. Man must accept the moral responsibility of properly using the power machines he has devised.

3

CHAPTER 1

THE AUTOMOBILE

THE AUTOMOBILE HAS CHANGED OUR LIVES

FOR TRANSPORTATION, the automobile is man's most popular power machine. But its service and satisfaction depend on how well and fairly he uses it.

The American public has accepted the automobile with open arms. Over 55 million motor vehicles are registered in the United States; nearly two-thirds of our families now own cars. Nearly one-half of all employed persons use passenger cars in connection with earning a living.

Because of the automobile, greater changes have occurred in transportation in the last few decades than had occurred in the entire previous history of the world. For business and pleasure, we consider the car a necessary part of our daily life. It has become such an important and common tool in our civilization that training in skillful and sportsmanlike driving is now a necessary part of one's education.

Little more than half a century of the automobile has changed our entire civilization almost beyond recognition.

"Get a horse," people shouted only a generation ago, amused when the early "horseless carriages" broke down.

But the motorist has had the last laugh, for the old carriage society has completely changed to an automotive civilization. The American family has come to think

DO YOU KNOW:
What power means to man?
How the automobile has changed our lives?
Where we have failed in using it?
What we can do to correct the failures?

AND ITS DRIVER

of the automobile as a necessity. American business has thrived on it. The automobile is used more and more for commerce, convenience, and pleasure. We are a people who like to be on wheels.

Civilian use of the automobile suffered a setback during World War II, as is seen clearly by the drop in car registrations shown in Fig. 2. The supply of cars was cut off; gasoline was rationed, travel restricted, and a halt was put to the normal growth in the use of cars.

At the close of the war, rapid increase in traffic volume again got under way. As fast as manufacturing plants could be converted from wartime to peacetime production, people bought new cars, trucks, and buses.

Fig. 1.
"Get a Horse!"

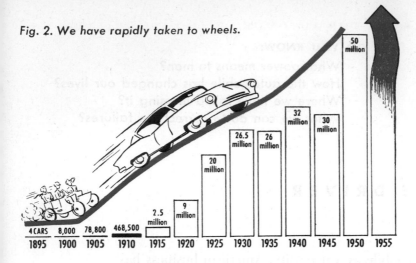

Fig. 2. We have rapidly taken to wheels.

												50 million
4 CARS	8,000	78,800	468,500	2.5 million	9 million	20 million	26.5 million	26 million	32 million	30 million		
1895	1900	1905	1910	1915	1920	1925	1930	1935	1940	1945	1950	1955

Motor vehicle registration has increased almost 60 per cent since the close of the war. It has been mounting at a rate of from 3 to 4 million cars a year.

The automobile is a fine asset to civilization. But it also creates many new and perplexing problems, and it has made a good many changes in our manners and morals.

Changes in Family Activities — AMERICAN FAMILIES have learned to depend on the automobile. Everyday errands by car, driving to work, Dad's fishing trip, the family's summer vacation, an after-dinner drive, or the week-end motor trip—all are accepted features of modern American life. Many parents daily drive their children to school. Large numbers of older students drive themselves.

The car has greatly enriched the leisure-time activities of wage earners. A drive to the baseball park, a swim, or a game of golf can be a matter of a moment's decision on a summer afternoon. Motor trips have become a widespread American custom. Approximately 75 million persons annually take to the road as tourists. Many tourists practically take their homes with them by living in auto trailers.

The car has made everybody in the family so independent and flexible that it tends to lessen what was once a close-knit family life. Family disputes arise over who shall have the car on Saturday night. The car has com-

6

pletely changed social customs, family activities, and
domestic points of view.

ALTHOUGH the automobile has added greatly to the en- **The Automobile**
joyment of life, it has also brought annoyances, incon- **and the City**
veniences, and hazards. **Dweller**

City traffic has become congested and dangerous. Too
many city streets are ill-suited for the motor age. They
were designed for horse-drawn vehicles and are now
called upon to serve a flood of passenger automobiles,
trucks, and buses. In most cases, cities lack both space
and funds to do a satisfactory job of redesigning their
streets to take care of the great masses of present-day
motor traffic. Only where new cities are growing up, or
where new streets are being added in expanding cities,
do we generally find streets well planned for modern
traffic.

The volume of city traffic steadily increases. Space
needed for traffic flow is used up by cars parked at curbs
and the loading and unloading of trucks and buses. The
demand for parking space on city streets far exceeds the
supply. Congestion causes increasing delay and irritation.

The automobile is rapidly changing the city as a place
of residence. Quiet residential streets are often trans-
formed into noisy, dangerous, fume-filled traffic arteries,
which most people like to avoid for residences. In greater
and greater numbers, city dwellers move their residences
away from the central parts of cities.

Fig. 3. Who gets the car!

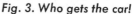

The automobile makes it practical for people to live at considerable distance from their places of employment. So suburban residential areas spring up many miles away from the central city. Such areas have been growing three times as fast as cities. Moving heavy volumes of suburban dwellers to and from cities both morning and evening is creating many new transportation and traffic problems.

The automobile has made a greater need for city playgrounds and neighborhood parks. Playing on city streets has become extremely dangerous to children.

How can we improve city streets and their use for this motor age? How can residential areas be protected? How can traffic be routed, controlled, and kept in flow? How can parking demands be met? These are among the problems that we face in the motor age.

If You Live in the Country HIGHWAYS and automobiles have brought town and country closer together. Farmers and their families easily drive to town on shopping tours.

Larger and more modern rural and suburban communities are being built, with the village or town as the center. Stores, theaters, libraries, and other institutions are expanding in these centers. Churches in the open country are closing; centralized village churches are increasing in membership and activities.

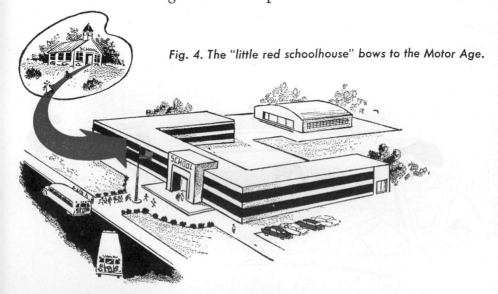

Fig. 4. The "little red schoolhouse" bows to the Motor Age.

Fig. 5. Motor buses will take you anywhere.

The "little red schoolhouse" is giving way to centrally located consolidated schools, built to serve larger areas and provide better teaching facilities. This educational improvement is made possible by good roads and transportation by school bus. Children can now go to school from long distances and in almost any weather.

Good roads and motor transportation have brought improved mail and parcel post service to rural areas. The isolation of the farmer and country folks is a thing of the past.

WITH THE RAPID development of the motor bus, thousands of communities now have good intercity and interstate travel service. A national network of connecting bus routes makes it possible to travel comfortably, conveniently, and economically to almost any point in the United States. More than 25,000 towns in the United States depend entirely on highway transportation. *Travel by Bus*

Passengers annually carried in regular passenger buses and in school buses now number in the billions. School buses alone daily serve approximately 8 million pupils. One out of every four school children rides a school bus to and from school.

The motor bus competes with the railroads but also supplements and "feeds" them. Railroads themselves operate an increasing number of buses, especially for short hauls and to provide "feeder" service for main lines.

Fig. 6. The automobile broadens the business area.

Buses can be routed anywhere. This flexibility of routing assures the bus a permanent place in modern transportation.

There has been a steady growth in the number of buses operated by local transit companies. In a large number of cities, street cars have been entirely replaced by buses, although, in some industrial areas, the street car continues to be a convenient means of mass transportation.

The Motor Truck Just as the car makes man's social community broader, the motor truck extends the area over which he conducts his business affairs.

The truck has rapidly come to the front in carrying both "short-haul" and certain "long-haul" freight. It is flexible in routing and can change its schedule to provide quick, effective service over both short and long distances.

Railroads use trucks increasingly for "door-to-door" freight handling. Trucks enable them to furnish services to the shipper or receiver which were available a few decades ago only by means of slow, horse-drawn drays.

Stores deliver their merchandise by truck over a wide shopping radius. Free delivery service has become flexible and prompt. This has greatly increased trade.

Motor trucks speed up the marketing of agricultural products. Food on the American table today is fresher and more varied than in the days of four-miles-an-hour horse-and-wagon transportation. Farmers deliver daily to markets, creameries, and wholesale food distributing centers. The truck has brought orchards, farms, and dairies close to city residents.

THE AUTOMOBILE is responsible for the employment of great numbers of people. In a short period it has created a vast industry of its own. One out of every seven employed persons receives his income directly or indirectly from the automobile industry.

The Automobile and Employment

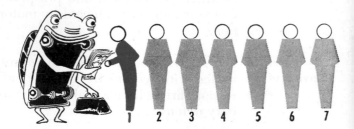

Fig. 7. The auto is there when pay day comes.

The manufacture of automobiles has become a major industry. The sale and distribution of cars means tremendous business growth. Many related industries and businesses have also grown to enormous size. Gasoline production and sale is one example of a business development brought about by the automobile. Tire business is another. So also is the mechanical servicing of cars. In addition, many miles of roadway in the United States have been paved or improved because of the demands of motor traffic. Installment plan purchasing of automobiles has greatly increased the business of banks and finance companies. One business in six is due to the automobile. The automobile is a mighty factor in our economic life.

It is estimated that 10 billion dollars are spent annually by motoring tourists. Many people make a business of serving them. Tourist travel has built up resort areas, developed new towns, and brought about an active and wholesome spirit of competition among cities and states.

11

Good modern hotels and motor courts have been constructed along main highways, to meet the demands of tourists and vacationists. Some 45 thousand comfortable and well-equipped "motels" offer the motorist very attractive accommodations. Rapid growth of this new form of lodging has brought about inspection and control to promote high standards of sanitation.

Millions of dollars have been invested in resort areas, golf courses, sport facilities, state and national parks, and other attractions for the motorist.

In fact, it is difficult to name any business or industry in which employment and prosperity have not been directly or indirectly affected by motor vehicle transportation.

Protective Services of the Auto THE AUTOMOBILE provides many protective services, connected with such matters as law enforcement, crime detection, fire fighting, health and rescue service, and military defense.

Crime Detection In some ways the automobile has made crime easier. With good roads and fast cars, the criminal can act rapidly and make a quick "getaway" to a distant hideout. Legal cases involving car thefts and hit-and-run traffic violations have increased with the rapid growth in use of cars.

Law enforcement officers are greatly aided by motor vehicles. Police cars equipped with two-way radios, and dispatched by means of efficient police broadcasting stations, enable policemen to capture criminals before they can make a "getaway." Fleeing criminals are caught in radio-arranged dragnets. Two-way radio equipment keeps officers in police cars constantly in touch with police headquarters.

Motorized patrol wagons, squad cars, and motorcycles speed to places where police are needed. Stolen cars are detected, burglars tracked down, and criminals speedily caught. Suburban and semi-rural districts now enjoy police protection that was impossible before modern highways and motor vehicles.

Fire Fighting Fire departments move motorized apparatus quickly, even to places far removed from fire stations. Thousands of rural and suburban homes, which once would have been doomed if fire broke out, are now protected.

Health and Rescue Service Safeguards for life have been extended. The motorized ambulance quickly answers a call of distress. Physicians and nurses travel rapidly to scenes of disaster. The car enables the family doctor to visit many more patients and to meet an emergency much faster than his predecessors in the "one-hoss-shay." Motorized rescue units save many lives and are now an important part of Civil Defense Programs across the nation.

Military Service Spectacular advances in recent warfare have closely coordinated the work of mechanized units and aircraft. Motorized units move artillery and other heavy military equipment and also transport troops. Radio-equipped cars control the movements of convoys and play a very important role in battle. There are motorized kitchens, bathhouses, supply units, trucks, ambulances, and command cars.

Huge searchlights are rapidly moved by motorized units to locations where needed. Electric power for their operation is generated on mobile, motor-driven power plants. Antiaircraft equipment, brought up by motor vehicle, can be quickly placed in operation where it will be most effective.

Mechanized tanks and flame-throwers have become the foremost spearhead of lightning-fast military operations. Heavily-armored tanks have earned the name of mobile land forts.

Equipped with all-wheel drives, motorized units are not limited to the highway. They are built with the power and traction to go across country where getting through would seem impossible. They can operate on deserts, on and under water, in the tropics, in the arctic. Some units have automatic transmissions with eight forward speeds and two reverse. Many improvements in civilian cars originate from lessons learned on military vehicles. Land operations of the Navy and Marine Corps make full use of motor vehicles.

The protective service of motorized units was indeed spectacular during World War II. These units will remain equally indispensable in any time of war.

38,000 Killed
1,200,000 Injured
$3 Billion Property Damage
178,500 Pedestrian Injuries and Deaths

Fig. 8. Traffic tragedies in a single year.

TRAFFIC ACCIDENTS

THE AUTOMOBILE, unfortunately, is not always used with proper control. At such times, it is anything but protective. In fact, it has greatly increased the hazards to life, limb, and property.

The number of highway casualties in recent years has been appalling. Between 35 and 40 thousand persons are killed annually in traffic accidents. Over 100 thousand persons are permanently disabled. Over one million suffer lesser injuries. Traffic accidents, in a year's time, injure or wipe out the equivalent of the entire population of a large city. Neither numbers nor words can express the suffering and sorrow involved in these statistics.

Furthermore, it is estimated that, for each fatal accident, there are 150 accidents involving only property damage. The annual economic loss to the American people has been estimated to be three and three-fourths billion dollars. This is a staggering amount of money to be lost in such a needless way. It is more than half the annual cost of operating our system of public schools.

No amount of money can measure the value of a father or mother lost in a traffic accident to the future of a family. No sum can be set to measure the value of the contributions a young man or woman prematurely killed in traffic might have made to humanity.

Why do we suffer this destruction and maiming of human beings? Is it necessary to pay such a price for the better transportation the automobile has brought? The history of the railroad does not indicate that this is so. Fifty years ago, railroad accidents killed some 400 passengers a year. Then railroad companies began to make safety a major goal. The number of deaths by railroad accident sharply declined. Conditions on the highway are vastly different, but it seems reasonable to believe that automobile accident rates also can be greatly reduced by well-planned, united efforts.

IMPROVING TRAFFIC SAFETY

THE EFFORTS of motorists, pedestrians, traffic officers, traffic engineers, and all people concerned with street and highway use are needed to improve the traffic safety picture.

There are several possible ways of attacking the many problems. The most promising approach of all is thought to be that of giving proper training to every driver before he is granted a driver's license.

IT IS THE DRIVER who has the responsibility of controlling the power of the car. In our country, there is a vast army of drivers to shoulder this responsibility. Sooner or later most United States citizens drive cars. About 2 out of every 5 persons are drivers. Annually nearly 2 million young people come of age to drive. Nearly half of them promptly get licenses. There is no doubt about it, we are a nation of drivers!

Educating the Driver

15

With such a large percentage of our citizens driving cars, it is time for all of us to be concerned about the way people learn to drive. Are most people well prepared to drive by the time they get their driving licenses?

Table I below shows the results of a poll taken at a large city Automobile Show. Ninety per cent of the nearly 8 thousand drivers polled had learned to drive without a systematic driving course. Thirty-eight per cent had taught themselves. What connection can there be between this trial and error kind of driver preparation and the appalling picture of our tragic traffic accidents?

HOW PEOPLE LEARN TO DRIVE		
Self taught	3,030	38%
Taught by a friend	2,300	29%
Taught by an auto salesman	354	4%
Taught by a relative	1,533	19%
Taught in a driving course	781	10%
Total	7,998	100%

TABLE I

Six distinct groups of drivers are in need of sound, well-guided driver training programs:

▶ New young drivers
New adult drivers
Violators of traffic regulations
Accident repeaters
Commercial drivers
Drivers of small powered vehicles

New Young Drivers EVERY YEAR, more high schools give instruction to young beginning drivers. This is thought to be the most promising single way of improving traffic safety.

Young citizens of this country need to learn all they can about automobiles and modern traffic conditions. They will meet the problems, decide on the improvements, and determine the traffic conditions of the future. They will be the highway, traffic, and automotive engineers of tomorrow. An important and interesting part of

Fig. 9. A Driver Education class tests reaction time.

their civic duty is to know the facts of the motor age and to help deal with its growing problems.

Learning to drive means much more than acquiring the easy skills needed in driving operations. A good course in driving gives you valuable information about your car, helps you understand traffic regulations, establish good traffic habits, and develop right attitudes toward traffic responsibilities.

High school driver education produces good results. Studies made in Pennsylvania compare the driving records of two groups of high school students. One group of 3000 students received driver training in high school; the other group of 3000 did not. The trained boys had 45 per cent fewer accidents than the untrained boys.

Fig. 10. Supervised practice pays big dividends.

The trained girls had 53 per cent fewer accidents than the untrained. Similar studies, made in many other states, give evidence that systematic classroom driver education, together with well-supervised driving practice in a dual control car, promises to reduce the traffic accidents and arrests of young drivers by 50 per cent or more.

Driver education will produce better drivers for the motor age.

TO TALK ABOUT:

1   Can you think of any other single invention that has so speeded up the tempo of American civilization as has the automobile?

2   What adjustments would have to be made if suddenly there were no cars in your community?

3   Discuss how various types of business have been affected by the automobile. Can you name any type of business not affected?

4   What are some of the costs of the delays that arise from traffic congestion: to the public; to the average motorist; to the business man? If you were a "traffic dictator" in your community, what would you do to eliminate or reduce congestion?

5   Cite and discuss instances: (a) when the automobile is a civic liability; (b) when it is a civic asset. Can you defend the proposition that it is the driver who determines which?

6   Compare the number of automobile fatalities last year with all other types of fatal accidents in your state or community. What seem to you to be the principal answers to the traffic accident problem?

7   Why have so many people learned to drive in a haphazard manner? What effects has this had on traffic?

8   Discuss the advantages of a dual control car from the point of view of: (a) the learner; (b) the instructor.

TO DO:

1   Make a survey among members of your group to determine how many parents or close relatives work directly or indirectly for the automobile industry.

Visit a market to see the kinds of produce carried by trucks **2** and to find out where the produce came from and how long it was enroute. Report to your group.

Visit a modern motel or motor court to see how it is ar- **3** ranged. Observe from their license plates where the tourists are from. What features are offered to trailer owners.

Find out the number of U.S. traffic casualties suffered last **4** year: (a) persons killed; (b) persons injured. What cities have populations with approximately these numbers?

Divide the class into groups, each group to study and re- **5** port on a different protective service of the automobile: (a) Crime detection; (b) Fire fighting; (c) Health services; (d) Rescue service; Civil Defense Units; (e) Military uses.

Ask several passenger car operators how they learned to **6** drive. Pool your findings with those of others in your group and make a chart showing the methods by which most present drivers were prepared. What probable relationship is there between the preparation of these drivers and the number of traffic accidents on our streets and highways today?

If a friend of yours wished to learn to drive, how would you **7** recommend he go about it? Map out a complete course of instruction for him to follow.

Make a comparative study of the traffic accident and viola- **8** tion records of a number of students in your school who have completed the driver education course and an equal number who, during the same period, got drivers' licenses without the training. Write up the findings for the school paper.

TO LOOK UP:

A Car Traveling People. Automobile Manufacturers Association, Detroit, Michigan, Revised 1954. 48 pp.

Accident Facts. National Safety Council, Chicago, Illinois. Annual Publication.

Automobile Facts and Figures. Automobile Manufacturers Association, Detroit, Michigan. Annual Publication.

Driver Education Proves Its Worth. American Automobile Association, Washington, D.C. 1955.

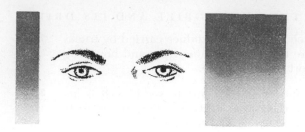

CHAPTER 2

THE EYES

GOOD EYESIGHT AND THE DRIVER

GOOD VISION is one of the most important tools a driver can have. It is a tool which should be sharp!

The car goes where the driver decides to steer it. Where he steers depends, to a large extent, on what he learns through his eyes about changing traffic situations. Seeing a danger is the most frequent signal which sets off a driver's emergency stopping reactions, change of course, or whatever maneuver will avoid an accident. Visual signals must therefore tell the driver what to do, and tell him quickly.

When eyes have normal vision, sight signals give the driver the truth about the situation. But the eye is a delicate organ with many parts, and various parts may work imperfectly. When this happens, the driver may get un-

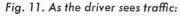

Fig. 11. As the driver sees traffic:

A. With clear vision

DO YOU KNOW:
How important eyesight is to driving?
What every driver should know about his eyes?
How you can test for visual defects?
How to correct or compensate for visual defects?

OF A DRIVER

satisfactory sight cues, make delayed or faulty reactions, and be thrown into an emergency or even an accident.

Eyes furnish the signals for a driver's actions in relation to:

The number, position, or movements of other vehicles, ◄
    pedestrians, animals, or objects.
Distances.
Speeds of other cars or of pedestrians.
Color of traffic signals.
Meaning of traffic signs.

Accurate sight signals mean better judgment and therefore better and safer driving.

In most states, your eyes are tested when you are examined for a new driver's license. Some states require a visual check when you renew your license. If you wear glasses, your eyes are tested both with and without them.

B. With poor vision

21

This test determines whether or not you will be permitted to drive and whether or not you will be required to wear your glasses when driving.

If your seeing is not normal and your visual cues are likely to be delayed or incorrect, take these precautions:

▶ *1.* Consult a competent eye specialist immediately.
2. Learn the nature of your eye defects.
3. Have your faulty vision corrected as far as this is possible.
4. For uncorrected eye defects, learn what kind of misjudgments you are likely to make.
5. Learn how to compensate for uncorrectable eye defects.

Compensation for eye defects generally means *slower driving* and *greater alertness*.

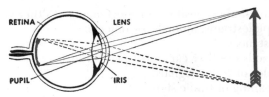

RETINA LENS PUPIL IRIS

Fig. 12. Visual "cues" must be right.

HOW THE DRIVER'S EYES MUST FUNCTION

1. Clearness of Vision THE MOST obvious function of your eyes is to give a clear picture of what is in front of you. Ability to see details clearly is called *visual acuity*. People differ considerably in visual acuity. One person may be able to read a highway sign from a distance greater than 300 feet while another may not read it until he is within 60 feet. Many persons have vision considerably below normal without realizing it. They have never had their eyes examined carefully. But such a test is simple to make, and no one should drive without having had one.

Test for Clearness The easiest and most frequent test for visual acuity is made with a Snellen Chart. The person with normal vision can read standard Snellen letters that are 0.349 of an inch high at a distance of 20 feet. This is called 20/20 vision. Many people have better than 20/20 vision and can see the same letters farther away. Far-point vision is very important in driving.

Most Snellen charts consist of several rows of letters of various sizes, and your visual acuity is scored by the *size* of the smallest letters you can read. With other charts, your score may be determined by the *distance* at which you read the letters.

Use the chart in Fig. 13 to test your vision. Have it held in good light about 15 feet away. Cover one eye with a card and walk slowly toward the chart until you can read 8 letters out of 10 correctly. Carefully measure the distance from your eyes to the chart. Multiply this distance in feet by 10 and you will have your approximate visual acuity rating in per cent.

Fig. 13. Test your visual acuity.

If you can read the letters at 10 feet, your vision for the eye tested is normal, or 20/20 vision. If you can read the letters at 12 feet, your rating is above normal. If you can read them no farther than 8.5 feet, then your rating is below average. Then test the other eye in the same way, except that you should read the letters backwards to eliminate remembering the order of the letters.

If your vision is much below normal (75 per cent or below), consult a competent eye specialist. Early correction may prevent vision defects from becoming serious, and also may prevent the kind of accident that comes to persons whose below-normal vision keeps them from properly meeting emergency situations.

State licensing agencies consider visual acuity of such great importance that most of them have established minimum standards. The most common *minimum* requirement is 20/40 vision.

2. Seeing Out of the Corner of Your Eye YOU LOOK directly at an object to see it sharply and in detail. Off to the side you see objects in less detail. In other words, you can see "out of the corner of your eye." The area which you see to either side, while looking straight ahead, is called your *field of vision.* Your vision to the side, "out of the corner of your eye," is called your *peripheral vision.* This vision is very important in driving, as a driver must be aware of everything going on around him.

People differ in field of vision. Some people have wider fields of vision, or see farther to the side, than others. It is greatly to a driver's advantage if he can detect objects and motion over a wide field. He can more quickly detect vehicles, persons, animals, etc., approaching from the right or left.

Your *peripheral,* or side, vision is better for moving than for stationary objects or for color. Fortunately, it is movement off to the side that it is generally most important for a driver to detect.

A few persons have such narrow visual fields that they are said to have "tunnel vision." They see only straight ahead, as one would if he were looking through a tunnel or through binoculars. They are at a great disadvantage when cars are overtaking them to pass, when they are driving through intersections, and at all times in heavy traffic.

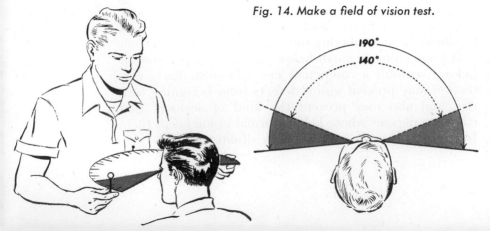

Fig. 14. Make a field of vision test.

190°

140°

Test for Field of Vision Test your field of vision by making a cardboard protractor with a radius of 10 inches. (See Fig. 14.) Hold it up to the bridge of your nose with the o directly ahead and the 90° marks to the right and left. Now look at a fixed point some distance straight ahead. Have someone move a pencil slowly from back to front along the edge of the protractor until you can see the movement of the pencil out of the corner of your eye while still looking straight ahead. The point where you first saw the movement of the pencil can be noted in degrees. Have several trials made and the average reading in degrees determined for each side. The sum of these two figures will indicate your total field of vision in degrees.

Fig. 15. This driver's tunnel vision obscures the speeding car coming from the side road at the right.

Most persons can see more than 90° to each side, making a total field of vision of over 180°. A field of less than 140° is generally considered a serious handicap to safe driving. However, a person who knows about such a handicap can do much to compensate. He can:

1. Reduce speed at all points where vehicles or pedestrians might be approaching from the side. ◄

2. Turn his head slightly to look both ways at intersections and at all other dangerous points.

COLOR is often used to give traffic information to the driver:

3. Judging Color

Red light signals for "stop," and green for "go." ◄
Red flags, lanterns, or flares at roadway hazards and obstructions.

Red flags to show loads extended beyond the ends of vehicles.
Red taillights on cars.
Flashing red taillights as turn signals.
Yellow or red blinker lights at dangerous crossings.
Colored road signs, route markings, and curb markings.

Persons unable to distinguish the colors used for traffic situations are definitely handicapped. It is estimated that about one man in twenty has some difficulty in distinguishing certain colors. Defective color vision is about 5 times as frequent among men as among women. Fortunately, the percentage who have difficulty in distinguishing between red and green traffic signals is very small.

If tests show that you have a definite color-vision weakness, especially in red and green, learn to compensate for this deficiency. Here is what you can do:

▶ *1.* Keep a sharper lookout for signals at intersections.

2. Know the *arrangement* of signals in localities where you do your driving. In most states and cities, signal positions follow the national standard—red at the top, yellow in the center, and green below. Unfortunately, position cannot always be relied upon, for there are still places with a nonstandard arrangement.

3. Pay closer attention to the actions of other drivers at intersections with traffic signals.

4. Learn to interpret the *shape* of traffic markers and signs as a guide to what you may expect ahead. Learn what the different shapes signify—circle, octagon, diamond, and rectangle.

Test for Color Vision   One color-vision test is the Ishihara test. This consists of several circular areas filled with spots and dots of various colors. Spots of a given color are arranged in patterns to form numbers. Persons with defective color vision are unable to distinguish some of the figures from the background. The nature and extent of their color blindness is determined by which numbers they cannot read. See Fig. 16A.

Fig. 16. Two color vision tests:

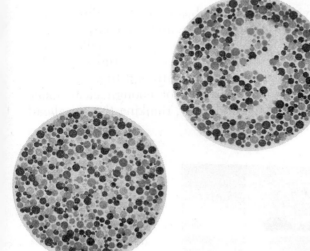

B. The Colorater

The Ishihara test detects minor degrees of color blindness, many not serious enough to interfere with safe driving. But if this test indicates some color blindness, you should be tested with actual traffic signals.

A color-vision testing device which requires the same kind of color identification that a driver needs for reading traffic signal lights is the Colorater, shown in Fig. 16B. A small motor within the box turns a disk containing sections of traffic signal glass. A light illuminates each section

as it becomes visible through a small opening. The colors appear in random order, each exposed for about two seconds. To pass the test, you must name the colors correctly as they appear.

4. Judging Distance IN NORMAL vision, you see objects in three dimensions. You are able to judge size, shape, and distances.

A person with faulty depth perception usually cannot judge distances accurately. He may overestimate the distance of an approaching car and attempt to pass the car he is following when there is not enough clear space ahead. Or he may stop suddenly, thinking the car ahead is closer than it is.

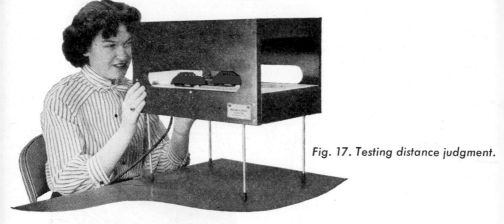

Fig. 17. Testing distance judgment.

Test for Distance Judgment One of several tests available for measuring depth perception is illustrated in Fig. 17. When you look into the eyepiece of this test, you see miniature cars in a mirror. The mirror is placed 10 feet from the test and the cars appear to be 20 feet away. As quickly as you can, you move the cars forward and backward until they appear to be side by side.

Unless your distance perception is considerably below normal, you should have an error of less than one inch in lining the cars up side by side in this test.

If you have below-average ability in judging distances, you should allow additional space between your car and other cars on the highway. In other words, do not follow other cars closely or overtake another car to pass, unless there is much more clear space ahead than you appear to need. If you know your distance judgment is faulty, allow for it.

YOUR EYES make adjustments so you can see in different degrees of illumination. Like the diaphragm of a camera, the pupil of the eye controls the amount of light that enters. The retina also adapts itself to different degrees of light.

5. Seeing at Night

 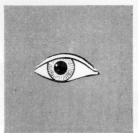 

Fig. 18. The pupil of the eye works like the shutter diaphragm on a camera.

Entering a dark theater in daytime, you find it very difficult to see at first, but gradually objects become visible. Here is what happens. In the daylight, the pupil of your eye contracts to prevent too much light from falling on the retina. (See Fig. 18.) Then, when you enter the dark theater, the pupil opens up fairly rapidly to allow more light to enter. But the sensitivity of your retina has become dulled by exposure to the brightness of day. During the time required for the retina to recover the sensitivity needed for seeing in low illumination your sight is dull.

The eye adjusts much more slowly to darkness than to light. In fact, although most of the adjustments may take place in the first few minutes after you enter the dark theater, complete adjustment to dim light can take as long as half an hour.

Even though your daytime vision is normal, you may have difficulty seeing objects distinctly at night. To driving, this is very important, especially in view of the fact that nearly three-fourths of the fatal traffic accidents occur during hours of dusk and darkness.

Glaring headlights complicate night driving.

Fig. 19. Use low-beam lights when meeting other cars.

A. Headlight glare hides the pedestrian.

B. With low lights the same pedestrian shows.

The headlights of an approaching car greatly reduce your ability to see. When oncoming bright, upper-beam headlights are about one hundred feet away, it is very difficult to see objects beside or beyond the approaching

30

car. Even after the glaring lights have passed, some time is required for your vision to return to normal.

Your stopping distance should never be greater than the distance in which you can clearly see ahead. Too many drivers try to drive at night at the *same speed* as in the daytime, instead of with the same *factor of safety*. They *overdrive their headlights*, going at a speed from which it is not physically possible to come to a complete stop in the distance of their clear vision ahead. Then, in an emergency, they are unable to avoid trouble. *Speed should always go down with the sun.*

At night, the available light to see by is very limited. In daylight, you often have some 10,000 foot candles of light with which to see. At night, 100 feet from your car, you have only 7 or 8 foot candles of light. Out ahead, at 1,000 feet, you have only $\frac{1}{14}$ of a foot candle.

Anything which reduces the small amount of light entering the eye at night makes seeing more difficult. For that reason, *sunglasses should not be worn for night driving,* and dark-tinted windshields can prove dangerous, especially to persons with subnormal vision. They reduce the effectiveness of the visual cues which help a driver see the road and all the objects along or on it. With some colors the driver may have an illusion of greater visibility or better seeing, whereas actually his seeing is reduced. His chances for night driving accidents are increased in proportion, as the color or tint in the glasses cuts down the light which enters his eyes.

The Night Visibility Committee of the Highway Research Board has stated, "In the light of present knowledge, it is concluded that any media, except clear corrective spectacles, introduced at night between the eye and an object or situation on the roadway are not to be recommended for night driving."

The age of a driver is important in night driving. Various experiments have shown that ability to see in dim light becomes poorer as people grow older. The eyes of older persons are also less able to see correctly in the glare of oncoming headlights. They are also slower to recover from glare.

Various tests give evidence that, as drivers grow older, they are less and less safe when driving at night, unless they decrease night driving speeds. Many elderly drivers, whose vision may still be satisfactory for *daytime driving* but whose night vision has become poor, *should never drive at night*.

The difficulties and handicaps of night vision have to be taken seriously by all ages. The fatal accident rate, on the basis of miles driven, is *three times* higher at night than during the day. Inability to see well enough is without doubt a major factor in the many accidents which occur after dark. Lessen the accident danger in your own driving in these ways:

1. Drive at night only after you have so mastered driving that you can keep your eyes on the road.

2. Drive at a lower speed than in the daytime.

3. Drive at night only when rested. Fatigue impairs your night vision.

4. Know the range of your headlights and what you can see at given distances.

5. Be able to stop within the visibility range of your headlights.

6. Avoid dark or colored glasses which reduce the amount of light entering the eye.

7. When facing glare from approaching headlights: reduce speed; avoid looking directly at the lights; and guide your steering by the right-hand side of the road and the center line. Keep speed reduced until your eyes recover from the effects of the lights.

8. Always depress your headlights when meeting other cars. This is not only common courtesy, but it lights the road directly ahead and to the right, where you most need it lighted. A driver blinded by high-beam headlights tends to crowd the light. He may sideswipe your car.

9. Depress your lights when following another driver. The glare caused by your lights shining in his rear-vision mirror can reduce his vision enough to cause an accident.

DEPRESS LIGHTS
WHEN FOLLOWING

10. Keep battery, lights, and electrical system in good condition.

LIGHT INSIDE CAR

11. Avoid lighting matches or using bright lights in the car. Keep bright interior lights off.

12. Keep your headlights properly adjusted so that the depressed beams are not high enough to hit the oncoming driver's eyes.

13. Keep the windshield and headlamps clean.

Tests for Night Vision Ability to see at night varies greatly among individuals. Two persons may have the same visual acuity during the day, and yet, at night, one may be able to see much better than the other.

A number of devices have been developed to measure ability to see at night. The best tests are those which most nearly duplicate night driving conditions.

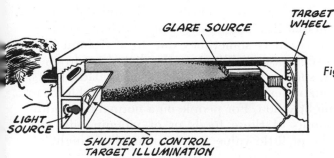

GLARE SOURCE

TARGET WHEEL

LIGHT SOURCE

SHUTTER TO CONTROL TARGET ILLUMINATION

Fig. 20. Testing night vision.

One test measures three things about ability to see at night: (a) vision under glare conditions; (b) ability to see objects in low illumination; and (c) recovery of vision after glare. This test is illustrated in Fig. 20.

(a) *Glare Vision*—The subject looks through the eyepiece at the target wheel and, as the wheel turns, reports the direction of the opening in the "C's," or broken circles, whether right, left, top, or bottom. Two small glaring lights shine directly into the subject's eyes. The examiner manipulates a shutter which controls the amount of light on the target wheel. He slowly reduces the illumination on the target until the subject can no longer

33

identify the breaks in the circles correctly. The level of illumination at which the subject fails to give correct responses gives a measure of his glare vision.

(b) *Vision in Low Illumination*—The glaring lights are turned off so that the subject no longer faces them. The light on the target wheel is then slowly reduced until the subject cannot identify the breaks in the "circles." This measures the degree of illumination required by the subject to see under night driving conditions.

(c) *Glare Recovery*—The subject identifies the breaks in the "circles" while facing glaring lights similar to the glare he faces on the highway. Then the glare lights are turned off and the examiner reduces the illumination on the target to the degree of illumination required by the subject in test (b) above. A built-in timer then measures in seconds the time required for the subject to recover from the glare and be able to identify the breaks in the "circles."

Some persons are so seriously handicapped by poor night vision that they should avoid night driving entirely. Poor night vision is sometimes due to a vitamin deficiency. In such cases, addition to the diet of food rich in Vitamin A, such as fresh vegetables, green salads, fruits, milk, cream, butter, cheese, eggs, meat, liver, and fish can improve night vision. For people on a normal diet, additional amounts of these foods or of vitamin pills will probably be of little value in improving their night vision.

DANGER IN EYE FATIGUE

CONTINUOUS use of your eyes for long periods of time puts a heavy strain on the muscles and results in eye fatigue. This is especially true in driving, because of the strain of constant watching and the need to change focus for near and far distances. A headache after a long drive is often a symptom of overused eyes or deficient vision. Such fatigue can cause poor driving for the following reasons:

1. Tired eyes tend to make one drowsy and bring on ◄
   sleep. "Dozing at the wheel" is known to cause many
   accidents.
2. Ability to judge distance is often reduced by eye
   fatigue. Most persons have better vision in one eye
   than in the other. In case of eye fatigue, the dominant
   eye tends to take over the main burden of seeing. The
   result is something like one-eyed vision, and ability to
   judge depth and distance is greatly reduced.
3. When the dominant eye takes over the burden of
   seeing, the field of vision is greatly decreased. Objects
   approaching from the side of the less-used eye are not
   so likely to be seen.
4. When you are fatigued, it is difficult to keep your attention focused on the road ahead.

You cannot afford the risk of driving when your eyes
are tired. On long drives, occasionally give your eyes a
rest. Stop the car off the roadway, close your eyes, and
press your fingers lightly over the eyelids. This helps re-
lieve fatigue caused by eye muscle strain.

Keeping your eyes steadily in a fixed position brings on
drowsiness. Learn to let them shift easily over the whole
area of your vision while driving, keeping constantly
aware of what is going on in the entire area. Learn to see
quickly, accurately, and broadly. This is highly efficient
seeing.

TO TALK ABOUT:

Discuss the question: Should a person with 20/40 vision   1
drive half as fast as a person with 20/20 vision?

What vision tests are required in your state before a license   2
can be obtained? Discuss how the testing might be improved.
Should testing of night vision be included? If it is not included, find out why.

Discuss the advantages of a wide field of vision.   3

In what ways can a mirror help a person with a narrow   4
field of vision?

Assemble clippings of traffic accidents and discuss the part   5
that defective vision may have played.

TO DO:

1 With the use of a Snellen chart, or the chart in Fig. 13, carefully test the vision of each member of the class and make a table showing the visual acuity for each eye for each person.

2 Measure the height of the letters on a STOP sign. At what distance away could these letters be read by a person with 20/20 vision? At what distance could they be read by a person with 20/50 vision?

3 Make a cardboard protractor as illustrated on page 24, and measure the field of vision of each member of the class. Make a chart showing the range. How far around can a person see if he has only one eye? What should such a person do in driving?

4 The eye adjusts to light much more quickly than to darkness. If your eye is adjusted to darkness, it will require several minutes to recover most of the sensitivity lost by exposure to a bright light for only a few seconds. You can perform an interesting experiment to prove this. After spending 15 minutes in a dark room, cover one eye and shine a flashlight in the other for five seconds. After doing this, quickly test the sight of one eye and then the other and notice the difference.

5 Seeing with two eyes, or so-called binocular vision, is a great help in depth perception. To illustrate, ask a friend to hold a pencil with the point up, about 30 inches in front of you. With your arm outstretched, hold your hand a few inches above the pencil; then attempt to touch the point with your index finger: (1) with the right eye closed; (2) with the left eye closed; (3) with both eyes open. Describe what happens.

TO LOOK UP:

Age and the Ability to See at Night. Allgaier, Earl. American Automobile Association, Washington, D.C. 1953. 14 pp.
The Seeing Factors in Traffic Safety. Lebensohn, James E., M.D. National Society for the Prevention of Blindness, New York 19, New York. 1949. 12 pp.

DO YOU KNOW:
The effect your general health has on your driving?
What disabilities handicap a driver?
How a driver can compensate for disabilities?

CHAPTER **3**

PHYSICAL FITNESS

AND SAFETY

GENERAL HEALTH

SOME small part of a car can bend or break or lose its adjustment and ruin the performance of the whole machine. A driver is much like that. He gives a more satisfactory performance when all his parts are in first-class condition and working together smoothly.

A driver complains bitterly when vital parts like the carburetor, generator, or brakes of a car are not working properly. It would be interesting if the car could complain of the driver whose "parts" are out of order!

Physical fitness means the proper working together of sound body organs. In such a condition one is at his best. He is efficient; his thinking is clear; his reactions are steady. His driving is much more likely to be reliable.

Major illnesses, such as influenza, ptomaine poisoning, fevers, and infections, can reduce or even destroy one's ability to drive well. Alertness may be decreased, clearness of vision reduced, power of judgment lessened, and reaction time slowed down.

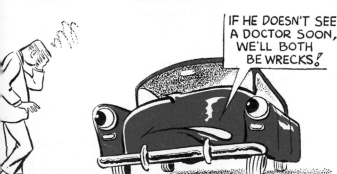

IF HE DOESN'T SEE A DOCTOR SOON, WE'LL BOTH BE WRECKS!

Fig. 21. If cars could talk!

37

Even minor troubles, such as worry, headache, indigestion, a sore throat, or a throbbing tooth can be distracting and affect one's driving ability.

No one in poor health or worried or distracted should be driving an automobile. If it is absolutely necessary to drive under such circumstances, only greatly reduced speed and exceptional caution can in any way help make up for the driver's poor condition.

PHYSICAL UNFITNESS

PHYSICAL disabilities that can create hazards and interfere with driving can be classified as:

   ▶   A. Permanent disabilities, for which there can be corrections or compensations.
       B. Major disabilities, with no satisfactory corrections or compensations.
       C. Disabilities that temporarily disqualify a driver.

Examples of disabilities in the first group are defects of eyes and ears, certain effects of advancing age, and physical handicaps. In the second group are serious disabilities that can cause loss of control, such as epilepsy, mental disorders, paralysis, syphilis, and heart diseases. In the group of temporary disabilities are such conditions as fatigue, drowsiness, intoxication, and emotional disturbance.

Permanent Disabilities, with Possible Corrections or Compensations

1. Defects of the Sense Organs *Vision*—Defective vision can greatly handicap a driver, as was shown in Chapter 2. You may know drivers with such defective vision that they cut in too quickly, back into things, or bump into objects ahead, endangering themselves and others. Obviously, licensing regulations should require whatever corrections of vision are possible, and the driver should use every compensation.

Hearing—Poor hearing also handicaps a driver. It can prevent him from hearing other vehicles or horn signals from cars about to pass. Railroad grade crossings offer an especially great hazard to the deaf.

Totally deaf persons learn some compensations. Since

they cannot depend on hearing, they learn to be exceptionally alert and cautious. The partially deaf are in greater danger, especially those who have only recently suffered serious hearing losses and scarcely realize their handicap. They should compensate in the same way as the totally deaf, by being more alert and cautious than persons with normal hearing.

Hard-of-hearing drivers can make some compensations by:

Using their peripheral, or side vision, for all it is worth. ◄
Being exceptionally alert and watchful.
Using an additional rear-view mirror.
Using properly-adjusted hearing aids.

Test your own hearing acuity by means of an audiometer. Or, if you have no audiometer, use a simple watch test. Use a watch with a fairly loud tick. Find the average distance at which several people known to have good hearing can detect its tick. Test each of your ears separately by bringing the watch toward the ear until you can just hear it. Then measure the distance from which you heard it tick. Get a rating of your own hearing stated in per cent by dividing the average hearing distance for the watch into your own score and multiplying by one hundred.

2. Advancing Age Advancing age can bring serious driving disabilities. With it can come failing eyesight and hearing, high blood pressure, temporary lapses of attention, or stiffness of movement. Glare resistance and glare recovery tend to grow increasingly difficult with age.

With age, reaction time grows slower. This does not mean that all young drivers have faster reaction times than older drivers. They do not. But each adult's reaction time tends to lengthen as he grows older. He cannot, with equal safety, drive as fast as he once could.

There are great individual differences as to when age begins to interfere seriously with driving efficiency. With some persons, interference may begin to show in their 50's; with others, not even at 65. Some persons demonstrate competence to drive when very much older. The chief compensations for the lowered driving efficiency and reduced safety of elderly people are lower speeds, greater caution, and constant attention to traffic conditions.

3. Physical Handicaps Under right conditions, persons with certain physical handicaps can operate cars efficiently and safely.

Some states grant restricted licenses to persons with physical handicaps. Such licenses may permit driving when corrective glasses are worn, when the car is equipped with an extra rear-view mirror, or when special levers, buttons, or extensions have been built into the car.

Fig. 22. ". . . and I advise you not to drive for the present."

Wars have produced so many veterans who have suffered losses of eyes, legs, arms, or hands that automobile engineers and manufacturers, working with Army surgeons and orthopedic specialists, have designed new levers and switches to give driving control to the physically handicapped. On cars where gearshifting must be done, special levers and switches have been designed for use in all the driving operations. A special steering knob makes steering possible for persons with artificial hands. Automatic transmission cars prove a great help to the handicapped, especially to persons with amputations.

Drivers who must use special devices to compensate for handicaps can, with special training and right driver attitudes, achieve a safe degree of driving skill.

LICENSING programs should weed out persons with cer- *Major Disabilities* tain major disabilities for which there are no satisfactory *with No* corrections or compensations. People who suffer from *Corrections or* the following disabilities should be prevented from driv- *Compensations* ing cars:

1. Epilepsy—Sudden attacks may, at any time, result ◄ in loss of control or even in unconsciousness. Even minor epileptic attacks can produce brief periods of unconsciousness during which a car can get completely out of control.

2. Mental Illness—Even comparatively mild mental ◄ disturbances that are difficult to detect can menace the safety of the highway. Persons who are so seriously ill mentally that they may be unaccountable for their behavior should be prevented from endangering the safety of others. This means, they should be refused a license to drive a car.

3. Paralysis—Paralysis results in loss of muscular con- ◄ trol. Where certain muscles are affected, safe driving is obviously impossible.

4. Syphilis—This disease may affect the brain centers ◄ and result in a progressive childishness, unreasonableness, loss of judgment, and tendency to hallucinations. It may result also in a form of paralysis. In some stages of the disease, driving is unsafe.

5. Heart Trouble—Any heart disorder which is likely ◄ to cause sudden collapse makes a person obviously unsafe at the wheel. He should never drive.

It is very significant that the American Medical Association is urging doctors to realize the important role they can play in reducing traffic accidents. They are urged to detect in their patients physical conditions that make them unfit to drive and to warn them of their unfitness.

The profession regards disorders of the nervous system as especially dangerous to driving. They list among conditions with which persons should be warned not to drive: narcolepsy or an uncontrollable tendency to fall asleep, epilepsy, brain hemorrhages, Parkinson's disease, the effects of operations involving brain incisions, paraly-

41

sis of nerve centers which control muscles, high blood pressure, effects of heart attacks, disorders of the main artery in the neck, and angina pectoris.

Disabilities that Temporarily Disqualify a Driver SOME TEMPORARY physical conditions make a driver so unsafe that he shows good judgment if he disqualifies himself and does not drive until the conditions are corrected.

1. Fatigue or Drowsiness Serious fatigue should disqualify a driver.

As you work and exert your body, changes take place in the chemical make-up of your tissues. They collect "fatigue poisons." When sufficiently filled with fatigue poisons, you become drowsy and finally lose consciousness in sleep, even though you struggle against it

Fatigue poisons make such important changes in the chemistry of the blood that extracts made from the muscles of a seriously fatigued animal and injected into a rested animal will cause the latter to show signs of fatigue.

When you rest, your body produces chemical substances which counteract fatigue products, and it is only during rest that these substances can be supplied in sufficient quantity to restore your tissues to normal.

The poisons that cause fatigue slow down the working of the different parts of the body. The fatigued driver becomes less vigilant and loses judgment as to depth, distance, and speed. His reaction time is slowed down. He is less able to resist glare. A study of interstate truck drivers by the U.S. Public Health Service shows the increasingly bad effects of long hours of driving. Driving efficiency

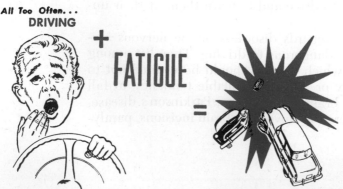

All Too Often. . . DRIVING + **FATIGUE** =

Fig. 23. Inviting accident.

falls with increasing fatigue. Finally, nodding at the wheel is inescapable. Accidents almost invariably follow.

Cars that are wrecked with the driver asleep at the wheel are generally very badly wrecked. With the driver unconscious, no effort is being made either to prevent or to lessen the accident.

Drivers struggling against fatigue and determined to stay awake a little longer have had so many and such serious accidents that many commercial concerns now limit the number of consecutive hours their bus or truck drivers are allowed to drive. Some states have adopted laws limiting driving hours. As early as 1939, the Interstate Commerce Commission limited the hours of driving by bus and truck drivers under their jurisdiction to 10, after which 8 hours must be taken off duty. A passenger car driver should restrict himself as rigidly. Under no circumstances should he drive when sleepy or fatigued.

The chart below (Fig. 24) shows how the accident rate varies according to the hour of the day and night. Accidents tend to increase as the day and evening wear on. They reach their peak in the early evening and remain frequent during the first half of the night.

Fig. 24. Hours of darkness increase the hazards.

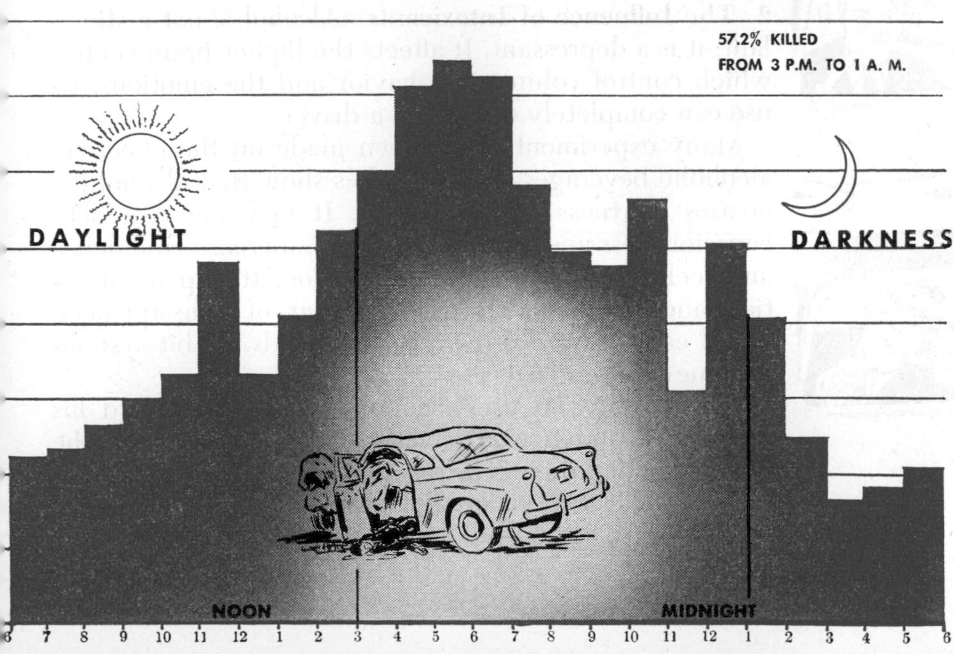

57.2% KILLED FROM 3 P.M. TO 1 A. M.

DAYLIGHT   DARKNESS

NOON   MIDNIGHT

6   7   8   9   10   11   12   1   2   3   4   5   6   7   8   9   10   11   12   1   2   3   4   5   6

Of course many things help cause this increase of accidents after dusk. Dusk and darkness greatly decrease driving visibility; more alcoholic drinking is done in the late afternoon and evening; workers returning home greatly increase traffic volume. But, undoubtedly, fatigue from the day's work or from long driving is also a big factor in increasing accidents at the end of day and in the night. The longer or later one drives, the better his driving performance needs to be. But, as he grows more fatigued, he becomes less able to do his best at the wheel.

The way to prevent crashes caused by fatigue is to *refuse to drive when fatigued. Stop and rest,* or turn the wheel over to someone who is rested.

Here are some ways to help offset drowsiness, if you are driving for long periods:

Keep plenty of fresh air in the car.

Engage in conversation.

Pull off the road as soon as drowsy, and take a nap.

Park the car, and rest your eyes by pressing gently on your eyelids.

Drink coffee or strong tea.

Avoid alcoholic drinks, which cause further drowsiness.

Rest frequently by getting out of the car and walking around.

2. The Influence of Intoxicants Alcohol is not a stimulant; it is a depressant. It affects the higher brain centers which control voluntary behavior and the emotions. Its use can completely disqualify a driver.

Many experiments have been made on the effects of alcoholic beverages. These studies show that alcohol decreases alertness and efficiency. It may decrease self-consciousness and, at the same time, increase confidence and feelings of ease and of relaxation. It impairs attention and judgment. It destroys fear of consequences. Usual cautions are thrown to the winds. Habit systems become disorganized.

The driver who uses alcohol tends to disregard his usual safety practices. He may not even be aware that he is disregarding them. His reaction time slows down; normally quick reactions are not possible for him. To make matters worse, he may not realize he is slower. His eye muscles may be so affected that his vision is not normal. He cannot correctly judge the speed of his car or of any other car. He cannot correctly estimate distances being covered by each. He becomes a highway menace.

Driving under the influence of an intoxicant is *criminal* carelessness. In most states, the penalty is severe.

The Uniform Vehicle Code provides that every person who is convicted of driving while under the influence of intoxicating liquor "shall be punished by imprisonment for not less than 10 days or more than 1 year, or by fine of not less than $100 or more than $1,000, or by both such fine and imprisonment. On a second or subsequent conviction, he shall be punished by imprisonment for not less than 90 days or more than 1 year, and, in the discretion of the court, a fine of not more than $1,000. The commissioner shall revoke the operator's or chauffeur's license of any person convicted under this section."

It is unintelligent even to consent to ride in a car driven by a person who, although not drunk, "has been drinking." He may be hilarious in spirit, but he is generally poor in judgment, slow in reaction time, and not very alert. This combination produces emergencies when the driver is altogether unfit to cope with them. A forced stop under such conditions generally means disaster. Alcohol and driving simply do not mix.

Accurate statistics on the number of accidents where alcohol is involved are, at present, very limited. Some studies indicate, however, that alcohol plays a much greater part in traffic accidents than is generally realized.

Fig. 25. Alcohol and driving do not mix.

Tests for Intoxication An intoxicated person cannot conceal his condition when certain tests are made. Properly given, these tests help protect the innocent and convict the guilty by giving scientific evidence of the absence or presence of alcohol in the system. The tests are impersonal and impartial. They are being used increasingly to keep alcoholic drivers off the highways. Here is how they work.

Alcohol requires no digestion. It is absorbed into the blood directly, rapidly, and unchanged, from the stomach and intestines. The blood then carries it to all parts of the body, including the brain.

Some of the alcohol is eliminated after drinking, in breath, perspiration, and urine. Some is converted, in the body, into water and carbon dioxide; some is destroyed by a process of oxidation.

Alcohol is absorbed so rapidly into the blood that it shows up in a minute or two after it is drunk. Because the rate of absorption is more rapid than the rate of elimination and oxidation, alcohol appears in the blood in different degrees of concentration. The amount of concentration in the blood depends on many conditions:

Amount of alcohol taken.
Kind of alcoholic beverage taken.
Amounts of other fluids in the body.
Size and weight of the drinker.
Contents of the stomach.
Speed of the drinking.
The time since the drinking took place.

Fig. 26. Breath test for intoxication.

The tests indicate the concentration of alcohol in a person's blood. This concentration is used as a measure of degree of soberness or intoxication.

There is a close relationship at any time between amount of alcohol in the brain and amounts in the blood, breath, and urine. So the tests determine the amount of alcohol in either the blood, breath, or urine.

The breath test is most frequently used. The person being tested blows up a rubber balloon. The "breath" in the balloon is then passed through a solution of sulphuric acid and potassium permanganate in measured quantities. If alcohol is present, the chemical solution changes from purple to light brown. The volume of breath required to change the color of the solution determines the concentration of alcohol in the breath.

Different persons react differently to alcohol, and the reactions of even the same person vary considerably under different conditions of drinking. But medical and legal authorities have set up practical standards to use in stating the soberness or drunkenness of persons who are tested.

In setting up these standards, many cases were studied. The alcohol concentration in the blood of many persons was measured. Degrees of soberness or intoxication generally found with different degrees of blood-alcohol concentration were determined. Table II gives the standards that were set up in this way. These standards are recognized by both medical and legal authorities and are used in many localities.

Notice, in Table II, that certain degrees of blood-alcohol concentration make it questionable as to whether or not the person is legally "under the influence" of an intoxicant. Further evidence is required. At higher concentrations, the person is considered "under the influence." Even in such cases, other supporting evidence is customarily presented in court.

Many states and cities now admit such test information as evidence. Actually, because the tests give objective data, they can help protect the innocent. For it is known that certain injuries, illnesses, and drugs tend to make the behavior of a person look much like that of an intoxicated person, even though he has not been drinking. Proof of the absence of alcohol in the blood of such a person reduces or eliminates the chance of an unjust charge.

TABLE II

BLOOD ALCOHOL CONCENTRATIONS

MEDICO-LEGAL INTERPRETATIONS AS TO WHETHER PERSONS TESTED ARE "UNDER THE INFLUENCE" OF AN INTOXICANT *

Alcohol Concentrations in the Blood	Medico-Legal Interpretation
0 to .05%	Not evidence of being "under the influence" of an intoxicant.
.05% to .10%	Inadequate evidence requiring further support. Possibly "under the influence."
.10% to .15%	Probably "under the influence."
.15% or more	Definitely "under the influence."

* Standards recognized by the American Medical Association, the American Bar Association, the National Safety Council, and other organizations. Also found in the Uniform Vehicle Code, Act V, Sec. 54 (b) paragraphs 1, 2, 3.

According to studies made by the Northwestern University Traffic Institute, a driver with a 0.15 per cent concentration of alcohol in his blood is 33 times as likely to have an accident as a man who has not had a drink. We can draw a simple conclusion. Persons who are going to drive motor vehicles should not drink alcoholic beverages.

Consider well the many ways in which alcohol makes a person incompetent to drive:

It acts as a narcotic, dulling the driver.   ◄
It quickly affects his brain, destroying good judgment.
It breaks down motor skills.
It slows down reaction time.
It interferes with vision.
It breaks down emotional control and a person's real personality.

There is *nothing* about alcohol that recommends it for the driver. The drinker should not drive. The driver should not drink.

3. Drugs   It is interesting to note that displays dealing with traffic safety attract increased attention at meetings of the American Medical Association.

The medical profession asserts that some drugs prescribed for various ailments can be as hazardous to driving as the ailment itself. They list, as especially likely to make a person unfit to drive: sedatives, narcotics, alcohol, antihistamines, anticonvulsants, and some of the antibiotics.

Very serious accidents have come from drivers falling unexpectedly asleep after even light use of some of these drugs. If you have to use any such drug under doctor's prescription consult the label as to whether or not it is likely to bring about drowsiness. Do not drive while you are using it.

The most harmful drugs are the narcotics, which cannot be secured legally in any quantity or form, unless prescribed by a specially licensed physician. Even then they are used with extreme care because of their dangerous habit-forming nature.

THE DOCTOR WARNED HIM NOT TO DRIVE AFTER TAKING THAT MEDICINE!

Fig. 27. The medical profession is alert to the danger.

Marijuana and the opium derivatives, morphine and heroin, are extremely habit-forming, and, in short time, destroy one's personality, health, and even sanity and life. Needless to say no user of these narcotics can possibly be a safe driver or have a moral right to try to drive.

Some narcotics have a brief stimulating effect, during which they give a false sense of courage, make a person reckless, and cause him to do things which show bad judgment and lack of will power. Then comes abnormal drowsiness; the functions of the nervous system are destroyed; the whole mental state of the person is made completely unreliable.

The Food and Drug Act requires that patent medicines containing certain drugs or barbiturates must be labeled: WARNING—MAY BE HABIT-FORMING. Watch for these labels, and be especially careful not to use these medicines when driving. They may produce sleepiness, slow down reaction time, destroy alertness, and cause serious accidents.

4. Carbon Monoxide Poisoning   Driving along a rural highway, a man suddenly heard a crash, felt a bump, put his hand to his head, and felt moisture. He looked at his hand and saw blood. He looked about him and discovered, to his confusion, that he was sitting in his car in the middle of a creek. How he got there he never knew. The doctor found that his blood was poisoned by carbon monoxide.

Fig. 28. The horn saved his life.

A family was awakened on a winter night by the blowing of a horn. Their seventeen-year-old son was found sitting in the car in the garage slumped over the steering wheel. He had driven in and kept the engine running while he sat reviewing the events of the evening. The wind had blown the door shut. Lapsing into unconsciousness, his body fell on the horn button, and the horn brought the puzzled family to the garage. Artificial respiration saved his life. Few cases of carbon monoxide poisoning end so fortunately.

Carbon monoxide is found in the exhaust gases of all automobiles. It is produced by the incomplete combustion of gasoline. Excessive amounts come from poor ignition and faulty carburetor adjustment. It is a colorless, tasteless, odorless gas and can be deadly even in small amounts. In a very short time, it can impair a person's mental reactions. He loses coordination of muscles and cannot safely operate a car.

A motor running at idling speed, in a closed garage, can generate enough of this gas in a few minutes to overcome a person and cause death. Cues to the presence of carbon monoxide may be mental dullness, absent-mindedness, sudden perspiration, headache, drowsiness, dizziness, or nausea. The odor of exhaust gas is one of the cues to the presence of carbon monoxide.

Simple rules to prevent carbon monoxide poisoning:

1. Run your engine as little as possible inside a garage ◄ and then only with the doors open.
2. Always have plenty of fresh air in your car while driving.
3. Have the entire exhaust system inspected: floor boards, heater system, muffler, tail pipe, and the "seal" between the body of the car and the engine to discover carbon monoxide leaks.
4. Be sure there is adequate ventilation if you run the engine to keep warm while the car is standing still, especially in a snow bank. The snow around the car may "pocket" the gas and cause it to seep into the body of the car. If you must keep the engine running

while standing in snow, shovel the snow away for an area of about two feet all around the car.

5. If ventilators are at the front, close them if you are kept standing in a line back of cars with motors running. Otherwise, these vents act as funnels, pouring into your car the exhaust gases from cars in front.

6. Replace mufflers or tail pipes that are clogged or damaged by corrosion. Have tail pipe straightened, repaired, or replaced, if bent or broken.

7. If holes are drilled in the fire wall between the engine and the passenger compartment to install new accessories, be sure adequate seal is made around the hole to prevent engine fumes from entering car.

8. Keep the car engine in proper condition to reduce amount of carbon monoxide developed.

Carbon monoxide may be a greater factor in causing accidents than is commonly realized.

To function properly, the cells of the brain have to be well-supplied with oxygen. Carbon monoxide acts in the body to rob the blood stream rapidly of its oxygen. The brain cells are then not supplied and the brain operates inefficiently. The driver becomes groggy. His reaction time is slowed down. He has been known, with carbon monoxide poisoning, to drive off the road or into oncoming traffic.

The first thing to do with a carbon monoxide victim is to get him into FRESH AIR. Send for a doctor. In the meantime, apply artificial respiration.

5. Worry or Distractions   Driving requires constant alertness. People are not alert when they are worried or distracted or when their minds are preoccupied with other things than their driving.

Home trouble, serious worries, serious illness in the family, or personal fears make a driver more likely to have an accident. Strong emotions can work the same way. They tend to absorb one's attention. It becomes more difficult to be as alert and watchful as one should be when controlling a fast, powerful car.

Fig. 29. Better wait and "cool off."

Persons who have just had quarrels or are angry should allow for a definite "cooling off" period before driving a car. "Taking it out" behind the wheel is very poor judgment.

It is possible that the frequent "crack-ups" of criminals who attempt automobile getaways are caused as much by the desperate condition of the driver's mind as by the car speed.

Worry and safe driving do not mix. If you are worried, nervous, or depressed, let someone else do the driving.

O TALK ABOUT:

Discuss the meaning of "compensate" as it is used in this chapter. **1**

How can a deaf person check his horn? **2**

Discuss whether or not it would be desirable to require drivers who reach a certain age to pass periodical physical examinations and driving tests before renewal of their operator's license? What age? Why? **3**

Can you cite instances of disabled persons who, because of compensation, drive as well as other persons? Explain how they compensate. **4**

What is the policy of your state about refusing licenses to people with disabilities? **5**

"Disqualify" is a strong word. Discuss the fitness of its use here, after reading through the four sections on Fatigue, In- **6** fluence of an Intoxicant, Carbon Monoxide Poisoning, and Worry and Distractions.

7   Discuss the effects on driving of: anger; fear; distraction or preoccupation; worry. Give examples, if possible.

TO DO:

1   By means of an audiometer, test the auditory acuity of each ear of the members of your group.

2   Interview 25 drivers and report on the means they use to ward off fatigue. Can all of them be recommended for common use? Which ones can be? Explain.

3   Construct and exhibit posters or cartoons on the subject of physical fitness and the driver.

4   The Bureau of Motor Carriers of the Interstate Commerce Commission has set up regulations restricting the time companies are permitted to allow their drivers to operate. Secure a copy, study the regulations carefully, and summarize them. Then determine a set of regulations which you think your state should adopt. Report to the group for discussion, making sure you can defend your proposal.

5   Have the chemistry class demonstrate how the addition of alcohol changes the color of a solution of sulphuric acid and potassium permanganate, as in the breath test for intoxication.

TO LOOK UP:

Carbon Monoxide—Your Car and You. White, Andrew J., Motor Vehicle Research, Inc., South Lee, N. H. 1953, 35 pp.
Evaluating Chemical Tests for Intoxication; a Report of the Committee on Tests for Intoxication. National Safety Council, Chicago 11, Illinois. 1953. 16 pp.
What Happens to Alcohol in the Body. How Alcohol Affects Psychological Behavior. Lay Supplements No. 7 and No. 11. Quarterly Journal of Studies on Alcohol, Yale Center of Alcohol Studies, 52 Hillhouse Ave., New Haven, Conn.

CHAPTER 4

STOPPING DISTANCES

AND THE DRIVER

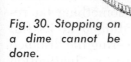

Fig. 30. Stopping on a dime cannot be done.

HOW FAST CAN YOU STOP A CAR?

IT IS difficult to believe that you cannot "stop on a dime." The truth is that the best driver, with the newest car and the best brakes, can do nothing of the sort.

Suppose you are driving along and have to bring your car to an emergency stop. What determines the best you can do? What are the factors that determine how far your car will travel before you can stop it?

Suppose we use as an example an emergency stop made necessary by the fact that a pedestrian has stepped into the path of the car, under conditions where the driver must stop the car as fast as possible or the pedestrian will be hit. In such an emergency, an inevitable series of 5 things must happen. Every one of them takes time. During every one of them, the car continues toward the pedestrian.

First of all, the driver has to *see* the object in his path. Second, he must *recognize* the object as a pedestrian who will be struck unless the driver does something fast. Third, the driver must then *decide* to stop. Fourth, he must then *react,* by moving his foot to the brake pedal.

55

Fifth, he must *brake*, pressing the brake pedal down until the car is finally stopped. Each step takes time—during which the car moves on ahead.

Figure 31 shows these 5 stages in emergency stopping very well. Study it carefully. Suppose we examine better what happens in each stage.

Seeing An Object in Your Path LOOKING at Fig. 31, let us say that, at CAR POSITION 1, an attentive driver with good eyesight could have seen the object in the path of his car if he had been "driving ahead," that is, if he had been completely attentive to his driving and alert to the situation ahead.

Let us suppose he was not attentive. Perhaps he was looking at the scenery, had his mind on conversation, had poor eyesight, or was thinking about something far removed from his driving. His car continued at its full speed toward the object in its path, covering the distance marked "X" and arriving at POSITION 2. Inattention shortened the distance the driver could have had for use in the emergency stop, had he been attentive and had he seen the hazard earlier.

Recognizing the Object as a Hazard EVEN AFTER the driver sees "something" ahead, time elapses before he recognizes it fully, before he attaches meaning to what he sees and perceives it to be what it really is. In our example, he now perceives the object to be a man in the path of his car.

During the time required for the driver to perceive the object as a pedestrian in his path, the car continued, probably at full speed, over distance "Y" and arrived at POSITION 3, making even shorter the space the driver will have left for emergency stopping.

Deciding to Apply the Brakes AT POSITION 3, the driver has not even decided to apply the brakes and stop. Even though it may seem like an instantaneous matter, time is required to make this decision. The driver is choosing what to do. Choosing requires time.

By the time the driver has decided to meet the emergency by coming to an emergency stop, his car has gone

56

farther along, perhaps at a somewhat reduced speed. It has covered distance "Z," and arrived at POSITION 4.

THE DRIVER now moves his foot from the accelerator to the brake pedal. This reaction also requires time. It is called the *braking reaction time* and is measurable. **Applying the Brakes**

The important fact about a driver's braking reaction time is the distance the car moves ahead while the reaction is taking place. In our example, the car moves during this period over distance "A" and arrives at POSITION 5.

The distance left for the emergency stop has shortened even more, and the car has not yet stopped, or even started to slow down.

The length of distance "A" in Fig. 31 depends chiefly on two things:

1. The reaction time of the individual driver who is ◄ making the stop.
2. The speed his car is traveling when he decides to apply the brakes.

An average person has a simple braking reaction time of 0.75 of a second. This is true under conditions of knowing in advance what stopping signal to expect and exactly what to do when the signal appears. Many people have slower reaction times; some require even 1.5 seconds, or twice the average time, to react. The longer the driver's reaction time, the longer is distance "A," the distance the car travels while the driver's reaction is being made.

BY THE TIME the car being stopped in this emergency has come to POSITION 5, the driver has pressed on the brake pedal and the brakes have started to play their part in stopping the car. Time is required for them to stop the car. During that time the car travels over distance "B" and finally stops at POSITION 6. **Braking the Car to a Stop**

The length of distance "B" depends chiefly on:

1. The braking force available. (Based on the grip of ◄ the brakes on the drums and the friction grip of the tires on the road.)
2. The speed the car was traveling when the brakes were applied.

57

WHAT A DRIVER FACES IN

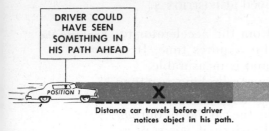

DRIVER COULD
HAVE SEEN
SOMETHING IN
HIS PATH AHEAD

POSITION 1

X

Distance car travels before driver
notices object in his path.

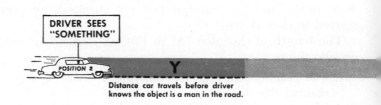

DRIVER SEES
"SOMETHING"

POSITION 2

Y

Distance car travels before driver
knows the object is a man in the road.

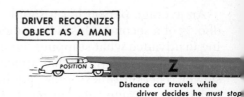

DRIVER RECOGNIZES
OBJECT AS A MAN

POSITION 3

Z

Distance car travels while
driver decides he *must* stop

DRIVER DECIDES
HE *MUST* STOP

POSITION 4

Fig. 31. What happens in an emergency stop.

MAKING AN EMERGENCY STOP

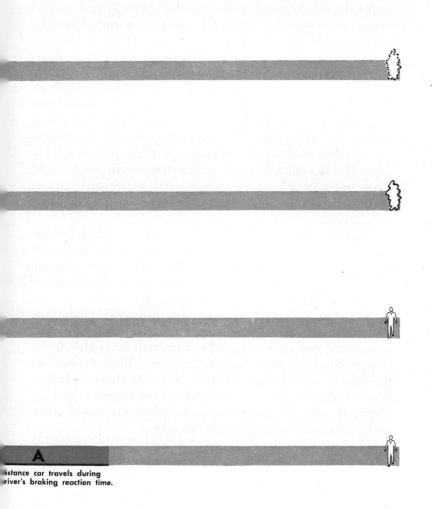

A

Distance car travels during
driver's braking reaction time.

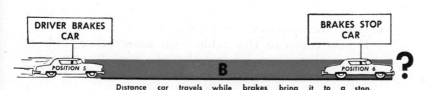

DRIVER BRAKES
CAR

POSITION 5

B

BRAKES STOP
CAR

POSITION 6

?

Distance car travels while brakes bring it to a stop.

THE STOPPING DISTANCE

AT THIS point in the story about our pedestrian who stepped into the path of the car and caused the driver to make an emergency stop, we want to know: Was the pedestrian hit?

Was the Pedestrian Hit? WHETHER or not he was hit depends on whether or not, when the driver saw him, the pedestrian was *inside* or *outside* distance Y + Z + A + B. If he was inside that distance, he was hit. If he was outside it, he was saved.

Had the driver been fully attentive, the pedestrian would have had a better chance in the emergency, because the stopping distance at the driver's disposal would have been X + Y + Z + A + B. An inattentive driver builds up odds against saving the life of any pedestrian caught in an emergency-stop situation.

Distance "X" is an unknown distance. It depends on such things as a driver's alertness when at the wheel. It depends also on whether or not the driver has built up the good driving practice of noticing everything ahead within any possible range of danger.

Distances "Y" and "Z" are also unknown distances. They depend on such things as the sharpness of the driver's senses, and on the speed with which he is able to interpret what comes to his eyes and ears. They depend on the driver's speed of perception. Actually these distances depend also on the driver's general intelligence and his ability to size up situations, make judgments, and come to decisions about what action to take.

When it comes to distances "A" and "B," it is possible to arrive at rather definite measurements, provided you know the driver's average reaction time for braking, know the available braking force, and the car speed.

Table III shows total stopping distances at different speeds, after you decide to apply the brakes. It gives definite measurements for distances "A" and "B."

If you compare this table with some other table of stopping distances and find that the two do not agree, this does not mean that either table is incorrect. In gen-

Miles Per Hour	Reaction-Time Distance	Braking Distance	Total Stopping Distance
5	5.5 Ft.	4 Ft.	9.5 Ft.
10	11.	9	20.
15	16.5	15	31.5
20	22.	23	45.
25	27.5	33	60.5
30	33.	45	78.
35	38.5	61	99.5
40	44.	81	125.
45	49.5	105	154.5
50	55.	133	188.
55	60.5	167	227.5
60	66.	206	272.
65	71.5	252	323.5
70	77.	304	381.

MINIMUM STOPPING DISTANCES
at
DIFFERENT SPEEDS

(To nearest half foot)
Reaction Time 0.75 second

These distances are based on tests made by the Bureau of Public Roads. The chart below shows how greatly braking distances increase when you increase your speed.

Reaction Time Distance
Braking Distance

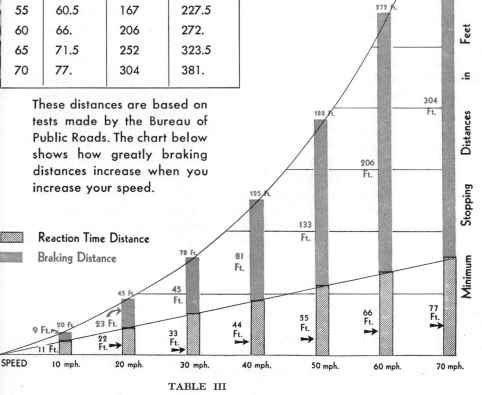

TABLE III

eral, both will show the same thing about the seriousness of stopping distances. But they may be based on different average braking reaction times or on brakes of different efficiency. Some tables are arrived at by using a formula which assumes that braking distances vary as the square of the speed. Table III is based on actual stopping tests made by the Bureau of Public Roads. It assumes a driver with an average braking reaction time of 0.75 seconds and brakes in good condition.

Braking Reaction Time Distance   IN THE column under Braking Reaction Time Distances, Table III shows how distance "A" in Fig. 31 lengthens at higher speeds, with the driver's reaction time remaining the same. Notice that the braking reaction time distance increases as the speed increases. If the driver's reaction time is longer than the 0.75 seconds used in setting up this table, the distance the car will travel at these different speeds, before the driver gets his foot off the accelerator pedal and on the brake pedal, will be longer.

Measuring Braking Reaction Time   YOUR braking reaction time is important in driving. A device such as the one shown in Fig. 32 can be used for measuring it. The clutch, brake, and accelerator pedals are arranged on the device as they are in an ordinary automobile. When you are being tested, you sit down and place your right foot on the accelerator. You are directed to move your foot from the accelerator pedal to the brake pedal as rapidly as possible when a red light appears. The distance an electrically-run timing hand travels, after the red light appears, until you step on the brake gives a measure of your braking reaction time.

After a few practice trials, at least ten real trials should be given and the average used as a measure of your average braking reaction time. People vary so much from trial to trial that the average of only two or three trials is not a good enough measure of one's reaction time.

Reaction time varies with the type of test used and the way it is given. For the test just described, the average reaction time is about 0.40 of a second. Some people are much slower to react than this.

In the test just described you know ahead of time what to expect and exactly what to do. When the red light comes on, you make just one movement.

Under actual driving conditions your reactions are not so simple. You are not always watching for a signal to stop. You may have to make a left turn to avoid hitting an obstacle, give a hand signal, and slow down, all at one time. Or you may have to choose whether to brake hard or spurt ahead out of trouble.

Fig. 32. Reaction time testing device.

Because actual driving situations are more complicated than this simple test situation, the driver's reaction time is longer. Under simple driving conditions, when the driver is watching for a signal to stop, the average braking reaction time is found to be around 0.75 of a second.

IN THE COLUMN under Braking Distances, Table III shows **Braking Distance** how greatly distance "B" lengthens with higher car speeds. This is the distance the car goes from the time the driver applies the brakes until it comes to a stop.

Although this distance depends also on the braking force available, the speed of the car is the most important factor in determining the length. *This braking distance increases approximately as the square of the speed of the car between 20 and 55 miles per hour. At higher speeds, the braking distances increase even faster than the square of the speed.*

Total Stopping Distance THE REACTION Time Distance and the Braking Distance together make up the total stopping distance, after the driver decides to stop.

Study Table III and the interesting diagram under it. The curve which shows how minimum stopping distances increase as you speed up your car rises *sharply.* Every ten miles added to your speed gives you a far more serious emergency stopping problem than the preceding ten miles. There is no escaping the fact. It is part of smart, intelligent driving to know this and to know how to choose speeds that suit conditions.

The Brake Reaction Detonator THE BRAKE Reaction Detonator is a good device to use in measuring distances "A" and "B" at various speeds. It makes all the more real the fact that no driver can "stop on a dime."

With this device, you can test your own stopping distances for different speeds after you have learned to drive. These test distances, however, will generally be shorter than in actual driving emergencies. For in actual driving situations, you are making more complex judgments, and they require longer times.

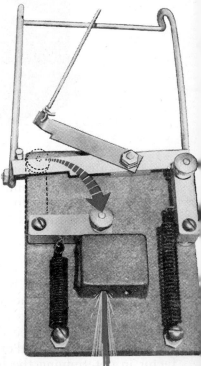

Fig. 33. A brake reaction detonator.

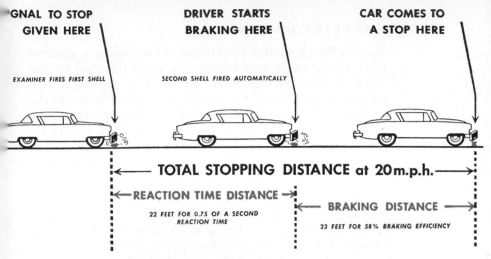

GNAL TO STOP
GIVEN HERE

DRIVER STARTS
BRAKING HERE

CAR COMES TO
A STOP HERE

EXAMINER FIRES FIRST SHELL

SECOND SHELL FIRED AUTOMATICALLY

TOTAL STOPPING DISTANCE at 20 m.p.h.

REACTION TIME DISTANCE

22 FEET FOR 0.75 OF A SECOND
REACTION TIME

BRAKING DISTANCE

23 FEET FOR 58% BRAKING EFFICIENCY

Fig. 34. How to use a brake reaction detonator.

In this test, you are "tipped off" beforehand as to what to expect and exactly what you are to do when a signal is given. So it is called a *simple* brake reaction time test.

In ordinary driving situations, you are not "tipped off" ahead of time as to dangers and reactions. You have to be on the lookout for anything to happen. The traffic picture is often very complex. You must constantly make judgments. You are often confronted with alternative choices as to what you will do. Under such circumstances, both your reaction time and your reaction time distance will be longer. So it is well to realize that, in this detonator test, you are measuring a much simpler, faster reaction than you can hope to make behind the wheel in most traffic situations.

The Detonator is hung on the front or rear bumper of the car in which you are tested. Two .22 blank cartridges loaded with yellow marking powder are inserted in two miniature gun barrels which point down toward the street. The person who is testing you sits beside you in the front seat of the car and tells you to drive at a given speed, such as 20 miles per hour, and to stop as quickly as possible when you hear a shot fired. After you have driven awhile, and unknown to you, he pulls a string or presses a button to fire the first shell in the Detonator. This explosion forces the marking powder in the first

65

capsule down to the pavement. This makes a powder mark at the exact spot where you were directed by the "shot" to step on the brake. At the first explosion, you take your foot from the accelerator pedal and hit the brake pedal as quickly as possible. Pressure on the brake pedal automatically fires the second shell in the Detonator, making a second powder mark on the pavement. This second mark indicates exactly where the front or rear bumper was when you got your braking started. Measure the distance between these two powder marks on the pavement, and you have your *simple brake reaction time distance.* Then a white chalk mark is placed directly below where your bumper comes to a stop. The distance between the second and third marks is your *braking distance.* The sum of the two distances is your total *stopping distance.*

If you are an average driver with a simple brake reaction time of three-fourths of a second (0.75 of a second), and if you are traveling at 20 miles per hour, the distance between the two marks will be some 22 feet. In these 22 feet, you have not even slowed down the car. You have merely moved your foot off the accelerator pedal and put it on the brake pedal.

Try the test at a speed of 30 miles per hour. Your reaction time distance will be found to have increased greatly. It is now 33 feet in length before you even start to brake. The distance your car travels while you react to a signal to stop varies directly as the speed.

Suppose you are driving on the open road at 40 miles per hour. Just as you begin to pass a line of three cars standing bumper to bumper along the roadside, a child darts out from in front of the third car. Even if you see him at once, you will have traveled 44 feet, or nearly the total length of the three cars, and be upon him by the time your foot has just begun to press the brake. Even in split-second reaction, your car covers this astonishing distance.

There is still the braking distance to be traveled before your car is brought to a stop. No, a driver cannot stop on a dime.

Fig. 35. A danger zone always stretches out in front of your car.

THE DANGER ZONE

THE STOPPING distance represents a *danger zone* which always stretches out ahead of every moving car. It is the distance within which you cannot stop.

A driver who is not alert and who is late in seeing an object in the path of his car increases the probability that, as the car approaches it, the object will be *within* the car's stopping distance or danger zone. He greatly increases the probability that the object will be hit.

The slower the reaction time of the driver, the longer is the danger zone. As the speed of the car increases, this zone of danger stretches out very much farther. Adverse road and brake conditions make it still longer.

When driving, you always have this danger zone to deal with. You cannot escape it. Your driving must always be in terms of it. In fact, your car is never in actual control unless you are managing it with this danger zone in consideration.

You help decide the length of the danger zone ahead of your own car by:

Your driving alertness.
The way you care for or neglect your brakes and tires.

The physical and mental condition in which you keep yourself.

The speeds at which you drive.

The danger zone should NEVER be allowed to become greater than the length of the roadway ahead which you believe will remain clear of hazard.

Controlling the Stopping Distance THERE IS nothing you can do to *eliminate* either the reaction time distance or the braking distance. You can, however, do much to *reduce* these distances by choosing proper speeds.

Reaction time distance depends on the way a human being is put together. In ordinary driving situations, you can help keep it down by being always alert for traffic dangers, by becoming very familiar with the car and its performance, and by establishing good driving habits. By paying close attention to traffic, you recognize dangers sooner. When you are familiar with the car and use good driving practices, your reactions become partially automatic. Very often you don't have to "stop and think" in order to make the proper reaction.

Braking distance can be decreased by keeping the brakes in proper adjustment, the tires in good condition, and by replacing worn brake linings and tires. It cannot be eliminated. It depends on mechanical factors which are unavoidable.

Fig. 36. The passenger gets "the brakes"!

Brakes have been greatly improved by skillful engineering. But there comes a point beyond which their power to control a mighty force like a rapidly moving car cannot go. Indeed, braking can be too hard. Too rapid deceleration, not only makes passengers uncomfortable, but can be unsafe—throwing them out of their seats, or causing objects which many people wrongly carry on the rear shelf of a car to fly forward and hit them.

The stopping distances of small, motor-powered vehicles are extremely important and are often not recognized by their drivers. The braking and stopping distances of different makes and types vary greatly and should be determined by actual tests. Most of these vehicles have only a rear wheel brake. This in itself makes the braking and stopping a special matter. Overloading, by carrying more passengers than the vehicle is designed for, increases the difficulty of stopping quickly in tight spots. The stopping distances of one of these vehicles can be controlled only by having it equipped with adequate brakes and driving it at reasonable speeds, without overloading.

IS YOUR REACTION TIME ALWAYS THE SAME?

WE HAVE been talking about *average* reaction time. But each person must consider his own.

Even when you are in a normal condition, your reaction time may vary considerably. Some people have a more consistent reaction time than others. They are less likely to be involved in collisions if they also use good judgment in choosing speed. If you find out, by test, that your own reaction time is likely to vary considerably from time to time, be guided by your longest reaction time in estimating your stopping distances.

The physical condition of the body varies from time to time, and reaction time changes with physical condition. This can be shown by actual measurement.

Laboratory tests have proved that reaction time is measurably increased by:

▶
1. Distractions.	*5.* Carbon monoxide.
2. Alcohol.	*6.* Eyestrain.
3. Low visibility.	*7.* Drugs of various kinds.
4. Fatigue.	*8.* Age.

Day-dreaming, worry, sorrow, business or social planning, conversations, or concentration on radio are all distractions.

In the case of alcohol, experiments reported by the Laboratory of Applied Physiology of Yale University showed that visual reaction time, or the time it takes you to react to a visual signal, rapidly became much longer as more alcohol was consumed. In some cases, visual reaction time was found to be lengthened, after drinking, by 34 per cent.

In driving, a 34 per cent increase in visual reaction time means that, traveling at 50 miles per hour, it would take about 19 feet more road space to bring the car to a full stop after a visual signal to stop. This is one powerful argument against the use of alcohol by drivers.

The Council on Pharmacy and Chemistry of the American Medical Association agrees that certain drugs, such as barbital, veronal, phenobarbital, and luminal, have a dulling effect on reaction time and mental processes. A driver does well not to use such drugs without medical advice and never to use them when driving.

MARGIN OF SAFETY

REALIZE your limitations in stopping a car, and provide safe margins of stopping distance when driving:

▶
1. Behind other cars.
2. With unfavorable road conditions.
3. At night.
4. Where there are pedestrians, especially children.
5. In built-up sections.
6. Near intersections.
7. In a strange car.
8. On unfamiliar roads.
9. When under par physically or mentally.

With professional drivers, it is a matter of pride to be familiar with such technical points in driving and to act accordingly. The driver who frequently has to make sudden stops is not allowing adequate margins of safety.

Dangers can loom up instantaneously, but perceiving the danger and stopping a car can never be an instantaneous matter. By choosing speeds with good judgment, the driver can provide the *margin of safety* to prevent sudden danger from ending in catastrophe. Expert drivers provide just such a margin.

TO TALK ABOUT:

Discuss the driver's chances to improve his reaction time. **1**

Discuss all the factors which affect the braking distance of **2** a car.

Describe situations which make an accident certain, be- **3** cause of the reaction times and braking distances involved.

Show that the "danger zone" is a flexible matter and that **4** the driver controls the length of it almost as he would a rubber band stretched between two fingers.

How do you account for the fact that reaction times differ: **5**
(*a*) in different individuals?
(*b*) in the same person at different times?

Why are you likely to underestimate your true reaction **6** time under general driving conditions?

To what extent is the "braking distance" at any particular **7** speed dependent upon the driver?

TO DO:

Have the members of the group join hands to form a **1** "chain." Have a leader in the chain press the hand of the person next to him. Have each one relay the "squeeze" to his neighbor as soon as he receives it. With a stop watch, or the second hand of an ordinary watch, measure the time it takes the "squeeze" to travel around the chain. Divide the time in seconds by the number of people in the chain to find the average "touch" reaction time per person.

2   Secure a Brake Reaction Detonator and make stopping distance tests at 20 and 30 miles per hour in a place where there is no other traffic.

3   If a Brake Reaction Detonator is not available, measure, along a curb, the total stopping distances shown in Table III for 20 m.p.h. and 30 m.p.h., so you will realize how far a car travels at these speeds before you can stop it.

4   Make a table showing the reaction time distances at 20, 40, and 60 miles per hour for: (a) a driver with a slow reaction time of 0.90 of a second; (b) a driver with a very slow reaction time of 1.2 seconds.

5   Copy Fig. 37. Using a scale of one inch for every fifty feet of roadway, measure off, on the copy you have drawn, the danger zones of cars which are being driven at different speeds by a driver with average (or better, *your own*) reaction time. Color the danger zones red.

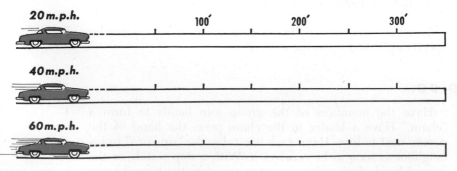

Fig. 37. Mark off the danger zones for different speeds.

20 m.p.h.

100′   200′   300′

40 m.p.h.

60 m.p.h.

If an average parking space of 20 feet is being used by **6** each car, show how many parked cars the driver will have to pass from the time he perceives danger ahead and decides to make an emergency stop, until he can bring his car to a complete stop, if his reaction time is 1 second and his car is moving at the rate of 40 miles per hour.

TO LOOK UP:

Age and Complex Reaction Time. Allgaier, Earl. American Automobile Association, Washington, D.C. 1953. 4 pp.

Let's Drive Right. Halsey, Maxwell. Scott, Foresman and Company, New York, New York. 1954. 465 pp.

Man and the Motor Car. The Center for Safety Education, New York University. Prentice-Hall Publishing Company, New York, New York. 1954. 367 pp.

Reaction Time in Automobile Driving. Baker, James Stannard. National Safety Council, Chicago, Illinois, Public Safety Memo No. 95. October, 1948.

The Fundamental Principles of Driving. Tysor, James H. Banks Upshaw & Co., Dallas, Texas. 1953. 346 pp.

CHAPTER 5

THE PSYCHOLOGY

WHY DRIVERS DIFFER

NO TWO persons behave in exactly the same way.

Man cannot be standardized as the car has been. He is not constructed of machine-like parts. The part that is strong in one person may be weak in another. Each person develops a special combination of abilities, habits, and attitudes, depending on his background.

Why the driver behaves as he does is a problem of driver psychology. How can you avoid the mental twists or psychological weak spots that produce the kind of driver behavior that causes most highway accidents? How can you develop driver behavior that is mature and shows good judgment and of which you can be proud?

Fig. 38. What makes a driver tick?

DO YOU KNOW:
Why drivers differ?
Why some drivers tend to have accidents?
Who are psychologically unfit to drive?
What mental qualities lead to top-notch driving?

OF THE DRIVER

BEHIND THE SCENES IN THE DRIVER'S MIND

CAN WE GET "behind the scenes" in the driver's mind and learn about his mental weak spots?

When a car fails to perform as it should, technical experts analyze the situation, find what the car troubles are, and correct them. Can we do as well with the driver? Can we get "behind the scenes" and analyze him to discover what it is about him that causes trouble at the wheel? Can we find out also what makes a *good* driver "tick"?

To some extent we can. The psychologist, the physician, the judge, the traffic engineer, and the enforcement official have all been studying what it is in a person's make-up that gets him into traffic troubles. It is known that some drivers are much more likely than others to have accidents. We call such drivers "accident-prone."

Studies made by the U.S. Bureau of Public Roads, as well as by commercial concerns operating large fleets of trucks and cars, show that some drivers suffer emotional or other disturbances that make them accident-prone. On a fleet of vehicles, for example, a small group of accident-prone drivers may prove responsible for most of the accidents.

Any person may be temporarily accident-prone due to some temporary condition. Some persons are generally unfit to drive because habitually wrong attitudes or emotional weaknesses make them bad risks as drivers.

The ideal results of driver trouble-shooting would be to:

▶ 1. Sort out accident-prone drivers and revoke their driving privileges—take them right off the road—until their weaknesses are corrected.

2. Test drivers and prospective drivers for certain mental and emotional weaknesses and "spot" accident-prone persons before they have accidents, or even before they begin to drive.

3. Show individuals how to recognize and correct traits in themselves that cause accidents.

HOW ACCIDENTS ARE REDUCED

WHEN ACCIDENT-PRONE DRIVERS ARE WEEDED OUT

Year	Miles Traveled	Number of Accidents
1st year	2,400,000	176
2nd year	2,680,000	173
3rd year	2,640,000	137
*4th year	2,880,000	69
5th year	2,394,000	55
6th year	2,373,000	45

* In this year, accident-prone drivers were put on other work.—From Highway Research Abstracts.

TABLE IV

BAD RISKS AS DRIVERS

The Egotist ALL BABIES are normally self-centered. They have not learned how to be unselfish. They have not learned how to share. They are good examples of the perfect egotist.

As people grow out of babyhood, they learn that self is really not the center of the universe. If they develop normally, they become more social; that is, their interests spread out and away from self, and they see things more and more in the light of public good. They acquire *social attitudes.*

With his normal psychological make-up, the baby would make the worst possible driver. He would consider nothing but his own interest and immediate desires.

The babyish adult makes a miserable driver for the same reason. He has never outgrown his babyish egotism. He may have had the kind of childhood training that makes grown-up persons act like babies.

Fig. 39. The egotist thinks the world revolves around him.

On the highway, this egotistical, babyish type of person betrays himself by such practices as:

Pulling out of line to the confusion of others.
Stopping or making turns without signaling.
Making turns from improper traffic lanes.
Cutting in too closely after passing.
Not staying on his own side of the road or in his traffic lane.
Boasting of breaking traffic laws.
Acting as though accidents happen only to others.
"Chiseling in," out of turn.
Demanding the right-of-way.
Using influence and "pull" for ticket fixing.
Parking double, for his own convenience.
Parking his car so that it occupies almost two parking spaces.
Pulling out from the curb without signaling or looking for approaching cars.

77

The egotist is a psychological misfit in the traffic picture. He is easily spotted. He is never admired. The habit of thinking of others can keep you from being one.

The Show-off LIKE THE egotist, the show-off discloses that he has never properly grown up. He has never managed, no matter what his age, to get both feet on the ground and to see himself in his proper place among other men and women. He is like the child who enjoys dangling his lolly-pop in other children's faces! He is competitive and boastful. Often he is suffering from a sense of inferiority which he is covering up by trying to appear superior. He doesn't stop to realize how ridiculous he looks to others.

Fig. 40. The unpopular show-off breezes by.

The show-off is a bad risk as a driver because of practices like the following:

▶ Driving too fast for conditions.
Driving more recklessly the larger his audience.
Creating near emergencies to prove that he can get out of them.
Boasting of his car's speed and power and of his own skill.

Boasting of the time he makes between places.

Acting more for showmanship than for sportsmanship.

Passing other cars at risky places and talking about his luck.

Painting his car with "loud" colors and smart remarks or plastering it with stickers.

Being ready to prove he can "stop on a dime."

Being ready to take a chance or to "try anything once."

Being willing to turn the highway into a race track.

Boasting that he can drive just as well after a drink or two.

Always taking a dare.

Passing red lights and stop signs with an air of bravado.

Trying to give the impression that he drives like "a man who has been around a lot."

Admired by none, the "smart-aleck" is likely to think he is admired by all.

Fig. 41. "Baby Blow-Horn" plows through.

The U<small>NCONTROLLED</small> emotions are another sign of immaturity.
Over-Emotional A baby does not have the problem of controlling his emotions; he just expresses them. Ability to control emotions and remain calm under stress should develop as you grow older. With proper training and a desire to be mature, such emotional control should show by the time you reach your later teens.

But some persons are never more than adult-sized babies as far as their emotions are concerned. They take the slightest criticism as a personal offense. They whine and sulk and become resentful. Unimportant trifles seem big to them. We say they "make mountains out of molehills." Their emotional development has been stunted. They have never really grown up. We call them "unstable," because they cannot be depended on.

Persons with stunted emotional development show characteristic driving faults. Psychological trouble-shooters can spot them because they:

▶ Lack presence of mind in emergencies.
Get "upset" over trifles, or are nervous in unusual situations.
Lose their temper and, consequently, their judgment.
Express anger by driving recklessly.
Show impatience in traffic jams and start irrational horn-blowing.
Flash their lights in the eyes of oncoming drivers.
Talk loud, or use profanity.
Call traffic officers by abusive names.
Resort to boorish crowding and pushing others out of their lanes.
Are easily distracted from the main business of driving.

Fig. 42. Shouting patches no fenders.

Childish giving away to emotions is responsible for a great many traffic emergencies and accidents. Regardless of age, people with childish emotional behavior are not worthy of driving licenses.

THEN THERE IS the person who never learns to face facts squarely. He finds it easy to see a thing the way he wants to see it, rather than the way it really is. He will not admit his own faults. If involved in an accident, he blames the driver of another car, the traffic regulations, the road, a "backseat" driver, his own car—anyone and anything but himself. He lacks courage to admit his own faults.

The Rationalizer

Such a person is clever at finding plausible-sounding arguments to excuse everything—even though obviously wrong. We call him a "rationalizer." He fails conspicuously in sportsmanlike driving.

SOME PERSONS do absurd things to compensate or make up for failure.

The Thwarted

There is a strong desire in man to be masterful, to achieve something, to assert himself and display his power. If circumstances prevent him from showing mastery in one situation, he tries to show it in another. A familiar example is the man who does not amount to much at the office or shop and so tries to lord it over everybody at home.

The unimportant fellow looks for a chance to appear powerful. The really important man doesn't need to hunt for artificial outlets, for his desires for mastery and self-expression are being satisfied normally.

Fig. 43. Mr. "Milktoast" borrows power.

But watch the thwarted man step into a car. Here is power at his disposal! What will he do with it? The psychological trouble-shooter will find him:

► Insisting on the right-of-way.
Arguing a traffic point endlessly.
Talking "big" to traffic officers and other drivers.
Showing the road practices of the egotist.
Bullying other drivers and pedestrians.
"Giving his dust" to smaller or older cars.
Edging in to cheat someone out of a parking space.
Making pedestrians scramble to safety.
Not moving over when another driver signals he wants to pass.
"Getting even" with drivers who pass him.

He is always trying an artificial boost to his puny self-esteem.

Of course, he shows himself up as an unimportant fellow who is borrowing a feeling of personal power from his car. But the foolish things he does may lead to tragic or expensive accidents. It is disagreeable to be with "rationalizers." It is worse to find *you* are one. Forming the habit of facing facts, even though disagreeable, keeps you from being one.

THE MENTAL MAKE-UP OF A TOP-NOTCH DRIVER

FROM a psychological point of view, the top-notch driver has, not only motor skill, but *balance* and *self-control*. He has good social attitudes. He shows good adjustment and maturity. These characteristics show up in evidences of his:

► **Acceptance of responsibility**
Self control
Good sportsmanship
Forethought
Controlled attention
Good judgment
Good sense of humor

CREASED HORSEPOWER . . .
CREASED RESPONSIBILITY!

150 h.p.

85 h.p.

h.p.

"EARLY DAYS"   In the 1940's   "NOWADAYS"

Fig. 44. Today's driver controls galloping horsepower!

IT IS DIFFICULT to draw a sharp line between good sports-manship and a sense of responsibility.

Good sportsmanship is found in people who show fairness, courtesy and reasonableness. Such traits come from a desire for *fair sharing*. This desire is an indication of social maturity. It means that the driver senses the traffic situation, not merely from his personal point of view, but from the point of view of other highway users. His driving practices are quite the opposite of those of the babyish, egotistical, over-emotional, unbalanced trouble-makers we have been analyzing. He, too, is easily spotted on the highway. His good attitude and sound actions reflect his mental and emotional maturity. Sound driver instruction helps produce this kind of driver.

Responsibility and Sportsmanship

GOOD *judgment* is not the mysterious "gift" that some people suppose. It comes, to a large extent, from a good background of sound training in home and school.

You think more soundly about subjects you thoroughly understand. The business of driving an automobile in traffic is no exception. A background of driver education is the foundation for good driving judgment. Experiences in well-supervised practice driving are good building blocks. They help build both skill and sound attitudes in the top-notch driver.

A driver of good judgment is constantly sizing up the traffic situation and is not caught unawares. He has developed *traffic imagination* and insight. He makes de-

Judgment

83

cisions and reactions that help keep the traffic pattern sane and safe.

Attention   A QUALITY that shows in the driver of mature psychological make-up is *controlled attention*.

The person who cannot control his own attention is not fit to drive a car. Imagine a man steering a fast-moving object on a shared highway with his attention like that of a child, at the mercy of any accidental happening! Attention has to be directed into place and held there.

The psychologically fit driver is able to attend to business. His business is the total traffic pattern. He "drives ahead." That is, he knows everything that is happening in his whole field of vision that could possibly affect the driving picture. His attention is focused constantly on *the path that his car should take,* considering all the other factors in the situation.

It is a fact that there is a strong tendency to steer toward the spot to which you attend. The muscles of your body tend to adjust toward the goal of your attention. You have seen a bicycle rider, for example, turn his wheel toward the spot where he is looking, without knowing he does it. A driver whose attention is so poorly controlled that he turns his head toward distractions is likely to steer his car unconsciously in the same direction.

John Doe was a man of childish, uncontrolled attention. While he was driving, his dog, in the back of his

Fig. 45. Mrs. Snippy hunts a house number.

car, made a commotion. John Doe immediately gave it his attention. He looked over his *right* shoulder, and took his eye from the road. In a split second, his car had crashed into a telephone pole at the *right* side of the road.

Mrs. Doe thought she could drive down a city street and, at the same time, watch for an obscure house number on the *left*. She crashed into a car traveling in the *left* lane, because she unconsciously steered that way.

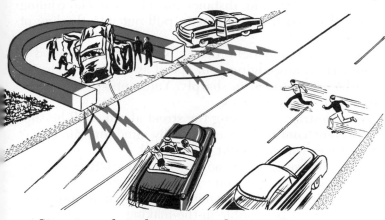

Fig. 46. The scene of an accident can distract the attention of drivers and pedestrians.

Situations that threaten to distract the uncontrolled attention of drivers may be:

The scene of an accident
Novel things along the route
Fine views
A member of the opposite sex—in or out of the car
A back-seat driver
Arguments
A bee or wasp in the car
The radio program
A hat blowing off; or things placed on the seat sliding around
Sharp light reflections
Pets and children in the car
A thousand and one other things

Control, whether of emotions, attitudes, or attention, is a distinguishing characteristic of the person who is psychologically mature.

Foresight THE BEST drivers develop a high degree of traffic imagination and foresight. They see and think ahead. They keep control and avoid trouble by recognizing *trouble-in-the-making*.

PLAYING
IN STREET

School children are walking or playing along the road. One is about to catch a ball. Suppose he misses it. Will he dart after it into the road? The driver who foresees this possibility may save the child's life.

A parked car some distance ahead has smoke coming from its exhaust. Is it about to pull out into the line of traffic?

EXHAUST SMOKE

Ahead, an impatient driver is nosing out around a truck. He is misjudging your speed as you approach. He will be forced to cut in sharply. Your anticipation of the situation avoids a wreck.

A pedestrian is crossing the street ahead. Will he slip, or become confused, or change his mind and direction? The driver with foresight is prepared.

You observe a slight movement at the left front door of a parked car. Someone is about to step out on the wrong side without knowing that your car is approaching. This may be trouble-in-the-making.

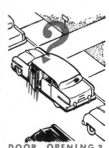

DOOR OPENING?

The driver you are following is erratic. His speed is not steady. He slows down at unexpected places without signaling, and then darts on ahead. He does not keep to his side of the center line. You prepare to take no chance with him.

Some distance ahead you see a strip of icy road, a section of wet pavement, a large puddle of water. You anticipate what could happen if you were compelled suddenly to apply your brakes on that particular spot.

A SUDDEN GUST

The road is emerging from a deep cut through a hill. You know it is a windy day and there will be a strong cross-wind at the edge of the cut. There may be a powerful sideward thrust on your car because of the wind. Your foresight makes you ready for it, and you will not be caught napping at your steering.

You are on a through-traffic street or highway. Ahead is an intersection with a "stop" sign protecting you.

You see a car on the cross road moving too rapidly toward the "stop" sign. Will the driver be able to stop where he should? Does he even see the sign? You are aware of the situation. Whatever the other driver does, you are prepared. You are showing foresight.

WILL HE STOP?

Driving skillfully and safely in modern traffic is no "cinch."

The mechanical operations are not difficult for most people to learn. They have become simpler than ever with automatic transmission cars. But there are at least five important factors, other than mechanical skills, that make expert driving of an automobile a challenging job:

1. The power and the limitations of the car.
2. The physical features of roads and streets.
3. The behavior of other highway users.
4. Changing light and weather conditions.
5. The make-up of the driver himself.

The driver is the most important factor in keeping driving from being a "cinch." Automotive engineering may make the car easier to drive. Highway engineering and traffic engineering may make the highways and streets safer to use. Safety devices and clever inventions may help lessen the hazards in unfavorable weather conditions. But, in spite of all such improvements, first-rate driving will always demand that the driver act in accordance with SPORTSMANLIKE ATTITUDES.

The mental make-up of a driver is often more important than his skill. It determines what he will do when he has power in his hands.

THE THRILL OF POWER

MOST persons like strong, powerful things and forces. They like mighty seas and high mountains. They are fascinated by brilliant fires and thundering waterfalls, by strong men and forceful machines. They identify themselves with mighty things and get a thrill of reflected power. This is a normal human trait.

Fig. 47. Keep power under control.

So it is not surprising that the power of the automobile is a source of thrill. You can identify yourself with this machine, step into it, drive it yourself, and seem to "step-up" your power. Here, indeed, is an opportunity for glorified self-expression through borrowed power!

But there are two important things for a man to remember when he uses power:

▶ 1. Power has constructive value only when in control. Out of control, it is destructive.
2. How one uses power discloses just what kind of a person he is, and the degree to which he has reached maturity.

Man is reduced to a weak and foolish-looking creature when the power he is supposed to be directing runs away with him. He faces this fact now with the fission and thermonuclear bombs he has created. Either he controls the power, or it destroys him. Instead of the satisfaction of mastery, he could suffer the disaster of obliteration. It is not simply power that man wants; it is *power under control.*

All drivers gain a sense of power. Only top-notch drivers gain the sense of *power under control.*

Any power—whether of money, office, political prominence, or of a fine car—makes a foolish man look more foolish and a wise man look wiser.

What you do wrong as a pedestrian may be mild enough to deceive yourself and others, but when you get behind the wheel of a powerful car, every personal quality you have, good or bad, is magnified. Power in your hands shows up the real YOU!

O TALK ABOUT:

1. What is an "unstable" person? Give examples of the conduct of unstable persons whom you have met. In what situations would they make bad risks on the highway?

2. Discuss the proneness of some people to blame the other fellow for mistakes and accidents: (a) in sports; (b) in the home; (c) when driving.

3. Explain the rudeness some drivers show to pedestrians and small-car owners. How different is their behavior when encountering heavy trucks and fine cars? Explain.

4. Discuss the drivers in the following traffic incidents. Explain the psychology of each:

    ◄ M is approaching an intersection. He sees that the light is about to turn green. He speeds on the wrong side of the street and cuts in front of waiting vehicles.

    ◄ R has the reputation of always getting to the game first. This time a car is ahead of him. A pal dares him to prove he is the fastest driver in the group. He takes many chances, breaks traffic regulations, takes unfair advantage of a stop sign, and crowds ahead.

    ◄ C approaches an intersection at about the same time as a car turning from the cross street on his right. The other car passes through first. C crowds it to the curb, "bawls the driver out," takes his license number, and threatens to report him for not yielding the right-of-way.

    ◄ S tries to pass a truck near a hillcrest. A fast car approaches from the opposite direction and a three-car crash results. S defends himself by saying that the driver of the truck ahead signaled him to pass.

5. Describe other cases of bad risks as drivers and try to explain their psychology.

6. Report instances where the driver lost control of the car and the situation because of uncontrolled attention.

7. Report on accidents caused by small distractions.

8. Discuss, "Power in your hands shows up the real YOU."

TO DO:

1. Map out a plan of self-training that would help anyone with a self-centered, egotistical attitude acquire a more social point of view.

PERSONAL RATING PROJECT—

(a) Rate yourself.

(b) Have someone else rate you.

(c) Compare the two ratings.

TABLE V

SIGHT AND HEARING ABILITIES
OF
IMPORTANCE TO DRIVERS

Add other personal abilities for which you can secure measurements by use of psychophysical testing devices.

ABILITY	READING ON DEVICE	RATING			COMMENTS Corrections or Compensations
		Above Average	Average	Below Average	
Visual Acuity (with glasses) Right eye Left eye Both eyes					
Field of Vision Right eye Left eye Both eyes					
Color Perception Both eyes					
Depth Perception Both eyes					
Auditory Acuity Right ear Left ear					
Night Vision					
Etc.					

PERSONAL CHARACTERISTICS

Add other items of importance to driving which you can rate reasonably well.

CHARACTERISTIC	RATING			COMMENTS Importance to Driving
	Above Average	Average	Below Average	
Health				
Emotional Stability				
Control of Attention				
Reliability				
Courtesy				
Observation				
Presence of Mind				
Sportsmanship				
Etc.				

Extend these three tables using this textbook to help you select additional items.

TABLE VI

Study your own responses in traffic situations. Do you show **2** any tendencies to act like persons who make "bad risks" as drivers? This is a very difficult project to carry out. It is not easy to analyze oneself with fairness. But it is decidedly worthwhile doing. If you show tendencies of a person with a poor psychological make-up, what can you do about it?

Draw two diagrams of the same traffic situation: (a) as it **3** is first seen in the distance; and (b) as it changes into a hazard by the time the driver reaches it. Show how proper foresight can, in such a case, avert trouble.

TO LOOK UP:

Driver Characteristics and Accidents. Highway Research
    Board, Washington 25, D.C. 1953. Bulletin No. 73. 60 pp.
The Motor Vehicle Driver—His Nature and Improvement.
    Eno Foundation for Highway Traffic Control, Saugatuck,
    Conn. 1949.

DRIVING ABILITY—A SELF-RATING

List additional items. The more items you check, the more helpful will be your driving ability self-rating.

DRIVING SKILLS AND PRACTICES	Self-Rating			COMMENTS Suggestions for Improvement
	High	Fair	Low	
Mechanical operations: Shifting gears, Steering, etc.				
Observing traffic laws, signs, and signals.				
Keeping in correct traffic lane.				
Choosing speeds right for conditions.				
Avoiding driving when fatigued.				
Never mixing drinking and driving.				
Good judgment in: Overtaking and passing, Following, etc.				
Always "driving ahead."				
Regular inspection of car's safety equipment.				
Etc.				

TABLE VII

PART TWO

HOW WE LEARN

THERE ARE good and poor ways of learning. The *way you learn* has much to do with the quality of your later performance.

Poor learning methods stunt skill. Good learning methods lead to high-quality skill. So it is a good idea to know the difference between poor and good learning methods.

Top-flight football players, swimmers, typists, or golfers do not arrive at the top merely by reading books, watching others perform, or taking instruction from unskilled persons.

Skill must be developed by means of well-guided practice. You learn to do a thing by doing it. You learn to do it exactly as you practice. How you practice makes a lot of difference.

Practice without system and guidance is learning by "trial-and-error." It is a hit-or-miss process of trying out first this method and then that, until, by accident or luck, you happen on something that works after a fashion.

Left to themselves, beginners almost always follow a trial-and-error learning method. But such learning is inefficient. It wastes time and effort. It gives no assurance that the skill will ever be of high quality. It is likely to produce "dubs."

LEARNING HOW TO DRIVE

Trials and errors are not fatal if you are learning to play the saxophone, drive a golf ball, or do the latest dance step. The family may suffer—as will your disposition! But all will recover. Learning to drive a car is a different matter. Only competent drivers should be on our streets and roads. So only the best methods, under the supervision of competent instructors, should be used in learning to drive.

What makes a good driver? What, a poor one? It is more and more evident that people who "pick up" driving by themselves have greater difficulty in understanding their cars and in acquiring sound driving practices. Frequently they fail to understand the regulations and practices that keep traffic patterns orderly. Too often they fail to observe traffic laws voluntarily. Too often they are the cause of traffic accidents.

Systematic driving practice, under the supervision of a good instructor, gives you the best chance to become a top-flight driver.

WAIT FOR ME!

CHAPTER 6

BEFORE YOU STAR

AT THE WHEEL

SLIP behind the wheel of the car. Whether you are a beginner or have already done some driving, you probably find yourself grasping the wheel with a pleasurable thrill. "Let's go!" is your feeling.

Hold on a moment, please! Take a look at the instrument panel in front of you. Take a glance at the pedals and the button on the floor by your feet. Do you know what all those "gadgets" are for?

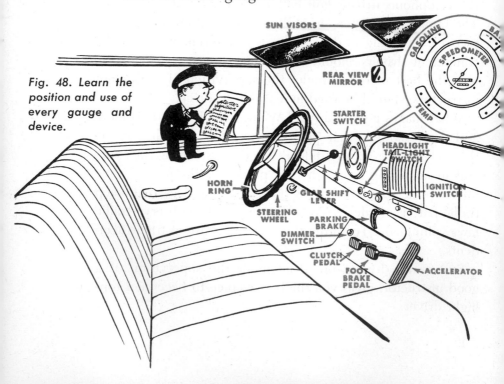

Fig. 48. Learn the position and use of every gauge and device.

SUN VISORS

GASOLINE

SPEEDOMETER

REAR VIEW MIRROR

TEMP

STARTER SWITCH

HEADLIGHT TAIL-LIGHT SWITCH

HORN RING

GEAR SHIFT LEVER

IGNITION SWITCH

STEERING WHEEL

PARKING BRAKE

DIMMER SWITCH

CLUTCH PEDAL

FOOT BRAKE PEDAL

ACCELERATOR

HE ENGINE

It is only by means of some of these devices that you are able to handle this powerful "giant" with anywhere from 80 to over 200 horsepower. It is only by consulting the gauges that you can check as to whether or not your car is in proper operating condition.

We can classify the driving devices in the car as:

A. Gauges
B. Safety Aids
C. Starting Devices
D. Control Devices

Identify each one on your car, and get thoroughly acquainted with its use.

THE GAUGES

YOUR CAR has a "diet" of five items: gasoline, air, water, oil, and electricity. Four gauges on the instrument panel measure the supply or condition of these indispensable items.

1. Gasoline Gauge A glance at this gauge tells the approximate amount of gasoline in the tank. Keeping the tank well-filled is a good practice, not only to prevent the embarrassing situation of an empty tank, but because excessive condensation of moisture tends to take place when the tank is not well-filled, and you will have water in the gasoline.

95

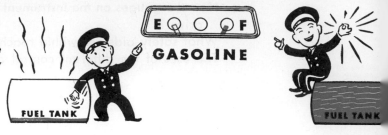

Fig. 49. Keep the fuel tank happily full.

GASOLINE

FUEL TANK

FUEL TANK

2. Temperature Gauge The "power plant" under the hood of your car normally gets very hot when it runs. Cooled water from the radiator is pumped through it constantly to help prevent overheating. This gauge indicates the temperature of the water.

WATER

Fig. 50. The temperature gauge can warn of trouble.

Most engines operate normally with water temperature between 160 and 180 degrees Fahrenheit. If temperature rises close to the boiling point—212 degrees—take care! You may be able to put your finger on the cause of the trouble, or you may need help from a mechanic. Excessive temperature can be due to a great variety of possible causes:

▶ *1.* Connected with the water cooling system—
  Insufficient water in the radiator
  Clogged, punctured, soft, or weakened hoses
  Poor circulation of water in the system
  A worn or broken water pump
  A leaking radiator
  Failure of the thermostat to operate properly
  A broken or slipping fan belt so that the pump cannot operate

2. Connected with air cooling— ◀
   A broken or slipping fan belt so that the fan does
      not run
   Radiator clogged with mud or insects
   Engine idling for a long period with the car stand-
      ing still

3. Connected with lubricating system— ◀
   Insufficient oil in the crankcase
   Clogged oil line or defective oil pump

4. Miscellaneous causes— ◀
   Improperly timed ignition
   Incorrect "gas" mixture
   Excessively heavy pulling

3. Oil Pressure Gauge No doubt you have been oiling things for years—roller skates, bicycle, lawn mower, sewing machine, or other household, shop, or farm devices.

Oil is indispensable for the automobile engine. Rapidly moving parts must be constantly bathed in it. Take the protective film of oil away, and the terrific friction would wear out the parts and ruin the engine.

The *oil pressure gauge* shows whether or not there is sufficient pressure to pump the lubricating oil to where it is needed. Normal oil pressure varies somewhat in different makes and models of cars. Consult your Owner's Manual.

Fig. 51. Low oil pressure brings a car to grief.

L ○ ◉ ○ **H**

**OIL
PRESSURE**

Fig. 52. A well-charged battery gives you a snappier car.

4. Ammeter   The ammeter is an instrument to measure the flow of electric current to and from the car's storage battery.

Compare the electrical system of your car to the nerves of your body. Electric current, flowing through these "nerves," sounds the horn, starts the engine, provides the lights, and operates several other of the car's devices. The car *battery* serves as a reservoir for the electric energy produced by the car's *generator*. The ammeter shows whether the supply of electric energy in the battery is being used up faster than the generator is producing it or whether it is being produced and stored faster than used.

When everything is in good working order, the pointer on the ammeter indicates—

▶ CHARGE—When the engine is running at speeds above from 15 to 20 miles per hour. This indicates that more current is being produced by the generator than is being used and that the surplus is being stored in the battery for future use.

▶ DISCHARGE—(1) When the engine is idling and electric current is being used but not enough current is being produced. (2) When the engine is not running, but the lights are on, or the horn is being used, or the ignition switch is turned on, or other devices are using up the energy stored in the battery.

▶ ZERO—(1) When the engine is not running and no part of the electrical equipment is being used. (2) When the generator is producing just enough current to offset that which is being used at the moment.

If the ammeter shows DISCHARGE when all the electrical switches are turned off, there is a short circuit, or "leak" of electrical energy. If it shows DISCHARGE when the engine is running rapidly, some adjustment is needed and an expert mechanic should be consulted.

In some cars the ammeter is replaced by a small red light which comes on only to indicate discharge. This light is normally on at idling speeds but should go out at higher car speeds, if the electrical system is in good order.

The battery itself needs to be checked regularly and supplied with clean water, preferably distilled, to keep the level of the liquid above the battery plates. To assure regular checking, it is good practice to check the water level in the battery each time you have the gasoline tank filled. If the plates become dry, the life of the battery is greatly shortened.

5. Speedometer This instrument shows, in miles per hour, the speed at which the car is traveling.

6. Odometer This instrument indicates the numbers of miles the car has traveled. It is generally found mounted with the speedometer.

Most of these gauges are important indicators of the state of well-being of your car. One instrument, the speedometer, is an important indicator of the state of health of your driving. Check with it frequently.

Fig. 53. Whoa there! Watch that speedometer!

Always choose speed in relation to stopping distances and all the traffic conditions under which you are driving. Like an aviator, expert drivers frequently check their instruments.

SIX SAFETY AIDS

WITHIN easy reach of the driver are six safety devices:

1. Light Switches: Upper Beam; Low Beam; and Parking It is a far cry from the days of a swinging lantern on a wagon to the electric lights on the modern car. The

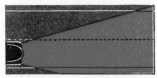

Fig. 54. No car proaching—hig beam light.

OPEN ROAD — NO ONE COMING

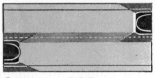

Car approachir —low-beam lig

MEETING ANOTHER CAR

light switch is generally mounted on the instrument panel. By moving it to different positions, you get various combinations of lights:

      a. Parking and tail-lights on
      b. Head and tail-lights on
      c. All lights off

An additional light button is on the floor under your left foot. Stepping on this button causes a shift from the raised-beam lights which would glare-blind an approaching driver to a low-beam, "non-glare" passing arrangement. Stepping on it again, after the car has passed, returns you to the raised beam arrangement. Rest your left foot lightly on this switch when driving at night. Always use it as a courtesy when another car approaches or when you are following close behind another car. This is required by law in most states.

Most cars have a small, red-colored light to indicate that the high-beam, glare-producing lights are on. Some cars are equipped with an electronic "eye," which automatically shifts the lighting pattern to the low-beam, non-blinding arrangement when sufficient light falls on it from the headlights of an approaching car.

The instrument panel is lighted either by a special switch, or, on some cars, when any headlight beam is on. The driver can control the brightness of the instrument panel lighting either by twisting the light-control knob or, on some cars, by means of a separate knob.

2. Rear-view Mirror Not having eyes in the back of your head or a neck like a turtle's, you keep track of what is happening on the road behind you by glancing in the mirror, usually near the top of the windshield. You must know conditions behind your car, especially when you want to:

Stop, or slow down	Pass other vehicles ◀
Park	Pull out from parking
Turn around	Change lanes
Make right or left turns	

If a car overtakes and passes you by surprise, you have not used your rear-view mirror properly. It is an important safety device.

3. Windshield Wipers When rain streaks down your windshield or sleet begins to form, you pull, push, or turn a little knob and set windshield wipers to work. This knob has no standard location. Learn where it is and how to operate it.

Keep good rubber blades on the windshield wipers, and keep them properly adjusted to give a clear windshield.

4. Sun Visors Driving is both difficult and dangerous if you are blinded by sun-glare. Most cars have sun visors above the windshield that can be pulled down in front or tipped to the side for shading the eyes. Both the comfort and the safety of driving are increased by visors. They can be easily installed in cars that do not have them.

5. Windshield Defrosters On most cars, defroster slots are built into the top of the instrument panel. Hot air is blown against the windshield from the heater through these slots. This prevents accumulation of snow or ice on the outside of the windshield and "fogging" of the glass inside. Learn the position of the control button for this device.

Other defrosting devices are sometimes used—either electrical heating arrangements or fans to keep warm air in circulation. In freezing temperatures, a dependable defrosting method is very important for safe driving. If your car does not have defrosting devices, opening windows on both sides may be of some help.

Fig. 55. The horn-ring is handy. Watch your manners!

6. Horn Button The horn is usually sounded by pressing either on the hub of the steering wheel or on a large metal ring inside the steering wheel.

The horn is not there to blow pedestrians or cars out of the way. Good drivers are not horn tooters. Use the horn only when necessary. It can, of course, be indispensable in an emergency and should always be in operating condition.

STARTING DEVICES

STARTING devices are four in number:

1. Ignition Switch The car's ignition must be turned on before you can start the engine. Insert and turn a key in a keyhole on the instrument panel or on the steering wheel column, depending on the make of car.

"Back stage" behind the panel, turning the key closes an electric circuit. The starting motor can then start the engine when the starter switch is operated.

2. Starter Switch The powerful electric motor which starts the engine is put in motion by using a starter switch after the ignition has been turned on.

This starter switch is not standardized either in form or position. It may be a hand button on the instrument panel; it may be a foot switch. On some cars, the accelerator pedal serves not only for feeding gasoline to the engine, but as a starter switch as well. One make of car is started by pushing all the way down on the clutch pedal. In some cars, turning the ignition key clockwise as far as it will go closes the switch that starts the engine. Learn the position and use of the starter switch on the car you drive.

Never press the starting switch when the engine is running or you may damage the starting motor. If the engine is so quiet that you don't know whether it is running, touch the accelerator pedal lightly. A glance at either the oil pressure gauge or the ammeter can also tell you whether or not the engine is running.

3. Choke To start a cold engine, the mixture of gasoline and air must be rich in gasoline, because gasoline does not vaporize so quickly when cold. The *choke* is a device for enriching the gasoline-air mixture. It lives up to its name; it "chokes" the amount of air going into the carburetor.

Most cars now have automatic chokes designed to adjust themselves, without the help of the driver, according to the changes of temperature in the engine. Where

103

there is a manual choke button, it is generally found on the instrument panel.

4. Hand Throttle A hand throttle is used on some cars to regulate the flow of gas-air mixture while the engine is being started. On cars which have them, the knob is generally on the instrument panel.

CONTROL DEVICES

YOU NOW know the gauges, the safety aids, and the starting devices. Other instruments that are of great importance to the driver, are the *control* devices:

1. Steering Wheel Most people have grown up steering kiddie cars, tricycles, wagons, and bicycles. So they know from early experience that, whether moving forward or backward, the vehicle turns to the right if the top of the steering wheel is turned to the right, or clockwise, and that it turns to the left if the top of the steering wheel is turned to the left, or counter-clockwise.

2. Clutch Pedal This foot pedal is found on gearshift cars and on cars with semi-automatic transmissions.

Think of your automobile as made of two major units: (*a*) the engine; (*b*) the body and chassis.

Each unit can run independently of the other. On a grade or by pushing, a car can be set in motion while the engine is still; the engine can run while the car remains stationary. Or, we can make the engine move the car by hitching them together. This hitching or unhitching is controlled by the *clutch pedal.*

On gearshift cars, the clutch pedal is operated with the left foot. How to use it will be explained in greater detail in Chapters 8 and 9. It is used principally:

▶ *a.* When starting the engine.
  b. When shifting from one gear to another.
  c. Together with the brake pedal, when bringing the car to a stop.
  d. Together with the accelerator pedal, when backing the car.

3. Gearshift Lever, or **Selector Lever** On cars where the gears must be shifted by hand, a *gearshift lever* is mounted on the right-hand side of the steering wheel column. With this lever, the driver changes gears according to his changing needs for power, speed, or direction. Proper use of the lever is explained in Chapter 8.

On cars equipped with automatic and semi-automatic transmissions, the gearshift lever is replaced by a *selector lever,* generally mounted also on the right-hand side of the steering wheel column. Use of this lever is explained in Chapter 9.

4. Accelerator Pedal This device is operated with the right foot. It controls the amount of gas-air mixture fed into the engine and so regulates the speed of the car.

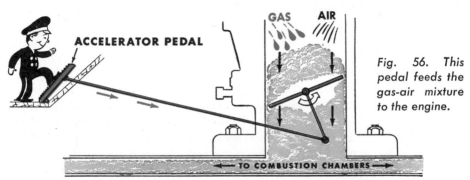

Fig. 56. This pedal feeds the gas-air mixture to the engine.

Learning to accelerate with the foot in a comfortable position on the accelerator pedal is a great help to smooth, well-controlled driving. The pressure should be applied with the ball of the foot high on the pedal, the heel serving as a pivot on the floor of the car.

Some cars have hand throttles or accelerators also, but the foot accelerator, not the hand throttle, is used while the car is in motion.

5. Foot Brake Pedal The brakes on all four wheels of the car are operated simultaneously, by pressure of the foot on the brake pedal.

There are five types of foot brakes: mechanical, hydraulic, air, vacuum, and electrical. Hydraulic brakes,

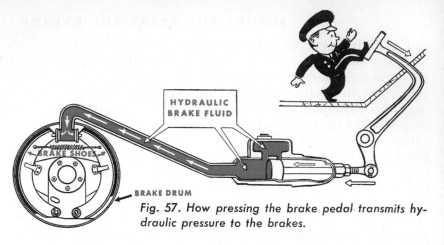

Fig. 57. How pressing the brake pedal transmits hydraulic pressure to the brakes.

and, in a few cases, mechanical brakes, are the types
commonly found on passenger cars. Air, vacuum, and
electrical brakes are common on trucks, buses, and trac-
tor-trailers.

Mechanical brakes transmit the pressure of the right
foot, greatly increased through a number of mechanical
units, to the brake "shoes" at the wheels. With hydraulic brakes, the foot pedal forces a piston into a cylinder,
causing compressed brake fluid to transmit pressure
equally to the four brakes. This is the type now used on
practically all passenger cars. Air brakes are operated by
a piston driven by compressed air. Vacuum brakes are
operated by the suction of a partial vacuum.

6. Parking Brake This brake is used in parking and in
one method of starting on hills. It is usually a lever to
the left or right of the steering column. On some cars, it
is applied with an additional foot pedal to the left of the
driver and released by a hand knob.

On some cars, this brake operates on the drive shaft of
the car and is independent of the foot brakes. On other
cars, it provides an independent mechanical means of
operating the brakes on the rear wheels.

Neglecting to release the parking brake fully when
driving can be expensive. If it is left on, the engine must
pull against it. Furthermore, the brake linings can be
burned.

INSTRUMENTS ARE IMPORTANT

BECOME thoroughly acquainted with the gauges, safety aids, devices that start the car, and those that control it in action. Go over them until you know just where they are and know their uses well. Sit in the driver's seat and touch or use each one until its position and "feel" are familiar.

These devices are so simple that, before long, use of them becomes automatic. Even the simplest is highly important for safe and efficient car operation. The last group, the control devices, can be mastered only by actual practice driving.

TO TALK ABOUT:

1 A man driving along notices that his car is becoming sluggish. He notices an odor like hot metal and oil. He glances at the water temperature indicator and discovers that it registers overheating. What shall he do at once? What are some of the things that might be wrong? Which can he correct himself? Under what conditions will he need a mechanic?

2 There are several "home-made" ways of treating a windshield to prevent ice and snow from collecting on it and reducing visibility. Make a list and discuss the effectiveness of any methods you know.

3 Discuss the importance of a thorough knowledge of the purposes and operation of each of the gauges and control devices.

4 Why does the oil pressure gauge give a higher reading when the motor is cold than when it is hot?

5 What would you suspect might be the trouble if the car is operating satisfactorily but the ammeter registers zero at all times?

6 Why should the water level in the battery be checked more frequently in summer? Why should the degree of battery charge be watched more closely in the winter?

7   Explain how a glance at the oil pressure gauge or at the ammeter can let you know whether or not the engine is running.

8   Which is more important, a gauge which shows the amount of oil in the crankcase or a gauge which shows the oil pressure? Why?

9   Explain the meaning of low-beam headlights and the importance of using them. Explain the "electronic eye."

10   How, from inside your car, can you make certain that your stop light is working?

TO DO:

1   Compare the gauges and safety and control devices on an old model car with those on the latest model of the same make. List the major changes. Why have these changes been made?

2   Make a list of all additional car devices of which you have heard. Which would increase safety and which are merely "gadgets"?

3   Visit a first-class repair station and observe the servicing of both hydraulic and mechanical brakes.

4   Make diagrams and compare the panel and control devices of different makes of cars.

TO LOOK UP:

Owner's Manual. For the car you are driving. Supplied with the car.

DO YOU KNOW:

How power is produced in a gasoline engine and harnessed for use?

What preserves the engine against excessive wear and tear?

How engine power is transferred to the rear wheels?

CHAPTER 7

HOW THE AUTOMOBILE RUNS

UNDER THE BODY

THE SHINING, streamlined body of a new automobile is an object of beauty and pride. But it is under the body that you find "the works." Strip off the body and you disclose the *chassis*.

Examine the stripped car and you find it made up of units held firmly together and designed to work in harmony:

1. The frame and running gear
2. The engine or power plant
3. The power transmission system
4. The systems for various special functions, such as—

Fuel	Braking
Ignition	Lubricating
Exhaust	Cooling
Steering	Lighting

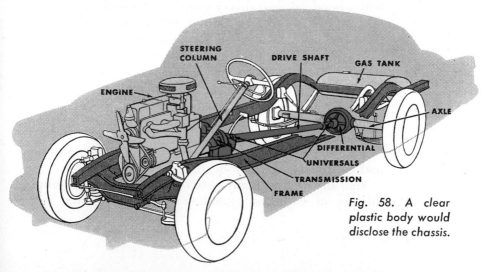

Fig. 58. A clear plastic body would disclose the chassis.

The chassis *frame* is the skeleton of your car. It is mounted on the springs, axles, and wheels. On it are mounted the body, engine, power transmission system, and some control devices. The frame supplies backbone and firmness to your car and holds the parts in place so they can function as a stable working unit. Some cars are so constructed that the frame and body are welded together in one assembly.

By means of a chart, or, better still, an actual cutaway car, become thoroughly familiar with the various chassis units. Learn their locations, their special functions, and their functional relations to each other. As a driver, you will find great value and satisfaction in an ability to identify and understand the principal units of your car.

Fig. 59. Under the hood. You too?

UNDER THE HOOD

DID YOU ever pass a car stalled by the side of the highway—hood up, and driver gazing sadly within? Suppose you were in the driver's shoes. What does a look under the hood mean to you? Is the automobile engine a sort of No-Man's-Land to you, or do you understand its various parts?

When you first see the many complicated-looking parts under the hood, you expect the principle of the gasoline engine to be hard to understand. Actually, it is a very simple principle.

The secret of automobile power is in the production and control of fuel combustion.

Man discovered many years ago, that when a proper mixture of vaporized gasoline and air is heated suffi-

ciently by a spark, it burns with explosive force. These
"explosions" mean power. The trick was to harness this
power—to confine it in closed chambers and make it do
work, make it turn wheels. This is just what man did
when he invented the gasoline engine.

MOST of the parts under the hood are there for one of **The Power Plant**
four purposes:

1. To prepare the gasoline for burning with explosive
   force.
2. To furnish a place in which the "explosion" of the
   gasoline-air mixture can be confined.
3. To furnish the spark which ignites the gasoline-air
   mixture at just the right time.
4. To harness the force of the "explosion" and convert it
   into mechanical energy that will turn the wheels.

The largest block of metal under the hood is the engine block. It looks solid. But if you look inside, you discover a number of hollow *cylinders* or tubes—six in a
six-cylinder car, eight in an eight-cylinder car, etc. Study
Fig. 60.

The cylinders are closed, at the top, by cylinder heads
which hold spark plugs. Closing the other end of each
cylinder, but able to work up and down in it, is a movable *piston.*

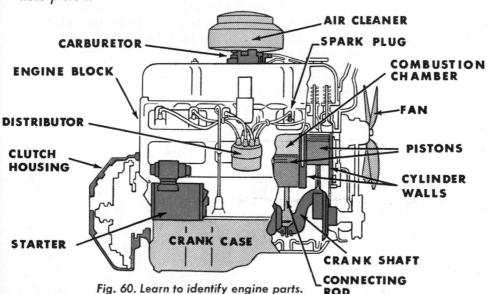

Fig. 60. Learn to identify engine parts.

CARBURETOR

AIR CLEANER

SPARK PLUG

ENGINE BLOCK

COMBUSTION
CHAMBER

DISTRIBUTOR

FAN

CLUTCH
HOUSING

PISTONS

CYLINDER
WALLS

STARTER

CRANK CASE

CRANK SHAFT

CONNECTING
ROD

A fountain pen can be used to illustrate the cylinder and piston idea. Hold up the cap of a pen and move the barrel up and down inside the cap. The cap represents the cylinder and the barrel represents the piston. Notice that when the barrel moves *up*, the space inside the cap gets smaller; when it moves *down*, the space gets larger. That space corresponds to the combustion chamber of an engine, and the combustion chamber is the place where the "explosions" of the gasoline-air mixture take place. See Fig. 60.

A fuel pump receives the gasoline from the tank in liquid form and sends it through a cleaner, or filter, to the *carburetor*. Gasoline will not burn with explosive force in a liquid form. So it has to be prepared for the combustion chamber by being atomized and mixed with air. See Fig. 56. The carburetor is the device for this precision mixing of particles of gasoline and air in correct proportions. By means of jets, it creates a spray of gasoline and mixes approximately fifteen parts of air with one part of gasoline. The proportion of gasoline and air is regulated by means of the *choke*, which on some cars is automatic. The driver controls the amount of gasoline and air mixture which goes into the combustion chambers by means of the accelerator pedal. As you feed more of this mixture, engine power increases.

After the gasoline is properly mixed with air, it enters the combustion chamber where it is to be fired. But the gasoline-air mixture will not burn by itself. A hot electric spark is used to fire it.

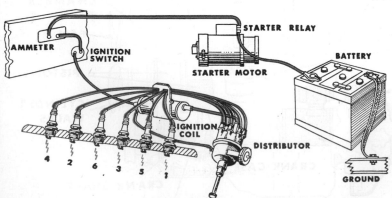

Fig. 61. The ignition system.

This spark is supplied by means of a spark plug at the top of each cylinder. Electric wires run to the spark plugs from a unit of the ignition system called the *distributor*. When the engine is running, electric current at high voltage flows along these wires. At the bottom of each spark plug are two metal points which do not quite meet. This creates a gap which the high voltage electric current must jump. Jumping the gap causes the spark. The spark is produced in the combustion chamber which contains the gasoline and air mixture, and causes the mixture to burn with explosive force.

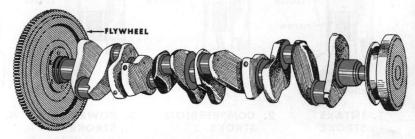

CRANKSHAFT WITH COUNTERWEIGHTS AND BEARINGS

Fig. 62. Parts of the crankshaft and its bearings are shown in color.

How is this gasoline "explosion" harnessed to drive the wheels?

When the gasoline "explodes" in the combustion chamber, it exerts terrific pressure in all directions. But only the piston which forms the bottom of the cylinder is movable. So the pressure of the explosion gives the movable piston a "power shove" downward.

This downward shove of the piston is the beginning of the power that turns the wheels. For the pistons are fastened by connecting rods to the *crankshaft*. See Fig. 62. The downward strokes of the pistons rotate the crankshaft, just as the power strokes of the legs of a bicyclist cause the main sprocket to rotate. The turning crankshaft drives other mechanisms which "make the wheels go 'round."

Perfect Rhythm A GOOD tap dancer must have perfect *timing*. So must a fine dance orchestra. Timing is just as important to a gasoline engine as it is to a tap dancer's nimble feet.

Smooth running of the engine depends on everything working in perfect timing. The sparks in each cylinder must be introduced at just the right split second. Valves in the combustion chamber must be opened and closed in perfect rhythm. How is this done?

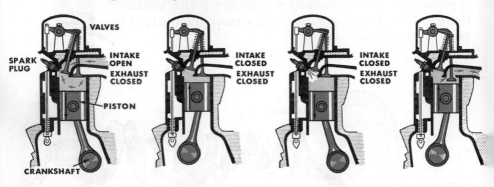

1. INTAKE STROKE　　**2. COMPRESSION STROKE**　　**3. POWER STROKE**　　**4. EXHAUST STROKE**

Fig. 63. The four-stroke power cycle.

For each explosion of gasoline in the combustion chamber, the piston must make two round trips in the cylinder —that is, twice up and twice down. Each one of these four strokes of the piston plays an important part in producing power. The four strokes of the piston take place in each cylinder as follows:

▶ *1.* The piston is drawn down by the turning crankshaft. As this occurs, an accurately timed intake valve opens and the mixture of gasoline and air is sucked into the combustion chamber at the top of the cylinder. This is called the *intake stroke.* Fig. 63 (1).

2. The intake valve closes. The piston is then pushed up in the cylinder by the turning crankshaft. With this stroke, the piston compresses the gas in the combustion chamber, creating a great pressure in a very small space. This is called the *compression stroke.* Fig. 63 (2).

3. By exact timing, the spark is now introduced and the compressed gas burns explosively. This forces the movable piston down, causing the third piston stroke. This is called the *power stroke*. Fig. 63 (3).

4. The last of the four strokes is upward. At this time, an *exhaust* valve opens and the second upward stroke of the piston forces the burned gases out of the cylinder. This is called the *exhaust stroke*. Fig. 63 (4).

This completes one four-stroke cycle, and another cycle immediately follows. These cycles of four strokes take place in each of the car's cylinders in well-timed rhythm.

A well-balanced *fly wheel* is attached to the counter-balanced crankshaft. See Fig. 62. This helps give the crankshaft momentum as it rotates, and keeps it turning smoothly between the power impulses.

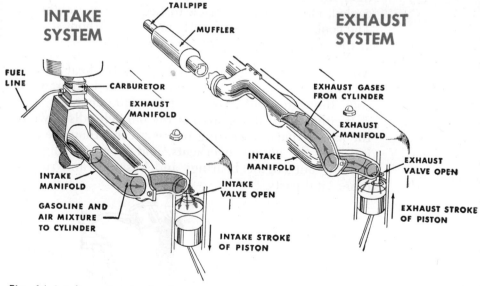

Fig. 64. Intake system and exhaust system.

YOU WOULD think that, with continuous operation, an en- *Reducing Wear* gine would knock itself to pieces or burn itself out. You *and Tear* would expect tremendous wear and tear. This would happen were it not for two systems built into the car—the cooling and the lubricating systems.

The explosive burning of the compressed mixture of gasoline and air creates tremendous heat, some of which is converted into mechanical power. Parts of the car subjected to this heat are made of especially durable, heat-resisting metals. But this is not enough. The engine must be supplied with a cooling system to keep these parts from being destroyed by overheating. Both water and air are used for cooling. Oil also helps.

Water The water put into the radiator of a car is pumped through water jackets around the engine to keep down the temperature. The engine block described on page 111 has many carefully designed water passages which carry water around the outside of each cylinder, the cylinder head, and the valves. By continuous circulation, the water is returned to the radiator where it is cooled, and then flows back to help cool the cylinders. The cooled water is constantly needed! Without it, parts of the engine would rapidly become red hot.

Air Air drawn in by the fan helps keep the heat down in two ways. See Fig. 65. A draft of air through the radiator cools the water and blows heat from the engine.

If either the water system or the fan belt falls down on the job, so that the heating rate is greater than the cooling rate, the engine overheats, and there is danger of burning out engine bearings and bushings and ruining other vital parts.

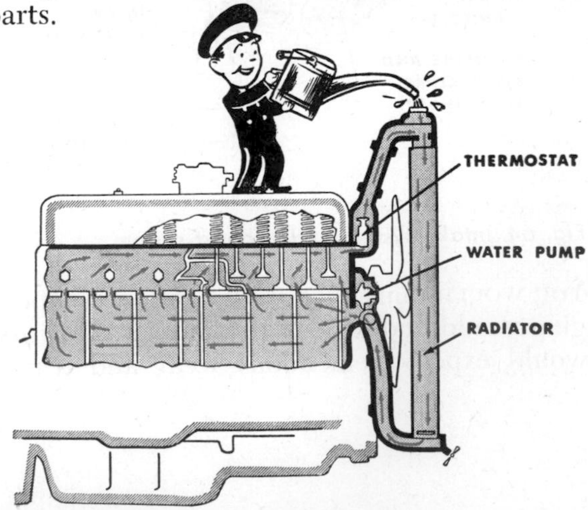

Fig. 65. Water circulates through "jackets" around the engine.

THERMOSTAT

WATER PUMP

RADIATOR

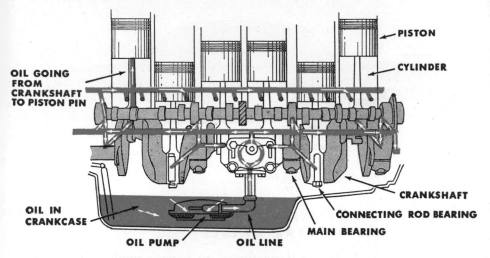

Fig. 66. Oil is pumped to all moving engine parts.

Oil The lubricating system helps reduce wear to a minimum. Serious engine wear can be caused by the rubbing together of metal surfaces. Wherever such rubbing would occur, lubricating oil must be used to provide a slippery film between the surfaces. Study Fig. 66 and find where such lubrication would be needed.

In one type of lubricating system, the rotating crankshaft and the connecting rods splash into a basin of oil at the bottom of the crankcase and scoop it up. By this means, moving parts are bathed in oil. This is called the *splash system* of lubrication.

Another type of lubricating is called the *pressure system.* Oil is pumped from a well in the bottom of the crankcase to the points where it is needed. The pressure system is used in most cars and is the system diagrammed in Fig. 66.

The proper amount of oil has to be kept in the crankcase for the lubricating system to work. The amount of oil can be checked by a dip-stick on the side of the engine block. Oil level has to be checked regularly. If the oil level gets low and lubrication fails, it can mean an over-heated engine, burned-out bearings, and repair bills.

Keep the cooling and lubricating systems of your car in order.

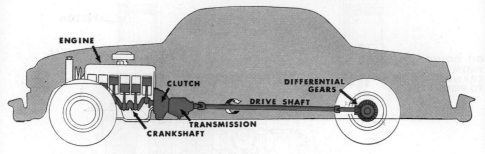

Fig. 67. The power train.

TRANSFERRING THE POWER
TO THE REAR WHEELS

THE POWER produced in a car's engine, by the explosive burning of vaporized gasoline and air, has to be transmitted to the rear, or driving, wheels of the car. This conveying of power is done by means of the parts of the car which make up the *power train*. See Fig. 67.

The delivery of the engine's power to the rear wheels of the car is not a simple matter. It is complicated especially by two requirements:

►
1. Sometimes you want the engine running while the car wheels stand still. So there must be a means by which the driver can disconnect the two.
2. Sometimes, for power, you want the engine to turn many times faster than the rear wheels. At other times, for economy, you want the engine to turn more slowly, without reducing the speed of the rear wheels.

The *clutch* and the *transmission* take care of these requirements.

The Clutch THE CLUTCH is the device which permits the engine and the car wheels to be connected or disconnected so that the former can run while the latter stands still. There are many clutch designs in cars of different makes, but, in principle, they can be classified as: (1) *a mechanical clutch;* (2) *a fluid clutch.* Generally, gearshift cars use the first kind of clutch; automatic transmission cars use the second.

To understand how the mechanical clutch works, put

a small rod through the holes in two phonograph records and hold the rod horizontally. If you leave a little space between the discs, you can spin one without spinning the other. Now press them close together. Rotate one, and you rotate the other. The clutch discs in the gearshift car work on the same principle.

A friction plate is fastened to the fly wheel at the end of the engine crankshaft. Another plate is attached to the forward end of the shaft which runs into the transmission. When the engine is to move the car, these plates are held firmly together by strong springs. Spin the forward plate and you spin both plates.

In a gearshift car, when you want to disconnect the driving wheels of the car from the engine so that only the engine will be running, you press the clutch pedal all the way down. This separates the two friction plates, and the motion of one does not affect the other. Engine power does not get back to the car wheels.

In automatic transmission cars, this connecting and disconnecting of engine power and rear wheels is accomplished by a *fluid coupling*, sometimes called a *hydraulic clutch*. This kind of clutch makes use of the ability of liquid in motion to transmit power. Oil is set in motion by a rotating unit connected with the engine. This oil in motion causes a second unit which is connected, through the transmission, to the driveshaft to rotate.

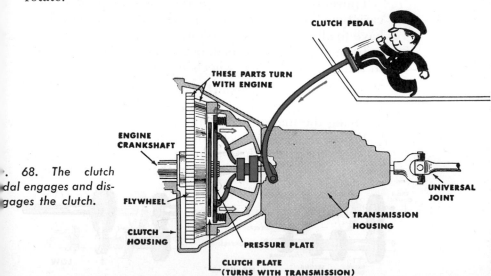

68. The clutch pedal engages and disengages the clutch.

CLUTCH PEDAL

THESE PARTS TURN WITH ENGINE

ENGINE CRANKSHAFT

FLYWHEEL

CLUTCH HOUSING

PRESSURE PLATE

CLUTCH PLATE (TURNS WITH TRANSMISSION)

TRANSMISSION HOUSING

UNIVERSAL JOINT

You can easily demonstrate the way this fluid clutch works by placing two electric fans face to face and turning only one on. The moving air produced by the rotating fan will cause the other fan also to turn. In much the same way, the oil set in motion by the one rotating unit of the clutch causes the facing unit to rotate also. Oil, driven by a rotating unit connected with the engine crankshaft, causes a second unit connected with the driveshaft to revolve.

In most cars having a fluid clutch, the connecting and disconnecting operations performed by the clutch take place automatically, and no clutch pedal is needed.

The Transmission Gears IN TRANSFERRING engine power to the rear wheels, the second important requirement is that the engine and rear wheels can rotate at different speeds.

An engine develops more power as it speeds up. For heavy pulling, a lot of engine speed is needed to develop power, but the car's rear wheels must, at the same time, move at slow speed. The engine must be able to turn rapidly while the car is moving slowly.

On the other hand, when the car is cruising along on the open highway, only a relatively little power, or engine speed, is needed to keep it moving in the usual speed range. Fuel is saved and driving made smoother and more quiet because car wheels can move rapidly without the engine being speeded up to the same extent.

Transmissions have to be designed to permit these variations between engine speed and car speed. They have to allow the twisting effort, or *torque*, of the engine to be multiplied, as needed, before delivering it as power to the rear, or driving, wheels of your car.

Transmissions in Gearshift Cars You can understand the way the transmission in a gearshift car works by studying the marginal drawings.

When two cogwheels of different diameters are meshed together, they turn at different speeds. The larger one revolves more slowly than the smaller one.

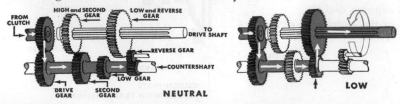

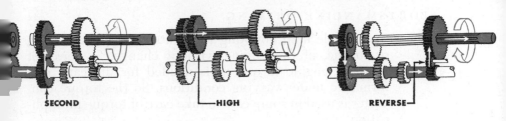

SECOND   HIGH   REVERSE

A larger wheel with twice as many teeth as a smaller one makes only one turn while the smaller wheel is making two. Transmission gears make use of this principle. Gears of different sizes, or ratios, can be meshed by means of the gearshift lever.

In automobile transmissions, there are several possible combinations of gears in different ratios to each other, depending on need. When you want the rear, or driving, wheels to turn slowly and powerfully, as when starting the car, you use the first, or "power" gear. To pick up more car speed, you shift to second, the "pick-up" gear. For cruising speed, shift to third or high gear. To reverse the direction of rotation of the driveshaft, so that the car can back, you use the reverse gear.

Transmissions in Automatic Transmission Cars The changes between engine speed and car speed take place, in automatic transmission cars, with much less attention from the driver.

In gearshift cars, when the driver realizes the need for a different gear ratio, he decides which gear to use and makes the shift with the manual gearshift lever. In automatic transmission cars, the selection and the shift take place automatically, by means of mechanical devices about which the driver never need think—such as valves, speed governors, gear brakes, and hydraulically-operated clutches.

There are many variations in the design of automatic transmissions. Some cars have actual forward gears of different sizes to multiply engine torque to meet the various driving needs for speed or power. Others do not have all the usual forward gears but get the same results by means of a special kind of fluid coupling called a *torque converter.*

A simple fluid coupling transmits the twisting effort, or torque, of the engine without change. It does not multiply engine torque as is needed for the car's performance under varying conditions. So the torque converter is used in some cars to take care of torque multiplication.

The torque converter operates on the principle of a turbine. Within a housing, its parts run in oil. The parts are turned by oil currents set up when a pump driven by the car's engine puts the encased oil in motion. In its simplest form, it is made up of a *pump* (the member which drives), a *turbine* (the driven member), and one or two intermediate units called *stators*. All of these members have blades or vanes. See Fig. 70.

The pump is turned by the engine crankshaft. The turbine turns the parts which rotate the car's driveshaft. The vanes of the pump direct streams of oil in rapid motion into the vanes of turbine and stators. The vanes of all members are ingeniously curved and designed so that, as engine speed changes, they control the direction and force of oil flow. This produces the multiplication of engine torque, or twisting effort, as required to give the car get-away, power, or speed as needed. Because this device multiplies, or converts, engine torque, it is rightly named a *torque converter*.

Since the torque multiplication takes place by means of oil currents acting on the turbine blades, rather than by means of a limited number of actual gears, the effect is like an infinite number of "gear ratio" changes brought about as the driver uses the accelerator pedal to change engine speed.

Fig. 69. An automatic transmission with a hydramatic system.

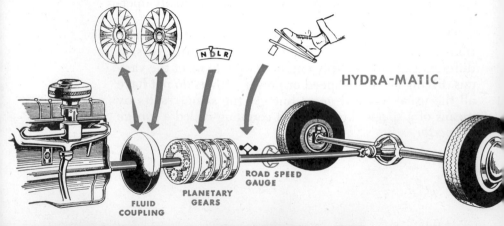

HYDRA-MATIC

ROAD SPEED GAUGE

FLUID COUPLING

PLANETARY GEARS

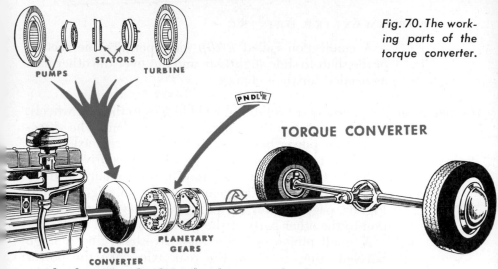

PUMPS STATORS TURBINE

PNDL'R

TORQUE CONVERTER

Fig. 70. The working parts of the torque converter.

TORQUE CONVERTER

PLANETARY GEARS

This brings us back to the driver, with whom, no matter what the make of car or how automatic the transmission, the ultimate control of the car's performance still rests. For it is the driver's shifting of the selector lever and the pressure of the driver's foot on the accelerator pedal, changing the speed of the car's engine, that puts any of these carefully-engineered power-transmitting units into action. So, even with the automatic transmission car, the driver still remains "in the driver's seat."

WHAT KEEPS the straight, revolving driveshaft of a car from breaking itself to pieces when the rear axle of the car moves up and down in going over bumps?

The Universal Joints

If the entire driveshaft were rigid, it would break. But, just as a person's arm has wrist and elbow joints for flexibility, the driveshaft has *universal joints*. These joints enable the shaft to adapt itself to the bobbing of the rear wheels as the car goes over bumps.

The *length* of the driveshaft has to be variable too. Bumping over road irregularities makes slight, constant changes in distance between the transmission and the rear axles. So slight changes in length must be possible in the driveshaft.

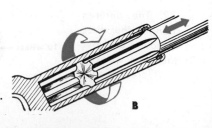

Fig. 71.

A. Universal joint.

B. Slip joint.

A

B

A connection called a *slip joint* permits one section of the shaft to slide slightly in and out over the other part as needed for such changes.

The Differential THE DRIVESHAFT rotates at right angles to the rear wheels.
Gears This presents another engineering problem. The *direction* of the power has to be changed. The rear axles must be made to rotate at right angles to the driveshaft in order to turn the car wheels. This is accomplished by means of the differential gears. See Fig. 58, page 109, and Fig. 67, page 118, for the position of these gears in relation to the other parts of the power train.

A small pinion gear on the driveshaft, and a large beveled "ring gear" on the rear axles take the power "around a corner," so to speak. This mechanism works somewhat similar to the gears on an old-time ice cream freezer, or on an egg beater. Power applied in one direction works in another.

When a squad of soldiers marches around a corner, the outside man walks farther and faster than the inside, or pivot, man. In the same way, when a car goes around a corner, the rear wheel on the outside must turn faster than the one on the inside. The differential gears on the rear axle make this possible. The gears allow the wheel on the inside of the curve to slow down while the one on the outside increases speed. Both wheels, however, are driving, even though one is turning faster than the other.

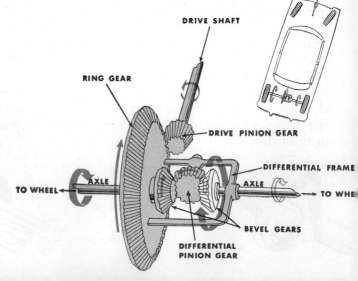

Fig. 72. The differential changes the direction of power and permits the rear axles to turn at different speeds.

DRIVE SHAFT

RING GEAR

DRIVE PINION GEAR

DIFFERENTIAL FRAME

TO WHEEL AXLE

AXLE TO WHEEL

BEVEL GEARS

DIFFERENTIAL PINION GEAR

This completes a picture of the major parts by means of which the automobile is put in motion and kept in motion. Now, how can a moving car be stopped?

THE BRAKES

STOPPING is done by friction forces. This will be explained further in Chapter 11.

When you apply the brakes, friction slows down the car wheels by means of lined brake shoes at each wheel. The shoes expand against the interiors of the brake drums. With mechanical brakes, the shoes are forced against the drums by a system of levers. With hydraulic brakes, fluid under pressure does the same thing.

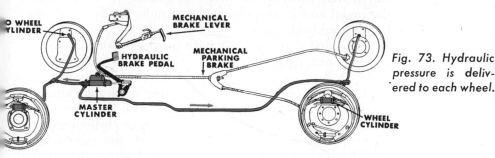

Fig. 73. Hydraulic pressure is delivered to each wheel.

Maximum braking comes about just before the wheels reach the locking point, which means the point at which they stop rotating and begin to slide. As you apply brakes for maximum or emergency stops, try to keep pressing the pedal *just short* of locking the wheels. When rear wheels lock on slippery pavements, a skid is likely to result. When front wheels lock, you no longer have steering control. Good drivers try to brake with no sudden locking of the wheels.

POWER BRAKES are designed to take more of the effort out **Power Braking** of braking and to reduce driver fatigue. Supplementary power is added to the force applied by the driver's foot on the brake pedal. This reduces the force which the driver must use in applying the brakes. The source of this added power is the engine vacuum created by the pistons on their intake strokes.

Power brakes combine vacuum units and hydraulic units. Pushing down on the brake pedal opens a valve. This permits air at atmospheric pressure to act against one side of a piston in the power brake cylinder while vacuum is applied to the other side. This force, combined with the force you apply to the brake pedal, operates the piston in the hydraulic brake master cylinder. The pressure is then transmitted to the hydraulic cylinders at each of the four wheel brakes. This forces the brake shoes against the brake drums, as in any hydraulic system. You control the braking effort by the way you use the pedal.

Stopping distances with power brakes are shorter than stopping distances with conventional brakes only to the extent that you can save time in getting your foot onto the pedal and in pushing it down more easily to obtain the desired braking.

When first driving a car with power brakes, carefully try them out. Apply the pedal several times with the car going at slow speed, to get the feel. Be especially careful not to over-apply the brakes and cause sudden locking of the brakes and too sudden stopping, with the danger of skidding if the pavement is slippery or of throwing passengers violently forward. As is always the case when first driving a car differently equipped, drive cars with power braking at reduced speeds until you are used to getting quick brake action with very little foot pressure. On the other hand, drive slowly and with special care when changing from a car with power brakes to one without them, or you may at first lengthen your stopping distances by under-braking.

Power brakes are designed so that, if the engine is not running and creating the vacuum, or if the power system fails, the unassisted brakes still operate. Moreover, on some cars, a reserve vacuum tank provides sufficient reserve to supply power braking for a few applications even after the engine stops running. On others, an electrically driven vacuum pump goes into operation.

Fig. 74. A plan showing how power brakes work.

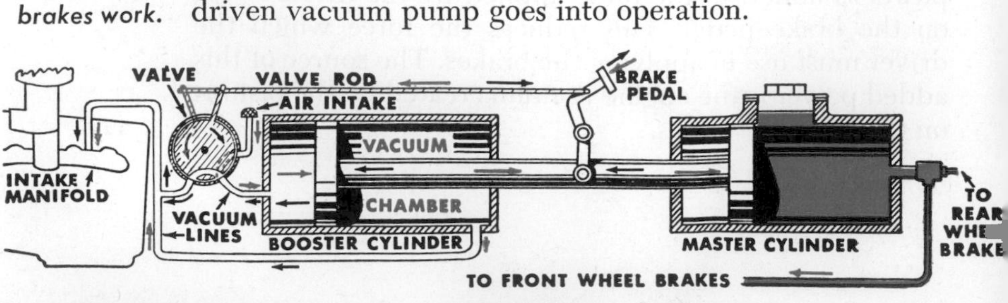

VALVE VALVE ROD BRAKE PEDAL AIR INTAKE VACUUM INTAKE MANIFOLD CHAMBER VACUUM LINES BOOSTER CYLINDER MASTER CYLINDER TO REAR WHEEL BRAKE TO FRONT WHEEL BRAKES

Without the vacuum booster power, you must press very much harder on the brake pedal. So it is a good safe-driving practice, for those who drive cars with power brakes, to try stopping the car with the ignition switch off and the transmission out of gear. Choose a safe spot *away from traffic* and discover how *very much greater* foot pressure you must apply without the power assist. A little practice in braking the car by leg pressure only will avoid the unsafe surprise you might otherwise get in case of power failure.

With some power brake systems, the brake pedal is lowered to about the same plane as the accelerator pedal and needs to be pressed down for only a short distance. With such a pedal, you can operate the brake and accelerator pedals by swinging your foot on the same plane from one to the other, or even by pivoting your foot on its heel. This somewhat reduces your reaction time in getting your foot onto the brake pedal, thereby helping you to stop quicker. When driving a car with such a short-range pedal, keep your heel on the floor and operate the pedal with toe pressure. This provides better control. But always keep in mind that, if a power failure occurs in a system using the short-range pedal, you must then exert *even more* pressure on the pedal than with conventional brakes. This is because the reduced lever length of the short-range pedal decreases its mechanical advantage. With the pedals on the same plane, be careful not to press quickly on the accelerator pedal, thinking your foot is over the brake pedal. Again, it is a matter of driving with special care and attention until you are thoroughly accustomed to the particular car.

To keep the brakes on your car in an efficient condition, careful, smooth braking is as important with power as with standard brakes. Over-driving traffic conditions and having to cut down car speed repeatedly by sharply applying brakes is misusing any kind of brakes. You pay extra costs for such bad driving practices, because tires and brake linings wear out quicker. Extra quick stopping causes almost as much excess tire wear as "jack-rabbit" starting.

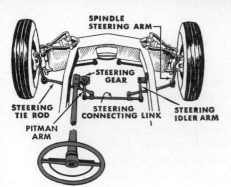

SPINDLE
STEERING ARM

STEERING
GEAR

STEERING
TIE ROD

STEERING
CONNECTING LINK

STEERING
IDLER ARM

PITMAN
ARM

Fig. 75. The steering mechanism.

THE STEERING SYSTEM

THE PRINCIPAL parts of the steering system are the steering wheel, steering column, shaft, steering gear, and a group of ingeniously-linked rods and arms.

When you turn your steering wheel, you turn a worm gear, or a cam, inside the steering gear housing at the lower end of the steering column. This causes motion of the pitman arm attached to the steering gear shaft. The pitman arm is connected by means of rods to arms attached to the spindles on which the front wheels are mounted. So, moving the pitman arm causes the front wheels to turn right or left.

The steering system, like the braking system, is a critical part of your car. It is a most important control mechanism and must be maintained in good working order.

Power Steering POWER STEERING uses power from the car's engine to do some of the work of steering. It greatly reduces driver effort and makes driving less fatiguing, especially when parking in limited curb space, in city driving where many corners must be turned, or on long trips.

Power steering units operate hydraulically. They are made up of a hydraulic, or power cylinder, high-pressure hoses, valves, and an engine-driven, high-pressure pump.

In one type of power steering system, the control valve and the hydraulic power cylinder are built in, as part of the steering gear, in the housing at the lower end of the steering column. In another type, the power cylinder is separate from the steering gear and is installed beneath the car and linked up with the steering system. With either system, the hydraulic power cylinder is double act-

128

ing. When a small amount of effort is applied to the steering wheel, the position of a control valve is changed, and oil is forced into one end or the other of the hydraulic cylinder. This moves the piston in whichever direction is necessary to steer the wheels in the desired direction.

Although the steering effort of the driver is reduced with power steering, it is not eliminated. Power steering provides assistance only after the driver has exerted a certain amount of force on the steering wheel. The amount of driver effort required before the assisting effort occurs is different on different makes of cars.

Power steering units are so designed that, should anything about them fail, the non-powered steering mechanism still operates as on a car without power steering.

Power steering provides easier and safer control in case of a front tire blowout where keeping a car on its course suddenly may become difficult, in emergency situations requiring very sudden turns, when driving on crowned roads, or in case one or both right wheels get off the paved road onto soft or rough shoulders.

When you first drive a car with power steering, drive with special care and attention. Practice taking corners at slow speed until you feel thoroughly accustomed to the decreased steering effort needed and the quick car response. On some cars with power steering, considerably less turning of the steering wheel is required than in cars with conventional steering to accomplish the same degree of turning of the front wheels. Until you are accustomed to power steering, you may have a tendency at first to over-steer.

In the same way, when you change from a car with power steering to one without it, be cautious at first. You may expect the car to turn faster than it does and so may under-steer.

It's always safer to drive any strange car slowly until you get accustomed to the steering as well as the brakes —the two most important controls on the automobile.

TO TALK ABOUT:

1   Explain the function and the working of the carburetor.

2   Just how is the power of the engine increased by depressing the accelerator pedal?

3   Why is the third stroke of the piston in a four-cycle engine called the "power stroke"?

4   Explain clearly by what means the up and down motion of the pistons is changed into rotary motion.

5   Explain the function and the mechanism of the low, second, and high gears in the ordinary passenger car.

6   What principal changes must be made in cars which have front wheel drive? Would this construction make the differential gears unnecessary? Explain.

7   How would you diagnose the trouble when you see a driver starting out with a succession of rabbit-hops? How could he correct this? What explanation could there be, other than the one you have given?

8   What are the advantages and disadvantages of an increased number of cylinders in automobile engines?

9   Why does gasoline burn explosively less readily when the engine is started in cold weather?

10   Explain how "riding the clutch" can cause damage.

11   Why is it dangerous to coast downhill in neutral?

12   Automatic transmission cars are said to make driving easier. In what ways do they accomplish this?

TO DO:

1   Prepare a simple model with which to explain the four piston strokes. Write out a description of what is taking place with each stroke.

2   Make as large a list as you can of the mechanical devices commonly used in or around the shop, farm, and home, that could illustrate the principles of the: piston, crankshaft, flywheel, valves, carburetor, spark plug, radiator, fan, gears

that allow connected parts to rotate at different speeds, gears that change the direction of power, and friction brakes.

Write a summary explaining the principles of the automo- **3** bile engine in not more than 100 words.

Write out the "life history" of a drop of gasoline from the **4** time it is put into the tank at the filling station until it has been fully utilized by the car.

Devise some mechanical set-up to demonstrate the princi- **5** ple of the simple disc clutch.

Make a list of all the automobile parts mentioned in this **6** chapter. Divide your study group into two sections as in an old-fashioned "spelling bee." Let the instructor give out the terms in the list as he would give out spelling words. If a student cannot explain the term given him to the satisfaction of the instructor or group, he is "out" and the term goes to the next side. See which side can get the better score.

From local dealers, secure manufacturers' booklets describ- **7** ing new developments in the transmission of automobile power. Have individuals or groups volunteer to study the principles of these new mechanisms and discuss them with the class.

TO LOOK UP:

Automotive Mechanics: Principles and Practices. Heitner, J. D., Van Nostrand Company, Inc., New York 3, N.Y., 1953. 501 pp.
Automotive Mechanics. Crouse, William H., McGraw-Hill Book Company, Inc., New York, N.Y., 1951. Second Edition. 1483 pp.
Electricity and Wheels. Richardson, Ralph A., General Motors Corporation, Detroit, Michigan. 1939. 32 pp.
How the Wheels Revolve. General Motors Corporation, Detroit, Michigan. 1952. 29 pp.
Motor Service's New Automotive Encyclopedia. The Goodheart-Willcox Company, Inc., Chicago 5, Illinois. 896 pp.
Owner's Manual. Obtained for different makes of cars from local automobile dealers.

CHAPTER 8

ACTION: IN CARS WITH

IS YOUR CAR READY?

THE TIME has come for actual driving. First, check your car for good driving condition. Take a tip from the railroad engineer and the airplane pilot. Their machines are checked over carefully before they take them out.
Be sure that:

All tires, including the spare, are inflated to the right pressure.

The radiator is filled with water.

There is enough oil in the crankcase.

Fig. 76. "X" marks the spots.

DO YOU KNOW:

How to check your car for good driving condition?
How to signal for starts, stops, and turns?
The best techniques for steering a car?
The best techniques for starting and stopping?
How to shift gears smoothly?

MANUAL GEARSHIFTS

Battery plates are covered with water.
There is enough gasoline in the tank.
All lights are working.
Brakes are in sound operating condition.

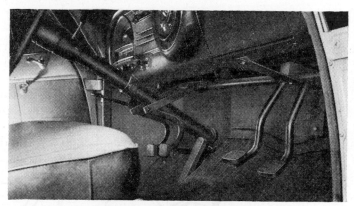

Fig. 77. Dual controls for a practice driving car.

The car in which you learn should be equipped with dual-control brake and clutch pedals. This is important both for ease in instruction and for safety.

ARE YOU READY?

DO YOU know the positions and uses of all pedals, buttons, and levers? Sit in the driver's seat and locate them. Learn to find them by "feel." Operate them with the correct hand or foot and review what each one does:

Ignition switch—Turns on electric current.

Starter switch—Causes starting motor to crank the engine.

Clutch pedal—Disengages the clutch.

Gearshift lever—Selects gear positions: first, second, third, reverse, and neutral.

Accelerator pedal—Feeds the gasoline-air mixture to engine.

Brake pedal—Slows down or stops the car.

Parking brake—Holds the car in place after it is stopped.

Light switch—Turns lights on and off.

Low-beam light button—Lowers the headlight beams.

Horn button or ring—Sounds the horn.

Windshield wiper control—Starts or stops wiper blades.

A DEMONSTRATION FIRST

A GOOD introduction to practice driving is a demonstration by your instructor. Watch him handle the car. Ask him to do things slowly. Follow every move carefully as he starts the engine, starts the car, shifts gears, signals intentions, steers the car, and brings it to a smooth stop.

Keep a sharp eye especially on the directions in which his right hand moves in shifting gears.

Fig. 78. Drive by "touch"—eyes front.

It is important to learn to shift gears without looking at the lever. Study Fig. 79. Notice where the knob on the gearshift lever must be for the different gear positions. Notice that the gear positions on the boxed-in "H" are the same for both the floor and steering column type of gearshift lever.

The gearshift lever selects the different-sized gears in the transmission to give various combinations of speed and power. Study the diagram below until, with your eyes shut, you can visualize the five positions of the knob on the gearshift lever—the positions for low gear, second, high, reverse, and neutral.

In a car with a clutch pedal, *never move the gearshift lever without first pressing the clutch pedal all the way down with your left foot. Keep the pedal firmly pressed down until you finish changing the lever to the new position.*

The reason is very important. Pushing the clutch pedal down completely disengages the clutch. It disconnects the engine from the transmission until the change is made to gears of a different ratio. Failure to disengage the clutch fully causes a loud grinding of gears, and gear teeth can be broken or "stripped" by such clumsy shifting. You have heard the ugly grating noise unskilled drivers make when shifting gears. For quiet, smooth gearshifting, *keep the clutch pedal down.*

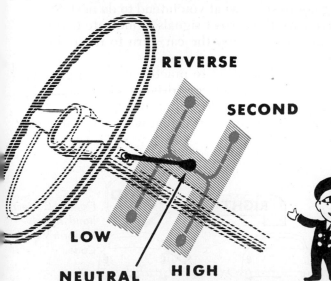

REVERSE

SECOND

LOW

NEUTRAL **HIGH**

Fig. 79. Gear-shifting movements follow an "H" pattern.

135

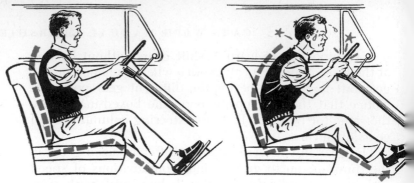

Fig. 80. Good seat adjustment and posture reduce fatigue.

BEHIND THE WHEEL

WHEN you know the different positions of the gear-shifting lever for the various gears, take your place in the driver's seat for a first practice. Place books, purse, or other articles on the back floor to avoid the distractions, confusion, and hazards of having them on the front seat.

Does the seat fit you? Is it high enough? Be able to see the road *over* the steering wheel—not through the spokes. Be able to see the road to the back through the rear-view mirror. If necessary, adjust the seat, or use firm cushions, so you can reach the clutch pedal easily, without having to strain. You will then be well-adjusted to reach all the control devices.

Signaling Your Intention FROM THE START of your driving, form the habit of giving correct signals to show what you intend to do next. Study Fig. 81 and learn the correct signals to indicate to others that you are going to stop the car, turn to the right, or turn to the left.

It is extremely important to practice correct signaling from the very beginning of your driving. Good signaling is a built-in part of the driving habits of expert drivers. It should be so thoroughly learned that it is practically automatic.

Fig. 81. Correct hand signals— Uniform Vehicle Code.

Follow the simple rules:

Signal for all stops, for slowing down, and for all turns. ◄
Always signal for starts before pulling out from the curb.
Give signals that are correct and clear.
Give the signal early enough to allow other traffic to adjust to your intentions.

The correct signal when starting the car depends on circumstances. When starting from the curb, give the appropriate turn signal, depending on the direction you must turn to get into the line of traffic. When starting in reverse to back out of a parking position, a tap on the horn is the starting signal.

Many cars are now equipped with mechanical signaling devices. If your car is one of these, *learn the hand signals also.* Practice operating the device from the start, but use the hand signals as well for all practice driving. Some states require signaling by hand, even when the car is equipped with mechanical signals.

Now THAT it is time to learn to start the engine, start the car, and do some actual driving, you must be ready to steer properly. Before starting the car, study Fig. 82 which shows how the car turns when you turn the steering wheel. **Steering the Car**

Most people find learning to steer easy. They have steered toy vehicles or bicycles all their lives. Keep in mind the simple fact that the car goes in the same direction as you turn the top of the wheel, whether the car is moving forward or backward. The car will turn to the right if you turn the top of the wheel to your right, or clockwise; it will move to the left if you turn the top of the wheel to your left, or counter clockwise.

Keep in mind these simple rules for good steering:

Keep your eyes on the road. ◄
Keep your hands on the wheel.
Stay on the right side of the road.
Guard against over-steering, or turning the wheel too far, in your early practice.

137

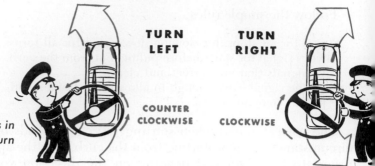

TURN LEFT

TURN RIGHT

COUNTER CLOCKWISE

CLOCKWISE

Fig. 82. The car turns in the direction you turn the wheel.

The best position for hands on the steering wheel varies with the length of arms of the driver. The main point is to keep your hands well apart and in a position that will give sufficient turning space in either direction with both hands, or with either hand. Hands need not remain in any one position on the wheel; they can be moved about for steering efficiency and driving comfort. It is better, for the sake of flexible steering in either direction, to keep them on opposite sides of the wheel rather than together at the top or bottom.

Hold the wheel firmly, but don't grip it as if it were struggling to get away!

At first, you won't know how far to turn the steering wheel to make the car go where you want it to go. Beginners tend to over-steer. But practice gives you judgment and soon corrects this. Practice until you know exactly where the wheels of the car will go.

Keep your eyes always on the road for well-controlled steering, even when using the pedals and levers. Begin at once to drive on the right side of the road. This is an important habit that should be started from your very first practice at the wheel.

Starting the Engine

Now FOR ACTION!

The steps in starting the engine, as given below, should be practiced in the car under the supervision of the instructor. Don't be in a hurry. Learn the series of operations in starting the engine in their correct order before going on to the steps in starting the car. Be sure the parking brake is set before starting the engine.

Let's start the engine. Study Fig. 83. Then:

a. Depress the clutch pedal all the way down with the   ◀
   left foot.
b. Check the gearshift lever for neutral.
c. Turn on the ignition.
d. Use the starter, releasing it when the engine starts.

The engine is now running, and you can slowly release the clutch pedal. Never touch the starter device when the engine is running.

Press the accelerator pedal down gradually and notice that added pressure speeds up the engine and that releasing the pressure slows down the engine.

To stop the engine, release the accelerator pedal and turn the ignition key to the "off" position.

Start and stop the engine several times until it is easy to remember these four steps.

If the engine is cold and your car is not equipped with an automatic choke, you may have to pull out the choke knob before you press the starter. After the engine is started and is getting warm, you can gradually push the choke back. Push it all the way in as soon as the engine runs smoothly without choking. Most passenger cars now have automatic chokes.

Before starting the car, warm the engine slowly, running it no faster than necessary to keep it from stalling.

For any make car, when starting the engine, follow the directions found in the Owner's Manual.

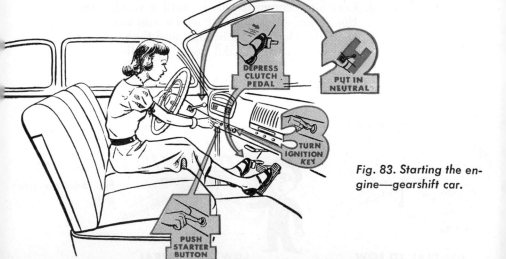

Fig. 83. Starting the engine—gearshift car.

If the engine fails to start after you have used the starting device several times, release the starter and look for the cause. Using the starter repeatedly for a long time soon runs the storage battery down.

Failure of an engine to start might be due to:

▶ 1. Lack of gasoline.
2. Failure to turn on the ignition switch fully.
3. Too rich or too lean a fuel mixture.
4. Moisture on ignition parts which can be wiped off.

It would probably take a mechanic to remedy more complicated troubles such as:

5. A clogged fuel line.
6. A broken or disconnected wire in the ignition system.
7. Fouled spark plugs.
8. Improper carburetor adjustments.

Starting the Car FOR YOUR first actual driving, you will need a wide, quiet, level street or road away from traffic. Or you may be fortunate enough to have a marked-off practice area.

After you have started and warmed the engine, follow these steps:

▶ *a.* Depress clutch pedal.
b. Shift to low gear—palm up.
c. Check mirror.
d. Release parking brake.
e. Check "blind spot" by turning head and looking to the left rear, and signal.
f. Let clutch come up slowly until it reaches the "friction point"—the point at which you can feel it taking hold. Hesitate an instant, and then,
g. Slowly let clutch pedal come up fully, and, at the same time,
h. Increase pressure slightly on the accelerator.

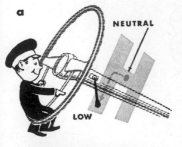

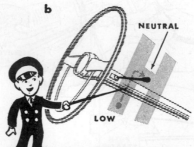

Fig. 84. Low gear shift.

NEUTRAL TO LOW   **LOW TO NEUTRAL**

In step *e*, by the "blind spot" is meant the section of the road to your left rear (just back of your left ear) that is hidden by the "post" or construction panel between the car's left window and rear window. A car coming up to pass can be completely hidden in this spot. A check should always be made, by a slight turn of your head, before starting up from the curb or turning to the left.

Fig. 85. Check the dangerous "blind spot" at the left rear.

In step *f*, you are harnessing the engine for its work of moving the car. So you must accompany it with step *g*, and give it gas to do the work. If the car starts with jumps or jerks, the clutch pedal has not been released properly. If the car jerks, depress the clutch pedal immediately, and practice releasing it more gradually until you can start the car smoothly.

Drivers who shift gears noiselessly and smoothly, without jumping the car, stalling the engine, or grinding gears, have learned to sense and use the *friction point* of the clutch. At the very instant when you reach this point where the clutch takes hold and your car starts to move, press very lightly on the accelerator pedal. Then, while you let the clutch pedal come on up, gradually feed more gasoline.

If you feed gasoline too soon, your car will tend to jerk at the friction point. If you feed gasoline too late, or after the friction point, the engine will not have enough

141

speed and power to pull the car and there will be a series of slow, bumpy jerks or even a stalled engine.

Learning to use the friction point skillfully is one of the secrets of smooth, finished driving in a gearshift car.

When the car is under way and you want to go a little faster, merely increase pressure slowly on the accelerator pedal.

When you have carried out the above steps, your car will be moving in first, or low gear, and you must attend closely to steering.

Stopping the Car from Low Gear You are driving along in low gear, and you want to stop the car. This is what you do:

► *a.* Check traffic through the rear-view mirror.
b. Signal for a stop.
c. Depress clutch pedal.
d. Release accelerator pedal.
e. Apply brake pedal and gradually press down.
f. Shift to neutral. (Follow dotted line shown in Fig. 84, b.)
g. Apply parking brake, and remove feet from pedals.

Learn to carry out step *d* at just about the same time that you are pressing down on the clutch pedal. When in low gear, take your foot off the accelerator pedal *just slightly later* than you press down on the clutch pedal. This prevents jerkiness.

In step *e,* ease up slightly on the brake pedal just before you bring the car to a full stop. This gives you smoother stopping.

After step *g,* keep the gearshift lever in the neutral position until you are ready to start again. This practice is recommended at all times and is especially important at traffic lights, stop signs, and places where there are pedestrians. Serious accidents have occurred where the car has been kept in gear while standing and the foot has slipped from the clutch pedal.

Shifting from Low to Second Gear When you can start the engine, start the car in low gear skillfully, and bring it to a stop, you are ready to learn to change from low to second gear. Start the car in low gear, as you have now learned to do. When it is running smoothly in low gear, *keep eyes up* and—

  a. Press the accelerator until the car is running approxi- ◀ mately 8 mph.
  b. Depress the clutch pedal, and at the same time,
  c. Release the accelerator pedal.
  d. With palm down, move the gearshift lever forward to the position of neutral; then tilt it away from the steering wheel and forward into second gear.
  e. Release the clutch pedal slowly, hesitating for an instant at the friction point. At almost the same time,
  f. Gradually press the accelerator pedal.

. 86. Second gear shift.

LOW TO SECOND   **SECOND TO NEUTRAL**

In step *a,* the accelerator must be pressed until the speed of the car is sufficient to let it run on momentum while the clutch is disengaged during the shifting of gears.

In moving the gearshift lever forward in step *d,* use a slight pressure away from the steering wheel, so that the lever will by no chance move past the neutral position and into reverse position. Follow the dotted path shown in Fig. 86 (a). Notice the hesitation point, and practice observing it.

When you have carried out these steps, you are driving in second gear and must carefully steer the car, keeping it on the right-hand side of the street.

To bring the car to a stop from second gear, proceed as

143

you did when stopping from first or low gear, except that you move the gearshift lever to neutral in the direction shown by the dotted line in Fig. 86 (b).

Practice until you can skillfully shift from first to second and stop from second gear. Then you are ready to learn to shift from second to high gear.

Shifting from Second to High Gear   PROCEED as above until you have the car running smoothly in second gear. Then, *with eyes up:*

    a. Press gradually on accelerator to a speed of about 15 mph.
    b. Depress clutch pedal.
    c. Release accelerator pedal.
    d. Shift to high gear—palm down.
    e. Let clutch pedal come up smoothly, and, at the same time,
    f. Gradually press accelerator pedal.
    g. Slide foot from clutch pedal to floor.

SECOND TO HIGH

HIGH TO NEUTRAL

Fig. 87. High gear sh

In step *a,* your car must be given sufficient speed—approximately 15 miles per hour—to carry it along while the engine is disengaged during the shifting of gears, and to keep it from laboring when it first goes into high gear.

In step *d,* move the gearshift lever as shown by the dotted line of Fig. 87 (a).

In step *g,* form the good habit of sliding your foot back from the clutch pedal rather than lifting it straight up. The weight of your sliding foot helps you release the pedal gradually. This avoids the "clunk" you hear when the transmission and differential are strained unnecessarily by improper releasing of the clutch pedal.

After you have carried out these steps, you are driving the car in high gear. You will find the steering easier. You will learn also to make smaller turns of the steering wheel. At higher speeds, less steering is needed to change the course of the car. Practice until you know just how far the car will turn as you turn the steering wheel. *Keep to the right side of the practice street. Keep eyes on the road.*

To STOP from high gear:

Stopping from High Gear

a. Check traffic in the rear-view mirror.
b. Signal for a stop.
c. Release accelerator pedal gradually.
d. Press brake pedal, slowing car to approximately 10 mph.
e. Depress the clutch pedal.
f. Continue braking, easing up slightly just before full stop.
g. Move gearshift lever to neutral. (As shown by dotted line in Fig. 87, b.)
h. Apply parking brake and remove feet from pedals.

Notice the order of steps *d* and *e*. When stopping from third gear, you use the foot brake *before* you depress the clutch pedal. Then, as you take your foot from the accelerator pedal, the engine slows down and helps brake the car. If you depress the clutch too soon when in high gear, you lose this braking power of the engine.

The complete operation of shifting from low through second to high gear should, under ordinary conditions, be completed in about 12 seconds and within a distance of about 175 feet.

SOMETIMES, when you are driving on hills, turning corners, or are slowed down in traffic, it is necessary to shift from high gear to second.

Shifting from High to Second Gear

Never hesitate to shift into second, if you feel that you can keep your car in better control by doing so. Shift on

145

upgrades if it is evident that the engine may labor under its load.

When you shift from high to second, you need greater engine speed to match car speed. This is how the shift is made:

▶ *a.* Release pressure on the accelerator, while you—
   b. Depress the clutch pedal.
   c. Shift from high gear to second. (Reversing the direction shown in Fig. 87, a.)
   d. Press accelerator pedal to increase engine speed.
   e. Release the clutch pedal, and *at the same time,*
   f. Increase pressure on the accelerator pedal.

Step *d* is necessary to increase the speed of the engine because second gear requires a faster engine speed than high gear. Only practice gives you the feel of the proper engine speed.

If your car is climbing a hill during the shift from high to second, make the shift quickly enough to maintain momentum. This avoids a "stalled" engine. A shift from high to second should generally be made only when the speed of the car has dropped to 15 or 20 miles per hour.

Sometimes a *downgrade* proves steeper than it looks. A shift to second should have been made *before* starting down. But suppose the shift was not made, then the problem is how to make it while on the downgrade. The procedure is the same as shifting from high to second on an upgrade, except that, immediately after step *a,* you apply the foot brake to slow down the car, so there can be a smooth shifting of gears. Here, again, you need practice to learn to downshift smoothly. If the shift is to be made to low gear, it is better for beginning drivers to stop the car before shifting.

Much well-guided practice away from traffic brings results. Practice the simple, straightforward driving operations described in this chapter until they are easy. Then you are ready for the more complicated driving maneuvers.

SHIFT
FROM HIGH
TO SECOND

TO TALK ABOUT:

Explain why you must *never* shift gears without fully disengaging the clutch and keeping it disengaged. **1**

What are the most suitable practice driving conditions for first lessons in driving? **2**

Why, during shifts to higher gears, must the car be going fast enough to run on momentum? **3**

If the gearshift lever is hard to "jiggle" when in the neutral position, how would you make sure that it is in neutral? **4**

Why is it sound practice always to depress the clutch pedal fully when starting the engine? **5**

When stopping the car in low gear, why should you step on the clutch pedal before applying the brake? **6**

Discuss why the steering wheel should not be held rigidly. **7**

TO DO:

Examine the transmission gears in a gearshift car, to see how the shifting takes place through neutral to the four gear positions. Then restudy the diagrams in this chapter to link them up with your observation. **1**

List circumstances which would cause a good driver to: **2**
a. Keep his foot on its heel ready to move to the clutch.
b. Poise his right foot above the brake pedal.
c. Hold his hand over the horn button.
d. Make especially sure his hands are in good positions on the wheel to turn it quickly either way.

Chalk-mark a line on the road. Practice until you can stop accurately at the line. This practice develops skill and confidence. **3**

Chalk-mark a spot on the road. Practice until you can drive either front wheel over it accurately. **4**

TO LOOK UP:

Owner's Manual. Supplied with each car.
Practice Driving Guides for Use with Gearshift Cars. American Automobile Association, Washington 6, D.C. 10 pp. **147**

CHAPTER 9

ACTION: IN CARS WITH

DRIVING CARS WITH AUTOMATIC TRANSMISSIONS

THE PRINCIPAL purpose in developing automatic transmissions for cars has been to make driving easier.

This purpose has been accomplished. Cars equipped with automatic transmissions are easier to drive. Getting under way, picking up speed, and stopping can be done with fewer hand and foot operations than in gearshift cars. This means greater driving ease.

All cars with automatic transmissions have much in common as far as driving operations are concerned. Driving one make is practically the same as driving another. There are, however, a few differences. So always study the Owner's Manual for your own car. The chief difference is that some have clutch pedals and some do not. Because of this, it is necessary, in setting up steps to follow in practice driving, to give alternate lists of steps. Choose the steps to follow, depending on whether or not your car has a clutch pedal.

THE SELECTOR LEVER

YOU HAVE already learned, in Chapter 6, the meaning and uses of the gauges, safety aids, starting, and control devices. With the exception of the conventional gearshift lever and, on most makes, the clutch pedal, you will find the same gauges and control devices on your auto-

DO YOU KNOW:
What automatic transmissions mean to driving?
How to use the selector lever positions?
What are good practices in driving these cars?
How to protect the transmission when towing or
push-starting your car?

AUTOMATIC TRANSMISSIONS

matic transmission car. The principal difference is in the *selector lever*.

Cars with automatic transmissions have no conventional gearshift lever. Instead, they have a "selector lever." The selector quadrant, or mounting for the selector lever, is usually on the steering column just under the steering wheel, as you see in Fig. 88. On a few cars, it is on the instrument panel.

There are four or five lever positions on the selector, depending on the make of car. These positions are marked by letters, as explained below. As the lever is moved, an indicator shows the driver where it is positioned. Some indicators are illumined so they can be clearly seen in night driving.

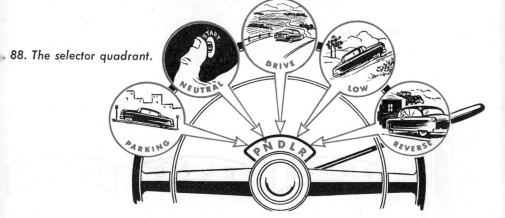

88. *The selector quadrant.*

Here are the general meanings of the selector positions:

▶ N—*Neutral Position*—
   Transmission gears are disengaged.
   The engine is disconnected from driving parts of the car.
   When starting the engine, the lever must be at **N**.

▶ D or **Dr**—*Driving Position*—
   Most forward driving is done in this position.
   The lever is placed in this position after the engine has been started and it is time to start the car.
   The engine cannot be started, in most cars, with the lever in this position.

▶ L or **Lo**—*Power, or Low Gear Position*—
   In this position, the car uses low ratio gears.
   It is for heavy going:
     In mud, sand, over extremely rough road, etc.
     On very steep upgrades.
   It is used for increased engine braking on long, steep downgrades.

▶ R—*Reverse Gear Position*—
   This position is for use in backing.
   Lever must be slightly raised to permit moving it to the **R** position.
   On Hydra-Matic cars, this is the parking position when the engine is stopped.

▶ P—*Parking Position*—
   In this position, a pawl drops into place and locks the transmission so that the car cannot move.
   This position can be used with or without the engine running.
   The engine can be started when the lever is in this position.

Fig. 89. Selector positions are not standardized.

Fig. 89 shows several different selector patterns. Notice that positions for identical purposes are differently placed in relation to each other on cars of different makes. This can cause confusion when persons familiar with a particular selector pattern first start to drive a car with another pattern. Notice especially the **R** or Reverse position. On some selectors, it is on the extreme right; on others, on the extreme left; on others, in an intermediate position. If, because of a habit, the driver switched to **R**, thinking the switching was to **D** or **L**, this could create a serious hazard.

It is certainly desirable from both the driver's and the car owner's points of view that selector positions be standardized. As it is, carefully examine the selector on every automatic transmission car before you drive it and keep the positions well in mind when driving.

BEGINNING with 1952 models, the selectors on some cars have a Dual Range driving pattern. That is, they have two positions at **Dr**, and the driver selects between them according to driving needs.

Dual Range Positions

Study the marginal illustrations for variations in Dual Range designs.

In general, the positions are the same as described on page 150. The only additional explanation needed is for the Dual Range **Dr** positions:

Left-Hand **Dr** Position— ◄
  Provides four forward speeds.
  Automatic shifting takes place all the way to 4th gear.
  The position is used for all ordinary driving.
  Use of 4th gear reduces engine speed and increases economy.

Right-Hand **Dr** Position—(**S** on Oldsmobile) ◄
  Provides three forward speeds.
  Automatic shifts take place to a top of 3rd gear.
  For use in congested traffic and for mountainous driving.
  Reduces automatic shifting in traffic and on hills.
  Increases braking effort on long, steep downgrades.

There is one exception to this description. Even with the lever in the right-hand **Dr** position, an *automatic* shift occurs to 4th gear if the car is accelerated to a very high speed.

The control lever can be moved from one position to another within the dual driving range at any car speed. A change from either of the **Dr** positions to **Lo** can be made safely at moderate speeds on *dry* pavements. It should not be made on wet, slippery pavements.

Lo position provides two forward speeds, 1st and 2nd gears. Uses are the same as described on page 150.

IN THE DRIVER'S SEAT

COMPLETE car control is an outstanding mark of good drivers. The time to acquire it is during the practice periods when you are learning to drive.

The driver sitting behind the wheel and operating the safety and control devices must be the "boss" of everything his car does. All responsibility for what his car does in traffic rests with him. That is why there is so much meaning in the expression, "in the driver's seat." It is a seat of power and control; but it is also one of obligation and of trust. No one deserves "the driver's seat" unless he knows exactly where his car should be and what it should be doing in every traffic situation and can make it obey his will.

Learn *control* of your car by making it move very slowly. Practice inching it along smoothly, at a "snail's pace," both forward and backward. Learn to keep its

Fig. 90. Learn "snailp control—forwards and backwards.

INCH BY INCH

speed down at your will, to bring speed up very gradually from the creep, to decelerate just as gradually back to the creep, and to stop exactly when and where you choose. This practice gives you the kind of car *control* that the best drivers have in traffic. It is a skill worth learning, not only for safety, but for smooth, expert driving. Now that the time has come for actual driving practice, take things slowly enough and practice long enough to acquire car *control*.

At this point, before you begin actual practice driving, review pages 136 and 137 on Signaling Intentions and Steering the Car.

Make the adjustments needed to give you an easy, comfortable position in relation to the seat, steering wheel, foot pedals, and mirrors. Move the seat ahead enough so your heel still touches the floor when the ball of your foot is well up on the accelerator pedal. Good position helps you drive smoothly, safely, and without needless fatigue.

WHEN you have reviewed Signaling and Steering, have checked the gauges, and identified all control devices, you are ready for action. It is time to practice starting the engine. *Starting and Stopping the Engine*

A. **In Cars without Clutch Pedals** If you are learning in a car without a clutch pedal, study Fig. 91.

91. Starting the engine—automatic transmission car.

SET LEVER AT "N"

PRESS ACCELERATOR AND RELEASE

TURN IGNITION SWITCH

PUSH-STARTER BUTTON

Then practice the following steps:

▶ *a.* Check to be sure the parking brake is set.
  b. Place the selector lever at **N**.
  c. Press the accelerator pedal to the floor once to set the choke, and then release.
  d. Turn on the ignition switch.
  e. Use the starter, and release it when engine starts.

To stop the engine, turn the ignition key to the "off" position.

If the car has an automatic choke, the engine will start more readily when cold, if you include step *c* to set the choke. If the car has no automatic choke, omit step *c* and use the manual choke. If the car has a starting device operated by the accelerator pedal, pressing the pedal to the floor before turning on the ignition switch is not advised, as it may cause carburetor "flooding."

The accelerator pedal should never be "pumped" when starting the car. Nor should the engine be "raced." Warm it by light pressure on the accelerator pedal. Some cars run, when cold, at a fast enough idling speed without using the pedal.

If the engine fails to start, it may be due to any of the reasons listed on page 140. If the failure is because of "flooding," press the accelerator pedal slowly to the floor and hold it there while starting. In most automatic transmission cars, the engine will not start unless the selector lever is in the **N** or **P** position.

B. In Automatic Transmission Cars with Clutch Pedals
If you are learning in an automatic transmission car with a clutch pedal, practice the following steps:

▶ *a.* Check to be sure the parking brake is set.
  b. Depress the clutch pedal and hold.
  c. Place the selector lever in the **N** position.
  d. Depress accelerator pedal about ⅓ of the way down. Do not "pump."
  e. Turn ignition key fully to the right, as this activates the starting device.
  f. So it can return automatically to position, release ignition key as the engine starts.
  g. Release the clutch pedal.

The engine is now running. Most engines run when cold at a fast idling speed. Always let a cold engine warm up for several seconds at the idling speed for which it is set and without "racing," before starting to drive the car. This is a good economy measure.

If the engine fails to start because of "flooding," press the accelerator pedal down fully to open the throttle and eliminate choking. Keep the accelerator to the floor while you use the starter device until the engine starts.

Stop the engine by turning the ignition key to "Off."

A. In Cars without Clutch Pedals When the engine has been started and warmed by running a few minutes, it is time to practice starting the car.

Here are the steps:

Starting and Stopping the Car

a. Apply the brake pedal with the right foot. ◄
b. Set the selector lever in the **D** position.
c. Check traffic conditions in rear-view mirror.
d. Release the parking brake.
e. Check "blind spot" to left rear, and signal.
f. Move right foot to accelerator pedal and press down gradually.

The car is now under way, and you must attend carefully to steering. When you want to pick up speed, press down a little harder on the accelerator pedal. Most of your driving will be with the selector lever at **D**.

Some automatic transmission cars tend to move faster than expected, as soon as the selector lever is in **D** and the parking brake released. For this reason, *form the habit of always holding your right foot on the brake as the first step in starting the car.*

Be careful to press down on the accelerator pedal very gently and gradually in the early stages of practice driving in automatic transmission cars, especially if you are accustomed to gear shifting. These cars can get under way more rapidly than gearshift cars, and you may be out in traffic faster than you expect.

Bringing the car to a stop is a very simple process. Here are the steps to practice:

155

Fig. 92. Brief stops in traffic—automatic transmission car.

1. For brief stops in traffic on a level road—

▶
    a. Check in rear-view mirror.
    b. Give the stop signal.
    c. Ease up on the accelerator pedal.
    d. Apply the brake pedal to a full stop.

In braking, apply gradual pressure, and ease up slightly on the pedal just before the car comes to a full stop. This gives smoother stopping.

2. For long, "parking" stops—

    Follow through steps *a, b, c,* and *d,* as above. Then continue with three additional steps:
▶
    e. Move the selector lever to **P**, or to **R**, in cars without the **P** position.
    f. Apply the parking brake.
    g. Turn off the ignition, remove ignition key, and lock car when leaving it.

Learn to stop smoothly. Practice until you become skillful in gauging the pressure to use on the brake pedal. Practice the technique described above of slightly releasing pressure on the pedal just before the full stop. This avoids the "jolt" that unskilled drivers cause when stopping.

Practice until you can stop your car at any exact spot you choose. Pick out stopping spots in advance—a pole, tree, or other mark—and practice until you can stop every time with the car's front bumper exactly even with the spot chosen.

For "parking" stops, be sure to apply the parking brake, place the selector lever in the **P** position on cars so equipped, or in the **R** position on cars not so equipped, and turn off the ignition. Always have the car completely stopped before moving the lever to the **P** position.

In the above practice steps, you will notice that *the right foot* is used on the brake pedal. When cars without clutch pedals first appeared, there was considerable debating about which foot should be used on the brake pedal when stopping—now that the left foot had little to do but idle on the floor. At present, there seems to be consistent opinion among drivers experienced with these cars that using the *right* foot on the brake is better in ordinary stops and is a correct habit to form, in case you will be switching back and forth between gearshift and automatic transmission cars.

One reason for this is the matter of habit patterns. Using the right foot on the brake is a firmly established habit in drivers of cars with clutch pedals. In driving different types of cars, it is best to follow practices that will cause least disturbance to driving habits. Using your *right* foot on the brake pedal, even though your left is not operating a clutch pedal, is a good illustration of putting this principle into practice. It lessens habit disturbance when switching from one type of car to another.

Fig. 93. We switch from car to car.

On the other hand, many drivers who operate *only* automatic transmission cars and therefore will never be bothered with habit disturbance, say that they prefer using the left foot on the brake as a smooth, easy, and natural operation.

B. Starting Automatic Transmission Cars with Clutch Pedals When you have started and warmed the engine, practice these steps:

▶ *a.* Apply brake pedal with right foot.
 b. Depress the clutch pedal with left foot.
 c. Move the control lever to **D**.
 d. Check traffic in the rear-view mirror.
 e. Release parking brake.
 f. Check "blind spot" to left rear, and signal.
 g. Release foot brake.
 h. Let up on clutch pedal, and, at the same time,
 i. Press down gradually on accelerator. Your car will then be moving forward in 3rd gear. When car speed reaches from 11 to 15 mph, take one additional step:
 j. Lift up momentarily on the accelerator pedal.

Lifting up on the accelerator permits the automatic shift to occur from 3rd to 4th, or "cruising," gear.

Your car is now moving in 4th gear and you must attend to steering.

Pick up speed by pressing down gradually on the accelerator pedal. If speed drops below about 10 mph, an automatic shift takes place from 4th to 3rd gear. To return to 4th, or cruising, gear, increase speed, then release the accelerator pedal momentarily and the shift takes place.

Bring cars of this type to temporary stops in traffic in the same manner as cars with fully automatic transmissions.

To move again, transfer your foot back to the accelerator pedal, bring car speed to from 11 to 15 mph, lift up momentarily on the accelerator pedal, and you will again be in the 4th, or cruising, gear.

For prolonged, "parking" stops:

a. Check in rear-view mirror. ◀
b. Signal for a stop.
c. Ease up on accelerator pedal.
d. Move right foot to brake pedal and apply to a full stop.
e. Depress clutch pedal with left foot.
f. Move selector lever to **N**.
g. Release clutch pedal.
h. Set parking brake.
i. Release foot brake.
j. Turn off ignition, remove key, and lock car when leaving.

Practice stopping and starting until you have perfect control and can stop at any exact spot you choose.

USING LOW GEAR POSITION

ALTHOUGH all ordinary driving is done with the control lever at **D**, the **L** or **Lo** position is used for such purposes as:

Need for extra power ◀
Starting on very steep upgrades
Pulling slowly through sand, mud, or snow
Descending very steep grades
"Rocking" the car back and forth between **L** and **R** in deep sand, mud, or snow

Practice using the **L** position under the following conditions:

1. Starting the Car in Low In cars without clutch ped- ◀
als, set the selector lever at **L** and start the same as though the lever were at **D**. When your car is under way, shift the lever to **D** at any time.

In cars with clutch pedals, depress the clutch pedal and place the control lever at **L**. You will then start in 1st gear. To get an automatic shift into 2nd gear, bring car speed up to about 6 or 7 mph, lift up on the accelerator momentarily, and the shift will occur. To shift on into 3rd gear, depress the clutch pedal, move the lever to **D,** release the clutch pedal, and press down gradually on the accelerator pedal to pick up speed. Then lift up momentarily on the accelerator pedal and an automatic shift takes place into 4th gear.

If the car is to be started under slippery road conditions, better traction is available with the lever at **D.** The wheels have less tendency to spin than when lower gears are used.

► **2. Climbing Steep Upgrades in Low**   Shift the selector lever from **D** to **L,** if you are slowed down behind a slow-moving truck or line of cars on a steep upgrade.

This shift can be made smoothly at a moderately low speed, differing in various makes of cars. Shifts to **L** should *never* be made on wet or slippery roads until car speed is reduced to barely moving. Otherwise, the car can be thrown into a skid by the suddenly-introduced braking power of the engine.

In cars with clutch pedals, the shift to **L** must not be made except with the pedal depressed.

► **3. Using Low on Steep Downgrades**   If you are on a long, steep downgrade and need a lower gear ratio than can be had in the **D** range, brake the car down to the speed indicated in the Driver's Manual and shift to **L.** This shift prevents building up momentum and saves brakes by letting the engine serve as a brake. Never make the shift on wet or slippery roads without first bringing the car to a stop.

Never shift from a driving range into **N** and "coast." This can damage the transmission and is both illegal and unsafe.

► **4. Using Low for Heavy Pulling**   The low gear position is used also if you have to pull through deep mud, sand, or snow.

Think of the **L** position as one that gives you heavy pulling power for the rough, slow going required by bad weather or road conditions. It increases power and lessens strain on the engine.

5. Using Low to "Rock" out of Deep Sand, Snow, or ◄
Mud   To "rock" out of sand, snow, or mud, shift back and forth between **L** and **R**. In cars with clutch pedals, use the pedal when making each shift. Use gradual acceleration to avoid spinning the wheels.

DOWNSHIFTING TO LOWER GEARS

ON AUTOMATIC transmission cars, the downshifts to lower gears or "gear ratios" that are needed in all ordinary driving take place automatically with decreasing speeds of the car. Control valves act on hydraulic pressure, and the downshift results.

On some cars, you can force a shift to lower gear ratios at higher speed than occur automatically, if you want extra-fast pickup. This is sometimes called making a "kickdown" shift. This shift is used, for example, if you are back of a slow-moving car on a hill, have a clear, long view ahead, and need a sudden spurt of speed and power to pass.

Press the accelerator pedal quickly all the way to the floor. The downshift to a lower gear rapidly occurs, and you can pull around the slow-moving car. Your car automatically returns to a higher gear, or, on some cars, to

Fig. 94. A good situation for the forced downshift.

direct drive, as soon as you ease up on the accelerator and return to usual driving conditions. For each make of car, there is a top speed above which this forced downshift cannot be made. On some, it can be made up to 50 or 60 mph; on others, at even slightly higher speeds. Study the Owner's Manual for your car to learn at which speeds forced shifts can be made to lower gears.

PUSH-STARTING YOUR CAR

IF THE CAR battery fails and will not start the engine, the best plan is to have it started with a garage booster battery. If this is not available, the car should be pushed to start the engine, never towed. There is great danger with a towed car that, when the engine starts, speed will pick up so rapidly that the towed car will crash into the one doing the towing. *Push* the car for engine starting.

Study your Owner's Manual for the best method. Some manufacturers recommend starting with the selector lever at **D**, others, with the lever at **L**. They differ also as to the speed the car should be going when the ignition is turned on.

Cars with Hydra-Matic transmissions should be pushstarted as follows:

► Place selector lever at **N**.
Push to speed of from 20 to 25 mph.
Turn on ignition switch.
Move selector lever to **Dr**. (to **Dr** 3, or right-hand position, on Dual Range cars)
Do not put the lever in the **L** position.

Cars with clutch pedals should, in general, be pushstarted as follows:

► Put the ignition switch in the OFF position.
Depress the clutch pedal.
Place selector lever at **L**.
Push to a speed of from 10 to 15 mph.
Turn ignition switch to ON position.
Release clutch pedal.
Press accelerator pedal ⅓ down.

The engine should then immediately start. If the engine fails to start, depress and release the clutch pedal several times until the engine begins to turn over. If it does not start within a half mile of pushing, do not continue to try a push start. There may be some serious difficulty, and you might damage the transmission.

TOWING YOUR AUTOMATIC TRANSMISSION CAR

STUDY the Owner's Manual for your car to learn how it should be towed, in case towing proves necessary. *It is possible to damage automatic transmissions seriously by improper towing.*

Fig. 95. Tow automatic transmission cars with rear wheels elevated.

Cars must always be towed with the selector lever at **N**, and never at **D** or **L**. Tow at low speeds and only for very short distances, unless the propeller shaft is disconnected or the rear wheels are elevated. It is safest always to tow automatic transmission cars with the rear wheels elevated.

TO TALK ABOUT:

1   What are the most important things to learn about driving automatic transmission cars?

2   What arguments can you give to support the idea that young beginning drivers should all learn to drive both gearshift and automatic transmission cars? Will your arguments hold for all new adult drivers? Explain.

3   Discuss the use of the right or the left foot on the brake pedal of automatic transmission cars. What do you conclude?

4   Does it matter which type of car, gearshift or automatic, you learn on first? Support your opinion.

5   What habit disturbances can be expected when shifting from a gearshift to an automatic transmission car? From an automatic transmission car to a gearshift car? In which case would you expect the disturbances to be: (*a*) greater; (*b*) longer-lasting; (*c*) more hazardous?

6   The road is somewhat slippery; you are starting down a grade and decide it will be safer to have your car in a low gear ratio. Describe in detail how you will go about it, and explain.

7   Some experienced drivers of fully automatic cars start the car with the selector lever at **L** as an economy measure, switching to **D** after gaining a little speed. Explain why, in some circumstances, this may result in economy.

TO DO:

1   Talk with several drivers experienced with automatic transmission cars. Discuss in class what they have to say about: ease of learning; ease in driving; special driving precautions; habit disturbances when shifting to different cars; driving on slippery roads; care of the car.

2   Visit a machine shop or a car manufacturer's exhibit and examine either a torn-down automatic transmission, or a cutaway, or a plastic-encased model. Study its working parts and discuss in class.

Find out the extent to which the number of automatic **3** transmission passenger cars produced is increasing in relation to gearshift cars.

Find out the extent to which trucks and buses are being **4** produced with automatic transmissions. Give reasons.

Make a list of situations which call for special driver alert- **5** ness when switching back and forth between automatic transmission and gearshift cars.

TO LOOK UP:

Modern Automatic Transmissions. Articles from "Automotive Industries," published by Floyd Clymer, Los Angeles, California. 1950. 77 pp.

Motor Service's Automotive Encyclopedia. Goodheart-Willcox, Inc. Chicago, Illinois. 1954.

Owner's Manual. For the car you are driving. Supplied with the car.

Practice Driving Guides for Use with Cars with Automatic Transmissions. American Automobile Association, Washington 6, D.C. 10 pp.

CHAPTER 10

MANEUVERS

GOOD FORM IN DRIVING

WATCH fifty first-class golfers tee off. You are impressed by one thing—the great majority of them have good driving form. They take much the same position and go through much the same motions in hitting the ball. Indeed, *form* is one of the reasons why they are first-class golfers. In golf, good form helps produce good shots. Good form helps in any sport.

The same thing is true in driving an automobile. Certain ways of handling a car produce the best results. Failure in form marks the "dub" driver just as surely as it marks the "dub" golfer. A good foundation of form and practice is needed in such driving maneuvers as making turns, backing, turning around, parking, and starting on an upgrade.

RIGHT AND LEFT TURNS

ROAD practice, to this point, has consisted of driving forward. Now you must add practice in turning corners. When you practice turns, slow the car to very low speed, shifting into second just before the turn, if necessary.

DO YOU KNOW:
The proper techniques for:
Making right and left turns?
Backing a car? Turning a car around?
Parking? Starting on an upgrade?

EARSHIFT AND AUTOMATIC TRANSMISSION CARS

"Dub" drivers go around corners turning the steering wheel a few inches at a time in a series of jerky movements with both hands. Good drivers use a *hand-over-hand* technique, as illustrated in Fig. 96. One hand or the other is always on the wheel, firmly applying turning power.

As the turn is being completed, let your hands slide around the wheel to their normal driving positions while the wheel slips through them. The front wheels return automatically to a straight-ahead position. The speed of the return is controlled by the pressure of your hands on the steering wheel and by the speed of the car. You control the final alignment of the wheels with your hands.

IN PREPARING for a right turn, check traffic behind and on your right, signal for the turn, and move to the right-hand lane—either the one next to the right-hand curb or the one alongside the cars parked at the curb. **Right Turns**

Fig. 96. Learn hand-over-hand steering on curves.

RIGHT HAND IN POSITION TO START RIGHT TURN. — LEFT HAND TAKES POSITION ON WHEEL AND APPLIES TURNING POWER. — RIGHT HAND TAKES NEW POSITION AND APPLIES TURNING POWER. — TURN COMPLETED. BOTH HANDS RETURN TO DRIVING POSITION.

LEFT HAND SIGNALS FOR RIGHT TURN.

167

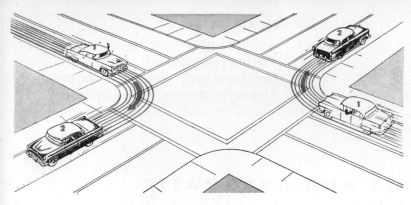

Fig. 97. Making right turns.

Where there are no parked cars, be from three to five feet out from the curb when you start to turn.

When should you start turning the steering wheel? If you start too soon, the rear right wheel may go up over the curb. If you start too late, the car will be out in the wrong lane when the turn is completed. As a general rule, start when your front wheels are opposite the point where the curb begins to curve. Follow the general curve of the curb as you complete the turn. Arrive in the right-hand lane of the street into which you turn.

Left Turns START LEFT turns from the lane nearest your side of the center line.

In preparing for a left turn, check traffic conditions to the left and rear, signal for the turn, and move to the proper lane. Just before turning, check traffic ahead and to both left and right.

Start to turn as the front wheels reach the pedestrian crosswalk. If you start too soon, you enter the cross street

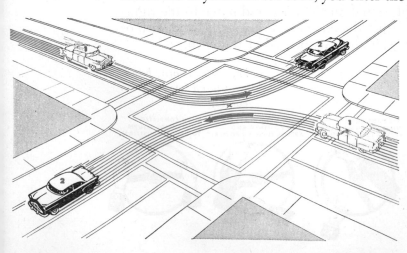

Fig. 98. Making left turns.

on the wrong side of the center line and interfere with pedestrians and traffic approaching from the left. If you start too late, you interfere with vehicles coming from your right or with the traffic turning left from the opposite direction. Start a left turn only after all approaching traffic near enough to interfere with the turn has passed. See Fig. 98. Arrive, after the turn, in the lane on the cross street corresponding to the one which you left.

Where markers, buttons, or signs have been installed at left turns, the course must be followed as marked.

BACKING THE CAR

WHEN a poor driver backs his car, turns around, or parks in a narrow area, lack of driving skill sticks out like a sore thumb! He embarrasses himself and his passengers. "Why doesn't the fellow learn how to drive?" they wonder.

The real question is: Why does he "muddle along," without good driving form? He needs to learn a good technique for *backing the car*—a skill required in both turning around and parking.

Whatever skill you have in "inching" your car forward in perfect control serves you well in backing, where it is especially important to have *complete control* every second and be able to stop instantly.

In steering backward, keep in mind the simple fact that your car will *turn in the direction you turn the top of the steering wheel,* just as when driving forward. Turn the top of the wheel to the right, or clockwise, and your car backs to the right. Turn it to the left, or counter clockwise, and your car backs to the left.

Fig. 99. The car backs in the same direction you turn the wheel.

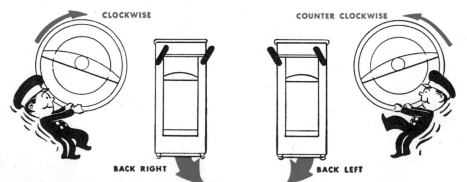

CLOCKWISE   COUNTER CLOCKWISE

BACK RIGHT   BACK LEFT

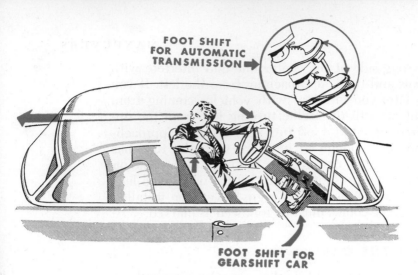

Fig. 100. Checking traffic conditions out of the rear window.

Before you practice backing, try turning yourself around on the seat so you can look through the rear window over your right shoulder. Keep both hands on the wheel as much as possible, and keep at least one hand on the wheel *all the time.* If you are short, you may have to swing your right arm up on the back of the seat and lift yourself up slightly. Keep in a position so you can easily reach the foot pedals. Under some circumstances, look over your left shoulder and out of the side window. In no case open the car door to look out when backing.

When you have practiced this until you can do it and still remain in a reasonably good driving position, you are ready to practice backing.

Here are some special cautions to observe when backing:

1. Take plenty of time, moving the car slowly.
2. Check traffic conditions carefully, front and rear.
3. Look out for pedestrians and other cars.
4. Pay careful attention to steering.
5. Avoid backing into main streets and highways and across pedestrian paths.
6. Back *up hill* rather than down, if a choice is possible when turning the car around.

1. Backing Practice backing in a place free from other vehicles and
Gearshift Cars pedestrians.

Backing requires control. In gearshift cars, control depends largely on skillful use of the friction point of the clutch—the point at which the car just begins to move. Where the car must be just barely moved, holding the clutch at the friction point provides control that allows you to stop almost instantly, if necessary.

Watch your instructor demonstrate several times shifting into reverse, starting the car slowly backward, and bringing it to a stop. Notice especially how he uses the clutch pedal. He releases it gradually to the friction point, using this point to control the speed of the car. Notice, too, that he always brings the car to a full stop before shifting into reverse gear. The shift to reverse is always *from neutral.*

Now take the wheel. Make sure the road is safe for backing, either by looking over the right shoulder and through the rear window or over the left shoulder and through the rear side window. Then practice shifting into reverse yourself. Here are the steps to practice:

a. Depress the clutch pedal. ◀
b. With palm up, raise the gearshift lever toward the steering wheel, and press it forward into reverse gear. (Follow the dotted lines shown in Fig. 101, a.)
c. Slightly increase pressure on the accelerator pedal, and at the same time,
d. Slowly release the clutch pedal to the friction point.

Keep the clutch at the friction point, so you can back smoothly and slowly without "killing" the engine. New drivers tend to feed gas too quickly. Then they release the accelerator pedal too suddenly in an effort to correct the error. Try to avoid doing this, by holding the accelerator steady with the engine running slightly faster than idle.

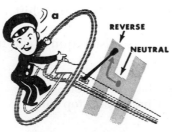
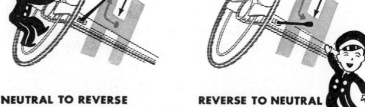

*. 101. Reverse
ar shift.*

NEUTRAL TO REVERSE   REVERSE TO NEUTRAL

Stopping from reverse requires the following steps:

▶ *a.* Depress the clutch pedal.
b. Release the accelerator pedal as you push the clutch pedal down.
c. Apply the foot brake.
d. Shift gears to neutral. (Follow the dotted path shown in Fig. 101, b.)

2. Backing
Automatic
Transmission
Cars

A. Backing Cars Without Clutch Pedals With the car completely stopped and the parking brake set, practice the following steps:

▶ *a.* Apply the foot brake.
b. Lift up the selector lever, and shift it to **R**.
c. Release the parking brake.
d. Check traffic conditions, front and rear.
e. Release foot brake, and press accelerator pedal down slowly.
f. When car starts, slightly release accelerator pressure.

Your car is now backing. You must pay close attention to steering, and constantly be ready to stop. Control the car by using the accelerator and brake pedals combined, to keep the car *barely moving.*

Always have your foot on the brake pedal when you move the selector lever to **R**. This precaution is strongly advised in automatic transmission cars because they tend to "creep," as soon as the lever is moved to a driving position.

On most cars, you have to lift up slightly on the selector lever when you shift it to the **R** position. This is a built-in safety feature to help guard against a move to **R** when you intend to move to **D** or **Dr**. On some cars, this lifting is not necessary, because the transmission is designed to block out any attempted shift to **R** when the car is moving forward.

Stopping from reverse also requires careful practice. Here are the steps:

▶ *a.* Lift foot from the accelerator pedal.
b. Apply the foot brake and stop car.

c. Move selector lever to **N** or **P**, after car is fully stopped.
d. Apply the parking brake.

Practice starting, steering, and stopping the car in reverse until you can stop exactly when and where you want to. Practice turning the car to the right and the left while backing. Practice, if possible, on a well-marked course, so you can judge your improvement and know when you have mastered these skills.

B. Backing Automatic Transmission Cars with Clutch Pedals Have the car completely stopped, with the control lever at **N**, and the parking brake set. Then practice these steps:

a. Apply the foot brake.
b. Depress the clutch pedal with your left foot.
c. Lift up on the control lever and move to **R**.
d. Release parking brake.
e. Check traffic conditions, front and rear.
f. Release foot brake.
g. Release clutch pedal, and, at the same time,
h. Press gently on accelerator pedal.

Move slowly; attend to steering; be ready to stop at any time.

To stop from reverse, follow these steps:

a. Depress clutch pedal with the left foot.
b. Let up on accelerator pedal.
c. Apply brake pedal and stop car.
d. Move selector lever to **N** position.
e. Release clutch pedal.
f. Apply parking brake.

Practice backing and stopping from backing until you have mastered the steps and can start, steer, and stop in complete control.

TURNING AROUND

AFTER you have mastered backing the car, you are ready to tackle the job of *turning the car around.*

Two methods are illustrated in Fig. 102.

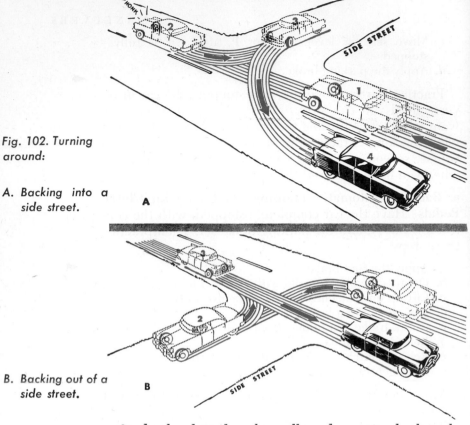

Fig. 102. Turning
around:

A. Backing into a
side street.

B. Backing out of a
side street.

Study the dotted paths well, and practice both techniques. You can use alleyways, farm lanes, or side streets in this type of turning.

Method **A** is preferred to method **B** because it avoids backing into a main roadway, which, in many places, the law forbids. With either method **A** or **B**:

▶ Choose places where there is little or no traffic.
Avoid backing into main highways and main streets.
If possible, avoid backing downgrade or toward a ditch.
Look carefully to see that your path is perfectly clear.
Sound the horn to signal your intention to back.
Move the car slowly, keeping constant control.

U-Turns SOMETIMES you want to make a **U**-turn, or turn in one complete sweep. Be sure it is in a place where **U**-turns are permitted, for in many places they are illegal.

174

When **U**-turning on country roads, be far enough away from a hillcrest or curve so that cars will not come upon you suddenly. On city streets, make sure no vehicles, pedestrians, playing children, or animals can get in your way. Even when you are satisfied that the way is clear, be ready to stop instantly.

TURNING around on a narrow street can be difficult. Here are the steps: *Turning Around on a Narrow Street*

    a. Stop close to the right-hand edge of the pavement.
    b. Be sure that the way is clear both ahead and behind.
    c. Signal for a left turn.

The next four steps are illustrated in Fig. 103.

    d. Go forward in low gear, turning the steering wheel to the left to bring the car to position 2.
    e. When the front wheels are about two feet from the curb and the car is still moving slowly ahead, turn the steering wheel rapidly to the right, and stop just short of the curb or road edge.
    f. Back slowly, turning the steering wheel to the right to bring the car to position 3 turning the wheel to the left just before stopping.
    g. Go forward slowly, completing the turn to the left, bringing the car to position 4.

In some states, the driver's license examination requires you to demonstrate turning on a roadway too narrow for a **U**-turn without touching the curb either in backing or going forward. Practice this maneuver until you can do it correctly every time.

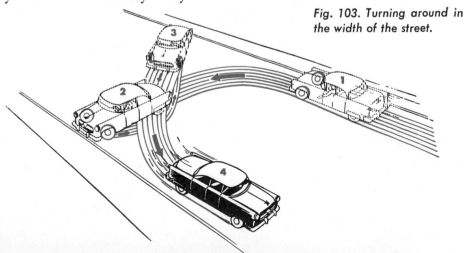

Fig. 103. Turning around in the width of the street.

The turning method you use at any time depends on such circumstances as traffic and the width and layout of the street. Choose the method which permits clear, unobstructed vision and causes least traffic interference.

Turning around is not permitted on some streets where it could be hazardous or might delay traffic. Sometimes, the simplest and best means of getting turned around is to drive around the block.

PARKING

THE "WATERLOO" of many drivers is parking in a limited space at the curb. Someone has paraphrased an old saying to, "Show me how well you park, and I will tell you how skillfully you drive."

There is a certain amount of truth in that. A driver who parks well has learned to control his car. He can put his car exactly where he wants it.

Practice parking first away from traffic. Set up stanchions to represent parked cars at each end of the parking space. Every time you touch a stanchion in practice, score a bent fender against yourself! Practice until you can park without touching a stanchion. Parking is a necessary driving skill.

Fig. 104. Angle parking:

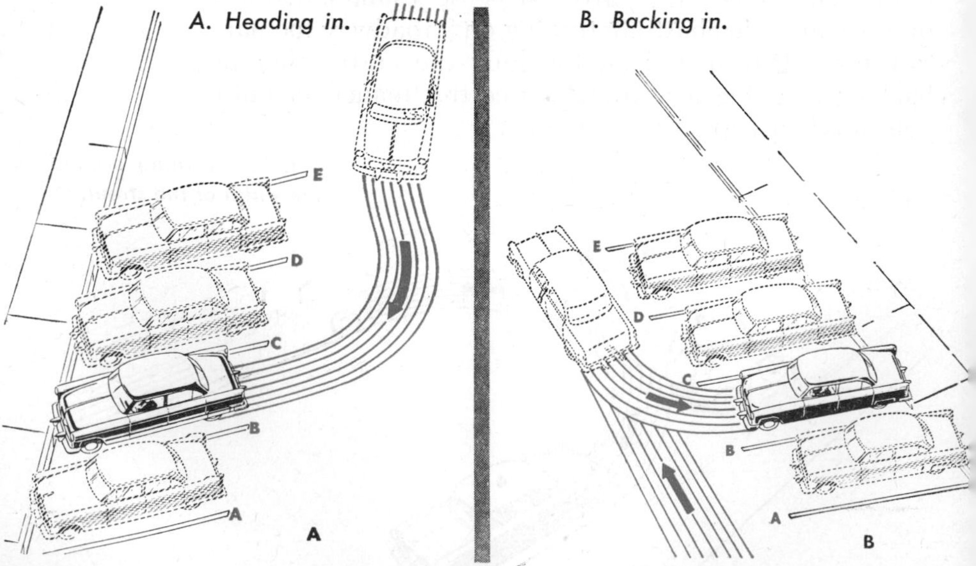

A. Heading in.   B. Backing in.

ALTHOUGH angle parking adds to street congestion and is **1. Angle Parking** hazardous, it is still used in some places. It may be "head in" or "back in" angle parking. Both are simple operations, but they require practice.

When entering a "head in" parking space:

a. Observe traffic conditions both ahead and behind. ◀
b. Signal your intention to slow down.
c. Move your car to the left at least five feet, bringing the rear of the car in position to clear other parked cars.
d. Steer sharply to the right, centering your car in the parking space as shown in Fig. 104 (A).
e. Continue forward slowly until the front wheel barely touches the curb. Do not hit the curb.
f. Place the gearshift lever or selector lever in either the reverse or the parking position.
g. Apply the parking brake.

In coming out of a "head in" parking space, move slowly and carefully because you cannot easily see approaching traffic. Be sure no car is approaching close in the lane into which you are backing. If pedestrian traffic is heavy, as on some parking lots, tapping the horn is a good extra precaution.

As a signal to other traffic, stop after backing about three or four feet. Continue backing until the left front wheel passes the rear bumper of the car parked on the left. Then turn the steering wheel sharply to the right. Straighten the wheels quickly as the car comes back into the line of traffic.

Although entering a "back in" parking stall is more difficult, it is easier and much less hazardous to drive out.

a. Drive slowly past the vacant stall, B-C, in Fig. 104 ◀ (B).
b. Signal, and stop with the right end of the rear bumper opposite the center of stall, C-D.
c. When traffic permits, back *slowly*, turning the steering wheel to the right as far and as fast as necessary to place the car in position to back straight in.
d. Ease in very slowly until the rear wheels barely touch the curb.

177

2. Parallel Parking LEARN, first of all, to judge whether or not the space left along the curb is sufficient for parking. A rough rule is that you need about five feet more than the over-all length of your car.

Assume that your car is number 1 in Fig. 105, and you are going to park at the right-hand curb between cars 2 and 3. Take these steps in order, carefully watching cues:

a. Signal for a stop. Drive alongside car 2, with about two feet of space between. Stop when the rear bumper of your car is beside the rear bumper of car 2. This beginning position is extremely important.

b. Back very slowly, steering sharply to the right, until your car is at nearly a 45 degree angle with the curb. Your right front door should now be opposite the rear bumper of car 2.

c. Straighten the front wheels. Continue backing into the parking space until the right end of your front bumper is opposite the left end of the rear bumper of car 2. The right rear wheel of your car is then about a foot farther from the curb than the right wheels of car 2.

d. Then turn the steering wheel rapidly to the left as far as it will go while backing slowly into the parking space. The rear wheel should now be close to the curb, but should not touch it.

e. Then go forward slowly, turning the steering wheel to the right to bring the car parallel to the curb. Stop the car after centering it at about an equal distance from cars 2 and 3.

Parking regulations in most cities require both front and back wheels of a parked car to be not more than six inches from the curb. If the wheels are too far from the curb, you have failed in one or more of the above steps. In that case, swing the car carefully out and follow 178 through all steps again. Or, if there is enough space in

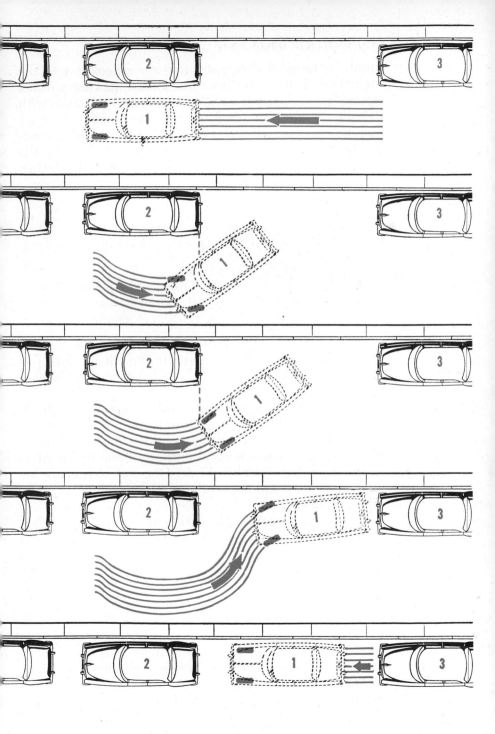

Fig. 105. A guide to *skillful parallel parking.*

front, go forward slowly, turning the wheel first to the right and then to the left, and finally backing parallel and closer to the curb. Parking too close to the curb, with wheels "frozen" against it, makes it very difficult to get out of the space. There is also a danger of scraping fenders on high curbs or of injuring tires. Avoid turning the steering wheel when the car is standing still, as this strains the steering mechanism and is wearing on tires.

After the car is properly parked:

▶ *a.* Apply the parking brake.
   b. Put the gearshift lever or selector lever in the reverse or parking position.
   c. Turn off the ignition switch.
   d. Take out the ignition key; turn off the lights; roll up the windows; and lock the car, taking the keys with you.

This kind of parking is required almost daily by the average driver in every community. Practice it until you are skillful and confident and need not hesitate to park in any adequate space.

If you park at the *left-hand* curb on a one-way street, you will follow all the steps given above, except that you will, of course, reverse all right and left directions. Practice parking at the left-hand curb until you can do it as easily as on the right-hand side. One-way streets are becoming more common, and so this maneuver is more often required.

Pull out from parking by reversing the steps described above. Check to the rear. Move slowly back until your car nearly touches the bumper of car 3. As you back, turn the steering wheel to the left as fast and as far as possible. Check traffic; signal; move forward slowly, steering to the left. Pull out at a 45 degree angle. When your front, right door is opposite car 2, turn your wheels to move in the direction of traffic.

Be sure to *inspect traffic conditions* before you move out from parking. The chief responsibility for avoiding a collision lies with the driver who is leaving a parking space.

If the street is carrying a stream of traffic, wait for a gap. If there are no gaps, edge your way into the traffic stream by "nosing" out little by little. Signal your action all the time. Give approaching drivers time to see what you are doing and to adjust their actions to yours. Finally, some car will stop or slow down so you can pull out.

To PARK on a downgrade, cramp the front wheels sharply *toward* the curb. Stop the car when the front wheels are *almost* against the curb. See Fig. 106 (A). On an upgrade on a street with a curb, cramp the front wheels sharply *away from* the curb. See Fig. 106 (B). On an upgrade with no curb, cramp front wheels *toward* the roadedge, so that, should the car move, it will back away from traffic. See Fig. 106 (C).

3. Parallel Parking on Grades

Leave a gearshift car in *reverse gear,* which has the lowest gear ratio, and with the parking brake applied hard. Leave automatic transmission cars with the selector lever at either the parking or reverse position, as directed in the Owner's Manual, and with the parking brake applied.

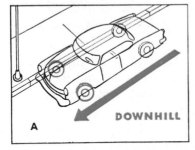
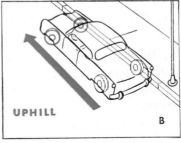

Fig. 106. Cramp front wheels when parked on grades.

181

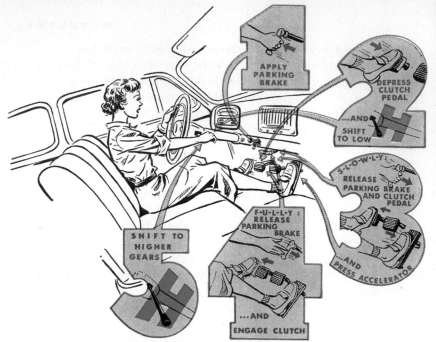

Fig. 107. Starting on an upgrade—gearshift car.

STARTING ON UPGRADES

SOMETIMES you have to stop on an upgrade and then restart. Learn to start on the grade *without letting the car roll back even slightly.* This skill is another mark of driver *control.*

A. In Gearshift Cars The best method for hill starting in a gearshift car is to use the hand brake and the accelerator pedal in combination. See Fig. 107. Here are the steps:

▶ *a.* Pull on the hand brake.
  b. Depress the clutch pedal and shift to low gear.
  c. At the same time:
        Press the accelerator pedal gradually.
        Slowly release the clutch beyond the friction point.
        Release the parking brake gradually, while feeding
            more gas so the car can start forward.
  d. Fully release the parking brake and engage the clutch
        as the car gets under way.
  e. Continue in low gear until your car has gained
        enough momentum to permit a shift to a higher gear.

If your engine stalls on an upgrade in a gearshift car, apply the foot brake quickly, depress the clutch, shift to neutral, and pull on the hand brake. Start your engine by stepping on the starter. Then follow with steps *b, c, d,* and *e* in the list above.

Avoid the panicky feeling unskillful drivers get when stopped or stalled on an upgrade. Practice away from traffic until you have developed skill and confidence.

On some cars, this problem is simplified by devices which prevent the car from rolling backward when stopped on an upgrade. You can then eliminate step *a,* and in step *c,* merely press the accelerator pedal and slowly release the clutch.

A different method for starting on a hill uses only the foot brake. It is good only on a slight grade, where the car will not easily roll back and the stop is short. Hold the car firmly with the foot brake. Shift into low gear. Let the clutch pedal come up to the friction point. Then move your right foot quickly from the brake to the accelerator pedal and release the clutch pedal slowly while accelerating to move forward.

The procedure for starting to back up a grade is exactly the same as the four steps listed above, except that the car is in reverse gear.

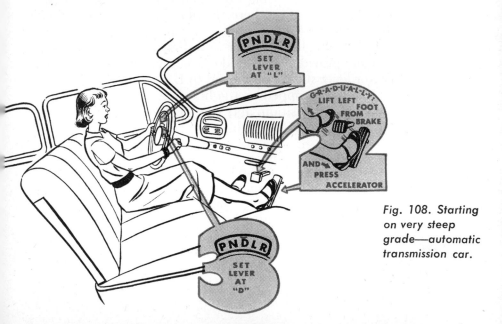

Fig. 108. Starting on very steep grade—automatic transmission car.

Follow the same method when backing out of a parked position on a downgrade, so as not to have to turn the front wheels while the car is stopped.

B. In Automatic Transmission Cars The method you use for starting on upgrades in automatic transmission cars will depend on whether or not the car you drive has a clutch pedal, on the steepness of the grade, on your experience, and on whether or not you will be driving both automatic and gearshift cars.

Regardless of the method, every good driver observes one practice on grades. He holds the car so firmly that it *never rolls back even slightly.*

Here are three upgrade starting methods for automatic transmission cars. Practice all of them.

1. *Restarting on Mild Slopes*—Make short traffic stops on mild slopes by moving your right foot from accelerator to brake pedal. When ready to restart, move quickly back to the accelerator pedal. Your car will not roll backwards during the brief time needed for this move.

Practice this easy method, *away from traffic.* Learn how your car behaves on slopes of different steepness. Never use this method where there is sufficient slope for the car to roll back even a slight distance.

2. *Restarting, Using the Hand Brake*—This method is for steeper grades where the car would roll back if you took your foot off the brake pedal. It is for use in cars without clutch pedals, or in automatic cars with clutch pedals, provided the grade is not so steep that the selector lever should be moved to **L.**

You have stopped on the hill, the selector lever is kept at the drive position, and your right foot is on the brake pedal firmly holding the car. Here are the restarting steps:

▶   *a.* Pull on the hand brake.
     b. Check traffic conditions.
     c. Move right foot from brake to accelerator pedal, and
     d. Press down gently on the accelerator, while you
     e. Gradually release the hand brake, getting the car under way *with no backward rolling.*

If the car has a clutch pedal and you change the lever to **L**, you must, of course, add the clutch pedal steps with which you are now familiar.

Practice this method *away from traffic*, until restarting is a smooth, safe operation and you can control every inch your car moves. It is a good method to use if you are going to drive gearshift cars some of the time. Using the right foot on the brake pedal helps prevent disturbance of your foot habit patterns when you switch back to a gearshift car.

3. *Restarting, Using the Left Foot on the Brake*— Some drivers experienced in automatic transmission cars satisfactorily use and advise using the left foot on the brake pedal when restarting on grades.

In this method, stop the car by using your *left foot* on the brake. Hold the car firmly with your left foot on the brake and your right foot slightly lifted above the accelerator pedal. You can then easily restart the car without rolling back, by merely releasing the brake pedal with one foot while pressing on the accelerator pedal with the other.

Smooth braking with the left foot has to be learned, just as with the right foot. With practice, braking can become as smooth with one foot as with the other. Here again, ease up slightly on the pedal just before you brake to the full stop.

ARE YOU READY TO DRIVE IN TRAFFIC?

IF YOU have mastered each practice step to this point, you now have confidence and skill in starting the engine, shifting the gears in a gearshift car and using the selector lever in an automatic transmission car, backing the car, turning corners properly, and turning the car around. You can start the car on an upgrade and park skillfully at the curb, at an angle between other parked cars, on the level, or on up or downgrade. When you can demonstrate skill in all of these operations away from traffic, you are ready for the best experience of all—driving in regular traffic.

*First drives in traffic should always be done with your
instructor or a licensed driver sitting beside you.* They
should be in a learner's car properly equipped, like a
learner's plane, with *dual controls.*

When you can soundly handle the car in traffic, you
are ready for your driver tests. If you pass your tests with
ease, you are ready to hold your operator's license and to
drop the pilot. You can then do "solo driving."

TO TALK ABOUT:

1   In what direction must the top of the steering wheel be
turned to back to the right?

2   Discuss the need for a thorough knowledge of starting,
stopping, and backing an automobile before learning how to
turn it around.

3   You are approaching a side street on the right and wish to
turn the car completely around. Describe the methods you
can use. Assuming the side street is on your left, describe the
best method.

4   Explain the best method for starting your car on an upgrade after stalling your engine: (*a*) in a gearshift car; (*b*)
in a car with an automatic transmission.

5   You are taking your driver's test. You are told to turn
around in the middle of the block. Describe and illustrate
how you would make the turn to demonstrate skill.

6   Give specific ways in which you must exercise the greatest
care with *any* method when turning a car around on a street.

7   Why is it advisable, in a gearshift car, to leave your gearshift lever in reverse position while parking on a downgrade?
On an upgrade? What determines where you should place
the selector lever in an automatic transmission car under the
same circumstances?

8   Explain the proper position of your car at a "stop" intersection if you wish to make a right turn; a left turn.

Describe the routine you would follow in parking your car **9**
parallel to the curb between two other cars.

What should you attend to before leaving a parked car? **10**

How should a driver signal his intention: to back; to slow **11**
down; to come out of a parked position?

TO DO:

Draw diagrams illustrating the paths of traffic which would **1**
be crossed in making a U-turn: (*a*) *between* intersections;
(*b*) *at* an intersection. Why is a U-turn often prohibited?

Draw a design for an off-street area for practice driving **2**
purposes. Include crosswalks, center lines, angle parking
lines, parallel parking lines, such signs as Caution, School
Zone, Stop, Right Turn, Railroad Crossing, etc.

Paint on a practice roadway a line 100 feet long and 4 **3**
inches wide. Then test your skill in knowing car position. In
going forward, keep the left front wheel on the line; then
drive backwards keeping the left rear wheel on the line. Try
the same maneuvers keeping your RIGHT wheels on the line.
Have someone check your performance.

Study the hand positions used by at least a dozen persons **4**
in holding the steering wheel while backing.

Study the methods used by different persons for checking **5**
traffic conditions to the rear and watching the path of the car
when backing. What recommendations would you make?

TO LOOK UP:

Learning to Drive Safely. A. R. Lauer, Burgess Publishing
  Company, Minneapolis, Minn. 1949. 141 pp.
We Drivers. General Motors Public Relations Department,
  Detroit, Michigan. 1949 Revised. 36 pp.

PART THREE

THE NEED FOR LAWS

ALL YOUR LIFE, laws of one kind or another control the things around you and what you do. This is to your advantage. For laws mean order.

Because of laws, you depend on certain forces of nature; you expect people to behave in ways you can depend on. Without laws, life would be lived in disorder and confusion.

Laws of nature control forces such as those that move the

winds and tides and stars. They account for the seasons and for day and night. They provide sources of natural power.

It is wise to treat the laws of nature with respect. For nature's laws always operate. They always enforce themselves. If you foolishly act as though nature's laws did not exist, you are always "caught"; you pay the penalty. Later, we shall see how this works out for drivers.

Man-made laws help people live and work together. Without them, we could not cooperate harmoniously with our fellow men.

Man-made laws determine good practice in matters of business, owning property, public education, and all the things in life that affect the welfare of many people. Using streets and highways is certainly one of these things.

Man-made laws, like nature's laws, should be treated with respect. They benefit the greatest number of people, even though they may sometimes seem inconvenient to individuals. Unlike nature's laws, man must enforce them. Otherwise, they are not effective.

TRAFFIC LAWS

Sometimes a law needs changing or should even be repealed. But as long as it stands as law, the greatest good comes to the greatest number when we all observe it. When a traffic law is not observed, the result too often is a traffic accident.

Our laws and customs give us the American way of life with its fine standard of living. With this, come the countless automobiles, the crowded streets, and the need for traffic laws and regulations.

Mature drivers understand the need for laws and cooperate in observing them.

CHAPTER 11

TRAFFIC LAWS

NATURE'S LAWS DEMAND OBEDIENCE

IN BOTH city and country driving, many accidents result from the driver's ignorance of natural laws.

Nature's laws work automatically. They are inescapable. Some of them affect driving so seriously that you cannot drive intelligently without knowing how they work. A driver must always deal with such natural forces as: friction, centrifugal force, the pull of gravity, and force of impact.

CENTRIFUGAL FORCE

LOSS OF FRICTION

FORCE OF IMPACT

FORCE OF GRAVITY

Fig. 109. Nature's laws enforce themselves.

DO YOU KNOW:
How nature's laws affect driving?
The importance of friction to driving control?
How to drive so as not to conflict with natural
laws?

MADE BY NATURE

FRICTION

THE ENTIRE control of a moving automobile depends
on the grip which four small areas of tire surface have on
the road. This grip is produced by *friction.*

Friction between the road and the tires enables an
automobile to start, stop, turn, or maintain traction.
When friction is reduced, there is little driver control. It
is then that an accident can readily result.

Friction between the road pavement and the driving
wheels of the car is brought into play whenever you start
or stop your car or keep it moving.

110. Control
ends largely on
r spots no big-
than the text-
k you are read-

191

The friction conditions between two surfaces sliding across each other change under different circumstances, as anyone knows who has skated or pulled a sled or a wagon. Some surfaces tend to grip or hold fast to each other. Some surfaces tend to slide very easily across each other. This fact is very important to car control.

If you measure in pounds the amount of pull needed to drag an object over a surface and divide that number by the weight of the object being pulled, you get a measure of the effective friction between them. We call this measure of friction the *coefficient of friction*. If we let C stand for the coefficient of friction, F for the pounds of force required to pull a car with its wheels locked, and W for the weight of the car, we can express a formula for finding the coefficient of friction as: $C = \dfrac{F}{W}$.

The higher the coefficient of friction between your car and the road surface, the easier it is for you to start or stop your car, or to keep it moving ahead.

When the pavement is dry and the tires are in good condition, the coefficient of friction is high and your chance to control your car is good. When, on the other hand, the pavement is slippery or the tires are worn, the coefficient of friction is low and your chance of car control drops sharply.

Here is one of nature's laws at work. Try as he will, the driver cannot exercise complete car control where adequate friction is not available. Of course he can, in many cases, help determine to what extent he will have friction available. By keeping his tires and brakes in first-class condition, he keeps the available friction at a higher level.

Starting and Stopping Friction THE FRICTION between the rear wheels of the car and the road surface enables the car to start. As the wheels turn, friction exerts a push that causes the car to move. Without friction, the wheels would merely spin, and there would be no resistance or push of tires on the road. The car would not start.

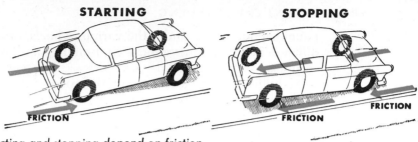

STARTING   STOPPING

ig. 111. Starting and stopping depend on friction.

Friction is equally important in stopping. When you apply the brakes, friction comes into play in two ways:

1. There is friction in the brakes between the brake ◀ shoes and brake drums.
2. There is friction between tires and road surface.

The stopping forces which the driver has at his command when he wants to stop his car depend almost entirely on these two sources. Actual ability to stop the car depends on the weaker of these two sources of friction. Even if your tires are good and the pavement is dry, worn-down or greasy brake linings give you a low braking force. But brakes in the best of condition will not provide much stopping force if the road pavement is so slippery that friction forces are low under the tires.

The amount of friction force available for car control varies, therefore, with the condition of: (1) brakes; (2) tires; (3) road surface.

This explains why a driver helps determine available stopping friction and increases his driving control by keeping tires and brakes in first-class condition, by applying brakes correctly, and by exerting whatever influence he has in securing roads that are properly engineered, built, and maintained.

ON A SMOOTH, level road, free from bumps and hollows, **Effects of Bumps** the force pressing the tires against the road is about **and Hollows** equal to the weight of the car. On uneven or bumpy roads, the wheels bounce up and down and various ones are at times actually off, or scarcely touching, the road surface. This causes variations in the pressure of the different wheels against the pavement. This results in un-

193

equal friction forces under the various wheels, producing difficult steering, unevenness in braking, and reduced stopping control for the driver. Skids easily occur.

At high speeds, variations in the road surface make these driving difficulties greater by further reducing friction forces underneath the tires. The driver can control this situation only by choosing a suitable driving speed. In fact, drivers who know the facts of friction know that it is important to reduce speed on a dry, bumpy road surface just as on a slippery, smooth one.

Soft springs, shock absorbers, and low pressure tires on a car all add to riding comfort. They help also to reduce the bouncing effects of bumps and hollows. They help keep the pressure of the tires on the road more constant. This makes braking more effective.

Friction is a fundamental fact of nature. Drivers who understand and respect its limitations are more successful in avoiding accidents.

TURNING ON A CURVE

Centrifugal Force Friction plays an important part also when your car is rounding a curve. But there is also another force at work—*centrifugal force.*

Fig. 112. When centrifugal force overcomes friction, the car skids.

A body moving straight ahead tends to keep on moving in a straight line. It moves in a curved path only when some force pulls or pushes it out of the straight path.

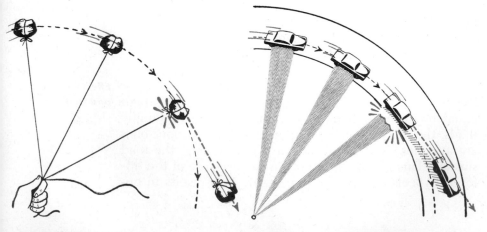

IF THE STRING BREAKS THE ROCK FLIES OFF.

IF THE FRICTION "BREAKS" THE CAR SKIDS OFF.

Try whirling a rock above your head on the end of a string. The pull of the string forces the rock to move in a curved path. You can, however, feel the force away from the center which would cause the rock to leave the curved path if the string were to break. This force away from the center is called *centrifugal force*—a force in nature with which every driver must deal when his car is rounding a curve.

When you steer around a curve, you are controlling the direction in which friction works. Because of centrifugal force, the car tends to go off in a straight line at every point along the curve. But the steered car is constantly kept to a curved path by means of the friction under its tires.

Friction does to the car what the string does to the stone in Fig. 112—holds it in a curved path. Road surface friction, pushing on the tires and toward the inside of the curve, counteracts centrifugal force. Without this friction, or gripping between tires and road, centrifugal force on curves would carry the car off the road.

Suppose, then, that you hit a slippery spot on a curve and have little or no friction between tires and road surface. Accurate steering becomes impossible; centrifugal force wins out; the car obeys nature's law and leaves the curve to follow a straight path, just as the whirled rock does if the string suddenly breaks. The result is an accident.

Fig. 113. Manage centrifugal force by controlling the speed of your car.

How serious an accident it is depends on the speed at which the car was traveling when friction gave way, and also upon whether or not banks, ditches, trees, large rocks, other vehicles, or pedestrians happen to be in its path when it goes out of control.

Available Road Friction on Curves A DRIVER can control his car around a curve depending on:

> Speed of the car
> Side-slope of the road surface
> Sharpness of the curve
> Road and tire conditions

Of the four, car speed is generally the most important. Fortunately, it is also the one over which you, the driver, have full control as you approach any curve. You must take the road as you find it; you cannot redesign the curve; you are depending at the moment on the tires you have on the car; you can, however, control car speed.

Speed of Car The faster a car moves around a curve the greater the centrifugal force tending to pull it off the road. Centrifugal force varies as the *square* of the speed. Here is an inescapable natural law.

As you round a curve, keep speed well below the point at which centrifugal force can win out. Safe speeds on curves depend, to a large extent, on the sharpness of the curve and the type of slope of the road surface.

Side-slope of Road Surface The kind of side-slope of the road on a curve helps determine the speed at which you can safely round it.

196

Fig. 114. Cross-sections of three types of curves.

The slopes of road surfaces on curves are principally of three kinds: (a) flat; (b) crowned; (c) banked. Imagine cutting straight across a roadway with a huge saw to make a road "cross-section." These three types of surface would look somewhat like the cross-sections in Fig. 114.

On *flat* road surfaces on curves, (a) in Fig. 114, there is very little road-push toward the inside of the curve. So friction easily gives way and centrifugal force easily wins out. With high speeds, you have difficulty holding your car on a curve constructed with a flat road surface.

On *crowned* curves, (b) in Fig. 114, a car on the outside lane tends to slide down the crown and away from the center of the curve. Car weight actually aids the centrifugal force tending to pull the car off the road. Only greatly reduced speed keeps a car on a poorly-engineered crowned curve.

The *banked curve*, (c) in Fig. 114, is the best construction. The banking toward the inside of the curve pushes the car toward the center. A greater friction force is available to assist in overcoming centrifugal force and help keep the car on the road. The public will demand correctly banked curves when it realizes that they are more comfortable and also safer.

Sharpness of Curve   The shorter the radius of a curve, the sharper the curve. Centrifugal force increases as the radius of the curve shortens. Then it is easier for the car to leave the road. This explains why sharp curves especially need correct banking and can be taken intelligently only at reduced speeds.

A driver who reduces speed for a sharp curve ahead shows an intelligent understanding of nature's laws. He is reducing centrifugal force.

Fig. 115. Banked vs crowned curves.

It is difficult for a driver to sense the sharpness of curves on sight. For that reason, safe speeds for curves are often posted. Posted speeds for curves should be observed.

Road and Tire Traction The friction forces that can be developed under the tires of a car to resist sliding on a curve depend also on the condition of tires and road surfaces.

With a curve free from bumps and hollows, tires with good tread, and a nonslippery road surface, good road friction is available and you get good traction. This is not true, however, on bumpy, muddy, wet, or icy roads, or with smooth, worn-out tires.

Entering any curve at too high a speed can put you at the mercy of centrifugal force. You are likely to slide off the curve or roll over before you can bring the speed down. Enter the curve at a speed that does not overtax the available friction. Never round curves with the car on the verge of skidding. Drive a curve at a speed that allows a generous factor of safety.

KINETIC ENERGY AND CHANGING SPEED

KINETIC ENERGY is the energy of motion. Any moving body, as, for example, a moving automobile, has kinetic energy. It is kinetic energy that keeps a car moving when you depress the clutch fully and the engine no longer pulls it.

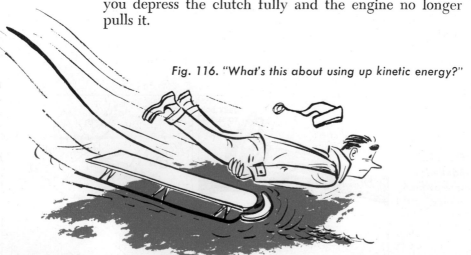

Fig. 116. "What's this about using up kinetic energy?"

The greater the speed of a moving object, the greater the kinetic energy. For *kinetic energy varies as the square of the speed*. Doubling a car's speed quadruples its kinetic energy. This is a very important fact when the car must be brought to a stop.

To THE DRIVER, the important facts about kinetic energy are:

Bringing the Car to a Stop

1. The only way you can stop a moving car is to *use up* ◄ its kinetic energy.
2. The greater the car's speed, the more kinetic energy you have to use up before you can stop it.

How can you use up the car's kinetic energy? One way is by merely *coasting* to a standstill. Kinetic energy then decreases little by little through air resistance and because of friction between moving parts.

But this method of using up kinetic energy takes too long for driving purposes. So you apply brakes to do it quickly. Brakes rapidly change the energy to heat. You can readily feel this heat on the brake drums.

Since the car comes to rest, in usual driving conditions, only when its kinetic energy is used up after the brakes are applied, stopping distance is always related to: (1) the speed of the car; (2) the available friction forces in the brakes and at the road surface.

If you are on a good, straight, clean, dry road and have good brakes, you can use up the kinetic energy and stop the car rapidly.

If the road is slippery, or the tires are smooth, no matter how hard you put on the brake, you may develop only a little braking force. Then kinetic energy is not used up so rapidly, and it is impossible to stop the car quickly. If, under such conditions, you can develop only about $\frac{1}{10}$ the usual braking force, your car travels about ten times farther than on dry roads, before the kinetic energy is used up and the car stops.

The kinetic energy that you must use up when stopping your car therefore bears an inescapable mathematical relation to the speed of your car.

199

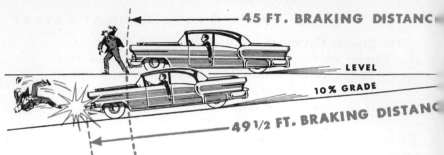

Under the same road and tire conditions, try as you may, a greater distance is always required to slow down at high speeds than at low speeds. An intelligent understanding of the facts about kinetic energy and stopping should make you a more intelligent driver.

The Pull of Gravity WITH THE SAME stopping force, you cannot stop so quickly on a downgrade as on the level. Part of the force must be used up to overcome the pull of gravity on your car. *Stopping distances are lengthened on a downgrade.*

The steeper the hill, the greater the gravitational pull and the longer the stopping distance. Add the factor of speed to the gravitational pull, and you build up a situation where it is difficult to use up the car's kinetic energy and bring the car to a stop.

Stopping force on a downgrade equals the braking force minus part of the car weight. Here is another case of a law of nature setting up a condition which every driver must take into consideration. *Your danger zone inevitably lengthens when you go over the crest of a hill even if you do not increase speed.* You can keep the danger zone from lengthening only by decreasing speed at the crest.

FORCE OF IMPACT

FORCE OF IMPACT gives us another inescapable physical law. It comes into play when objects hit each other, as when cars collide.

Force of impact is measured in pounds and is determined by:

200

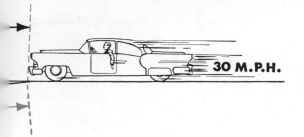

Fig. 117. Stopping distances lengthen with steeper down-grades and higher speeds.

a. The speed of the moving object.
b. The distance within which the object is stopped after hitting.
c. The weight of the object.

Speed is a very important factor, since the force of impact varies as the *square* of the speed. If speed is doubled, the force of impact is quadrupled. If speed is tripled, the force of impact is nine times as great. The damage resulting from the collision increases in the same proportion. This fact gives the driver great responsibility. The greater his speed, the more severe the damages are likely to be in a collision accident.

Force of impact varies inversely as the distance required to stop after hitting. Suppose a car traveling at 40 miles an hour is forced off the road and is stopped by small trees and bushes. There may be enough "give" to the bushes so that the car goes through them for a distance of ten feet before it is stopped. This distance will lessen the force of impact and also the amount of damage to the car and the passengers. If the same car at the same speed were to hit an object with less "give," such as a parked car, and be stopped within two feet after hitting, the force of impact would be five times as great (10 ÷ 2) and damages to car and passengers would likely be correspondingly increased. If a collision accident is inevitable, a driver may be able to lessen the impact by steering his car so as to avoid those rigid objects which would stop his car in a very short distance after hitting.

Fig. 118. Force of impact varies as the square of the speed.

20 mph.

40 mph.

60 mph.

A. The bushes provide a longer stopping distance after hitting.

Fig. 119. Impact is less where the stopping distance is longer.

B. The solid bus shortens the stopping distance after hitting.

To test the value of roadside planting for cushioning a crash, a car was driven into a heavy growth of specially chosen shrubbery. Another car was driven, at the same speed, into a heavy bus. The latter was greatly damaged; the former was relatively undamaged.

The "give" in the bushes was so effective that the force of impact was cushioned. This accounts for the fact that only minor damage was done to the car. This shows an important value for well-placed plantings on separator strips between roadways and along road edges where there are special dangers of skidding or running off the road.

The distance required for stopping after hitting is important when a passenger is thrown forward in a car. In a sudden stop, a passenger's head may be thrown against the dash. If the dash has a "give" amounting to $\frac{1}{8}$ of an inch, the person's head is stopped in a distance of $\frac{1}{8}$ inch. If the same dash were covered, to a sufficient depth, with an energy-absorbing material with enough "give" to let the head cover a distance of 1 inch before stopping, the force of impact would be only $\frac{1}{8}$ as great and the likelihood of injury would be greatly reduced.

Double the weight of an object colliding with another and you double the force of impact. This is an important fact to the pedestrian. Small wonder why he always comes out second best when colliding with cars 20 or 25 times his weight!

TO TALK ABOUT:

In what different ways can mud which has been washed   1
onto some part of a road by a heavy storm cause danger?
How should the driver meet this situation on a straightaway?
On a curve?

Why does a rapidly-moving car swerve if the wheels on   2
one side run off the pavement onto a soft shoulder?

What is the effect of the crown of a road on a car traveling   3
on the inside of a curve? The outside?

Compare the differences in feeling when riding in a car   4
rounding a flat-surfaced curve and when riding in one rounding a well-banked curve. Explain.

Explain why it is important to reduce speed at the top of a   5
downgrade.

Discuss the statement that "nature's laws enforce themselves." Illustrate the significance to drivers.   6

Explain how speed and kinetic energy are related and affect a driver's stopping distance.   7

TO DO:

1   To illustrate the tendency of a car to slide off the road on a curve, lay a bicycle flat on the ground. Let the tire of a wheel represent a miniature circular roadway. Place a penny on the tire to represent a car on the road. Turn the wheel slowly, then faster, until centrifugal force slides the coin off the tire. To illustrate the effects of "banking" and "crowning," lay three coins on the tire a few inches apart. Lay one on the highest part of the tire (as on a flat curve); one in towards the axle (as on a banked curve); and one on the edge near the tread (as on a crowned curve). Now rotate the wheel, starting slowly and speeding up, and note the order and relative speeds at which the coins slide off.

2   Find out what your state highway department has adopted as the maximum amount of banking per foot of width. List advantages and disadvantages of more banking than your state uses. Discuss with your city or state highway engineer.

3   Cut a block of wood with a square base and with a height 5 times its width. Stand this block on end on a level board laid on the floor of the car with one side of the block parallel to the direction of car movement. By driving at various speeds on several curves, determine the maximum speed at which you can take each curve without upsetting the block. This maximum will help guide you in selecting safe and comfortable speeds for various curves.

4   Cut out a piece of the tread of a discarded tire about four inches by six inches. Place on this a rock weighing about 5 to 10 lbs. Get the exact combined weight (W) of the rock and tire on a scale. Attach one end of a small spring scale (reading to 10 lbs.) to this rock and piece of tire and pull on the other end of the scale parallel to the road surface just enough to move the rock steadily ahead. Find the coefficient of friction by dividing the pounds indicated on the scale when the rock moves along by the total weight of the tire and rock. If, for example, the rock and tire weigh 8 lbs. and the pull is 5 lbs., then the coefficient is 0.625. Find, by this experiment, the coefficient of friction on various types of roads when muddy, wet, dry, and sanded. Try pulling uphill and downhill. If ice is available, try the experiment on ice. What type of surface do you conclude is most dangerous? Which is least dangerous?

Devise ways of demonstrating graphically to a group: (*1*) 5
why the danger zone lengthens at a hillcrest; (*2*) how much
farther it takes to slow down from 60 mph to 45 mph than
from 30 mph to 15 mph; (*3*) why excessive speed is more
serious on a curve than on a straightaway.

O LOOK UP:

Driving Can Be Safe. Smith, Truman S. Burgess Publishing
Company, Minneapolis 15, Minnesota. 1949. 136 pp.
Exploring Physics. Rucklis and Lemon, Harcourt, Brace &
Co., New York. 1953.
Let's Drive Right. Halsey, Maxwell. Scott, Foresman and
Company, New York, New York. 1954. 465 pp.
Man and the Motor Car. The Center for Safety Education,
New York University. Prentice-Hall Publishing Company,
New York, New York. 1954. 367 pp.
Modern Physics. Dull, Metcalf and Brooks. Henry Holt & Co.,
Inc., New York. 1953.

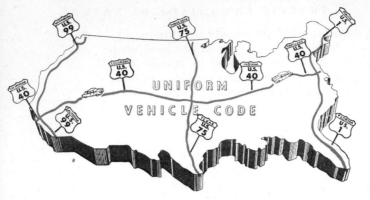

CHAPTER 12

TRAFFI

LAW

LAWS DEVELOP FROM CUSTOM

MANY of our traffic laws developed from custom. Driving to the right is a good example. Informal customs were later written down as laws and became the first formal highway regulations. Regulations have been added as needed. Sometimes, of course, regulations have to be revised because of changing traffic needs and conditions.

KEEPING LEGISLATION UP-TO-DATE

EVERY season, after the last football scores have been posted and the "All-American Team" has been picked, coaches meet to discuss the rules. For in all competitive sports, rules must be sound and uniform to protect players from confusion and dangerous practices and to encourage good sportsmanship.

Sound, uniform, up-to-date traffic regulations are even more important. In this motor age, with its rapidly increasing hazards and changing traffic conditions, traffic legislation must be kept abreast of the times.

Who Makes the Traffic Laws? WHAT units of government are responsible for making and changing traffic laws?

The right of each state to control certain acts of the people within its boundaries is fundamental to our system of government.

206

DO YOU KNOW:

How traffic laws are made and changed?
The basic rules of the road?
What determines legal speeds?
What the law requires of you:
　When you buy a car?
　When you get a driver's license?
Traffic laws for pedestrians and bicyclists?

...ADE BY MAN

Under our government, laws controlling private cars and their drivers are the proper responsibility of the states. There are good reasons why such control should not be by Federal law:

1. The Congress would face the impossible task of setting up laws which would satisfy the needs of different states and which would also comply with various state constitutions.
2. The huge corps of Federal police needed for enforcement of Federal motor vehicle laws could not be made available. Experience proves that state and local police officers have great difficulty enforcing Federal laws that are unwelcome in various states.
3. The Congress would have to devote much time needed for other work to enacting vehicle legislation for the entire country.

With our kind of government, it is best to keep the enactment of motor vehicle laws as close to the people as the state level.

Fig. 120. Many "rules of the road" grew out of early custom.

On the other hand, it is important that fundamental rules of the road be uniform from state to state so that, no matter in which state he drives, a motorist will not be confused.

In the early days, when problems of traffic were mainly local in character, local authorities set up the traffic rules. The result was a confused web of local regulations. There was little, if any, uniformity in traffic laws, and there were many different kinds of signs and signals. A motorist traveling through different cities was likely to violate some local traffic regulations, even before he realized that they differed from the laws of his own locality.

Gradually, as motoring became less local in character, states enacted *state-wide* motor vehicle laws. This reduced the conflict between the regulations of different towns in the same state. But it left a larger problem, since the laws of one state often conflicted with those of another. So, as motoring became nation-wide, there was a need for uniformity in the traffic laws, signs, signals, and markings among the states. Out of this need has come the Uniform Vehicle Code.

The Uniform Vehicle Code NATIONAL CONFERENCES on street and highway safety, held from time to time over the past several years, have resulted in the drafting of a Uniform Vehicle Code, a Model Traffic Ordinance for cities, and a manual of standards for traffic signs, signals, markings, and islands.

Many states have now studied their motor vehicle laws and regulations in the light of the Uniform Vehicle Code and have used this model as a guide in revising their laws.

Fig. 122. Let's fight with modern methods.

So motorists now traveling from state to state often find that the laws relating to registration, driver licensing, safety responsibility, and the traffic rules are similar to those in their home states.

Cities usually retain the right to regulate such *local* matters as parking, stops at intersections, and the use of certain streets for one-way traffic. But, even in these matters, many cities have now adopted parts of the Model Traffic Ordinance, so that motoring regulations tend to be fairly uniform in different cities.

The Federal Government also retains such power over traffic as the regulation of commercial transportation of passengers and property on roads that cross state lines.

Fig. 123. Only uniform laws can end the confusion.

The Federal Government is responsible for movement of Army vehicles in military maneuvers and in other defense activities. Also, it has control over bridges which cross navigable waters.

Steady progress has been made in recent years toward nation-wide adoption of the Uniform Vehicle Code, the Model Traffic Ordinance, and standard traffic signs and signals. This uniformity is very valuable to the motoring public. But, until all localities have adopted uniform regulations, it is necessary to know and obey all local regulations, when you drive in other states and cities.

Some state traffic laws still differ, and it is not possible to cover all local regulations in a book such as this. So SPORTSMANLIKE DRIVING is based on regulations in effect in states and cities that have adopted the Uniform Code and the Model Ordinance. If regulations in your state or city differ from those described here, you must, of course, be governed by your local law while driving within local boundaries. But you will no doubt find yourself interested in working for changes that will bring your state and city in line with uniform traffic regulations.

RULES OF THE ROAD

MANY states publish digests of the most important rules of the road, written in simple, non-legal style and well illustrated.

Fig. 124. How many lanes does a driver need?

Fig. 125. There are "rules of the road" for sea, air, and land.

These digests generally deal with such rules of the road as: speed requirements, traffic control signals, right-of-way regulations, turning regulations, pedestrian rights and duties, overtaking and passing, hand signaling, passing street cars, stopping, standing, and parking.

Without such rules, traffic on streets and highways would always be in a state of confusion. Rules of the road keep order in the traffic pattern.

Here are some common sense rules of the road:

1. Drive to the right of the road center.
2. Pass on the *left* a vehicle going in the same direction.
3. Pass on the *right* vehicles you meet.
4. Allow overtaking vehicles to pass.
5. If driving slowly, keep to the right-hand lane.
6. Signal intentions to slow down, stop, turn, and pass.
7. Always drive at a speed that is "reasonable and prudent" under existing conditions.

Most of these rules of the road are so basic that we scarcely think of them as laws. We observe them because of their obvious importance in avoiding accidents.

Any direction given by a traffic officer or an official sign, signal, or road marking takes precedence over the customary rules of the road. Where there is no special direction, the rules of the road are the proper guides.

IN GENERAL, right-of-way rules indicate *who shall yield* when there is a conflict between vehicles or between a vehicle and a pedestrian. In other words, such rules establish traffic priority.

Right-of-Way Rules

The driver of an emergency vehicle, for instance, warns of his approach with a siren or other special signal. He has immediate priority. It is the duty of all other drivers to yield the right-of-way. They must move as far to the right curb as possible, get out of the intersection, or otherwise clear the way for the emergency vehicle.

Here are some right-of-way rules:

1. The driver *approaching* an intersection shall yield the right-of-way to a vehicle which has entered the intersection from another highway.

2. If two vehicles reach an uncontrolled intersection at the same time, the driver on the left must yield the right-of-way to the one on his right.

3. Drivers must yield the right-of-way to pedestrians crossing at intersections in accordance with regulations, and on marked crosswalks between intersections.

4. The driver within an intersection and intending to turn left must yield the right-of-way to vehicles approaching from the opposite direction and within the intersection, or so close to it as to constitute an immediate hazard.

5. A vehicle emerging from a private driveway shall yield the right-of-way to vehicles on the street or highway.

Right-of-way does not mean the right to immediate use of the roadway! It is a duty of everyone to use the highway in such a way that he will not cause accidents. This *duty* is more fundamental than any right-of-way rule.

Fig. 126. An important right-of-way rule.

... YIELD **to the car
on your RIGHT!**

Fig. 127. The driver must yield his right-of-way where good judgment demands it.

Suppose, for example, that an elderly lady starts across the street on a red light. You are approaching on a green light. Your right-of-way does not mean you have the right to go honking and swerving past her.

Or, consider another interesting example. A green light gives the driver permission to turn right. It also gives the pedestrian the right to cross the street. Here is a right-of-way conflict. In this instance, the law provides that the driver shall yield the right-of-way to the pedestrian.

The driver who fails to yield his right-of-way in an emergency situation is flirting with the same sad fate as Mr. Gray—

> "Here lies the body of Julian Gray.
> Who died while taking the right-of-way.
> He was right, dead right, as he sped along,
> But he's just as dead as if he'd been wrong."

Fig. 128. "Says he had the right-of-way."

The driver of an automobile must always do everything he can to protect another driver or a pedestrian. Even when the actions of another motorist are foolish or illegal, a driver has no right to let such actions result in an accident which he has the last clear chance to prevent. Under some circumstances, he may be held accountable for an accident which he did not directly cause but could have helped avoid.

When it comes to safeguarding pedestrians, the motorist is subject to an additional principle. *The person who has the power to inflict injury also has a special responsibility to avoid inflicting it.*

WHO HAD THE LAST CHANCE TO AVOID THE ACCIDENT ?

Fig. 129. Where will the blame be placed?

The motorist can hurt the pedestrian. Therefore, the motorist must safeguard the pedestrian, if possible, even from the consequences of a foolish pedestrian act. Pedestrians even with physical or mental defects have the right to use the streets. The law places a great responsibility on the motorist to protect them.

Speed Control THE LEGISLATORS of a state face many problems when they try to set up speed laws. In general, there are two principal types of speed control through law: (1) Speed limits can be *fixed;* (2) Speed limits can be *flexible* according to driving conditions.

1. **Fixed Speed Limits** Under this plan of controlling speed, the belief is that certain definite speed limits are right for certain places at all times. So the legislators set

absolute limits, and motorists who exceed these limits can be arrested and penalized for speeding, regardless of the driving conditions at the time of arrest. Motorists who drive within the set limits are not subject to arrest for speeding, although they may be for reckless driving.

2. Flexible Speed Limits Under this plan of controlling speed, the belief is that no fixed speed limits are right *all* the time for a particular place. Whether or not a speed is lawful depends on driving conditions at the time. So provisional speed limits, called *prima facie* limits, are set to tell motorists and traffic officers what is considered reasonable and proper speed under normal driving conditions. You may be driving within these limits, but the conditions at the time really determine whether your speed is "reasonable and proper" or is unreasonable and therefore in violation of the law. So the *prima facie* limits are flexible and not absolute, and the traffic court judge must decide whether or not to hold a motorist guilty of the charge against him after hearing all the conditions.

If, for example, you are arrested for exceeding the *prima facie* limit, *you* have a chance to prove to the court that, even though you were exceeding the limit, you were not driving too fast for the existing conditions. If, on the other hand, an officer arrests you when you are driving at a speed lower than the *prima facie* limit, *the state* must prove that you were nevertheless driving too fast for conditions—as, for example, because the roads were icy or because a football game had just ended and the traffic was exceptionally heavy.

A *prima facie* speed law, as you can see, offers some flexibility in speed regulation, and it is favored by many traffic specialists.

A Basic Speed Rule—Drivers should control their own choice of speed according to a *basic speed rule* which we can state in a very simple way: *Never exceed a speed which is reasonable and proper for existing conditions, even where the law permits a higher speed than you are driving.*

This basic rule holds good no matter what kind of speed limits are set by law, or what type of speed control is used in the state in which you drive. Following this basic rule gives you the best possible protection. It is the kind of rule that intelligent drivers impose on themselves, regardless of whether there are fixed or *prima facie* limits where they are driving.

Safe, prudent speeds vary with such matters as driver reaction time, driver condition, brake efficiency, condition of pavement, weather, traffic congestion, and the whole traffic setup of the moment. A speed which is reasonable when there are few persons or vehicles on the street may be excessive in heavy traffic, or at hours when school children must cross the streets. Over the same stretch of roadway, speeds that are safe speeds at certain times are unsafe speeds at others.

Speed Control for Special Conditions Lower speed limits are sometimes set for night-time driving. In some areas, "speed zoning" is widely used. State authorities make studies and field observations and decide on reasonable speeds for certain stretches of highway, under normal, fair-weather, daytime conditions. Then they post signs showing the speed limit for each "zone."

Special speed limits may be set for residential and business districts, or for curves, intersections, and school

Fig. 130. Measuring car speed by radar.

zones. These limits are generally much lower than open-road limits.

Sound speed laws are of great importance. The basic speed rule is always sound. Much of the material in SPORTSMANLIKE DRIVING is designed to help you follow this basic speed rule: *Never exceed a speed which is reasonable and proper for existing conditions.*

RESPONSIBILITIES IN CASE OF ACCIDENT

AN ACCIDENT situation discloses your personality, character, judgment, and sense of social responsibility. Everyone involved has clear obligations.

Your first obligation after an accident is to "stand by." Running away from an accident is a cowardly, irresponsible thing to do, especially if someone has been injured and may need immediate attention. Hit-and-run drivers are held in lowest esteem by their fellow men. They show themselves to be without honor and sense of responsibility.

RENDER AID

A driver's obligations, when involved in an accident, are both moral and legal. His minimum duty is to:

Stop immediately.
Render assistance.
Obtain medical help, if needed.
Call an ambulance, if one is required.
Give his name, address, and license number.
Remain at the scene of the accident until he is sure no further help is needed.
Make accident reports promptly to the police and to his insurance representative, and to the Motor Vehicle Department, if required.

SHOW LICENSE

Use extreme care in assisting any injured person. Doctors and Red Cross first aid experts warn that unskilled handling, particularly where there are broken bones, may increase the injury and even cause death. Avoid moving an injured person hurriedly or lifting him into a passing automobile to rush him to the hospital. Unless you have completed a standard first aid course and know what is safe to do to an injured person, confine your first aid to keeping him warm and controlling bleeding.

REPORT

Every automobile driver should have systematic training in emergency first aid. Immediate, intelligent aid may save a life or help make the doctor's later care more effective. A first-aid kit carried in your car is very much worthwhile, especially if you have had good training in how to use it. Red Cross courses in first aid afford an excellent opportunity for this type of training.

...ALSO, THE MOTOR VEHICLE COMMISSIONER WILL REVOKE YOUR LICENSE!

JURY AWARDS $20,000 DAMAGES

Fig. 131. Heavy penalties for causing an accident.

Legal responsibilities following a traffic accident can be very heavy. Should you have an accident because of a traffic violation, you could find yourself involved in a criminal case resulting in a fine, imprisonment, or revocation of your license. If personal injury or property damage were involved, you could be sued in a civil case for damages. If you carry other people in your car, you may be held responsible for any injuries they suffer in an accident. If you are driving the car of another person and have an accident, both you and the owner may be held responsible for damages.

Fig. 132. A pilot's license should deserve respect.

OPERATOR'S LICENSE

LAWS CONCERNING CAR OWNERSHIP, LICENSING, AND SAFETY RESPONSIBILITY

You MUST meet certain requirements when you purchase a car. You must obtain a certificate of title and be issued vehicle registration tags or plates. To drive the car, you must possess a valid operator's license.

1. Vehicle Registration

When you purchase a new car, the dealer signs a bill of sale and registers it with state authorities. Most states retain this bill of sale, and issue a certificate of title which describes the car and names you as its owner.

This certificate should be carefully guarded, because you need it when you want to sell your car. Certificates of title are of great value to the car owner and to the state. Receipt of a *bona fide* certificate of title with the car assures you that you are not purchasing a stolen car. When a car is stolen, the thief does not secure the certificate of title unless the owner has been foolish enough to leave it in the car. Title regulations discourage thieves from stealing cars for the purpose of reselling them at a profit. In fact, in states which have adopted certificate of title laws, car thefts have declined.

When driving, your vehicle registration card must always be available to show at the request of the police or Motor Vehicle Department representatives. Do not leave this card in the car where a thief can find it.

Fig. 133. He kept his registration card in "a good, safe place!"

Vehicle registration tags protect an owner. Police in radio-equipped cars detect stolen automobiles through registration numbers. Your tags can also prove of unexpected value in helping locate you in emergencies and in supplying a means of personal identification.

2. Operator's License EVEN with a certificate of title and registration tags for your car, you must get a permit from the state before you may drive the car on a public highway.

You secure an application blank, fill it out, and send it to the state licensing agency with a required fee. If you are a beginning driver, in most states you must get a conditional permit as a "learner"—allowing you to drive for a designated period, provided a licensed driver is in the seat beside you. You must then take an examination and secure a regular operator's license before the learner's permit expires, or renew the permit.

When you present yourself to the state examiner for your license examination, you will be tested in various ways depending on the state regulations. Find out what your state requires. Here are tests that may be given:

▶ 1. A test on motor vehicle regulations in your state.
2. A test on your vision.
3. A check on knowledge of road signs, signals, and markings.
4. A driving test in your car to demonstrate satisfactory skill in such things as parking, turning around, turning at intersections, stopping on signal, and restarting on an upgrade.

It is necessary to carry your driver license card with you at all times and to show it to the police or a representative of the Motor Vehicle Department on request. When you change your address, you must notify the proper state office.

A good license test provides a "weeding out" process, to keep off the road persons who cannot drive properly, who are physically or mentally incompetent, or who are ignorant of traffic laws. Licensing tests are certain to become more strict. The competence of the licensed driver is a concern of everybody who shares the streets and highways and can suffer losses in traffic accidents.

In carefully set up licensing programs, drivers of motorcycles and motorized bicycles and scooters are also required to have operators' licenses. Special tests must be passed on a motorized cycle of the type the driver will ride before he is granted a license. This is as it should be. Drivers of small powered vehicles can cause serious accidents, and should be licensed only if they have special driving skills and sufficiently mature attitudes to take a proper part in the traffic picture.

Compare the automobile driver licensing requirements in use today with those of locomotive engineers or airplane pilots. Is society too liberal in granting the right to operate automobiles and in permitting certain drivers to continue driving? Do we give more weight to the keen desire of the individual to operate a car than to the welfare and safety of the general public? No doubt there will be improvements in the examination given new applicants. There is a trend toward re-examination of licensed drivers—especially of accident-repeaters, violation-repeaters, and the aged. Whether we like it or not, society will undoubtedly become more strict in granting and withholding the privilege to drive.

Fig. 134. Here's one to "sweat out"!

If a driver is convicted of any of the following serious types of offenses, some states make it *mandatory* that his license be revoked for a period of time:

► 1. Manslaughter by automobile.
2. Driving under the influence of intoxicating liquor or a narcotic.
3. Operating a motor vehicle to commit a major crime.
4. Failure to stop and give aid when involved in an accident resulting in personal injury or death of another, or failure to report an accident which involved personal injury or death.
5. Making false statements under oath involving any law covering ownership or operation of a vehicle.
6. Three convictions for reckless driving committed within a period of twelve months.

3. Safety Responsibility Laws ALL states and the District of Columbia have enacted laws requiring a driver, under certain conditions, to prove his financial responsibility. These are known as "safety responsibility" or "financial responsibility" laws.

Safety responsibility laws require that a driver's license and registration certificate be suspended:

► 1. If he has had a criminal conviction against him for certain serious violations of motor vehicle laws, and fails to show proof of future financial responsibility.

2. If he is involved in an accident resulting in death, or bodily injury, or substantial property damage, *and* does not show that he is able to pay the damages for which he may possibly be legally responsible.

Sometimes a driver must pay the damages and prove, before he is permitted to drive a car again, that he is able to take care of the costs of any future accident in which he may be involved. This is called "future proof," and is not to be confused with giving "security" before any legal judgment of liability is made. He can give this proof by having or taking out a suitable insurance policy, or providing a proper bond, or by depositing sufficient money or securities with the state.

Financial responsibility laws increase the safety of motorists and pedestrians. They help eliminate reckless drivers, as well as financially irresponsible ones, from streets and highways. No driver guilty of certain criminal convictions for violating motor vehicle laws can escape suspension of license under these laws.

To sum it up, safety responsibility laws help protect the public by:

Compelling payment of judgments for damages. ◄
Requiring motorists to make themselves financially responsible.
Requiring proof of such financial responsibility.
Eliminating criminally reckless drivers by suspension of their licenses.

REGULATIONS CONCERNING EQUIPMENT

THE Uniform Vehicle Code also includes regulations as to equipment on all motor vehicles. As more states adopt the Code, there is greater standardization of equipment. Chiefly, these regulations cover:

Number, intensity, and use of the lights on motor vehicles. ◄
The performance ability of braking equipment.
Warning devices permitted on different kinds of vehicles.
Mufflers and their condition.
Mirrors and their placement.
Windshields and windshield wipers and their condition.
Condition of tires used.
Kinds of window glass used.
Warning devices to be used on disabled vehicles.

Passenger automobiles, trucks, and buses are equipped by the manufacturer with at least the minimum devices required by law. The driver must then keep the devices in good working order and use them legally.

Small two-wheeled and three-wheeled vehicles with motors, such as motor scooters and motorized bicycles, are usually defined by traffic regulations as motor vehicles. They are subject to the same rules of the road as motorcycles and to some of the same equipment requirements.

Too often small motorized vehicles are not legally equipped. This is especially true of lights and brakes. When a motor is added to an ordinary bicycle, the brake is no longer safe. It can be either a hand or a foot brake, but it must be equal to stopping safely at the higher speeds made possible by adding a motor. Ordinary bicycle lights are no longer adequate when the bicycle is motorized. Especially where there is no storage battery, the lights may fail to give clear vision for the longer stopping distances.

TRAFFIC REGULATIONS CONCERNING PEDESTRIANS

ONE OUT OF every four persons killed in traffic is a pedestrian. In cities, often two-thirds or more of the traffic fatalities involve persons afoot. How best can traffic laws help protect them?

In some places, where a pedestrian crosses a street on a red light, he can be taken into court and fined. But, in many places, traffic regulations for pedestrians are so inadequate that they fail to protect. Better regulations are needed to control and protect pedestrians in traffic. Model regulations for the pedestrian are set up in the Uniform Vehicle Code and in the Model Traffic Ordinance. More and more cities and states are adopting them.

Fig. 135. Take two looks behind you, Mr. Walker!

Sound pedestrian practices, as well as sound driving practices, are largely a matter of knowledge and habit. The more uniform the regulations, the firmer the habits and the safer the pedestrian and the driver will be. When a different set of regulations is imposed on drivers and pedestrians by each locality, habit systems are interfered with.

TRAFFIC REGULATIONS FOR BICYCLE DRIVERS

BICYCLING has grown to such proportions that a national committee has developed model bicycle regulations for adoption by cities. Some of the main regulations are:

A bicycle license and license plate are required. ◀

Licenses are granted only if, on official inspection, the bicycle is found in safe mechanical condition.

Bicyclists using the roadway are subject to traffic laws.

Bicyclists shall ride on the regular seat, and shall carry no more persons than the number for which the bicycle is designed and equipped.

Bicyclists shall drive as near the right side of the roadway as is practicable.

Hitching to vehicles or street cars is prohibited.

No more than two bicyclists shall drive abreast on the roadway.

No bicyclist shall carry anything which prevents him from keeping both hands on the handlebars.

Parking of bicycles must be against the curb, in a sidewalk rack, against a building, or on the curb side, if on the sidewalk.

If a bicycling path is furnished, the bicyclist must use it and not the roadway.

Bicycling on the sidewalk is prohibited in business districts and posted areas.

225

When a bicyclist uses a sidewalk, he shall yield right-of-way to pedestrians and give audible signal before overtaking and passing pedestrians.

Bicycles used at night must have an effective light on the front and a red light or reflector on the back.

Bicycles must be equipped with a suitable bell or other signal device, but must not have a siren or whistle.

Brakes must be capable of locking the wheel on dry, level, clean pavement.

Many cities are adopting such bicycle regulations. Uniform bicycling regulations will benefit both bicyclists and motorists by reducing traffic confusion and accidents.

TO TALK ABOUT:

1   Why is the privilege of driving granted *by the state?*

2   What changes in your community might require new traffic regulations?

3   Should all traffic regulations within a state be uniform?

4   Why have traffic regulations not been made uniform by Federal laws?

5   If your state has not adopted the entire Uniform Vehicle Code, what can your group do to help secure its adoption?

6   There are some who believe that a left-hand right-of-way rule would be preferable to the right-hand rule when two vehicles approach an intersection at the same time. Discuss the advantages and disadvantages of the two types.

7   Motorcycles and motorized bicycles are all included in the definition of "motor vehicles" and come under motor vehicle laws and regulations. Discuss the common sense of this. To what extent must drivers of such vehicles be as responsible in traffic as drivers of automobiles, trucks, and buses?

8   What do you think should be the minimum legal driving age? Discuss this with a traffic police official, a judge, or a traffic engineer. Justify your opinions.

What should be the age for getting a learner's permit: **9**
Where there is a good high school course in driver education?
Where there is not? Justify your opinion.

Describe the procedure necessary in your state to secure an   **10**
operator's license.

Give illustrations of cooperative and non-cooperative prac-   **11**
tices in the use of streets by: (*a*) pedestrians; (*b*) bicyclists;
(*c*) motorists. What uniform traffic regulations would prove
of common value to all of them?

O DO:

List 8 important objectives that you believe society has in   **1**
view in setting up sound traffic regulations.

Find one or more provisions of the traffic law in your state   **2**
that are designed to meet each of the above objectives.

Study the Uniform Vehicle Code as to (*a*) right-of-way;   **3**
(*b*) overtaking and passing; (*c*) speed; (*d*) signals.

Examine your own state motor vehicle code. Find out any   **4**
important ways in which it does not conform to the standards
set up in the Uniform Vehicle Code. Make a list of changes
which you think should be made in your state's traffic laws to
bring about greater uniformity. Discuss this with your group.
What practical steps could be taken to secure such changes?

Secure a copy of the speed regulations in your own and   **5**
neighboring states. Find the number of arrests for speeding in
a given period in each of these states. Just what constitutes
the measuring stick as to when a person is speeding?

Secure a copy of the traffic ordinance of your city. Compare   **6**
its provisions concerning pedestrians with the state vehicle
law. Are your provisions wise? Adequate? Too severe? What
changes or additions do you think should be made?

Dramatize the scene of an automobile crash to bring out   **7**
what you should do when involved in a crash, whether you
are to blame or not.

8   Examine the tests given license applicants in your state. Are they sufficiently severe? Explain. Make a list of the tests you think should be used to determine the fitness of a person applying for an operator's license. Should tests for night vision be included? What kind of tests?

9   Study the equipment on different kinds of motorized bicycles and motorcycles. Notice particularly the brakes and lights. Report on such equipment from the point of view of: (1) safety; (2) traffic law. Discuss the need for just as adequate equipment on such vehicles as on other motor vehicles.

TO LOOK UP:

Digest of Motor Laws. American Automobile Association, Washington, D.C. Annual Publication. 120 pp.

Let's Drive Right. Halsey, Maxwell. Scott, Foresman and Company, New York, New York. 1954. 465 pp.

Local State Motor Vehicle Operators' Manual. May be obtained from your state Motor Vehicle Division.

Man and the Motor Car. The Center for Safety Education, New York University. Prentice-Hall Publishing Company, New York, New York. 1954. 367 pp.

Manual on Uniform Traffic Control Devices for Streets and Highways. U.S. Bureau of Public Roads. Purchase from Government Printing Office, Washington, D.C. 1948. 223 pp.

Model Traffic Ordinance. U.S. Bureau of Public Roads. Purchase from Government Printing Office, Washington, D.C. 1952. 41 pp.

Motor Carrier Safety Regulations of the Interstate Commerce Commission. Bureau of Motor Carriers, Interstate Commerce Commission. Purchase from Government Printing Office, Washington, D.C. 1952. 68 pp.

Safety-Responsibility Bill. American Automobile Association, Washington, D.C. 1953. 80 pp.

State Motor Vehicle Code. State Motor Vehicle Department.

Uniform Vehicle Code. National Committee on Uniform Traffic Laws and Ordinances, 1604 K St., N.W., Washington, D.C. 1954.

DO YOU KNOW:
Why voluntary observance is much better than enforcement?
How the public can be educated to better observance?
What enforcement practices are best?
The main obstacles to good enforcement?

CHAPTER 13

OBSERVANCE AND ENFORCEMENT

VOLUNTARY OBSERVANCE

TRAFFIC regulations grow out of experience. They are based on the practices which the majority of highway users have found to be good.

Practices found by experience to be good are finally enacted into laws. Most motorists realize that complying with such regulations is a good thing to do, and so they observe traffic laws voluntarily. They realize that traffic laws are designed to be protective. If they violate a law, they forfeit its protection. Therefore, they know that voluntary observance is only intelligent.

The protective nature of traffic regulations is shown by the fact that *practically every traffic collision involves at least one violation.*

Of course, not all violations result in accidents. But continued violation almost certainly leads to accidents. Take the case of Smarty-driver Joe who laughed off his

LIKE A TORNADO . . . THE MENACE MOUNTS WHEN THE DRIVER DISREGARDS TRAFFIC RULES

Fig. 136. The violator destroys the protective value of traffic regulations.

229

traffic violations with, "It's all right if you don't get caught." Gradually Joe became more careless and unlawful in his driving. Then one day—a hillcrest—Joe out of his lawful lane—a horrible crash—several persons painfully injured—Joe in the hospital, facing permanent crippling, a heavy fine, and large damage charges. By piling up bad driving habits, Joe had been bringing that collision closer every time he violated a traffic law.

Violations do lead to accidents. That is why intelligent police officials are more concerned with encouraging voluntary observance than with trying to enforce observance or with punishing offenders after accidents.

Observance Is Better Than Enforcement How MANY officers would be required in your community to *force* people to obey all the traffic laws? Your police chief will tell you that no city could possibly afford enough officers to enforce laws on an unwilling public. *No law can be successful in a democracy unless a large majority of the people obey it of their own free will.*

Getting the *voluntary observance* of drivers is a major goal in the work of traffic officers. Progressive police departments work toward informing motorists and pedestrians how they can help prevent accidents by observing regulations.

Obtaining Better Voluntary Observance DRIVERS and pedestrians are constantly choosing between observance and enforcement. If heavy enforcement is required in a community, it is a symptom that work is needed in educating the public on the value of voluntary observance and the penalties of non-observance.

Fig. 137. Drivers should find this choice easy.

Fig. 138. This levee must be made flood-proof.

Poor observance means, in addition to costly accidents:

Traffic disorder and delays.
Higher taxes to provide larger police forces.
Higher insurance costs.
Heavy enforcement, with its arrests, fines, license suspensions, and other penalties.
Less enjoyment in using highways and streets.

A community brings all these ill effects on itself when it does not voluntarily observe its protective traffic regulations.

The people in any community are more likely to give voluntary observance to traffic regulations if they have such aids as:

1. Reasonable, uniform, up-to-date traffic regulations.
2. Digests of regulations so simply stated that every driver and pedestrian can understand what he is supposed to do.
3. An understanding of why various regulations have been made and how they protect.
4. Realization of the serious results of non-observance.
5. Enforcement officials who can stimulate voluntary observance.
6. Education of the driver and the pedestrian as to the responsible part each has to play.

WHEREAS...COMPLAINANT...WILFULLY, WANTONLY, WITHOUT DUE REGARD... CONTRARY TO THE STATUTE IN SUCH CASE MADE AND PROVIDED...ETC. ETC. ...

I DON'T REMEMBER DOING THAT!

Fig. 139. Is it "gobbledygook" to the average driver?

When the public realizes how much injury, suffering, and loss are caused by the uncooperative minority of drivers, it will insist on removing from the highway those who will not "play the game" in accordance with the rules. It will want driving licenses made harder to obtain and to keep, and it will insist on suitable training of drivers and pedestrians for modern traffic conditions.

Driver education classes are a big help in preparing new drivers and specialized groups for intelligent observance of traffic regulations. But large numbers of persons are not reached by such programs. For them, we need mass education in observance.

Mass Education THE BEST programs for mass education in observance of traffic regulations are not those which make people fear law but those which increase understanding of the value of the law. Fear of being arrested and fined, or of being taken to court, or of having a license suspended can help only to a small extent.

Fig. 140. Public opinion can remove the violator.

People brought up, at home and school, as American citizens like better the self-discipline they *impose on themselves*. They want a clear understanding of the values of protective traffic regulations. They want to understand the reasons why we have the regulations. This gives a far better incentive to good driving than the presence of traffic officers along the highway.

Mass education for voluntary observance can take place in many ways.

Newspaper campaigns for better observance and accident reduction are good. Radio and television programs offer a very effective means for mass education.

"Live" panel discussions by teenagers, working with experienced moderators, are used successfully on television, following the showing of traffic safety films. High school students can dramatize accident cases on radio programs, emphasizing the value of voluntary observance.

Fig. 141. His choice will show up in his driving record.

Safety posters and cartoons in elevators, offices, stores, factories, and public places help boost observance. Warning signs on sidewalks can remind pedestrians to honor crossing regulations. Movie shorts have great educational value.

Good films encourage observance and help people develop safety habits. School groups, with good technical guidance, have made some useful traffic films them-

233

selves. A less expensive visual aid is the sound-slide film with a record on which the discussion is transcribed.

The interest of ministers in conserving human life through traffic law observance has led them, in some places, to take part in city or state Safety Sabbath programs, emphasizing acceptance of personal responsibility and courtesy.

Polls of public opinion on traffic matters help in mass education. They make the public think about traffic problems and then support activities which polls show are widely desired.

Polls, for example, show an interesting thing about public opinion on the "fixing" of traffic tickets and penalties. A judge may be told by selfish politicians that he should ease up in his sentences—that people want "soft" judges and like "ticket fixing." But polls of public opinion show that people want good observance and strict enforcement. In fact, such polls taken in a score of cities indicate that well over 90% of the people want stricter enforcement.

ENFORCEMENT

WHEN observance falls down, enforcement must step in.

Some people, fortunately the minority, either willfully or negligently fail to follow the traffic regulations which the majority have found to be protective.

Fig. 142. In public opinion polls, the people speak.

Fig. 143. A good job, if you can get it!

Where enforcement is needed, progressive police forces try to give most emphasis to the major violations which cause serious accidents. They use enforcement officers at places where the most serious violations and accidents occur, and at the times of day and night when they frequently occur. Officers are on hand to *prevent* violations. That is *selective enforcement* at its best.

Some Troubles with Enforcement

If some persons continue their violations, in spite of officers' efforts, fines, and other penalties, their driving privileges have to be suspended or revoked for the protection of all of us.

UNFORTUNATELY, not all enforcement is good. It may not be selective. It may not weed out the worst offenders and the worst violations. The number of convictions for serious violations may be too low in proportion to the number of accidents they cause.

Some enforcement is still carried on mainly for revenue purposes. "Fining mills" still operate, especially where the only source of pay for police officials and magistrates is fees paid by convicted violators.

"Fixing," where guilty, but influential, persons are not punished is still too common. Sometimes penalties are not effective. Too often the magistrate does not give serious cases enough consideration.

Fig. 144. Let's speak up for selective enforcement.

Fortunately, an increasing number of cities now have courteous, well-trained police and intelligent courtroom procedures and enforcement programs that command respect. In many places, however, there remains much room for improvement.

Improvement of Enforcement THE CHANCES of having high-grade, progressive traffic law enforcement are much greater in communities where newspapers and civic leaders support it. Influential, local politicians have to approve things which they believe the public strongly wants. So the public should speak up often and let it be known that it wants good enforcement.

Officials in charge of enforcement should have the power to advance police officers on the basis of merit and to transfer or dismiss incompetent officers. When the public fails to give police officers proper equipment and support, it cannot expect good enforcement. In order to be modern, up-to-date, and effective, enforcement programs must have:

    Adequate personnel
    Good officer training
    Adequate, intelligent supervision
    Proper equipment
    Court support
    Public support
    Adequate salaries, pensions, and insurance

Fig. 145. Traffic officers need specialized training.

IN CITIES, from 20 to 25 per cent of the total police force should usually be assigned to traffic. In many cities, police are so limited in numbers and have so many non-traffic duties, that it is not possible to shift them to traffic work. In such cases, the only solution to an inadequate traffic police force is to employ additional men for traffic duty. The Safety Division of the International Association of Chiefs of Police recommends for cities no less than the equivalent of four full-time traffic officers for each 10,000 of the population.

1. Adequate Personnel

UP-TO-DATE training of both drivers and traffic officers means increased respect and cooperation between them. This results in safer and more pleasant traffic conditions. Well-trained officers regulate traffic and save it from confusion. They serve as constant reminders of the value of voluntary observance and sportsmanlike behavior on the part of all who share streets and highways.

2. Officer Training

Traffic officers are trained to spot and control traffic "chiselers," and to correct and inform persons ignorant of the law. They are trained to weed out drunken drivers, reckless speeders, irresponsible violators, and jay-walking pedestrians. They must be well trained in attitude.

Fig. 146. The accident-investigation squad makes exact records.

237

An important part of their job is to give quiet, courteous help and advice to law-abiding drivers and to watch for opportunities to help educate the public in good driving practices.

Cities with progressive traffic programs have specially trained accident-investigation squads. These squads go immediately to the scene of an accident, aid injured persons, and determine the causes and conditions of the accident. They then get evidence to use in securing court convictions, if violations have occurred. They supply useful information and help set up better enforcement programs. There should be enough accident-investigation squads to investigate 85 per cent of all major traffic accidents. This requires one squad to about every five traffic fatalities per year.

Officers should be trained to use modern scientific equipment for intoxication tests. They must be prepared to use scientific crime detection techniques in serious accident cases. They should use modern, improved methods in preparing cases for court and in presenting the cases.

Some officers compile accident and enforcement records and study them to find improved enforcement methods. Others work with schools, giving talks and taking part in educational activities.

Traffic police work requires well-trained men. So progressive police departments have training schools. Various colleges now offer special police training courses.

Fig. 147. Traffic officers and the teenagers team up for sound driving.

Fig. 148. Moulage casts of tread marks help identify hit-and-run drivers.

A national traffic enforcement training center is conducted by the Traffic Institute of Northwestern University. Do your state and city have training schools for police? Have your traffic police officials had specialized training in traffic police administration?

ALL FULL-TIME traffic officers should be under the command of a ranking police official. To work well on a job, officers must be well supervised. Police officials in charge of traffic are handicapped when they have too few sergeants and lieutenants to do a good job of supervision. Adequate supervision is required for good enforcement.

3. Supervision

IN SOME localities, police are handicapped by lack of equipment. Compare the condition of the motorized fire apparatus in your community with that of the squad cars and motorcycles of the police department. In many cities, even where fire department equipment is excellent, as, of course, it should be, the police are expected to catch speeders, red-light runners, and hit-and-run drivers, in worn-out cars and motorcycles which should have been "turned in" long ago.

4. Proper Equipment

State patrolmen and city traffic police assigned to accident investigation should have cars equipped with two-way radios, a camera, a first aid kit, fingerprinting equipment, a spotlight, flares, and equipment for testing degree of intoxication.

239

Many police traffic headquarters lack even such essential equipment as modern files and record systems. The public cannot expect good enforcement work without modern equipment in good condition.

5. Court Support UNLESS the traffic court judge and the police cooperate, enforcement efforts fail. Good cooperation is most likely to come from the court if the judge is well-informed on traffic matters and traffic laws.

Sometimes there are too many cases to be handled for the magistrate to give each case the time it deserves. Enforcement can then be improved by having a Violator's Bureau handle the less serious, uncontested, first-offense cases by accepting fines without hearings. Also a separate Traffic Court can be set up for handling traffic cases only. Where there are not enough cases to keep a magistrate busy full time, certain hours or days can be reserved for handling all traffic cases.

Too many prosecuting attorneys and courts drop violation charges against drivers involved in accidents if they agree to pay the damages. In some communities, violators who cause serious accidents are much less likely to be convicted than violators not involved in accidents.

Many "fixed" cases never get to the judge at all. Offenders are simply not prosecuted. The records stay in the files; the case is never called out. "Fixing" has a very bad effect on enforcement officers as well as on those whose cases are fixed. How can a traffic officer be enthusiastic about risking personal injury or death to arrest speeders, hit-and-run drivers, and red-light crashers if his traffic cases are fixed.

Fig. 149. "Fixing" strangles observance and enforcement.

OFFICER ENTHUSIASM   RESPECT FOR LAW   COURT FAIRNESS   FIXING   INDIVIDUAL RESPONSIBILITY   SAFETY

Or, an officer may have to appear in court often on his own time. Who can expect officers to risk arresting privileged violators if they fear the result may be transfer "to the sticks" or to a remote section of the city for themselves?

THE MOST important aid the police can have in improving traffic law enforcement is public support. Excellent, intelligent enforcement can be expected where the public keeps demanding it. There will be less favoritism, influence, "fixing," bad politics, inefficiency, and similar abuses when the public acts against them. The policy of "no fix" but "face the music," if you violate traffic regulations, is being adopted in more cities and states. This policy improves observance, especially where the public gets information on what is done about all traffic tickets.

6. Organized Public Support

Public opinion can influence state leaders and city fathers to provide the men, money, equipment, and support needed for good enforcement. The public can get just about the kind of enforcement it *really wants*.

TRAFFIC enforcement work offers challenging vocational possibilities. Frequent obstacles confront earnest, modern enforcement work, due largely to the selfish interests of noncooperative individuals or groups. But intelligent, well-trained officers are definitely needed in greater numbers.

Enforcement Work as a Vocation

The scientific methods that are replacing old ways of doing police work require special training. The Federal Bureau of Investigation conducts excellent general training courses for state and local police in its National Police Academy.

Fig. 150. They cannot stand this searchlight!

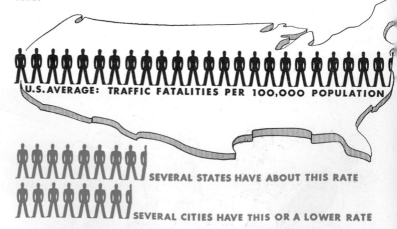

Fig. 151. With public support, these obstacles can be overcome.

Northwestern University and several other colleges and universities offer special traffic enforcement courses. Opportunities for well-prepared officers will continue to grow as the public increases its demands for traffic enforcement of high quality.

RESULTS OF VOLUNTARY OBSERVANCE AND EFFICIENT ENFORCEMENT

DO GOOD observance and enforcement reduce accidents and improve traffic conditions? Records of many cities and states prove that they do. Some states and cities have traffic fatality rates which are less than half the national rates. They are the ones with progressive enforcement programs, as well as sound legislation, engineering, education, and administration in traffic matters.

U.S. AVERAGE: TRAFFIC FATALITIES PER 100,000 POPULATION

SEVERAL STATES HAVE ABOUT THIS RATE

SEVERAL CITIES HAVE THIS OR A LOWER RATE

Fig. 152. Why do some states and cities have traffic death rates so much lower than the average for the country? Where do your state and city stand?

In all such places, good voluntary observance and an efficient enforcement program deserve a good share of the credit for the low fatality rates.

˚O TALK ABOUT:

What seem to you to be the best ways of influencing the **1** traffic behavior of the general public? Explain.

What are the advantages and limitations of the following **2** means of traffic education: (*a*) newspaper features and drawings; (*b*) radio announcements and radio programs; (*c*) television programs; (*d*) moving pictures; (*e*) permanent community organization for safety work; (*f*) posters in store windows, service stations, and elsewhere; (*g*) meetings and addresses; (*h*) special campaigns, such as safety week and courtesy week; (*i*) safe drivers' clubs; (*j*) adult education courses; (*k*) outdoor advertising?

Discuss the value of polls of public opinion for traffic edu- **3** cation. For what kinds of questions are the usual polls unsuitable? Why?

Do you think fear should be used to influence traffic be- **4** havior? Under what circumstances and to what extent?

Why do some people continue to make enforcement of traf- **5** fic regulations difficult?

How important is the enforcement of overtime parking **6** regulations in preventing accidents? Why is so much attention usually given to parking violations? Who benefits from parking enforcements? How?

What causes some people to believe, "It's all right if you **7** don't get caught"? How does this attitude make for trouble? How can it be changed?

What can your group do to encourage more voluntary ob- **8** servance and sound enforcement of traffic regulations in your city? Consider the value of organizing a Youth Committee for Traffic Improvement. What activities of such a committee would most likely produce results?

9   Should traffic police station themselves on side roads where they are not in plain sight of motorists?

10   Debate: "Resolved that clearly marked police cars are more effective in traffic law observance and enforcement than unmarked cars."

11   Discuss "selective enforcement." Give some illustrations.

12   Discuss observance on the part of drivers of small vehicles with motors. Are there any good reasons why traffic officers should overlook violations by such drivers?

13   How can the public be made to realize the bad effects of ticket "fixing"?

TO DO:

1   Invite your traffic court judge to talk to your class. What are his main problems? What does he think of fines? What does he think would help most to reduce accidents?

2   Invite an officer in your state highway patrol to meet with your class. Find out how many men are on duty at one time and what road mileage each man has to cover. Ask him to describe the services patrol officers give to motorists. Ask his views on observance and enforcement and on the problems and needs of the highway patrol.

3   Plan and put into effect ways for making traffic law observance "the thing to do" among members of your group.

4   Find out what five violations produce the most convictions in your town. Do you think these are the violations which need most attention? If not, which violations should have more attention? Why don't they?

5   List the best ways of promoting voluntary traffic law observance by the public.

TO LOOK UP:

Enforcement for Traffic Safety. National Safety Council, Chicago, Illinois. 1938. 48 pp.

How to Attack the Traffic Accident Problem in Your Community. Association of Casualty and Surety Companies, New York, New York. 1953.

Model Traffic Ordinance, Article II and Article III. U.S. Bureau of Public Roads. Purchase from Government Printing Office, Washington, D.C. 1952. 41 pp.

Report of Committee on Enforcement. President's Highway Safety Conference. Government Printing Office, Washington, D.C. 1949. 53 pp.

Traffic Engineering and the Police. Evans, Henry K. and Kreml, Franklin M. Traffic Institute, Northwestern University, Evanston, Illinois. Revised 1947. 103 pp.

Traffic Law Enforcement (1952 SAE Beecroft Memorial Lecture). Kreml, Franklin M. Society of Automotive Engineers, New York, New York. 1953.

Uniform Vehicle Code. National Committee on Uniform Traffic Laws and Ordinances, 1604 K Street, N.W., Washington, D.C. 1954.

PART FOUR

TRAFFIC HABITS

GOOD TRAFFIC practices come from good traffic habits.

Habits give you a reliable way of meeting the situations you face every day in walking and driving on streets and roadways. Having good habits is like having an army of helpers. They free you from the thousand and one details of daily life.

Suppose you had to stop and think out every movement of every muscle you must use when you back your car out of the garage. You would probably never get it into traffic!

You would be in the predicament of the famous centipede who managed his hundred legs with expert and unconscious skill until a curious fellow worm inquired how he did it. This question threw the centipede into such confusion that, according to the verse, he—

> ". . . Lay prostrate in the ditch,
> Not knowing which leg
> Came after which!"

Habits remove the need for countless little decisions from your driving.

SOUND TRAFFIC PRACTICES

During your practice driving lessons, you have been learning what driving habits should be formed—such as signaling intentions, driving in the correct lane, "driving ahead," showing courtesy, choosing speeds that suit conditions, and many other habits. Your driving practices will be sound only if they are backed up by good, reliable habits such as these.

Practically everybody thinks, now and then, about what kind of person he would like to become. What kind of person he becomes depends, in many ways, on what kind of habits he forms. It is that way also with a driver.

As a driver, you can be somewhat "custom-made." From the time you start to drive, you are actually deciding whether or not you will be a good driver.

Choose your early driving habits, and you are choosing whether your driving practices will be sound or unsound. Your day-by-day driving habits make the kind of driver you will be.

CHAPTER 14

''SOLC

SUCCESSFUL ''SOLO DRIVING''

WHEN you have your operator's license and start "solo" driving, your driving practices must be sound. Getting your license and starting off alone is serious business. A bad accident record can make it difficult and extra costly to obtain insurance. It may even make a driver non-insurable, so that it is difficult, or even impossible, for him to keep his driver's license.

Successful driving is a far more complicated matter than just managing to arrive somehow at your destination. How did you get there? What happened on the way? Were you master of your car every second of the time? Were your passengers always comfortable and safe? Were you driving according to traffic regulations? Did you treat other street and highway users fairly? Did you show driving sportsmanship?

Driving is top-quality only when it is sound in at least four different ways:

▶   Legally
        Technically
        Socially
        Personally

To be of top-ranking quality, driving must be sound in all of these ways at the same time and all the time.

248   You could drive in accordance with traffic laws and

DO YOU KNOW:

What makes a successful "solo" driver?
What conditions affect driving?
What is meant by a driver's responsibilities?
How to drive smoothly?
What kind of driving is sportsmanlike?

DRIVING''

still operate the car controls most inexpertly. Or, without violating a traffic law, you could do things that would interfere with and annoy other drivers. In each case, your driving would be unsound.

Joe Smith, for example, is driving his family along a two-lane suburban road on a Sunday afternoon, enjoying the scenery at 15 or 20 miles per hour. Joe is not violating the speed law or any traffic regulation; he operates the car controls in a technically sound and skillful manner, and he feels personal satisfaction. But behind him is a line of irritated drivers, held back and unable to proceed at a normal traffic rate without taking chances. They take the chances and create hazards. Joe's driving is socially unsound. He is not a top-quality driver.

Or Sam may punish his car with clumsy operating techniques. You've seen the kind—starting with a series of jerks, lurching around curves, dragging the clutch, grinding the gears on shifts, stopping with jolts that nearly throw passengers out of their seats. Sam is physically sound, and his driving practices are strictly legal.

Fig. 153. Team defense can break down at one weak spot.

Fig. 154. Three keys
to sound driving.

His consideration for other drivers is all that could be desired. But he lacks skills, and falls down in his driving technically. His driving is unsound.

Top-notch driving means that you always drive:

► With complete control.
  In accordance with conditions.
  In observance of traffic regulations.
  With smooth, skillful operation of your **car.**
  In good physical condition.
  Aware of and accepting your responsibilities.
  With fairness, courtesy, and general good sportsmanship.

COMPLETE CONTROL

THE GOAL of responsible drivers is complete control of the car during every moment behind the wheel. Every driver is a pilot. He must take full responsibility for whatever his car does. He should, therefore, be *ready* for the task in every way—as you expect a pilot to be. He should be alert and give full attention to the task of piloting. Only then is he a class-A driver.

Control is no half-way matter. If you have control, you are master of the situation. Your car obeys your will. Your passengers are at ease and safe when in your care. You control the speed of your car in such a way that the car's stopping distances always give you maximum opportunity to avoid accidents. You are not fooled into emergencies. No traffic accident will be due to your ignorance, lack of skill, disregard for regulations, foul play, show-offishness or carelessness. You keep yourself and as many other street and highway users as possible out of trouble.

KEEPING out of trouble is actually a matter of always driving according to conditions. You regulate car speed according to conditions. You know what conditions affect driving safety and drive according to them. This demonstrates your good judgment and maturity. *Driving in Accordance with Conditions*

Six principal things affect driving and must always be taken into account:

> Other traffic
> Road surfaces
> Weather conditions
> Degree of darkness and illumination
> Condition of car
> Your own condition—physical, mental, emotional

When you take into account every one of these factors and drive accordingly, you are doing the best driving you can do. If you are a young beginning driver, you then have the confidence of your parents, passengers, and traffic officers. Such a driver is a high-quality driver, no matter whether in his teens or fifties.

Fig. 155. There's no good substitute for complete control!

On the other hand, irresponsible drivers who disregard these factors are not A-1 drivers, no matter what their ages or experience.

Commercial drivers have to drive according to all these conditions if they expect to keep their jobs. Practically every accident is caused by drivers who fail to take one or more of them into account.

Chapter 17 about Driving Under Unfavorable and Special Conditions will give many practical suggestions for keeping your driving sound even when weather and road conditions make sound driving more difficult.

Driving in a Desert "THAT MUST be a misprint," you probably thought when you read the strange topic heading. "How many people spend their time driving in a desert?"

"Not many," is the answer. "That's just the point."

But some drivers behave as though they thought they were driving in a desert, without the slightest obligation to share the driving lanes with anyone.

Driving is a *social* undertaking. What you do in traffic when you solo behind the wheel is of concern to many people. One can argue that what a racing driver does in his own car on the wide-open unoccupied spaces of the

Fig. 156. Few people drive in a desert.

salt flats of Utah is a non-social affair and strictly his own business. Speed "at any cost" really means *at any cost to himself*. But that is a rare situation. Speed-record driving has few points in common with your solo driving in everyday traffic.

Social responsibilities and obligations pile up heavily when you undertake to drive on public highways and city streets. You are personally responsible for your own passengers, for the occupants of other vehicles, for playing children, other pedestrians, bicycle riders, and animals, and for properties bordering on the highway.

Without a sportsmanlike sense of *sharing the highway with other users*, one has no right to solo drive in traffic.

THE VERY large number of tragic traffic accidents makes us question to what extent drivers realize and accept their responsibilities. Surveys made by traffic officers give evidence that many drivers do not. **Driving Responsibility**

Look at what happens at turns. One survey showed that 7% of the turns made by the cars observed were from wrong traffic lanes. With traffic as heavy as it is, this percentage of drivers failing to use correct lanes can account for a great many crashes. Over 75% of the turns were made without hand signals. In bad winter weather, when signals were even more important, 99% of the turns were without hand signals. The protective values of the regulation requiring signals were put aside by these drivers. Such widespread disregard of a protective regulation creates dangerous situations for all of us on the road.

Do drivers stop at STOP signs? In the same survey, many drivers were observed disregarding STOP signs at intersections. Only one-third of all the cars fully stopped or even slowed down to less than 3 miles per hour at STOP signs. Many failed to slow down even to 15 miles per hour. In some locations, as many as two-thirds of the drivers paid no attention to the STOP signs. All of these drivers disregarded their responsibilities.

This survey disclosed also that drivers fail in responsibility at traffic light signals. Some passed through red

253

lights; some started before the change to green; 5% over-ran the STOP lines. Some drivers raced for the right-of-way and often took it even when rules required them to yield the right-of-way. Large numbers of drivers failed to reduce speed at dangerous locations. These are among the unsound driving practices of which accidents are made.

Other driver failures observed in such surveys are:

▶ Passing on the wrong side
  Cutting in
  Passing on hill-tops and blind curves
  Increasing speed when a car signals intention to pass
  Failing to give way to the car passing
  Driving in the wrong lane
  Straddling the center line or another lane line
  Failing to depress headlights when approaching other
    cars at night

Anyone can draw the obvious conclusion—*Accidents are heavy because too many drivers do not fully accept their responsibilities.*

No one is fit to "solo" drive or should be licensed to do so until he is ready to accept all his driving responsibilities. The driver who "fouls" or who repeatedly disregards protective driving practices is a bad driver. He is a menace on streets and roads, and he should not be there.

Fig. 157. Mr. Doe nearly misses a STOP sign!

There are four possible outcomes if drivers continue to fail to accept their responsibilities:

1. Accident records will grow worse, with more people killed and maimed.   ◄
2. Enforcement of traffic laws will have to be more strict, with more licenses suspended or revoked.
3. Licensing procedures will become much more strict, and larger numbers of applicants will be refused licenses.
4. The public will insist that every prospective driver be given sound driver training and then fully assume his driving responsibilities.

It will not take you long to decide which of these four outcomes are desirable.

"An AUTOMOBILE hit him," you read in the obituary. Did a ferocious car—angry, frightened, or thirsty for human blood—rise up like some gigantic animal and deal a mighty blow? *Responsibility Is Personal*

"The car dashed headlessly through heavy traffic," you see in the accident story. "She was run over by an automobile." "The car ran amuck." Is the automobile then a wild beast that must be tamed?

Fig. 158. But **I** don't do the driving!

The automobile needs no taming. It never does a wild thing of its own accord. By itself, it does not cause accidents, inflict injuries, or kill. Sometimes news statements of this kind obscure the fact: *The driver is personally responsible for everything his car does.* It is he or she who injures, maims, kills.

When you drive, you are so closely identified with your car as to be almost part of it. You decide what it shall do and direct it. The automobile is no more conscious, accountable, or responsible for its acts than a puppet pulled by a string. The driver is the responsible "puppeteer." The car never kills, injures, or causes property damage; it is always John Doe, Mary Doe, or the unfit "solo" driver, disregarding some driving responsibility—failing to signal, driving too fast for conditions, cutting in, using the wrong side of the road, showing off, committing some error in driving judgment, being careless or inattentive—being an unsound, inferior driver.

Driving Is a Privilege STREETS and highways are public property, and sharing them is a privilege. Proof of this is the fact that you can be refused the right to share the highway as a driver. Your license to drive can be refused, suspended, or revoked.

Any kind of license implies a privilege. It also implies that the holder will undertake some activity that could become a public menace if not subject to control. Wherever the public could suffer harm or loss from bad, unsound practice, a license is required. When granted, it is intended to assure the public that its holder can be trusted. The business practices of the licensed peddler have been examined; the training of the licensed doctor has met certain standards; the licensed plane pilot has satisfied requirements of preparation and fitness; the same is true of the barber, the beautician, or the pharmacist.

The public should be able to feel confident that a licensed automobile driver also has had proper training and has met standards sufficiently high to make him a dependable user of public roads. Driver licensing must not be thought of as merely a whim of officials. It must not be primarily a source of public income. Its chief purpose is to assure those driving standards that are known by experience to be protective and for the public good. Any license should be a badge of integrity and responsibility in the activity which it covers.

A license grants a privilege and should promise the public that the holder is a person of training, competence, and trust. So it is logical that incompetence, carelessness, or recklessness should be sufficient grounds for refusing or cancelling the license and denying or recalling the privilege.

Use of a privilege and a trust tests a person's judgment and maturity. The fit use a privilege properly; the unfit misuse it. The behavior of automobile drivers, regardless of age, gives a startling example of this fact. Some drivers have records that demonstrate good judgment and dependability. Some have records that prove the reverse. The record of a teenager who is just getting a license is still a blank. For this reason the concern of parents and older people is understandable. *A teenager has his or her driving record still to make.* What will it demonstrate? If a licensed teenager's driving behavior proves his or her competence and good judgment, of course there is every reason why he should have the privilege of driving his own or the family car and be respected as a successful driver. But in those cases where a teenager's driving behavior demonstrates recklessness, poor judgment, and childish immaturity, a license is not deserved. It should not be granted. If it has been, it should be revoked, just as the license of any malpracticing operator in any licensed business or profession should be revoked.

YOUR DRIVING RECORD — THE DAY YOU START TO DRIVE

IO YEARS LATER

Fig. 159. A new driver has his record to make.

Fig. 160. Smooth driving!

Smooth, Expert Driving

BY THE TIME you get your license and are ready to "solo," you should already have many of the driving qualities of experienced, expert drivers. In your road training or practice driving periods, you have been *refining* sound driving techniques. You have been acquiring skill, knowledge, and smoothness.

A poor, half-trained driver lacks smoothness. He overuses accelerator, brakes, and horn. He steps from accelerator to brake pedal and back to accelerator. He drives with "fits and starts," with alarmed passengers, and emergency blasts from his horn. Actually he is warning everyone on the highway to watch out, that a half-trained driver is on his way.

Expert driving is *smooth*. There are no sudden stops, jerks, and swerves. Passengers are at ease and confident. The expert driver does not create emergency situations. He "drives ahead." He accelerates evenly, and uses the clutch pedal properly in gearshift cars. He has learned smooth, even, efficient use of brakes.

If, at this point, your own driving skills and practices fall short of expert smoothness, you had better put in some extra supervised practice behind the wheel before you consider yourself prepared to "solo."

SPORTSMANSHIP AT THE WHEEL

SPORTSMANSHIP at the wheel, like sportsmanship in baseball, tennis, or any sport, is a combination of responsibility, fair play, and courtesy.

In every game, certain acts are recognized as fair play and others as fouls. Spectators watch fair play with admiration; they protest and boo at fouls. Try defending a player who habitually fouls. Spectators growl, "What business has he in the game, if he doesn't play fair?"

Sport has its own standards of fair practice; so has business. Automobile driving is no exception. You can draw a distinct line between fair and foul play.

"What business have they on the highway if they ignore the regulations and don't play fair?" traffic officers protest on the subject of violators. Officers are in a good position to know that fair play keeps traffic orderly and safe, and that foul play causes disorder and accidents.

Good sportsmanship goes even beyond fair play and sticking to the rules. In football, there is no rule that a player must help a fallen opponent to his feet after a tackle. No regulation in tennis, golf, or hockey says that you must congratulate your successful opponent, or recover another's out-of-bounds ball. Such things go beyond fair play; they are acts of courtesy.

Driving courtesy also goes beyond observance of rules. The strictly fair-play driver does not consciously break a traffic rule. He does not cheat at stop signs or red lights. He takes the right-of-way only when it is legally his. But the sportsmanlike driver goes further. He not only obeys the regulations; he drives in such a way as to protect others. He yields the right-of-way, even at times when it is legally his. He extends additional acts of courtesy that give other drivers and pedestrians every chance for safety. He belongs with the millions of good drivers who make motoring a pleasure.

A young driver who is exceptionally competent and has an enviable record expressed the courtesy and sportsmanship back of his driving philosophy very simply. "I'm never in such a hurry," he says, "that I can't give the other fellow a break."

Fig. 161. No pedestrian would get away with this. Why should a driver?

**VIOLATIONS OF 100 DRIVERS
INVOLVED IN FATAL ACCIDENTS**

Kind of Violation	Number of Times
Exceeding stated, or safe speeds	29
Driving on wrong side of road	9
Violating right-of-way	7
Under influence of alcohol	6
Passing improperly	3
Disregarding warning sign	2
Disregarding stop sign	3
Following too closely	1
Turning improperly	1
Disregarding an officer	1
Improperly parking or starting	1
Other improper driving	13
Total violations	76

62% of the drivers involved were violating.

Adapted from "Accident Facts," National Safety Council

TABLE VIII

Rude driving behavior is both disagreeable and dangerous. It has been said, after careful study of the causes of automobile accidents, that consistent road courtesy by every driver would reduce traffic accidents by at least one-half. Table VIII certainly indicates that violations of sportsmanlike driving practices are among the most common causes of traffic accidents.

Discourtesies cause a large proportion of the traffic accidents in which between 35 and 40 thousand persons are killed annually and nearly a million and a half are injured. This is a terrific cost for bad manners.

162. Where
he "park" his
nners?

Commercial organizations with fleets of trucks or buses insist on high standards of sportsmanship in their drivers. These organizations require their employees to drive, not merely within the law, but doing everything in their power to make highways safe and pleasant for other drivers. These companies so believe in the importance of road courtesy to public good-will and safety that they will not keep in their employ drivers who fail in courtesy.

Just as there are all kinds of pedestrians on the street, there are all kinds of drivers on the road. The drivers you meet differ in mental ability, physical fitness, experience, skill, emotional balance, acceptance of responsibility, and attitude. For this reason, you have to learn to drive defensively. Some drivers actually need your help if you or they are to get through traffic without accidents. You have to save them and yourself from their carelessness, ignorance, bad manners, and mistakes. When you retaliate with anger or discourtesy, you just add another bad driver to the scene!

A defensive driver takes no unfair advantage of the mistakes of others. He doesn't try to "get even" with show-off drivers. He knows driver psychology too well for that. He is willing to take every safe driving precaution, and, if necessary, even to help make up for other drivers' errors or difficulties. In doing this kind of defensive driving, he shows his maturity and intelligence.

Driver sportsmanship is made up of such sound driving practices as using the low beam lights when meeting other cars at night; passing properly; signaling intentions clearly; following at safe distances; driving at sensible speeds for the time, place, and conditions; driving in the correct lane; giving the other fellow a chance at intersections; and many other simple acts of fair play and courtesy.

TO TALK ABOUT:

1 When, in your opinion, is a driver ready to "solo" in the same sense that an airplane pilot is said to be ready to "solo"?

2 Develop the idea that "driving is a social undertaking."

3 What driving practices are properly classed as "fouls"?

4 Give illustrations of cooperative and non-cooperative traffic practices: (1) by pedestrians; (2) by drivers.

5 Which is more dangerous: (1) driving that is socially but not legally sound? (2) driving that is legally but not socially sound?

6 What sort of driver do you call "smooth"? What does he do that makes his driving smooth?

7 What characteristics in some drivers require special tolerance and understanding of other drivers?

8 What is the relation between loud and frequent horn-blowing and poor driving attitude?

9 Give examples of road courtesies you have seen extended by truck and bus drivers. Debate: The road courtesy of the majority of truck and fleet bus drivers is superior to that of the average passenger car driver.

10 What is meant by "defensive driving?" Give several examples.

O DO:

Observe drivers and try to spot the incompetent ones who 1
have not passed the learner stage and who, therefore, should
not be doing "solo" driving. What gives them away?

Make up a rating scale to be used by passengers in rating 2
drivers with whom they ride. Try it out with several passengers and drivers.

Observe the smooth, almost imperceptible starting of a first 3
class locomotive engineer. Practice slipping the clutch in a
gearshift car until you can start an automobile with the same
kind of smoothness and control.

To form an idea of how frequently a driver in your com- 4
munity must adjust himself to the faults of others, spend half
an hour at a street intersection and note the percentage of:
(a) drivers who "beat" the lights; (b) drivers who turn left
without signaling; (c) pedestrians who cross against the
lights. Discuss the kinds of "defensive driving" that are
needed to take care of these situations.

Check items in Table VIII that are violations of sportsman- 5
like courtesy and not merely of driving regulations. Work out
the percentage of accidents caused by discourtesies.

TO LOOK UP:

Driving Today and Tomorrow. Hyde, Margaret O. McGraw-
Hill Book Company, Inc., New York, New York. 1954.
143 pp.
How to Drive and Stay Alive. Williams, Frank. Harian Publi-
cations, Greenlawn, New York. 1952.
How to Drive Better and Avoid Accidents. Kearney, Paul W.
Thomas Y. Crowell Company, New York, New York. 1953.
Let's Drive Right. Halsey, Maxwell. Scott, Foresman and
Company, New York, New York. 1954. 465 pp.
Man and the Motor Car. The Center for Safety Education,
New York University. Prentice-Hall Publishing Company,
New York, New York. 1954. 367 pp.
Safe Driving Can Be Learned. Smith, Truman S. Burgess
Publishing Company, Minneapolis, Minnesota. 1952. 83 pp.
The Fundamental Principles of Driving. Tysor, James H.
Banks Upshaw & Co., Dallas, Texas. 1953. 346 pp.

CHAPTER 15

DRIVING ON

THE OPEN ROAD

YOU WOULD think that driving on a straight, open highway would be the easiest and safest kind of driving. But more than twice as many automobile accidents occur in rural than in city areas, and most of them on straight, open roads.

Large numbers of these rural traffic accidents are head-on or side-swipe collisions. Many are from running off the road on curves; even more are from running off straight, open stretches. This shows that a driver can never relax from his job—especially when he is out on the straight, open roadway and thinks the job is easy. He must be alert all of the time to keep in complete control.

Modern cars are easier to operate, but they are also more powerful, quieter, and have faster acceleration. Automatic shifting, power steering, power braking, automatic lowering and raising of windows, and automatic lowering of headlights all make the physical effort of driving easier. On the other hand, they in no way lessen the driver's responsibility to be alert.

In fact, with quiet, smooth acceleration, a driver has to be watchful on the open highway or he may wake up to the fact that he is driving at faster speeds than he realizes or intends. A smart driver sees to it every second that he drives his car—that his car does not drive him.

264

DO YOU KNOW:

What the main hazards are in open road driving?
How to interpret traffic signs and signals?
How to follow, pass, and meet other vehicles?
What is good practice at hillcrests?
How to drive smoothly around curves?
How to get out of a skid?

HE OPEN HIGHWAY

Good open road drivers size up traffic conditions far **Keeping on the** ahead. They are not taken by surprise. They plan a clear **Lookout** path for the car and for constant control of the situation.
Drivers who fail to anticipate hazards and trouble-in-the-making are always getting into trouble. They are like people who have to meet a "rainy day" with no savings. Knowledge of what can be expected on the road ahead is a driver's "savings." What will the situation ahead be by the time your car catches up with it? Every little sign of what is developing must constantly be observed.

Traffic signs give very important "tips" about the road **Standard Traffic** ahead. They warn of dangers you might not otherwise **Signs** know about. They show you where reduced speed is necessary, advise of traffic regulations, give route information, and show the kind of curve you are approaching. Whether on the open road or in city traffic, you must be able to recognize at a glance what all traffic signs and signals mean.

Fig. 163. Anticipate
conditions ahead.

Fig. 164. Learn the meaning of the shapes of standard signs.

In general, traffic signs have three main purposes: (1) to *regulate* traffic; (2) to *warn* of hazardous conditions; and (3) to *guide* as to direction. For quick identification, they should follow uniform standards in shape, color, wording or symbol, and in position along the street or roadway. Signs that are important for nighttime driving should be reflectorized or illuminated.

Even before you are close enough to read the lettering on a sign, you should recognize its general meaning by its standard shape. Every driver must know the following characteristic meanings of sign shapes:

> **Octagon—*STOP***
> **Round—*RAILROAD CROSSING***
> **Diamond—*WARNING OF HAZARD***
> **Rectangular—**
>   **(1) Longer horizontally—*INFORMATION***
>   **(2) Longer vertically—*REGULATION OF TRAFFIC***

Signs of these standard shapes are shown in Fig. 164.

Standard Signal Lights QUICK interpretation of traffic light signals is just as important as of traffic signs. Every driver must be familiar with the standard meanings and the standard positions of intersection signal lights. These are shown in Fig. 165.

In brief, the meanings of light signals are as follows:

> **Red—*STOP***
> **Yellow—*DO NOT ENTER THE INTERSECTION***
> **Green—*GO***
> **Flashing Yellow—*CAUTION; REDUCE SPEED***
> **Flashing Red—*STOP; PROCEED ONLY WHEN SAFE***

Fig. 165. Standard position of signal lights, and order of appearance.

The figures in parentheses in Fig. 165 give the standard order of appearance of red, yellow, and green lights.

You sometimes find flashing red or yellow signals where important streets or highways cross, or where there are special dangers. Come to a *full stop* at a flashing red signal, and proceed only after you have taken every precaution and know there is no danger. Greatly reduce your speed at an intersection guarded by a flashing yellow signal, and go through with special caution.

Traffic signs and signals are installed for the protection of motorists and pedestrians and to help produce a safe and orderly traffic flow. Be as familiar with them as you are with the control devices in your car.

DRIVING IN RELATION TO OTHER VEHICLES

ON THE open road, the important thing for every driver to learn is how to keep his own driving sound in relation to other vehicles. We can think about this under six heads: signaling your intentions, following, keeping pace with other traffic, passing other cars, meeting other cars, stopping along the highway.

DRIVERS must constantly adjust to the actions of others. They have a right to know what others intend to do.   **Signaling Your Intentions**

Puzzles and riddles have their place. But the little highway game of "What Do You Think I'm Going to Do Next?" is as dangerous as dynamite!

It may be perfectly clear to Bob in the truck that he's about to stop suddenly, or pass the car ahead, or dart into a side road on the left of the highway. But to the driver behind him there is nothing clear about it until the act is in progress—unless Bob signals his intentions.

WATCH OUT! HE'S GOING TO TURN LEFT

Fig. 166. Let's take the need for crystal-gazing out of the picture.

There are four common ways of signaling: (*1*) with the left hand; (*2*) by signal lights or mechanical arm devices; (*3*) with the horn; (*4*) by the lane position of your car.

A signal to turn may be given either with an electrical or mechanical device or by hand. The most common signal is the one given with the left hand.

Unfortunately, no one set of hand signals is in universal use. In some states, the arm is merely extended outside the window horizontally to warn of a change in either speed or direction. But this signal is not good enough. It is a too general warning. It does not tell other drivers exactly what you intend to do.

Three hand signals as shown in Fig. 81, page 136, are recommended by the Uniform Vehicle Code and generally required by state laws. Every driver should know them, and should use them unless other signals are required by the law of the state in which he is driving.

Another way of signaling for right turns is to extend the arm horizontally and rotate the hand at the wrist with a circular, beckoning motion, telling cars to come ahead. This signal is less generally used and is therefore less effective.

You may meet drivers from other states with different systems of signaling. So here is a sound rule to follow: *When an arm appears out of the window of a car ahead, be on the alert and prepare to slow down.* Of course, the driver *may* be knocking ashes off a cigarette, or waving to a friend, or pointing to a view—but he may also be signaling that he is about to change his course or speed. Be on guard.

Fig. 167. Signal intentions far enough ahead.

SAFE FOLLOWING DISTANCES

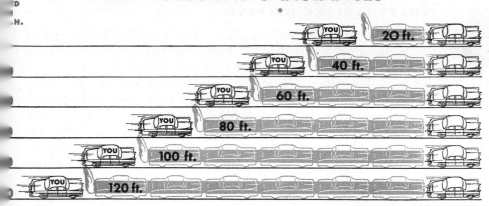

The lane position of the car on the road, especially at intersections, should help give correct information about a driver's intentions. Many state laws require that turns should be made only from proper lanes. The almost universal practice, as learned in Chapter 10, is to make right turns from the extreme right, and left turns from the lane next to the center of the road. Use lanes in such an expert way that other drivers will be aided by the position of your car as to what you intend to do.

Fig. 168. For every added 10 mph, fall back another car length.

The horn is merely a general signal to sound a warning or attract attention. It is useful chiefly in emergencies and should not be over-used. A driver has no right to "honk" others out of the way, simply because he can attract their attention with his horn. Skillful, mature, and sportsmanlike drivers are very sparing in use of horns.

The *time* when the signal is given is very important. If signals are to be of value, they must be given *soon enough* and continued *long enough* to be observed and acted upon. A late or too brief signal is only a little better than no signal at all.

FOLLOWING too closely is one of the most dangerous driving practices and also one of the most frequent causes of traffic accidents.

Following

The distance at which it is safe to follow another car depends on speed, road, traffic, weather and light conditions, car condition, and your own alertness, reaction

269

time, and physical condition. It is a greater distance than most drivers realize. At higher speeds, you have to keep cars much farther apart than you realize.

The driver ahead may stop quickly and unexpectedly. So, you must allow for reaction time and braking time and follow far enough behind to permit safe stopping in an emergency. If you use poor judgment and follow too closely, any mistake, sudden turn, or unsignaled stop by the driver ahead is almost sure to involve you in a tragic or costly crash.

Here is a simple rule of thumb: *Stay at least 20 feet, or slightly over one car length, behind the car you are following, for each 10 miles per hour of your speed.* Measure off and mark along the roadside the following distances shown in Fig. 168 for each added 10 miles per hour of speed, up to at least 60 miles per hour. Fix these distances in your mind. Taking time to do this can pay big dividends!

Many traffic crashes cannot be avoided because of drivers who follow too closely.

***Keeping Pace
with Other Traffic*** IT IS good driving to keep pace with the general speed of the traffic stream. Driving either considerably faster or slower than the general traffic causes entirely too much overtaking and passing. So they are dangerous practices, especially on high-speed traffic arteries. Your driving is much smarter and safer, and your trip is smoother, more enjoyable, and less fatiguing if you *keep pace* with other traffic.

Where traffic is heavy, it is especially bad judgment to try to travel at a faster rate than other traffic. A driver who weaves in and out of line, trying to get ahead of first one car and then another, gains nothing to offset the hazards and trouble he causes.

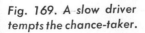

*Fig. 169. A slow driver
tempts the chance-taker.*

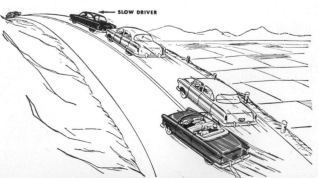

On the other hand, you are a nuisance, and often a menace, if you lag behind the normal stream of traffic and so tempt drivers behind you to overtake and pass in spite of dangers. Keeping pace with a reasonably moving traffic stream is generally the best rate of travel you can safely use. You get to your destination more relaxed, "all in one piece," and with a sense of having driven well.

PASSING is one of the most dangerous driving maneuvers. **Passing** To pass or not to pass! Here is where your judgment again comes in. Here the habit of *never taking a chance* pays off. Each situation is made up of different conditions, and judgment is constantly needed in deciding whether passing is safe or whether it means taking an unwise chance.

A slow vehicle crawls up the hill ahead of you. The driver beckons you to pass. If you pass "blind," you abandon your own judgment and trust his. If it results in an accident, you are the one who suffers and who pays the damages!

The rule for passing is a simple one: *"Overtake and pass only when you are sure you can easily make it safely."*

It is easy to underestimate the distance required to pass and get back on your own side of the road. Plan a *long margin of safety*. Drivers who pass in tight situations, especially on curves and at hillcrests, show bad judgment or ignorance of the distance needed.

To pass a car safely requires a minimum of about 10 seconds. If your passing speed averages 50 mph, you travel over 700 ft. from the time you pull out to pass until you can safely cut back into your own lane. If the car you are passing is going 40 mph, it will have traveled 587 feet, or approximately the length of 1½ average city blocks, by the time you have passed it.

If a car is approaching from the opposite direction at 50 mph when you start to pass, the space used up between your car and the one approaching, during the 10 seconds required for passing, will be over 1400 feet.

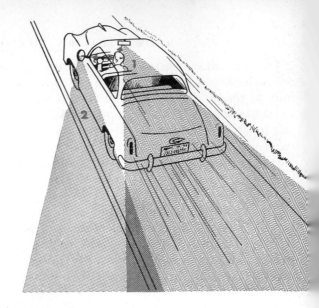

Fig. 170. Double check
traffic behind you before
you change lanes.

This means you will need approximately the length of 3½ average city blocks of unobstructed distance ahead to assure safe passing. Learn to estimate safe passing distances satisfactorily and you have added a very important factor of safety to your driving.

Know what is behind you before you start to pass another car. If a car has slipped up behind you and has already started to pass, you can be sideswiped if you suddenly swing out. A single hurried glance in the rear-view mirror may not tell you positively whether or not a car is passing. The "blind spot" caused by the back corners in closed cars can conceal a passing car.

Look in the mirror; check the "blind spot" by looking over your left shoulder; hand signal as for a left turn; and sound your horn, to tell the driver of the car ahead that you are going to pass. Then he will not decide at the same time to pass the car ahead of him and swing into your path.

Study Fig. 171. Driver A decided to overtake driver B, but gave no signal. Just as A drew out, B decided to pass C. A, in passing, had to guide his course by B. Suddenly A's car was in the ditch. Had A given warning, B could have waited before passing the truck, or could have warned A with his horn to wait while he passed first.

Before passing, check road conditions ahead for bridge approaches, narrowing pavement, pedestrian or bicycle traffic, intersections, or other conditions that would cause the car being passed to pull to the left or reduce your passing space in some other way.

If you wish to pass a car, but oncoming cars prevent it, drop back a little distance. Then, when you have sufficient clear distance ahead, you can build up your speed for a "running start," while still in your own lane. This reduces passing time and distance to a minimum.

After you have passed a car, return to your proper lane only when you can see the car you have passed in your rear-view mirror.

When a driver signals that he intends to pass you, courtesy calls for you to let him do it. In fact, the law prevents you from doing the things that would interfere with his passing. It prohibits you from obstructing the passing lane and from racing another car. Your responsibility is to help another driver pass you safely. Keep to the right, and *reduce speed slightly*. To want to interfere with another driver's right to overtake and pass shows childish immaturity. Sportsmanlike drivers give him the road.

ONE LANE of the roadway certainly is yours. But an approaching driver may not be fair about it. **Meeting Other Cars**

Are you going to risk a fatal or expensive accident by "standing your ground"? For all you can tell, the approaching "unfair" driver may be the worst driver in the state. He may be asleep, drowsy, inattentive, incompetent, or even drunk. If you don't like the way he is approaching, be *defensive* in your driving. Warn him with your horn and pull to the right-hand side of the road as far as possible. Good driving on your part means *yielding* the road and protecting yourself against him.

Fig. 171. Always signal intention to overtake and pass.

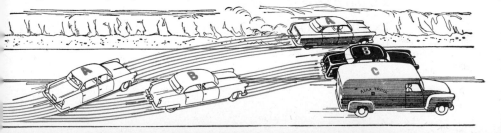

Anything that happens between cars that are meeting, happens in a hurry. *Two cars approach each other at a speed equal to the sum of their speeds.* This means that the mental reaction of both drivers must be very quick to meet any emergencies which occur between them.

Suppose a man is driving at 40 miles an hour on the middle lane of a busy three-lane highway. A car approaches in the same lane, also traveling at 40 miles per hour. The space between these cars is used up at the rate of 80 miles per hour, or 117 feet per second. If each driver has average reaction time, and each car has just average brakes, the drivers have to see each other and start trying to stop when at least 328 feet apart, if they have to stay in the same lane and bring their cars to a standstill without crashing. If an emergency arises within the 328-foot space and requires a full stop to avoid a head-on crash, *it cannot possibly be met.*

Is it surprising that so many accident victims report, "It was all so quick. I never knew just what happened"?

Stopping Along the Highway ON THE open highway, never stop so that vehicles from behind can come upon your car unexpectedly, or be forced to the wrong side of the road to move around you.

Always pull entirely *off the pavement* to the right to stop. In case of car trouble or a flat tire, *pull entirely off the roadway.* If the shoulder is too narrow, keep going until you can pull off where sight distances are good both front and back. It's a lot cheaper to ruin a tire than to have another car crash into yours.

Stopping entirely off the pavement is especially important at night. A driver who sees a taillight ahead may not realize soon enough that it is on a stopped car. This is particularly true if he is facing the lights of an approaching car. Stop *off* the roadway as a matter of habit.

ROUNDING CURVES

IN OPEN-ROAD driving, curves can show up good and bad driving.

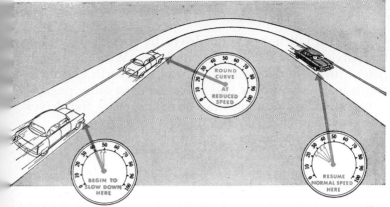

Fig. 172. Practice good speed control on curves.

The natural forces acting on a car are more complex on curves than on straight roads, as you have learned in Chapter 11. If you fail to slow down properly before entering a curve, your car may skid. Then there is real danger of leaving your lane, or even the highway.

Good drivers slow down *before* entering a curve, not while on it. A car is steadier on a curve when the engine is pulling than when coasting or slowing down. Therefore, enter the curve slowly enough so that your engine can continue pulling while rounding it. Use the brake *before* you are actually on the curve, if it is a curve that will require reduced speed. Then you will not have to brake when you are actually on the curve. This makes smoother, safer, more expert driving.

Having to brake *on* a curve is a dead giveaway. It shows unskillful driving. It means that you have put yourself in a foolish position. You have given yourself a difficult and needless struggle with physical forces of nature. The struggle can result in squealing tires, a rolling car, lurching passengers, a skid, difficult steering, or worse trouble. Take the curve the right way, so that your passengers are not even "curve-conscious," and you are doing a "finished" piece of driving.

Fig. 173. Ask the passengers to rate this driver.

"You can tell he's a good driver by the way he takes the curves." That's a remark one hears. With an incompetent driver, passengers slide back and forth clutching for straps or seat edges and apologizing to other passengers for all but slipping into their laps. It is the driver who should apologize. He's doing a miserable job.

Keep your passengers comfortable and safe by skillfully "easing" around curves, keeping to your own side of the road. Your passengers are more comfortable, and you display skill at the wheel.

Another obvious reason for special care is that curves shorten sight distance. The driver cannot see so far ahead. Emergency situations can develop very rapidly within the danger zones of cars that meet. The driver who is out of his proper lane or swerving on the curve is responsible if an accident occurs. *Stay in your own lane on your own side of the road on curves.*

In Fig. 174, "A" is going too fast. So he *has* to lengthen his radius in order to avoid skidding. He has to slow down *on* the curve and try to get back to the shorter radius. "B" has lengthened his radius to go around the curve without slowing down. In both cases, lanes belonging to other drivers are fouled. Speeds should be such as to allow you to follow the correct paths around curves.

GOING OVER HILLCRESTS

HILLCRESTS make another open highway hazard. You have no way of knowing what traffic conditions exist beyond the top.

Fig. 174. On curves, speeding drivers foul lanes—
A. To avoid skidding.   B. To avoid running off the road.

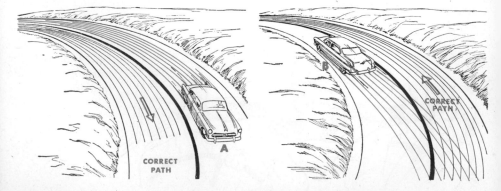

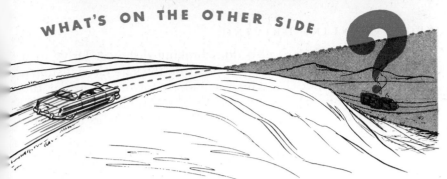

Fig. 175. Reduce speed as you approach a hillcrest.

The hillcrest may hide a recent collision, with wreckage strewn across the road. A car may be stopped on the roadway on the downgrade. An approaching driver may be using your lane, foolishly passing another car. You have to be ready to meet unexpected situations.

Never pass a car near the crest of a hill. As you ascend a hill, sight distance ends at the hilltop. You can NEVER safely cross the center line when approaching a crest.

Drivers find it irritating to follow slow-moving vehicles up a long, winding hill, especially if it means shifting into a lower gear. But where the only alternative is to pass without seeing far enough ahead, experienced drivers follow all the way to the hilltop and on over, control the irritation, and take the delay as just a necessary part of smart motoring.

With a little headwork, you may be able to avoid such an irritation. *Think ahead:* size up the speed of a slow-moving car; pass it far enough ahead of the hill to *have proper sight distance.* If that is not possible, keep well enough back so that you can pass the slow car just beyond the crest, before it picks up speed, if you see that the road is clear. Strategy of this kind marks the competent driver who is always alert to conditions well ahead.

You have the right to pass near hillcrests only on roads with four lanes or more. Even on such roads, unless there is a divider strip, hold down speed and pass only when sight-distance is adequate. For even on such a four-lane road, a wreck or blocked road over the crest may cause drivers to move over to your lane.

Reduce speed as you approach the top of a hill. As you go over the crest and start down, sight distance

277

increases, but so also does braking distance. Drive at a speed that will let you stop within the sure clear distance ahead. Otherwise, you surrender control and are at the mercy of circumstances. If the downgrade is at all steep, shift to a lower gear. Then the engine acts as a braking force and saves wear on the brakes.

On a long downgrade, if brakes are used, keep a light pressure on the pedal. This keeps the car from getting up speed, and less heat is built up in brakes and tires than when hard brake pressure is applied intermittently.

Coasting down hills with the gearshift lever or the selector lever in neutral or with the clutch disengaged should *never* be done. In many states, it is illegal. When coasting, the engine is not helping brake, and the job of slowing down and stopping the car is thrown entirely on brakes and tires. Stopping distance can become so greatly lengthened that control is lost. "Coasting" in neutral can also be very hard on your car. In gearshift cars, there is likely to be a severe jolt and strain on mechanical parts, if motor speed and car speed are not brought into step when the clutch is again engaged. In automatic transmission cars, the transmission itself can be expensively damaged.

RAILROAD GRADE CROSSINGS

GRADE crossings are a particularly dangerous kind of "highway intersection." About 1,500 persons are killed and 4,000 injured each year at railroad grade crossings. According to a study made by the Baltimore and Ohio Railroad Company, in about one-third of these accidents, the *automobile* strikes the locomotive or some other part of the train. In a large number of cases, the train is struck *behind the locomotive.*

Accidents of this kind may, in some cases, be due to lack of adequate, night-effective, advance warnings of the grade crossing. There are many kinds of warning devices provided to protect motorists at crossings. Some crossings have watchmen constantly on guard, although the trend is to replace them with automatic warning devices such as lights, bells, gates, or wigwag signals. Every driver should heed these warnings as well as the round, advance warning RR highway sign.

Many grade crossing accidents are due to inattention; others, to excessive speed. Often, the driver doesn't check to find out whether or not a train is coming before he starts to cross. He may fail to see the warning sign soon enough for the speed he is traveling. He may start across the multiple-track crossing after one train passes, only to be struck by a train on another track. Or he may overdrive his lights, traveling so fast that he fails to see the grade crossing in time.

At the usual grade crossing on the open road, the automobile driver must yield the right of way, or he may suffer serious consequences. A train, with its momentum and steel-on-steel stopping friction, requires many times the stopping distance of an automobile. In the interest of saving their own and their passengers' lives, drivers should: watch for and obey all grade crossing signs and other warnings; approach crossings at reduced speed and prepare to stop; look both ways before crossing; and stop completely for a thorough checking of the crossing when necessary, as under adverse driving conditions.

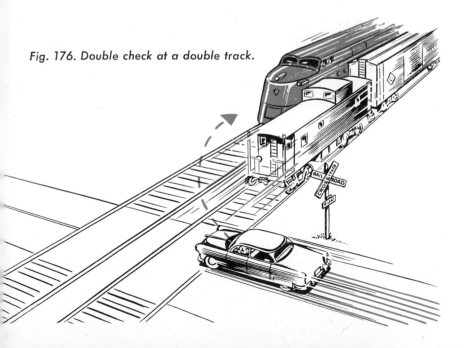

Fig. 176. Double check at a double track.

Fig. 177. Drive back on the pavement slowly and at a sharp angle.

PAVEMENT EDGES

IN OPEN highway driving, the edge of the road pavement sometimes causes very serious accidents. A ridge or difference in level between the road pavement and the road shoulder can easily throw a car into a skid. Drive so that the right wheels of your car are always on the paved surface.

If the right wheels get off the paved surface, use the correct technique for getting them back on. Study Fig. 177.

Never try to get back on the pavement at high speed. Avoid getting panicky and slamming on the brakes. Drive straight ahead, with the right wheels off the pavement, and slow your car down gradually. Drive at slow speed with the right wheels about two feet out on the shoulder. Look carefully to see that the roadway is clear behind you. Then cut back on the pavement by turning the front wheels sharply to the left. Jerking back at high speed, or attempting to get back while driving nearly parallel to the pavement edge, can ruin tires, can throw the car into a dangerous skid, or can cause it to roll over.

IF A TIRE BLOWS OUT

IF A tire blows out, the danger is usually so great that it is extremely important to keep control of yourself. This situation requires presence of mind.

The effect of a blowout depends on which tire blows out. If it is a rear tire, the back end of your car sways from side to side. If it is the right front tire, your car swerves to the right; if it is the left front tire, it swerves to that side—in either case, steering is very difficult.

Keep off the brake pedal, and let up on the accelerator. Steering is then the important thing. Grip the steering wheel hard and try to keep your car in as straight a path as possible. Only when your car is in complete control should you begin to brake. Apply the brakes very gently and slowly, keeping the car in gear so that the engine also helps slow down your car.

UNDERSTANDING ROAD MAPS

YOUR trip is more enjoyable if you know the make-up of road maps and how to take advantage of their useful information.

First study the "legend" which is generally found in one corner of the map. It shows the scale of miles, explains the symbols and markings, and indicates the kind of road.

To locate a particular city or town on the map, look it up in the map's index of place names—usually on the back of the map. After the name you will find a letter and a number, such as B-4, or K-10. These letters and numbers refer to the letters and numbers on the marginal edges of the map.

Fig. 178. Know how to use a road map.

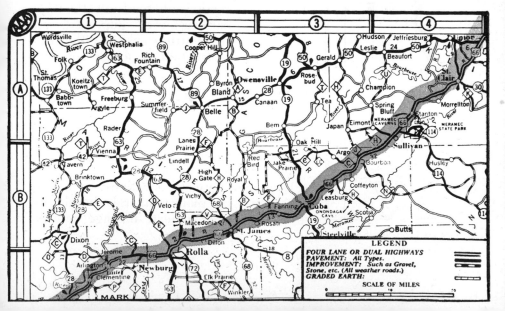

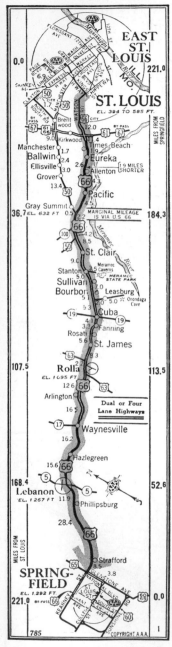

Fig. 179. Strip maps show details of the route.

For example, the town, Cuba, on U.S. Route 66, is indexed at B-3 on the back of the map of which Fig. 178 is a part. Find the marginal sections marked B and 3 on Fig. 178. Then run a finger directly across the map from each of these two sections until you find the place where the sections would cross. In that area, you will find the town, Cuba.

Usually maps are drawn with the north at the top of the map, but it is well to check with the north point symbol on the map to be sure.

The scale of miles on a map shows the degree to which the actual size of that portion of the earth's surface has been reduced for picturing on the map. The scale on a road map such as motorists use is generally a bar divided into several equal parts, each part marked to show the approximate distance it represents on the earth's surface. Usually it is marked in miles.

Lines of various widths, types, or colors indicate whether a road on the map is main, secondary, or minor. The legend explains how to tell by width or type of line or color whether a section of road on the map is paved, hard-surfaced, improved, all-weather, graded earth, earth, or either proposed for construction or under construction. Federal routes are shown by a number within a shield, like the shield-shaped route markers along Federal highways. State routes are indicated on maps by a number within a circle. Some maps show county roads by means of a number or letter within a diamond or rectangle.

Distances between locations on a map are shown by plain numerals beside the route lines; they indicate mileage between points or intersections marked by town outlines, diamonds, stars, or asterisks. See Fig. 178. By adding the mileage numbers shown along a route, you can easily determine the distances from place to place.

Where a body of water is crossed by a bridge, it is shown by a solid line the same width as the road leading to it. Ferries and steamship lines are shown by dotted or dash lines marked to show the type of service.

State and sectional road maps help you plan your trip and keep on your general course. Strip maps give information in greater detail about smaller areas along your chosen route. A strip map, or triptik, covering the part of U.S. Route 66 shown above is pictured in Fig. 179.

Learn to read a road map with ease and make use of the interesting and valuable information generally found on the reverse side of well-prepared maps. This information greatly increases the comfort, interest, and value of your trip.

Maps should be consulted *by drivers only when the car is not in motion.* If you are driving and have to consult a map after your trip is under way, always stop entirely off the roadway.

TO TALK ABOUT:

Accidents very frequently happen because cars follow too 1 closely. Discuss the circumstances of any such accidents about which you know.

Why should the "following distance" increase with in- 2 creased speed? What effect does darkness have on the proper "following distance"? Explain. How can you determine whether or not your following distance is long enough?

When you are traveling on a three-lane road, what are the 3 special dangers of passing near hillcrests? On curves? How should the road be marked at such places? What signs should be set up?

Make a list of discourteous acts of which some drivers are 4 guilty on hills; on curves; on straight, level roads. Discuss these discourtesies and decide which are the most serious.

5   What can a driver do to avoid or decrease the special hazards of changing a tire or doing other work around the rear of his car on the open road at night?

TO DO:

1   Find out what proportion of rural traffic fatalities in your state occur on straight roads; on curves; on hillcrests; in overtaking and passing. What driving faults or violations are most often involved in such accidents? Summarize your findings.

2   Prepare a list of ten sound driving habits for the open road, putting first the ones you consider most important. Watch drivers while riding with them and check their mistakes against this list. Do different drivers have about the same bad habits?

3   Draw a diagram, and indicate proper speed changes as a car approaches and goes over a hillcrest.

4   Draw a plan of a familiar intersection of two roads where there is obstruction to vision, such as buildings or shrubbery. Explain what may happen at such an intersection when driving at different speeds.

5   Secure samples of well-constructed state and sectional road maps and strip maps and study them until you understand all they show. Then plan a trip of about 300 miles and list the important things about this trip that you are able to learn from the maps.

6   Study the strip map in Fig. 179. List specific ways in which such a map can prove helpful on a trip.

TO LOOK UP:

Accident Facts. National Safety Council, Chicago.

Beyond the Highway Warning Sign. Smith, Truman S. Burgess Publishing Company, Minneapolis, Minnesota. 1952. 27 pp.

Driving Can Be Safe. Smith, Truman S. Burgess Publishing Company, Minneapolis, Minnesota. 1951. 136 pp.

State Motor Vehicle Code. State Motor Vehicle Departments.

Uniform Vehicle Code. See page 230.

DO YOU KNOW:
The special hazards in city driving?
What determines safe speeds in city traffic?
What are correct car lanes in city traffic?
How to reduce hazards at intersections?

CHAPTER **16**

CITY DRIVING

GETTING THE CAR INTO THE STREET

EVEN a short drive from your home garage to a parking space downtown calls for many driving skills.

Frequently cars are backed from the garage to the street. This creates a major hazard—the danger of not seeing someone in the path of a backing car. It has caused many tragic accidents, often to playing children.

Reduce this hazard as much as possible. Adjust the rear-view mirror to give a full view of the driveway. Be sure the back windows are clean. Look over your left shoulder and through the rear window. Examine conditions *on both sides* of the car. Lower the side window so you can put your head out and see better.

If children are playing nearby, see that they are in a place where you can watch them while your car is moving, and that their tricycles, wagons, skates and other toys are out of your way.

Fig. 180. Check all conditions, and make a double stop.

STOP

Never depend on children to look out for themselves. Touch the horn as a warning, and back very slowly.

Double-stopping is good practice, if you have to cross a pedestrian walk. Stop first before crossing the walk; stop again at the curb. The driver of a car coming from a private driveway must yield the right-of-way to pedestrians on the sidewalk. Vehicles entering the street from a private driveway must yield the right-of-way to vehicles already on the street.

On a quiet, narrow residential street, back out *gradually*, turning as you back so that the car is headed in the direction you wish to go. If the street is wide or traffic is heavy, back slowly into the nearest lane and proceed in the direction of traffic flow—even if you want to go in the opposite direction. It is better to go around the block than to back across traffic to the tune of screeching brakes, honking horns, confused drivers, or accidents.

DRIVING IN TRAFFIC

PEDESTRIANS, cross-streets, greater traffic congestion, and many other factors in built-up sections require greatly reduced speed.

Driving into a city from the open highway, consult your speedometer to be sure you reduce your speed enough. By contrast with open road speed, you may seem

Fig. 181. City traffic means busy streets, quick decisions!

to be merely "crawling along" when you are not even down to a safe or legal city speed.

In traffic, your mind must work fast—like that of the fastest running halfback. Tight traffic situations rapidly arise; the whole pattern of movement around you constantly changes; objects rapidly shift. You think "on the run," make decisions, and act quickly. It is a matter of seconds and split-seconds. Slower speeds, safe following distances, skillful techniques, understanding what the dangers are, good driving habits, wise judgments, quick decisions, and courtesy—these are your best assurances of safety in city driving.

Moving with the stream of city traffic, a driver must consider two very important factors all the time: (1) speed; (2) car position. How fast should he be going? Where should his car be in relation to others and to the turns he wishes to make?

IN CITY TRAFFIC, a normal rate of flow is set by the traffic **Safe City Speeds** conditions at the time. Traffic moves more smoothly and easily when all drivers adjust to the normal rate.

On a street too narrow to accommodate two lines of moving traffic in each direction, a driver who keeps below the normal rate of speed annoys the drivers behind him. On the other hand, the driver who tries to hurry ahead, cuts in and out of his line, gets on the wrong side of the street, and makes it necessary for approaching cars to slow down or stop, is both annoying and dangerous.

There may be times when you have to hurry along as fast as is safe in traffic. At such times, try to choose a less crowded route, even if it means driving a longer distance.

On a street where traffic is light and there are no special traffic controls, each driver has considerable freedom in deciding his speed, within any speed limit. No particular speed is right for all city driving. Under some circumstances, 25 miles an hour might be much safer than 15 miles per hour under other circumstances.

Correct speed for city driving is always a speed that is within the local traffic regulations and also in keeping with the traffic conditions at the time and place.

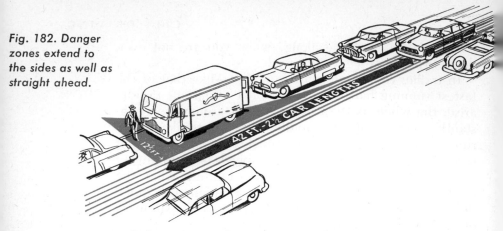

Fig. 182. Danger zones extend to the sides as well as straight ahead.

Safe city speeds give stopping distances that permit you to stop before hitting any object that could get into the path of your car.

Knowing how to choose safe city speeds depends partly on realizing how pedestrians and other vehicles are likely to get in your way.

You know, from Chapter 4, that the stopping distance creates a "danger zone" in front of your car. A car's danger zone extends also to the sides. You may be able to stop in what seems to be the clear distance ahead. But someone may suddenly walk or drive into your path from the side. This sidewise danger zone must always be considered in choosing city speeds.

The area in Fig. 182 represents the danger zone for pedestrians. If your car is going 20 mph and a pedestrian in the zone shown for that speed walks toward the path of the car at 4 mph, he will be hit. Even though you are attentive and see him, your reaction time is average, and your car has good brakes, you will not have control over the situation. You *cannot stop* your car in time.

As speed increases, the danger zone not only lengthens but increases in width as well.

In order to be relatively certain that no one will walk into the path of your car, *you must be able to see the entire area of your danger zone* at all times. If sight of the zone is obstructed by parked cars, drive farther away from the parked cars or decrease the sidewise danger zone by reducing speed.

THERE are some city streets on which speed is fixed by a *Correct Speed in*
progressive system of stop-and-go lights. The signals are *a "Progressive*
so timed that a driver moving at the speed indicated will *Signal System"*
have each signal light turn green as he nears it. He will
not have to stop at any intersection. The too-fast or the
too-slow driver will be caught by a red light at intersections and will have to wait for the green light. The
only satisfactory speed in such a system is, of course, the
speed for which the lights are set.

You can't beat this "clockwork," and the driver who
doesn't "keep in step" with such a signal system adver-
tises his lack of common sense and his poor driving. He
cannot beat the system, and he looks stupid failing.

INTERSECTIONS are places of special hazard. Some look *Speed Control at*
safe but are "trouble-makers." There may be obstructions *Intersections*
to vision so that vehicles come into the intersection suddenly, without being seen far ahead. One-way traffic may
start at the intersection, or traffic flow may be reversed at
different times of day, and you may meet vehicles in
unexpected positions at an intersection.

When approaching any intersection, a driver should
somewhat reduce car speed. This applies even to a car on
a "through" street approaching an intersection where
there is no obstruction to vision. A car from the opposite
direction may suddenly turn left, or may even fail to stop. *Fig. 183. Prac-*
For a good pattern to follow in reducing speed at inter- *tice good speed*
sections, study Fig. 183. Notice that lowest speed is *control at inter-*
reached as you come to the pedestrian crosswalk. *sections.*

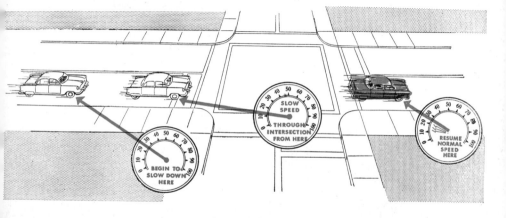

Adjust your speed so you can *stop before entering the intersection,* if stopping becomes necessary.

Keeping in One's Lane MANY heavy-traffic streets are marked off into traffic "lanes" by lines painted on the pavement. Streets are often marked to carry two lines of moving cars in each direction, in addition to providing space for parking at the curbs. On such streets, there are six lanes. Where streets are not marked off in lanes, imagine that lanes exist and constantly position your car accordingly.

Every car on the street should normally stay in a lane. Exceptions are when moving carefully from one lane to another in order to be in the correct place for making a turn, stopping at the curb, or moving to a faster or slower lane.

Skilled drivers do not wander over the roadway. They have intelligent reasons for choosing and keeping certain lanes. When traffic is light, they keep to the right, in order to let faster drivers pass without interference. When city traffic is heavy and there are three moving lanes in one direction, the lane to the left is often slowed **Fig. 184. Proper** down or stopped for left-turning cars. The lane to the **car positions on a** right is slowed or stopped for right-turning cars. That is **six-lane street.** why the middle lane is so popular with skilled drivers.

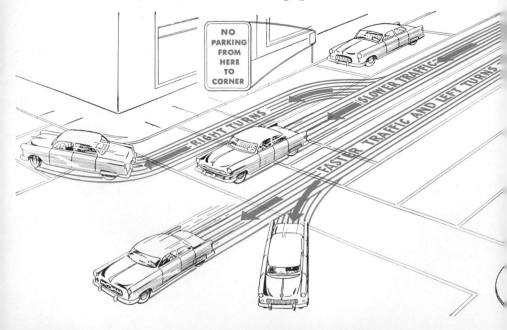

Fig. 185. A foul is a foul, wherever you find it.

Because left-turning cars cause serious delays, cities now tend to prohibit left turns on long stretches of important streets, at least at hours of peak traffic. When such turns are prohibited, the left-most lane is the fastest one.

The lane belonging to you can vary on some streets with the time of day. On main arteries leading into cities, inbound traffic is often very much heavier than outbound traffic in the morning peak period. Outbound traffic is much heavier than inbound in the afternoon peak hours. More and more cities provide extra lanes for these much heavier volumes of traffic by reversing the direction of traffic flow on either the whole street or on certain lanes of wide streets, according to the time of day.

Fig. 186 shows how these traffic peak loads are taken care of by what is called an *unbalanced* traffic flow. An artery with six lanes for moving traffic, for example, will have three lanes of traffic in each direction for the greater part of the day. But during the incoming and outgoing peak hours there may be four moving lanes in one direction and only two in the other. In such cases of unbalanced flow, stanchions or other clear markers must be used to indicate the point on the street where the traffic flow is reversed during definite hours of the day.

Such peak traffic loads are sometimes handled by changing the whole street from one-way in one direction part of the day to one-way in the other direction another part of the day. In this case too, special one-way signs must be used to show the permitted direction of flow.

Fig. 186. An extra lane is "borrowed" for rush hour traffic.

One of the best ways of doing this is by means of illuminated arrows. The heads show up lighted for one direction at certain hours, and at other hours another head at the opposite end is lighted. During mid-day hours no arrow is lighted and two-way traffic is permitted.

Avoid finding yourself turning dangerously against the traffic at city intersections by watching for all markings showing use of lanes, especially in unfamiliar cities.

Drive as far from parked cars as your lane permits. This reduces the chance of hitting a pedestrian should he step out from between parked cars, colliding with a vehicle suddenly pulling out from a parking space, or hitting a driver foolishly getting out of a parked car on the street side.

Making Right and Left Turns ALWAYS make turns from correct lanes. Otherwise, you are an unskilled, out-of-order driver and can easily cause an accident or confusion in the traffic pattern.

In city traffic, begin two or three hundred feet before reaching the intersection to prepare for turning right or left. The car should always be in the proper lane for the turn when it reaches the intersection.

The heavier and faster the traffic, the greater the distance required to work into the correct lane, and the longer in advance your signal should be given. When you give correct signals well in advance, other drivers have a chance to adjust their driving to your intentions.

Make turns at low speeds. All that was said above about having the car under control at intersections applies even more urgently to turns than to straight-through movements. Turning in city traffic is a more complex operation and is likely to involve more drivers and pedestrians than straight-through driving.

In the discussion of the rules of the road in Chapter 12, page 211, it was said that, in overtaking, one should pass to the left. There are exceptions to this rule. **When to Overtake and Pass on the Right**

When two continuous lines of traffic are moving in the same direction, it is undesirable for the entire right-hand lane of cars to have to stop if, for any reason, the left-hand line is delayed. So each line of vehicles moves independently of the other without confusion. This means that some cars pass on the right. Under such conditions, no abrupt, unexpected, unsignaled transfer from one lane to the other should be made.

When a vehicle is about to turn left at an intersection, it may be passed on the right-hand side. In some states, passing on the right is permitted under other specific conditions. Check your state regulations on overtaking and passing on the right, and always obey them.

City intersections are all alike in some respects: (*1*) the area is used by conflicting streams of traffic; (*2*) both pedestrians and vehicles use the roadway and must adjust their actions to one another; (*3*) the actions of each driver usually affect the actions of other drivers; (*4*) there are many opportunities for mistakes in judgment and for disregarding the rights of others. **Intersection Hazards**

There are, however, important ways in which intersections differ. So drivers have to use judgment and determine sound driving practices according to the special conditions at intersections.

Intersections are of many types: those controlled by stop-and-go lights or by an officer; those where "through" streets cross "side" streets having stop signs; those with no traffic control device, where everything is left to the judgment of individual drivers.

There are intersections with no obstructions to vision. There are "blind" intersections where shrubbery, parked cars, or buildings make it impossible for a driver to see across the corner until he is practically in the intersection. In addition to the customary right-angle intersection of two streets, there are "T" and "Y" and odd-shaped intersections, and "multiple" intersections where even more streets meet. So each intersection should be considered as a separate problem.

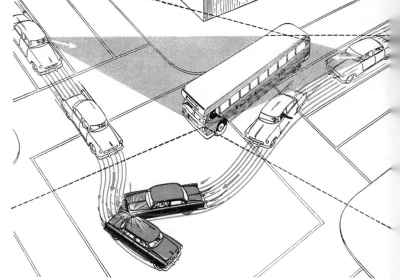

Fig. 187. The bus pulling out makes a "blind" intersection.

The "blind" intersection is likely to cause the most trouble, *especially if it does not look "blind" to the driver.* When you approach an intersection while driving at the side of a trolley, bus, or large truck, full view of certain pedestrians and cars may be cut off. This can create a "blind" intersection for the moment. If you speed ahead, driving "blind," you invite a collision with another car or injury or death to a pedestrian. This situation requires low speed and extra care. See Fig. 187.

As part of your preparation to be an intelligent driver, study different types of intersections and know their special hazards.

In city driving, a wrong technique in crossing street car *Crossing Street* tracks can easily cause an emergency. *Car Tracks*

Crossing car tracks from a position too-parallel to the tracks is likely to cause a skid, especially if the street is slippery. Drive entirely off the tracks, or straddle one rail. When you must cross, bring your car to a low speed and then turn the wheels *across* the tracks at a rather wide angle. As soon as the wheels have crossed, straighten them immediately. Be sure there are no other cars close enough to interfere with or be endangered by this maneuver. Fig. 188 shows the best path to follow.

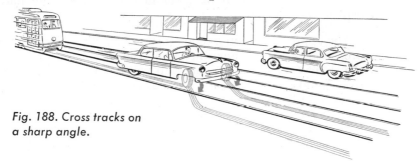

Fig. 188. Cross tracks on a sharp angle.

Parking the car on the street is one of the special ma- *Parking* neuvers of city driving. Correct techniques for parking and for pulling out from the curb after parking have been described fully in Chapter 10 on Maneuvers. It is not possible to be a good city driver without mastering these parking maneuvers.

Hand signaling is part of good parking. Move carefully into the correct lane, giving the "slowing down" or stopping signal well in advance. Use the rear-view mirror to be sure the signal is understood by drivers who are following. Then gradually maneuver the car into the parking place. Approach the curb slowly and with special care. Striking the curb hard is bad for both tires and steering mechanism.

In pulling out from parking, make certain your path is clear and that your signals make other drivers aware of your intentions. You can take personal pride in unbattered fenders. They announce the fact that you make

295

correct judgments. This is especially true if you drive a lot in heavy city traffic.

TO TALK ABOUT:

1 Are you ever justified in overtaking and passing other cars within street intersections? Consider streets with varying numbers of lanes, cars of different sizes and speeds, different types of intersections.

2 Discuss several intersections in your community with special driving hazards. Rank them in degree of danger and explain the ranking.

3 You approach an intersection just as a street car is also approaching it in the same direction. You are slightly behind the street car, but by speeding up you can pass it before it stops to take on passengers. There is no safety zone; the passengers are standing at the curb. Should you slow down? Stop? Or should you speed up and get by the street car before it stops? Explain. Does your traffic law have any provision covering this situation? If so, what is it?

4 Do your local traffic regulations permit right turns on a red light? Should they permit or forbid them? Is a green turning arrow used? Discuss the advantages and disadvantages, considering especially effects on *pedestrians*.

5 Consider the places on the streets of your community where parking is forbidden. Explain the restrictions. Do they seem wise?

6 Some drivers park their cars for a minute or two on the left side of a two-way street while they get a newspaper, or unload passengers at theaters, stores, etc. Is this good practice? Why, or why not? Have you ever observed difficulties caused by this practice?

TO DO:

1 A driver pulling out from the curb carelessly goes too far out into a street that has only one moving lane in each direction. Draw a diagram indicating the hazards to passing vehicles.

Select a street corner in a residential district where traffic **2**
is free to move at comparatively high speeds. Watch cars
making right and left turns. Note the cars making right turns
that start wide from the curb and swing wide to the wrong
side of the street into which they are turning. Does this practice seem to be due to excessive speed, to length of vehicle,
or to the driver's carelessness in laying out his course? Note
the added hazards when drivers "cut the corner" in turning
left. Report on your observations.

At the same corner, observe whether or not drivers show **3**
consideration to other street users. Note such practices as
turning without signals, turning from wrong lanes, and *disregarding pedestrian rights*. How do the attitudes of the average drivers of your community impress you on these matters?

Select a street in your community where many cars are **4**
parked. Observe how drivers pull out from parking spaces.
Do they signal, look, "nose" gradually into the stream of
traffic, and then stay in the proper lane? What are the most
frequent unsound practices?

O LOOK UP:

Local Traffic Regulations. From local Traffic and Police De-
   partments.
Model Traffic Ordinance. U.S. Bureau of Public Roads.
   Purchase from Government Printing Office, Washington,
   D.C. 1953. 41 pp.

CHAPTER 17

DRIVING UNDER UNFAVORABL

WHEN DRIVING IS DIFFICULT

BEGINNING drivers too often learn only under favorable driving conditions. Then, when they have to drive under unfavorable road, light, or weather conditions, they go right ahead with the only driving practices they have learned and run into trouble. You should learn what to do under every kind of unfavorable or special driving condition.

Unfavorable Conditions Lengthen the Danger Zone ADVERSE driving conditions put special responsibilities on you when driving. They lengthen your stopping distance or danger zone. Under unfavorable conditions, you must reduce car speed, merely to maintain the *same margin of safety* that you have at any given speed under favorable conditions.

Sometimes several unfavorable driving conditions occur at the same time. Each added condition makes your

Fig. 189. Several adverse conditions can pile up at one time.

DO YOU KNOW:
What conditions make driving difficult?
How adverse driving conditions can affect safety?
Good driving practices in winter weather?
Good driving practices in low visibility?
Good driving practices in mountain, plains, and
    desert driving?

R SPECIAL CONDITIONS

stopping distance longer for a given speed. Table IX shows what happens to your stopping distance when one unfavorable condition after another piles up against you.

Assume that your reaction time is average, 0.75 of a second, that your brakes are excellent, and that your car is traveling 50 mph under good driving conditions. After you decide to stop, your stopping distance, as shown in Table III, page 61, will be 188 feet. Now add other unfavorable driving conditions, one at a time. The increased stopping distances that result are shown in Table IX. Notice how a combination of bad driving conditions greatly lengthens the distance required for stopping your car.

Such piling up of unfavorable conditions is not uncommon in driving. At such times, the only possible way to maintain the *same degree of safety* is to *cut down on speed*.

Fig. 190. Each "gremlin" adds to stopping distance.

HOW STOPPING DISTANCES LENGTHEN

UNDER INCREASINGLY UNFAVORABLE CONDITIONS

Unfavorable Driving Conditions Piling Up	Stopping Distances (At 50 mph)
Excellent conditions: road dry and level, weather clear, daylight, car and tires new, braking force .625W,* you in an alert condition, your reaction time 0.75 of a second........	188 feet
Conditions as above, except that your car is now going down a 5 per cent grade...............................	195 feet
Conditions as just above, except that a wet pavement now reduces your braking force to .35W *..................	306 feet
Conditions as just above, except that smooth tires now further reduce your braking force to .30W *..................	347 feet
Conditions as just above, except that you are now fatigued and your reaction time is increased to 1.5 seconds........	402 feet

* W—Weight of car.

TABLE IX

The practical question for you, the driver, is: "To what must I drop my speed, under various unfavorable driving conditions, to keep my stopping distance from lengthening?"

Assume now that your reaction time is 0.75 of a second, that your brakes are excellent, and that you are driving at 50 mph. After deciding to stop, you have a stopping distance, or danger zone, of 188 feet under favorable conditions. To what speeds must you drop to maintain this same 188-foot danger zone, as unfavorable driving conditions pile up?

Study Table X and you will see that, with several unfavorable conditions present, you have to cut speed greatly to keep your danger zone from lengthening.

TO KEEP THE 188-FOOT STOPPING DISTANCE
WHICH YOU HAVE UNDER GOOD CONDITIONS
AT 50 MILES PER HOUR

Driving Conditions	Speeds, to Keep a Stopping Distance of 188 Feet
Hard, smooth, dry, level, straight road, clear daylight; you are alert, car and tires in good condition. (Assume a stopping force of .625W * and reaction time of 0.75 of a second)..	50 mph
Conditions as above, except that you are now going down a 5 per cent grade........................	49 mph
Conditions as just above, except that a wet road is now reducing your stopping force to .35W *..............	38 mph
Conditions as just above, except that now you are driving with smooth tires which reduce the stopping force to .30W *..	36 mph
Conditions as just above, except that you are now fatigued and your reaction time has lengthened to 1.5 seconds..	32 mph

* W—Weight of car.

Any intelligent, responsible driver who wants to be as free as possible from accidents and who wants a good driving record will know the facts shown in these tables and reduce his car's speed under bad driving conditions.

TABLE X

WINTER DRIVING

TRAFFIC deaths increase in winter months. They are heavier in the northern half of the country than in the southern half. Winter driving, with longer hours of darkness, is very hazardous, especially in states where snow and ice demand special techniques for winter driving.

Preventing Skidding on Slippery Roads RAIN, mud, wet leaves, oil, road bumps, loose gravel, or sand can cause loss of traction in any season. But ice and snow make skidding a special winter hazard.

Turn back and take another look at Fig. 110, page 191. Four small areas where the tires contact the road make all the difference in the world between driver control and non-control, and frequently hold the secret of safety or of accident. On slippery roads, or in winter weather driving, you can maintain "road grip" at those four areas chiefly by:

► *1.* Keeping car speed well below dry-road speed.
2. Keeping the car pulling steadily.
3. Making no sudden changes of direction, speed, gear-ratio, or use of brake.

Expert drivers generally stay out of skids. They know what driving practices cause skidding, and they avoid that kind of driving. They take into account slipperiness and irregularities of road surface, sharpness of curves, crown of the road, and car speed.

A car can readily go into a skid because of:

► Driving too fast on curves
Swerving suddenly from a straight course
Applying brakes too suddenly or too hard
Accelerating too suddenly
Sudden speed changes on slippery surfaces
A blowout
Driving too fast on rough roads, or while crossing the crown of the road
Driving with a wheel off the road pavement
Uneven braking on the four wheels
Changing to a lower gear ratio on slippery surfaces at too fast a speed

Notice how frequently *sudden changes* and *excessive speed* occur in these causes of skidding.

Speed is a killer on slippery roads. Stopping distances you can rely on under normal road conditions no longer apply. If something unexpected happens and you have to stop, you may find that you *cannot stop.* You have lost control; you are no longer the master of the car; speed

302

itself has become the master. When you let speed take over, you are the cause of any accident that results. Reduce your speed on slippery roads.

Fig. 191. Driver control vanishes when speed takes over.

To prevent skidding, avoid doing anything suddenly. Drive so that your car keeps up a steady, easy pull ahead. A driver who chooses speeds too fast for conditions must repeatedly check his speed. He repeatedly breaks up the steady push of his car. He is an up and down driver. He alternately accelerates and brakes. He is more likely to skid. On the other hand, a car kept pushing gently ahead, under slippery road conditions, tends to remain steadier and maintain traction at the four contact points between tires and road.

If your car is equipped with overdrive, lock out the overdrive and return to conventional gear under slippery road conditions.

Everything a driver does when driving on slippery roads must be done more deliberately, more smoothly, and *never suddenly*. There must be no sudden or jerky:

Steering
Braking
Stepping down on accelerator pedal
Letting up on accelerator pedal
Shifting to lower gears on gearshift cars without first
    stopping or slowing down
Moving selector lever to lower driving ranges on automatic transmission cars without first slowing down

WINTER
DRIVING RULES
TEST ROAD SLIPPERINESS CAREFULLY
① TEST ROAD SLIPPERINESS CAREFULLY
② DRIVE AT LOWER SPEEDS
③ FOLLOW AT LONGER DISTANCES
④ USE TIRE CHAINS WHEN NECESSARY
⑤ KEEP WINDSHIELD CLEAN
⑥ AVOID ALL SUDDEN DRIVING ACTS –
   STEERING, BRAKING, ACCELERATING, ETC.

Fig. 192. Follow Winter Driving Ru

Slowing Down on Slippery Roads

TESTS on glare ice show that "pumping" the brakes is best for slowing down or stopping with good steering control. Leave the car in gear; apply the brakes quickly for an instant; then fully release them for an instant. Repeat this rapidly once or twice a second until the car stops. This gives alternate short intervals of maximum braking, and short intervals of effective steering when the brakes are released and wheels roll.

If you must slow down on a slippery road that has large, bare, dry spots, pick out these places and apply the brakes on them. Even then, brake very cautiously. Where the whole road is slippery, you may be able to use the road shoulder. But do this only at very low speeds and on a firm, level shoulder.

Traction on a slippery road can be lost by sudden use of the accelerator pedal. Either accelerating or decelerating so fast that the speed of the back wheels is suddenly changed causes skidding. In fact, sudden decelerating is much like sudden braking, for the increased engine compression suddenly slows the car, and can make it skid.

Shifting to lower gears on slippery roads can cause very bad skids. Actually this is engine braking. In gearshift cars on slippery roads, wait until you have greatly reduced car speed before you shift to a lower gear. In automatic transmission cars on slippery roads, move the selector lever from the **D** to the **L** position only after you have greatly reduced speed. This is true also of moving to lower positions on cars with dual driving ranges.

The "kick-down" shift, or forced downshift, made on some automatic cars by pressing the accelerator pedal to the floor should not be used on slippery roads. It gives a sudden shift to a lower gear ratio, a sudden increase in power at the rear wheels, and a sudden spurt ahead. This is exactly what must be avoided under slippery road conditions. Reserve the forced downshift for bare, dry roads.

IN WINTER, the danger of skidding is at its worst with temperatures at or slightly above freezing. **The Effect of Air Temperature**

Roads are especially "slick" when the ice is wet or melting, even if the melting is caused merely by the pressure of tires passing over it. Tests made by Professor Ralph A. Moyer for the National Safety Council's Committee on Winter Driving Hazards showed that a car that could be stopped on ice in 110 feet at 20 miles an hour, when the temperature was at zero, required 250 feet when the temperature was at the freezing point, or 32° F. Ice that is barely frozen or beginning to thaw is more than twice as dangerous as dry, solidly-frozen ice.

At certain places in the wintertime, unexpected slippery spots are caused by temperature changes. With the temperature at or near freezing, moisture on a bridge can quickly change to ice because of wind sweeping under or around the bridge. Watch for slippery roads on bridges.

Or, with wintertime temperatures around freezing, there is another unsuspected source of danger.

Fig. 193. Slow down for shaded places in icy weather.

In rolling country, or where there are woods and cuts through hills, the roadway may be wet but perfectly free of ice where the sun hits it. But just over a hillcrest on a northerly slope, or around a bend where trees shade the road, or inside a cut where the sun is kept out, there may be ice, or, worse still, ice may just be forming. If you come upon these icy patches at too great a speed and try to stop or to steer sharply in some emergency, you can suddenly lose control of your car in a skid.

Drive at cautious speeds in freezing weather, and be on guard against such unsuspected icy spots.

Here is another special winter-driving precaution. On a fairly straight road covered with snow or slush, and with the temperature just above freezing, the front wheels may throw quantities of slush-ice up under the fenders. It may freeze and collect under there until there is a grooved, icy path just large enough for the tires to run in. Then when you try to make a sharp turn, your front wheels cannot turn. There is every chance that your car will leave the road. Make sure that the fenders are not carrying accumulated slush-ice which can trap your front wheels.

Getting Out of a Skid WHEN your car skids, you are in trouble. There are no standard steps which will always get you out successfully. Here, however, are some of the things that will help you most:

▶ a. *Keep YOURSELF under control.* Whatever is to be done to get out of the skid, *you* must do. You do it best if you don't "blow up." A person who cannot control himself in an emergency is an accident-prone driver.

▶ b. *Avoid braking.* Slamming the brakes on in a skid locks the wheels, causes loss of traction, and increases the skid. *Fix in your mind the determination not to slam on the brake pedal in a skid.*

▶ c. *Steer in the direction in which the rear end is skidding.* You can easily demonstrate what this does. Draw two chalk lines on the floor to represent a road. Push a toy car forward on the "road" and start the rear end skidding to the right. You will find that you must move the front end *to the right*, to straighten the car out. In the same way, you must turn the steering wheel of your car in the direction of the skid. As the car *begins* to straighten, straighten the front wheels also.

Fig. 194. Steer in the **same direction** as the skid.

d. *Avoid oversteering.* Turning the steering wheel too far "whips" the rear end into a skid in the opposite direction. ◄

e. *Keep the clutch engaged, or the selector lever in the **D** position.* Holding the car in gear helps reduce speed and produces maximum control throughout a skid. ◄

f. *Avoid lifting your foot from the accelerator suddenly.* Decelerating suddenly increases the skid because of the sudden braking effect of the engine. Some expert drivers even accelerate moderately to get out of a skid. ◄

Knowing how to handle a skid is valuable information, but never so valuable as knowing how to prevent one. Skidding is always dangerous business. As in the case of disease, prevention is the best cure.

307

Effects of Tires and Chains THERE are many opinions about the value of chains and different kinds of tires on starting, holding traction, and stopping on snow and ice.

The National Safety Council Committee on Winter Driving Hazards made 1,800 controlled field tests, with and without chains, and with tires of different construction and tread, to determine the effects on braking distances. The Table below shows some of the results.

BRAKING DISTANCES AT 20 MILES PER HOUR	On Hard-Packed Snow	On Glare Ice
Conventional Tires.....................	62 feet	209 feet
Winterized Tires.......................	59 "	188 "
Mud-snow Tires........................	54 "	201 "
Winterized Mud-snow Tires..............	51 "	190 "
Reinforced Tire Chains on Rear Wheels.....	38 "	77 "

TABLE XI

"Winterized" tires are constructed with materials such as salt, steel wool, sawdust, etc., added to the rubber. The "mud-snow" tires are made with extremely heavy tread or cleats. Winterized mud-snow tires have the features of both.

SNOW TIRE

Turn back to Table III, page 61, and you find that the average dry road braking distance at 20 miles per hour with the usual tires is 23 feet.

In Table XI above, you can see that braking distances at 20 mph on ice are so much greater than the 23 feet braking distance on dry concrete roads that, even when the best possible chains are used, only very moderate speeds can be justified on ice.

At times, chains are absolutely necessary, if you are to move or stop on snow or ice. On the other hand, some drivers expect entirely too much from chains. There are limits to the help they can give. Even with chains, it is necessary to drive at *greatly reduced speeds* on icy roads.

This shows up clearly in Table XII below. At 50 miles per hour, on a dry road and with ordinary rubber tires, you have a braking distance of about 133 feet. Consult Table XII to see how much you have to bring your speed down just to keep the same braking distance (133 feet) on hard packed snow or glare ice—even with chains on the wheels.

REDUCED SPEED REQUIRED ON ICE AND SNOW TO KEEP THE 133-FOOT BRAKING DISTANCE WHICH YOU HAVE ON DRY CONCRETE ROADS AT 50 MILES PER HOUR	Speed on Hard- packed Snow	Speed on Glare Ice
Average Rubber Tires..................	28 mph	16 mph
Winterized Tires.	29 mph	17 mph
Mud-snow Tires.........	31 mph	16 mph
Winterized Mud-snow............... .	32 mph	17 mph
(Reinforced) Tire Chains............	37 mph	26 mph

TABLE XII

If you use neither chains nor special winter tires, you have to cut speed on packed snow nearly one-half and on glare ice to less than one-third before you have the same braking distance control that you have at 50 mph on dry roads. This means that in slippery-weather driving, the distance at which you follow behind another car must be much longer than on dry roads.

The heavy winter accident rate will be cut down when motorists realize facts like these and drive accordingly.

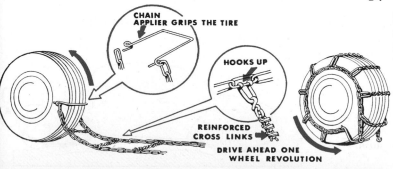

Fig. 195. A good method for applying chains.

Letting some of the air out of tires is found in tests to have little or no value in increasing traction for stopping, and it may increase the tendency of the car to skid sidewise.

Starting the Car on Mud, Snow, or Ice ON ANY slick roadway, it is often easier to gain traction by starting in a higher gear. There is less tendency for wheels to spin. Feed just enough gas to keep the engine from stalling, and ease the car along very gradually until you establish traction.

If you have to drive through water or on mud, loose sand, snow, or ice, try to *keep the car in steady motion.* Traction is much easier to keep than to regain. To keep traction, you want steady pulling and moderate power rather than speed. Shift into a lower gear in advance, and accelerate just enough for steady pulling.

Suppose you get stuck in mud, snow, or sand. Inexperienced drivers shift into low gear and step down hard on the accelerator. This spins the rear wheels and digs deeper into the slippery material. Keep cool, take your time, and apply power slowly. Direct the front wheels straight ahead so the pull of the car will be in a straight line. Sometimes, it is easier to back out in the car's own tracks than to pull out forward.

If the wheels have dug in, and efforts to start the car with straight ahead pulling fail, try to "rock" the car out. Start slowly in low gear. Just at the second when the car will go no farther ahead, shift rapidly to reverse gear and back until the wheels just start to spin. Then shift quickly to low. Repeat these shifts in rapid succession. Each "rock" may move the car a little farther, finally getting you out.

"Rocking" must be done carefully so the sudden shock will not break gears or other parts. It can be done in either a gearshift or an automatic transmission car. Attempts at "rocking" sometimes only spin the mired wheels. In that case, stop "rocking."

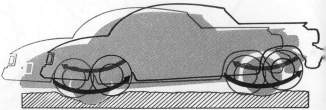

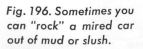

Fig. 196. Sometimes you can "rock" a mired car out of mud or slush.

Then your problem is to find a way to create traction. You will need to put rough material like gravel, cinders, branches, or burlap under the rear wheels. Sometimes you have to shovel out in front of the mired wheels to lessen the slope and then put down hard, rough material on which the wheels can climb.

Create better traction for *both* rear wheels. Because of the way the differential works, either wheel can spin by itself. Consequently, if one rear wheel is on solid material and the other is mired, the car is just as much stuck as though both wheels were slipping.

When you have placed rough material under both wheels, *apply power slowly* and steadily, using second or even a higher gear to diminish the power applied at the wheels. This helps them gain traction. In a gearshift car, if you try to get out using low gear, slip the clutch slightly. If you can get out in low gear, you have one advantage. As you move out, you have plenty of power to keep going and avoid stalling.

In winter weather, keep a few bags of sand and a shovel in the trunk for loss-of-traction emergencies.

DRIVING WITH LOW VISIBILITY

ANYONE who wants a good driving record takes special precautions when visibility is poor.

Take another look at Table X on page 301, which shows how greatly car speed must be reduced when driving conditions are unfavorable.

Suppose we add another unfavorable condition—low visibility. This gives us Table XIII. To maintain the *same degree of safety* you would have under good seeing conditions, you must now shorten your stopping distance by cutting down your speed. A speed of 50 mph, at which you could drive under ideal conditions, must be reduced to 20 mph when visibility is poor.

The thing to remember is that, even after you have reduced your speed to 20 miles per hour, the danger that you may collide with an object ahead remains practically

Your Driving Conditions	Permissible Speeds with Poor Visibility
Visibility distance—188 feet, 5 per cent downgrade, wet pavement, very low braking force, .30W,* your reaction time lengthened by fatigue to 1.5 seconds. (See Table X).	32 mph
Conditions as above, except that poor headlights or bad weather conditions now make your visibility distance only 150 feet.	28 mph
Conditions same as above, except that approaching glaring headlights now make it impossible for you to see objects farther away than 80 feet.	18 mph

* W—Weight of Car.

TABLE XIII

unchanged! If you fail to reduce speed under low visibility conditions, the chance of a collision accident becomes so much greater that no responsible driver will take it.

Driving at Night THE difficulties of night vision are serious to all drivers. The fatal accident rate is *three times as high at night* as during the day. Inability to see well enough is one of the most important causes of the great number of night accidents. It is appropriate to review here the ways to lessen the accident danger in night driving:

▶ *1.* Know the visibility range of your headlights.

2. Drive so you can always stop within the visibility range of your headlights.

3. Keep battery, lights, and electrical system in good condition.

4. Keep the windshield clean.

Fig. 197. Each "pirate" steals more sight distance.

5. Avoid tinted glasses or other devices which reduce light reaching your eyes.
6. Avoid lighting matches or using bright lights of any kind inside the car. Bright inside lights reduce your vision.
7. Drive at night only when rested. Fatigue impairs night vision.
8. Depress headlights when following another driver. Your lights, shining in his rear-vision mirror, reduce his vision.
9. Don't drive at night until you have become a good driver and can keep your eyes focused on the road.

Glaring headlights add an unfavorable condition to night driving. When you meet the glaring headlights of an approaching car, your ability to see is greatly reduced. With the headlights about one hundred feet away, seeing objects either beside or beyond the approaching car is very difficult. Even after the car passes, it is some time before your vision returns to normal. Sound driving practices for nighttime require that you:

1. Depress your headlights well ahead, when meeting ◄ other cars.
2. Keep your headlights adjusted so the depressed beams will fall below the level of the oncoming driver's eyes.
3. Greatly reduce speed when facing the glare from approaching headlights.
4. Drive at the reduced speed until your eyes recover from glare.
5. When meeting another car, keep your eyes on the right-hand edge of the road, not at the headlights of the oncoming car.

WATCH EDGE
OF ROAD

Fig. 198. Headlight rays don't bend around curves.

Drive so you can stop *within the distance clearly lighted by your headlights.* People who drive at night at the same speeds as in the daytime *over-drive their headlights.* They cannot possibly stop in the distance lighted. By the time they see that they must make an emergency stop, they cannot do it. They are the drivers who pile up the nighttime accidents.

Turn back to page 58 and look again at Fig. 31. Low visibility, like inattention, lengthens the distance marked "X," or the distance the car travels toward an object in its path before the driver even sees the object and realizes he must stop. Then the inescapable reaction time distance, "A," and braking distance, "B," are postponed until the car is nearer the object. This explains very well why speeds must be reduced whenever visibility is poor. *Speed should always go down with the sun.*

Fig. 199. Speed should go down with the sun.

Poorer visibility during twilight creates special hazards. Turn parking lights on at dusk. You may not need them to see, but they help others see your car and where it is. Sharp line and color contrasts show up a car very distinctly in the daytime. Such vision cues are not present during dusk. Pedestrians and playing children are harder to spot. Twilight is a dangerous time of the day for driving. The best way to lessen the danger is to increase alertness and lower speed.

Visibility in Bad Weather **Rain** For better seeing in rainy weather, keep windshields, windows, and headlights clean.

With rain beating on the windshield, it is difficult to see ahead. There is a longer danger zone. There is only one way to control the length of the danger zone. Reduce speed. In heavy rain, keep lower beam headlights on. Taillights are then on also, and the chance of a rear-end collision is reduced.

Dirt splashed back from rain-soaked streets by other cars speckles the windshield and greatly cuts down visibility, especially when so little rain is falling that the wipers cannot do a thorough job. Even when the wipers clean the sections of the glass over which they run, speckled areas remain on the sides. This produces wide "blind spots" and increases the danger that you will not see pedestrians or other cars coming in from the sides. Splash-back from the street also covers headlamps with flecks of mud which should be wiped off to keep satisfactory lighting efficiency.

Fog Visibility is at its worst in fog. The best rule for fog is: *Stay off the road unless the trip is absolutely necessary.* Giving up the drive is better than running the very real risk of giving up your life.

In dense fog, *creep*. Drive with *low beam* headlights. They throw the light down on the road where you need it, rather than out into the fog to be reflected back at you. Avoid sudden stops. Signal stops by tapping on the brake pedal to make your stop lights blink. Rear-end collisions are a special danger in fog.

Never assume a clear road ahead in fog, except for the distance you can see. Usually that distance is very short.

Fig. 200. Unwiped windshield areas widen the blind spot to the side.

Drive as though you may have to make an emergency stop within the distance you can see, no matter how short it is. In really bad fog, this means that you cut speed to a crawl—the only intelligent way to drive under fog conditions.

If the fog lies in patches, go into the patches at greatly lowered speed.

Drive as far as possible to the right of the center line, watching the road edge carefully, so you won't drive off the road, hit culvert heads, or hit pedestrians or parked vehicles.

The Windshield and Visibility In addition to the splashback of mud particles from the road in rainy weather, other weather conditions reduce windshield visibility.

Snow and sleet collect and sometimes freeze on the windshield. Wide "blind spots" occur because of the areas not wiped free of snow or sleet by the wipers. Side vision is greatly restricted—as though you had "tunnel vision."

Keep windshield wipers and defrosters in good working condition. They are bad weather safety devices. Driving without having them operating at satisfactory efficiency so increases danger that you may be guilty of contributory negligence if an accident results. If your car has no built-in defroster, you can install one at little extra cost. Or a fan can be mounted so it will blow the warm air of the car against the windshield. Glycerine or alcohol rubbed across the outside of the windshield helps prevent ice from forming for a very short time.

If weather conditions cause the windshield and side windows to fog over on the inside, reducing driving visibility, open a window slightly, or use the defrosting device, or wipe the windshield and windows with a specially-prepared defogging cloth.

DRIVING IN SPECIAL AREAS

OURS is a big country with all sorts of topographical features. Anyone who crosses it by car will drive over mountains, plains, and deserts. He will drive in highly industrialized sections and cross wide stretches of agricultural land. In some seasons, he will have all the problems of driving through snow-belt areas. In others, he may have to contend with floods, windstorms, dust storms, or droughts. Driving conditions vary greatly from place to place.

Some special driving practices are important to know and follow when you drive under some of these many special conditions.

In some parts of our country, mountains are steep and high, and there are long, steep stretches of narrow, winding roads. On such roads, the principal driving precautions are to *reduce speed* and *stay in your proper lane.* Chances should never be taken by trying to pass another car where curves ahead cut the sight distance down to the danger point. Going up the mountain, you may be able to stop quickly in an emergency because of the steepness. But a car coming down toward you and suddenly rounding the curve has a longer stopping distance, and the driver may not be able to stop before hitting you, if you are in his lane. Keep in your lane on winding mountain roads.

Driving in Mountainous Areas

Fig. 201. Mountain roads require correct-lane driving.

Slow down for sharp mountain curves, for the sake of your tires as well as for safety. Where corners are particularly sharp and also "blind," tap the horn.

Honor hillcrests by coming up to them always in your own lane.

On steep downgrades, shift into a lower gear in gearshift cars and into the low range or the lower of the dual driving ranges in an automatic transmission car. The engine then helps brake, and your brake linings last longer.

Driving on Plains and Deserts SPEED is the temptation on long, flat, open stretches where the roads are straight and "endless" and visibility appears unlimited. But these long, open stretches have their special hazards.

In the first place, it is easy for a driver to get sleepy or to become practically self-hypnotized by the monotony of the driving, the dry, hot air, and the speed and steady humming of the car. Speed goes up and alertness goes down. Without the change of pace that a driver gets on curves and hills, he tends to lose his sense of driving responsibility. He is said to be "velocitized." He becomes less keen in sensing road edges or even objects on the road. He drives faster than he realizes and then, when conditions develop where he should slow down, he just doesn't slow down.

Accident reports from plains and desert states show that the bad accidents which involve fatalities most frequently happen on good highways at long straightaways.

Fig. 202. In plains and desert driving, change pace frequently.

The majority of persons killed are in accidents involving only one car which simply *ran off the roadway*. The way to prevent this sort of tragedy from happening to you and your family is never to exceed posted speed limits, to choose speeds below the limits when it is "reasonable and prudent" to do so, and to drive with changes of pace and frequent rest periods to avoid self-hypnosis or becoming "velocitized."

In desert country, distances are often very long between service stations, and sometimes between habitations of any sort. You cannot risk driving in desert country except with a car in good condition and with plenty of gasoline in the tank. Tires should be good, and you should carry a spare in good condition. In case of car trouble, you may have to wait a long time before anyone will stop even to carry a message on to the next garage for help. Carry drinking water for use in such an emergency. In case of trouble, do not try to walk for help. The distances and the heat forbid it.

Tire pressure tends to build up in hot desert air. Then blowouts are more likely to occur in weak tires. If you have to change a tire, or if any trouble requiring a stop occurs, drive completely off the pavement to avoid a rear-end collision. It is a good thing, when driving across desert country, to carry a flat stone or hardwood board in the trunk to use as a foundation under the jack if you have to jack up a wheel.

In some states, there are desert-type, non-paved, side roads. You should not drive into these roads, if you are unfamiliar with them, without inquiring about them locally. These roads require very easy starts and stops and much lower speeds than paved roads. Unless you follow these precautions, you can easily find yourself stranded with ruined tires or a broken-down car in the middle of nowhere, facing a large towing bill—if you are lucky enough to get towed at all!

IN SOME agricultural areas, accidents are caused by cars hitting cattle, horses, or hogs wandering on the highway. *Driving in Farming Areas*

Fig. 203. Hidden dips may conceal animals or other cars.

Animals can be especially dangerous on routes where the highway has curves or dips deep enough to hide them until you are nearly on them. At times, cattle even bed themselves down in dips on the pavement where it is warmer. Cars at usual open-road speeds that strike bedded-down animals or low animals like hogs are likely to roll over or go out of control. Be alert for unrestricted domestic animals. Slow down at all places marked for cattle crossings.

Farm machinery or farm vehicles on the highway are another hazard to watch out for in agricultural sections. They usually travel more slowly than regular traffic and, if come upon unexpectedly around a "blind" curve or over a hillcrest, can cause an emergency. They are a special hazard at dusk or at night, because they may be without adequate lights or reflectors.

Fig. 204. Sometimes farm machinery is more than one lane wide.

Deer crossings also call for reduced speeds. In deer country, the animals are most likely to wander on the highway just before daylight or at dusk. They are likely to dart onto the road in front of the car lights, or to become confused by the lights and leap toward the car. The result is generally a badly damaged car, if not a serious accident.

In some states, drivers find winding, narrow, two-lane roads with bad shoulders, sharp pavement edges, poorly placed culvert heads, and one-lane bridges. The only intelligent way to drive on such roads is at greatly reduced speeds and with greater-than-ever alertness. Some old roads surfaced with black-top are especially treacherous if wet, and they may be pocked in the spring with potholes, or have so-called "frost boils." Good driving on them means slow driving.

CONGESTED truck traffic is likely to be a great hazard in areas of heavy industry. This is especially true if such areas are in states which have winding, narrow, two-lane roads. **Driving in Industrial Areas**

In such situations, forget hurry and take your time. Trucks hauling to and from factories may be so spaced on the road that passing one will merely put you behind another. Never take chances passing them. You need longer passing space if the truck is long, and often a truck is traveling faster than it seems to be.

In industrial areas, as in any heavy-traffic condition such as on city streets or on holiday weekends, or when crowds are leaving factories, large office buildings, theatres, or sports events, the best driving is *defensive driving*. When everyone drives to protect his car and passengers from damage and injury, there is far less likelihood of accident.

TO TALK ABOUT:

Discuss the difficulties you know some drivers have found ❶ themselves in because they learned to drive only under favorable circumstances.

2   What is meant by keeping a constant "margin of safety"? Illustrate how a driver would do this under two or three different driving conditions.

3   Why is it desirable to lock out overdrive under slippery conditions on cars so equipped?

4   Explain why using a "kick-down" shift under slippery road conditions can easily cause skidding.

5   How many reasons can you give for slowing down when driving at night through a cold, driving rain? If, in these conditions, you are on a stretch of road where 50 mph would be a proper good-weather, daylight speed, to what do you think you should now drop your speed?

6   Why is driving at or near freezing temperatures often more hazardous than driving in near zero weather?

7   A fellow motorist has driven into deep snow. He is trying in vain to drive out but merely spins his wheels rapidly and sinks in deeper. You come along and help him get out. Explain how you do it.

8   Discuss the value of properly-operating windshield wipers. Discuss the possibility of inventing some kind of wiper that will do a better job, leaving little or no unwiped windshield areas to serve as "blind spots" to the driver.

TO DO:

1   Plan a poster "Guide to Non-Skid Driving" that would be suitable for bulletin board display. Have the class choose 1st and 2nd prize winners and work out some way to make use of the winning "Guides."

2   *Away from traffic*, at *low* speeds, on a straight, level, wet road without side ditches, experiment with different braking techniques. Do this with great caution. This practice is to show you how the car behaves under different braking conditions, to help you discover the kind of braking that gives best control, and to help you acquire greater ability both to stay out of skids and to get out of skids.

Write a letter explaining to a beginning driver the values, **3** uses, and limitations of tire chains.

Describe a driving situation with as many unfavorable **4** conditions as you can imagine. List all of these conditions, starting with the least unfavorable and progressing to the most unfavorable. Check the point in your list where you think the driver would have to cut his speed in half to drive as safely as at the top of the list. Check the point at which he better decide to stay home!

Write a set of suggestions that you think should be fol- **5** lowed because of special driving conditions in your part of the country and which would help a strange driver do a good driving job when visiting in your area.

TO LOOK UP:

Age and the Ability to See at Night. Allgaier, Earl, American Automobile Association, Washington, D.C. 1953. 14 pp.

Cold Facts about Winter Driving. Aetna Casualty and Surety Company, Hartford, Connecticut. 1953. 13 pp.

Here Are the Facts! Committee on Winter Driving Hazards, National Safety Council, Chicago, Illinois. 1952. 17 pp.

Here Are Winter Facts for Passenger Car Drivers. Committee on Winter Driving Hazards, National Safety Council, Chicago, Illinois. 1953–54. 13 pp.

Motor Vehicle Driving Practices. Lord, Willard J., Newton Road, Ithan, Pennsylvania. 1955. 48 pp.

Winter Driving. Williams, Frank, Harian Publications, Greenlawn, L.I., New York. 1953. 29 pp.

\

CHAPTER 18

KEEPING THE CAR I

GIVING THE CAR A SQUARE DEAL

A PROMINENT surgeon says that too many of his patients arrive at the hospital because they fail to take care of themselves. "The human machine," he says, "doesn't get a square deal."

The same thing might be said of automobiles. Plenty of "sick" cars arrive at repair shops because they never get a square deal. The worst thing about it is that such cars are hazards on the road.

Keeping the car in fit condition is a driver's responsibility. It is good economy and a sound traffic practice. A driver may have taken a good driver education course; he may be in excellent physical condition to drive; he may have every desire to drive well. But the soundness of his driving and his good or bad driving record will depend also on how well he maintains his car. If he drives his car when it is not in a sound condition, he is guilty of an unsound driving practice.

Forty-nine exceptional drivers, representing each state and the District of Columbia, who had driven an accumulated 15 million miles without crashes or traffic convictions, were asked to list the main reasons for their excel-

Fig. 205. Some cars don't get a square deal!

AFE DRIVING CONDITION

lent driving records. *Keeping the car in a safe driving condition led the list.*

Drivers who pile up astonishingly good performance records give you three general reasons for keeping cars in sound condition and ready to perform:

1. Greater enjoyment in driving
2. Greater assurance of safety
3. Increased economy in car operation

In this Chapter we are interested chiefly in the first two reasons—enjoyment and safety. In Chapter 20, Your Automobile and Your Pocketbook, we shall be interested in the third—economy.

More of the cars you meet on the road have safety equipment in need of repair than is generally realized. This is especially true in periods of depression, war, or production control when it is difficult to replace worn-out parts. But in normal times there is little excuse for cars to be on the road in such bad shape that they are accident-breeders.

Fig. 206. Good inspection stations do a thorough job.

325

Keeping brakes in a safe condition can greatly reduce the far too numerous accidents caused by car defects.

Railroad locomotives, airplanes, steamships, elevators, bridges, and buses are given *periodic inspection* to assure safe, efficient operating condition. In many states, periodic inspection of the safety equipment of private automobiles is required by law. Everywhere, inspection to assure good car condition is required by common sense. Regular inspection takes little time and, in the end, is an economy as well as a safety measure. The cost is very low to each owner, when compared with the costs of needless repair bills and accidents.

CARE OF SAFETY AND CONTROL DEVICES

EVERY time you speed up your car, increase its momentum, and lengthen its stopping distance, you show great confidence in your safety and control devices. The higher your speed, the greater must be this confidence! These devices can save your life, or cause you to lose it.

1. Brakes BRAKES should be in sound condition always—instantly ready to perform. In an emergency stop, your brakes have to exert a force more powerful than the engine. Pull on the relatively weak parking brake, and try to start the car against it. In a tug-of-war between brakes and engine, your brakes must win.

For safety, brakes must always be effective. Unfortunately, not all of them are. Inspection station records show that, in spite of the easy standards of testing, *faulty brakes are found on nearly one-third of the cars tested.*

Sound brakes satisfy all of the following requirements:

▶ *1.* The grip on front wheels is equalized, and the grip on back wheels is equalized.

2. The braking takes place at all four brake drums at the same time, bringing the car to a smooth stop with no swerving, side-slipping, or skidding.

3. All tires have an equal grip on the pavement, assuming no slippery spots under one or more tires.

4. The brakes stop the car within safe standards of braking distance. See Table III, Chapter 4.

326

5. The brake linings are even, dry, free from grease or sand, and not unduly worn.
6. The brake drums are not warped from overheating, scratched because of sand and dirt, or scored by the rivets in worn-out linings.
7. The brake pedal cannot be pressed closer to the floor boards than about an inch and a half.
8. With hydraulic brakes, continuous hard application does not gradually lower the brake pedal.

Make sure that the brakes on the car you drive always satisfy these safety requirements.

Brakes out of adjustment can cause excessive wear on tires and brake bands. If brakes "drag," one or more brake bands may be in contact with the brake drums even when the brake pedal is not depressed. This holds back one or more of the wheels while the others roll freely. The result is uneven braking, and your car can easily swerve and involve you in an accident. Brakes should be checked several times a year by a competent mechanic and adjusted if necessary.

Make sure, with hydraulic brakes, that there is no leaking away of hydraulic fluid. Unless the master cylinder is full of fluid and the entire hydraulic system, including the cylinder at each wheel, is in sound condition, the brakes can suddenly fail. If you notice any decrease in braking power, have an inspection of the hydraulic system made at once.

Fig. 207. Neglected brakes can spell tragedy.

Hydraulic brakes may not lose their efficiency gradually. They can give out suddenly and result in a bad accident.

Testing the Brakes HERE is a simple method to use in testing four-wheel brakes. Try the test on a hard, smooth, level surface, *away from traffic*, and at a *low speed* of about 10 mph.

Press hard on the brake pedal to stop your car as quickly as possible. All four wheels should lock. Inspect the tracks made by the tires to see whether all four skid marks are the same length. If the skid marks are not equal or show that the car tended to skid or swerve to one side, the brakes are not properly equalized and need immediate adjustment.

For safe condition, test the brakes after you have forded a stream, after you have driven through slush or heavy rain, and if you drive immediately after the car has been washed. Wet brake linings may not hold evenly. If they are wet, dry them by gently applying the brakes while driving slowly, in low or second gear if necessary, until they respond properly.

If hard application of the brake pedal brings it to within less than an inch and a half of the floor-board, take your car in for brake adjustment, and for a complete inspection of the hydraulic system.

If the brakes squeak, the brake linings may be worn down to the rivets and be rubbing on the brake drums. Or the surface of the brake lining may be damaged from dirt or overheating. Grabbing brakes may indicate warped drums or dirt on the linings. "Chattering" is sometimes a clue to warped drums. All of these conditions are symptoms that your brakes are unsafe and need attention.

Proper Brake Care IF YOU want to protect your safe driving record, here is a summary of proper care and use of brakes:

▶ 1. Have brakes inspected regularly.
2. Have the brake system adjusted by expert mechanics several times a year.
3. Promptly replace damaged linings, drums, or linkage.

328

4. Keep sufficient hydraulic brake fluid in the system.
5. Prevent over-greasing in the differential and wheel packings. If grease works out onto the brakes, they become very ineffective.
6. Avoid over-use of brakes. The "brake driver" is a poor driver. He is hard on the braking system and on the tires. He alternately goes too fast and slams on the brakes. Over-used brakes betray poor driving.
7. Avoid the kind of driving that requires sudden stopping, which is hard on both brakes and tires. "Drive ahead"; know what the traffic conditions are; keep your car in constant control; avoid emergencies.
8. Use only tires with good treads.
9. Keep tires properly inflated.

Brakes are not crude mechanisms. They are carefully constructed and closely adjusted when a car is made. Brake bands are made to clear drums with the close precision of a few thousandths of an inch. If bad use injures parts or destroys this delicate adjustment, braking efficiency can drop way down. This reduces your control of your car in critical traffic situations. It can be the cause of a traffic accident. Driving with poor brakes is an unsound driving practice.

When you have brakes relined, be sure to get linings of good quality. Some linings on the market are of inferior material, and you cannot rely on them.

Proper brake maintenance pays the driver big dividends in safety. Give yourself a square deal by giving your brakes a square deal.

KEEPING correct air pressure in all tires is important to **2. Tires** tire life and safety. It helps reduce tire trouble. Check at least once a week to be sure that the pressure is right in all tires, including the spare.

Under-inflated tires can cause such driving troubles as:

1. Dangerous blowouts, because of excessive wear of tread and damage to tire side-walls caused by over-flexing, too much internal heat, and strain on side-wall fabric.
2. Hard steering.
3. "Side-rolling" on curves, reducing control.

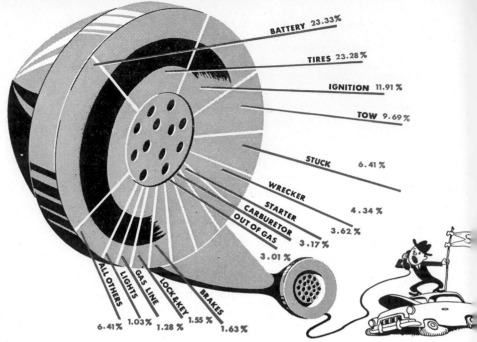

BATTERY 23.33%

TIRES 23.28%

IGNITION 11.91%

TOW 9.69%

STUCK 6.41%

WRECKER
STARTER 4.34%
CARBURETOR
OUT OF GAS 3.62%
3.17%
3.01%

ALL OTHERS 6.41%
LIGHTS 1.03%
GAS LINE 1.28%
LOCK & KEY 1.55%
BRAKES 1.63%

Fig. 208. American Automobile Association service calls
reveal the principal causes of on-the-road troubles.

Over-inflated tires can cause:

▶ *1.* Increased danger of blowouts in weak tires.

2. Excessive and uneven wear of tread.

3. Somewhat decreased road grip.

Badly worn tires are trouble-brewers. If the tread is
worn off, skidding is more likely on slippery surfaces. If
worn down to the fabric, sharp objects on the road can
easily penetrate the thin material. There is a constant
threat of a puncture or blowout, which means danger to
the driver, his passengers, and all nearby motorists or
pedestrians. Driving with worn-down tires is an unsound
driving practice.

Some motorists use reconditioned or recapped tires.
Recapping of tires has made tremendous strides. If the
"carcass" of the tire is sound, recapping can be satisfactory, if expertly done according to high standards and
before the fabric is worn or the cord structure broken.
330   Regrooving, on the other hand, is a process of cutting new

tread patterns deeper into worn tires and is generally not advisable. It weakens the tire and can injure the cord structure and result in a tire that is not dependable.

ALL the time you are driving, you depend on the steering **3. The Steering** mechanism for safe control of car direction. You roll **Mechanism** blithely along at 45 or 50 mph with very little space separating your car from a line of cars zooming by in the opposite direction at equal speed. This means a few feet of clearance and a 90 or 100 mph meeting speed. What confidence to put in steering equipment! It better be in good condition!

The checks and adjustments that have to be made in the steering assembly are so intricate and numerous that they should be made only by expert mechanics. Every driver, however, can learn to recognize symptoms of trouble developing in the steering mechanism and can have adjustments made at once.

Steering conditions give important warning cues:

1. Too much "play" in the steering wheel. If you can turn the wheel two or more inches before it starts to turn the front wheels, there is too much "play." An adjustment is needed.
2. Hard steering. This may be due to unequal or underinflated tires, inadequate lubrication, improper wheel alignment, or worn or improperly adjusted steering parts. Have all checks made.
3. "Shimmy," or rapid movement of the wheel from side to side. Check tire inflation and have wheel balance checked. If neither check solves the trouble, have a mechanic tighten connections, correct wheel alignment, replace worn parts, or balance the wheels.
4. The car wandering from side to side, or turning persistently to one side. This can mean unequal tire pressure, poor wheel alignment, and rapid tire wear.

Fig. 209. Front wheel "shimmy" is costly and unsafe.

Consult an expert mechanic *at once* when there is any symptom of trouble in the steering mechanism. No driver can afford the risk of steering failure.

4. Lights LIGHTS are comparatively easy to keep in a safe, efficient condition. Yet *many* drivers fall down on the job. In a high percentage of cars tested in vehicle inspections, lights are found to need attention.

A large number of serious accidents occur during darkness or under conditions of poor visibility. Driving at night or in low illumination, you need every possible help from lights in proper condition.

A simple and common lighting trouble is DIRT! Merely cleaning dirty headlamp lenses increases the amount of light to such a degree that it adds greatly to night driving comfort and safety.

On older model cars, not equipped with "sealed beam" headlights, tarnished or dull reflectors make the lights very poor. The dust or grit *inside* the headlights should be carefully wiped out. A soft, clean cloth should be used with light strokes to avoid scratching the reflector. Then the reflector should be carefully polished with lampblack and alcohol. Replace reflectors which are so badly worn or scratched that cleaning and polishing do not make them clear.

Dim lights on cars with old headlights can be caused by any of the following:

▶ Dirt on lenses, reflectors, and bulbs.
Old or incorrect bulbs.
Bad reflectors.
Low voltage at the bulb socket.

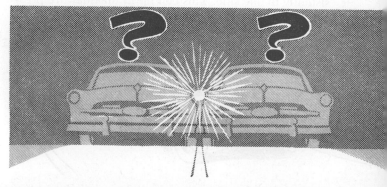

Fig. 210. One-eyed cars cause uncertainty and confusion.

Low voltage at the bulb socket may mean a weak battery, corroded battery terminals, or defective connections.

Sometimes a light burns out. The lamp must then be replaced. On the road, a one-eyed car is both annoying and dangerous. Check your lights frequently. Your car may be a "one-eyed menace" without your knowing it.

Suppose all car lights suddenly go out. The wiring may need repair. Or a fuse may be "blown," just as in the lighting system in your house. Always carry extra fuses and know the location of the fuses and how to replace them.

Fig. 211. Inspecting headlamp adjustment.

Fuses are not found in any standard place, and this may mean something of a hunt! In most cars, they are either up under the dash panel or mounted on the back of the dash panel under the hood. Find out where they are on your car from your Owner's Manual.

Inspection stations commonly find headlamps badly adjusted. If tipped up too high, they can blind the drivers of cars you meet. Open-road beams should be strong and

333

at the proper height, not rising sharply above the horizontal. Headlights should be tested for adjustment at least twice a year and with modern testing equipment.

5. Other Safety Equipment

ALL OF THE devices listed as safety aids in Chapter 6 should be kept in safe working condition, as a sound motoring practice.

Windshield wipers must be dependable, so they will clean the glass and keep visibility at a high level. New blades are sometimes needed. The spring which holds the wiper against the glass may need to be tightened or replaced. Sometimes a drop of oil is needed at friction points. If operated by vacuum, the wiper may stop on a hard uphill pull because suction is decreased. Lifting your foot from the accelerator an instant generally makes the wiper start again. If it fails to operate fast enough or will not work at all, there is probably a leak in the air line or trouble in the little driving motor. In either case, repairing it is a job for a skilled mechanic.

Horns, rear-view mirrors, and windshield defrosters should be kept in sound working condition all the time. Keep windshields and windows clean and unobstructed, for maximum visibility. Prevent frost or steam from collecting on windshield or windows by opening one window or ventilator slightly and using the defroster or a small circulating fan.

As a driver, you can well afford to take a tip from aviation and railroading in checking safety equipment. The motor of an airplane is gone over before every flight.

Fig. 212. Airplanes are thoroughly checked before a trip.

334

It is tuned up, oiled, greased, adjusted, and put in a reliable condition. Landing gear, all safety equipment, and other parts are carefully inspected. Railroad companies, with years of experience behind them, regularly inspect equipment before each run.

Inspection of a car's safety equipment takes very little time, especially if you establish it as a regular habit and do it systematically.

A driver can be proud of a car in good condition. In fact, car condition definitely indicates a lot about the personality and attitude of the driver. It helps show whether he is a responsible or careless person. It gives some indication as to his fitness to hold a driving license.

Whether or not your city or state has compulsory inspection of the safety equipment of motor vehicles, keep your car in a sound condition. Make it a personal responsibility. It pays you big dividends in safety. It helps safeguard your driving record.

Your personal driving record to which you add year after year, both with your state Department of Motor Vehicles and with your insurance company, can often depend on the condition of the control and safety devices on your car. They can help make and keep your driving record good. So take time frequently to check them.

TO TALK ABOUT:

What is the connection between a car in good condition 1 and a driver's sound traffic practices?

What is meant by a car that has had a "square deal"? If 2 you wanted to know whether a car has had a "square deal," what would you look for?

Give evidence: (1) that many automobiles now on the 3 road operate below minimum safety standards; (2) that this fact has considerable bearing on bad accident records.

Would you favor legislation requiring cars to be scrapped 4 after they have been used a certain number of years? Why or why not? After a certain mileage? Why or why not? What are the alternatives?

5   Debates: (1) It is worse for the steering system to go wrong than any other car part; (2) The braking system.

6   Discuss the proposition that a car with its non-engine parts in bad order can bring the driver as much grief as a car with its engine parts defective.

7   Report and discuss a serious accident caused by brake failure.

TO DO:

1   Set up minimum standards for automobile condition from the point of view: (1) of personal safety; (2) of the safety of other highway users.

2   Witness a thorough inspection at a garage or official inspection station and learn what devices and instruments there are for measurement of a car's condition and efficiency. Report your observations.

3   Try the experiment of driving for an hour or two with as little use of the brake as is consistent with good, safe driving. How many times were you compelled to use the brakes? Is it true that brakes need not often be used in well-controlled driving? Discuss this.

TO LOOK UP:

All About Your Car. Ed. of Popular Science, Garden City Books, Garden City, New York. 255 pp.

Auto Repair Kinks. Toboldt, Bill, Goodheart-Willcox Co., Inc., Chicago, Illinois. 1952. 221 pp.

Electricity and Wheels. Richardson, Ralph A., General Motors Corporation, Detroit, Michigan. 32 pp.

Everyday Automobile Repairs. Crouse, William H., McGraw-Hill Book Company, New York 36, New York. 1952. 296 pp.

How the Wheels Revolve. General Motors Corporation, Detroit, Michigan. 1952. 29 pp.

Owner's Manual. For the car you are driving. Supplied with the car.

Optics and Wheels. General Motors Corporation, Detroit, Michigan. 32 pp.

DO YOU KNOW:

Whether or not pedestrian traffic fatalities are decreasing?

When and where pedestrians are most likely to be in accidents?

What attitudes help pedetrians avoid accidents?

The traffic hazards of pedestrians at night?

How pedestrians can be protected?

CHAPTER 19 THE PEDESTRIAN

MAN-ON-FOOT IN THE MOTOR AGE

THE motor age has brought new problems to the man on foot.

A few decades ago there was relatively little danger in crossing the street or walking along the highway. Horse and wagon traffic gave pedestrians little trouble. The pedestrian had time to get out of the way.

Today, however, a pedestrian may have to wait several minutes before daring to cross a busy street or a rural highway. Even then he crosses with the jumpy feeling that a speedy 3,200-pound car may be on his heels at any second.

Motor vehicles have increased so rapidly that traffic conditions are often difficult and dangerous for drivers and pedestrians alike.

Safe walking on streets and highways has become a serious problem. The pedestrian is "on the spot." Drivers must help protect him, and he must be taught how to protect himself.

PEDESTRIANS IN CITY TRAFFIC FATALITIES

Fig. 213. The pedestrian fares badly in city traffic.

½ PEDESTRIANS NON-PEDESTRIANS

¾ PEDESTRIANS NON-PEDESTRIANS

IN AVERAGE CITY   IN SOME CITIES

Pedestrian Accidents Are Many ONE out of every four persons killed in traffic accidents in the United States is a pedestrian. In cities, the proportion is often much greater. The New York City Police Department reported that 72 per cent of the city's traffic fatalities in one year were pedestrians. Many were injured or killed while crossing the street against the red light, and many while crossing between intersections. In cities with over 500,000 population, usually 3 or more out of every 5 persons killed in traffic are pedestrians.

INJURIES OR DEATH RESULT ● ● ●

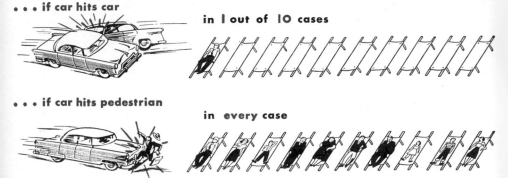

● ● ● if car hits car

in I out of IO cases

● ● ● if car hits pedestrian

in every case

Fig. 214. Pedestrians always come out second best.

Here, in round numbers, is a tragic picture of what the pedestrian is facing in modern traffic. In one year, in the United States, some 900,000 automobile accidents cause injury or death. In these accidents, over 200,000 adult and child pedestrians are hit by automobiles. Some 8,500 of these pedestrians are killed. Many times that number are crippled. It is clear that the Motor Age has given the man on foot some serious problems.

Man Versus Car IN ANY collision of pedestrian and automobile, the pedestrian is obviously at a great disadvantage. The automobile has the better of it on all counts—size, weight, speed, momentum, impact, and hardness of material.

Flesh and bones are no match for steel, glass, and rubber tires under pressure. The driver in his car is like a person encased in armor.

338

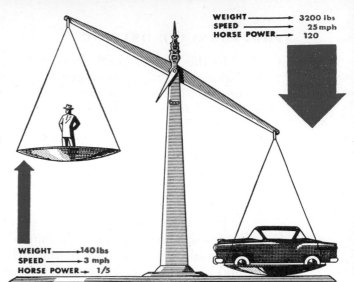

WEIGHT — 3200 lbs
SPEED — 25 mph
HORSE POWER — 120

WEIGHT — 140 lbs
SPEED — 3 mph
HORSE POWER — 1/5

Fig. 215. The pedestrian
is no match for the car.

If a driver so encased in his car collides with a pedestrian, it is the pedestrian who is injured. Personal injury occurs in only about one out of every 10 accidents where car crashes into car. But practically *every* accident where car and pedestrian crash involves an injury.

A 140-pound pedestrian walking at 3 or 4 miles per hour has no chance against the impact of a 3,200-pound machine traveling at the 25 miles per hour speed which is legal in most city traffic—to say nothing of the legitimate 50 to 60 miles per hour on many rural highways.

Accidents happen very fast. On city streets, the pedestrian has little chance to get out of the way once he has stepped into danger. In a recent year, 200,000 city pedestrians were injured or killed. Three per cent were killed.

JOE WALKER
140 lbs.

CARR N. DRIVER

3200 lbs.

Fig. 216. Pick the winner!

In the case of rural areas, far fewer pedestrians are exposed to traffic, but vehicular speeds are higher. Consequently, in the same year, 11,000 were injured or killed in rural areas, but 28 per cent of those hit were killed.

Whether on city streets or in rural areas, the traffic hazards of today's pedestrians are a very serious matter.

Pedestrian traffic accidents are so frequent that it is urgent for all to know why they happen, when and where they are most likely to happen, and what can be done to help prevent them.

If it takes you 20 minutes to read this chapter, 7 pedestrians will be seriously injured or killed while you are reading it. They will be the fathers, mothers, sisters, and brothers in families much like yours.

MEET THE PEDESTRIAN

SUPPOSE we take a look at the pedestrian. Who is he? Why does he behave as he does? Why does he all too often become the victim in a traffic accident?

In the statistics about accidents, the pedestrian sounds like some special creature whom you have never met. But he is not. He is any man, woman, child, or young person like yourself walking on a street or highway. He may be of any age; he may be normal in every respect; he may have any number of physical or mental limitations.

Many pedestrians have serious handicaps. They may have bad eyesight or hearing. Drivers should quickly recognize the white cane or the guide dog of a blind pedestrian. In many cities and states, the law requires a driver to stop for a pedestrian carrying a white cane.

Fig. 217. Meet the pedestrian!

Fig. 218. Is he deaf? Absent-minded? Confused?

Other pedestrians who have handicaps, such as deafness, are almost impossible to recognize in usual traffic situations.

Some pedestrians lack agility, balance, and walking skill; others have diseases that interfere with good judgment. Some have low intelligence; others have bad attitudes.

Some pedestrians are exceptionally slow in reacting. Even after they see danger, they cannot make quick, correct movements. The man crossing the street ahead of your car may be inattentive, in poor health, crippled, drunk, aged, preoccupied, or so tired that he will do the wrong thing. There are many possible physical and mental deficiencies.

A community of any size includes people with a wide range of intelligence, and they all use the streets. Some have exceptionally high intelligence; some are exceptionally dull and are not capable of guarding themselves in traffic. They fail to use caution. They lack good judgment, have very little foresight, and cannot analyze a situation to see its danger. Such pedestrians are no more to be laughed at or reprimanded for "stupid" acts than physically crippled persons are to be blamed when they cannot move fast. They need every assistance a driver can give.

Dozens of mental characteristics contribute to pedestrian accidents. Good drivers plan an extra margin of safety in stopping distance where there are pedestrians, realizing that the man walking in the street may be:

Afraid, or confused ◀
Bewildered on alighting from a bus or streetcar
Absent-minded, or ill
Inattentive, or distracted

In a hurry—suicidal in traffic!
Ignorant of traffic rules
Ignorant of the fact that traffic signals are for pedestrians also
Using poor judgment
Assuming bad attitudes of—
  Stubbornness
  Defiance
  Unfairness
  Selfishness
Over-optimistic—trusting too much to luck or to the ability of the driver to stop before hitting him
Intoxicated

Many pedestrians have little or no knowledge about the limitations of a driver in stopping his car. They do not realize that cars cannot be stopped on dimes! Several studies have shown that 9 out of every 10 adult pedestrians killed in traffic are non-drivers.

ONLY 1 OUT OF EVERY 10 PEDESTRIANS KILLED IN TRAFFIC...

Fig. 219. Pedestrian traffic fatalities are generally non-drivers.

... WAS A LICENSED DRIVER

The best attitude for a driver to take toward any pedestrian who seems awkward, out of place, inattentive, or slow in traffic is that he may be a handicapped person who needs consideration and assistance, or a non-driver who does not fully realize traffic hazards.

The Age of Pedestrian Traffic Victims A LOOK at Fig. 220 gives you a quick picture of how pedestrians of different ages compare in having traffic accidents.

The fact is that more pedestrians over 50 years of age

are *killed* in traffic accidents in proportion to their number in the population than in any other age group.

In proportion to their number in the whole national population, more persons in the two age groups, 5 to 14 years and 50 years and over, are *injured* in traffic accidents than at other ages. Pedestrians between 20 and 35 years of age have the lowest accident rate.

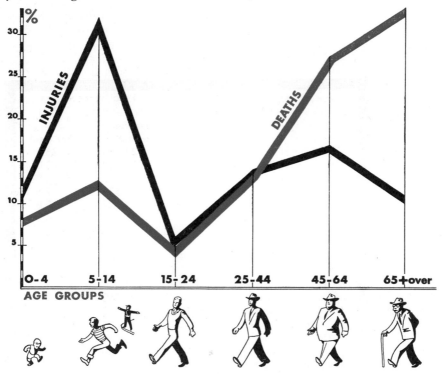

Fig. 220. Elderly pedestrians suffer the greatest number of traffic deaths; very young children have the most traffic injuries.

Elderly Pedestrians Persons past 65 years of age have the worst pedestrian fatality rate, the rate growing much higher with increasing age. About one-third of all pedestrians killed are 65 years of age or older. Yet only about 9 per cent of our population is of that age group.

Child Pedestrians In a recent year, of all pedestrians *killed* in traffic accidents, 21 per cent were under 15 years

343

of age, and 44 per cent of all pedestrians *injured* were under 15 years of age.

In one recent year, as many as 1,100 child pedestrians between the ages of 5 to 14 were killed by motor vehicles. Some twenty thousand others were crippled for life.

THE PEDESTRIAN ACCIDENT

BOTH pedestrians and drivers should know when and where most pedestrians are killed or injured in traffic, and what they are doing most often at the time of the accident.

WHAT PEDESTRIANS WERE DOING WHEN HIT	Number of Pedestrians	Per Cent
Crossing not at Crosswalk	28,783	26.3
Coming from Between Parked Cars	19,732	18.0
Crossing with No Signal	14,309	13.0
Crossing with Signal	10,535	9.6
Playing in Roadway	8,602	7.8
Crossing against Signal	7,354	6.7
Working in Roadway	2,274	2.1
Crossing Diagonally	2,004	1.8
Walking in Roadway with Traffic (Sidewalks not available.)	1,643	1.5
Walking in Roadway with Traffic (Sidewalks available.)	960	0.9
Walking in Roadway *Facing* Traffic		
(Sidewalks not available.)	701	0.6
(Sidewalks available.)	360	0.3
Getting on or out of an Automobile (Not streetcar or bus.)	1,414	1.3
Hitching on a Vehicle	703	0.6
Standing in a Safety Zone	573	0.5
Getting on or off Streetcar or Bus	260	0.2
Other and Unknown	9,724	8.8
TOTAL	109,931	100.0

Information taken from 1953 AAA Pedestrian Protection Contest reports from 42 states and the District of Columbia.

TABLE XIV

MORE pedestrians are killed on city streets than on rural roads, as you would expect because of greater vehicular traffic in cities and greater numbers of pedestrians.

Several studies have shown that a great majority of fatal pedestrian accidents occur near the victim's home. In a three-year period, nearly three-fourths were killed within three blocks of their homes.

The two most dangerous things that pedestrians do on city streets seem to be, from studies of accidents:

Crossing *between*, rather than *at*, intersections ◀
Walking or running out from between parked cars

If pedestrians, both young and old, would stop doing these things, we could expect pedestrian accidents in cities to take a big drop.

City pedestrians have to be especially watchful for cars making left turns. A study shows that two out of every three injured at intersections by turning cars were hit by cars turning left. Pedestrians are less alert for cars turning left, which often come upon them at greater speed than cars turning right. Also, the driver's attention is often on other vehicles when he is turning left. The driver who is turning left is also at a greater distance from the crosswalk, and he may not get the idea that the pedestrian has stepped into his path. Watch especially carefully for left-turning cars.

For children, a special danger in city traffic is playing in the streets.

The play habits of children between the ages of 5 and 14 are very active, and each year, as they grow older, the play is more and more independent of home protection. It is important to know that 1 out of every 3 injured pedestrians comes from this age group. Most of the accidents to these children happen at unprotected times and places; more often than not when they are playing in the street.

Studies made in New York have shown that nearly half of the accidents to children up to 14 years of age occurred after school and during the three-hour period from 5 to 8 P.M., when most of them were free for play.

In congested city districts without proper playgrounds, children of these ages often play in streets. They "hitch on" to trucks, "beat cars across the street," play catch, chase balls into the paths of cars, and dart out unexpectedly from between parked cars. In the excitement of play, they fail to watch for vehicles.

On Rural Roads MANY pedestrians are killed or injured each year while walking on a roadway. Two-thirds of those killed on the roadway were walking *with* the traffic. That is, they had their backs in the direction from which cars were coming. The simple habit of always walking facing traffic would prevent many, many rural pedestrian injuries and deaths.

Fig. 221. Walking on the left, the man on foot is "on the ball."

The Pedestrian DARKNESS makes the pedestrian problem much worse.
at Night The man on foot, especially if he is not a driver himself, is likely to think that, because the car lights seem to be on him, he can be seen by drivers from a far greater distance than is possible. Here, again, it is significant that 9 out of 10 pedestrians killed do not drive.

Car headlights look so bright to the pedestrian that he thinks he is easily seen by the driver. He does not realize that less than 5 per cent of the light which falls on him is reflected back to the driver's eyes, if he is wearing dark clothing and the background is dark. This small amount of reflected light is all that lets the driver see him.

Pedestrians are almost invisible to drivers at night until the car is dangerously close to them. This is true even under favorable night-seeing conditions. If rain, snow, fog, a dirty windshield, inefficient headlights, headlight glare, or other conditions reduce the driver's visibility, a pedestrian can be seen ahead only at a much shorter distance. His danger, if he depends on the driver seeing him, is shockingly great.

In fact, the months of the year that have longer periods of darkness also have higher numbers of pedestrian deaths and injuries.

A study made by the City of Los Angeles shows in a startling way that the majority of pedestrians are killed after dark. Three out of every 4 pedestrians killed in traffic lost their lives during hours of darkness. A Michigan study reports that 95 per cent of the teenage pedestrians killed in traffic had the accident between 6 and 12 P.M.

PEDESTRIAN FATALITIES BY HOUR OF DAY
(Report included 47 States and the District of Columbia)
SOURCE: NATIONAL OFFICE OF VITAL STATISTICS

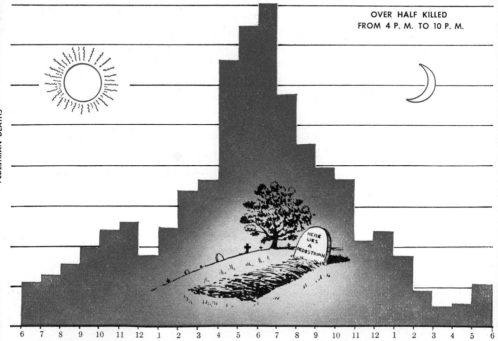

Fig. 222. Pedestrian deaths are heaviest in hours of darkness.

The easiest and most practical thing a pedestrian can do to protect himself against nighttime traffic accidents is to wear a conspicuous article of white or light-colored clothing, or carry a light. He can also be especially careful to follow sound walking practices in hours of darkness.

Alcohol and the Pedestrian AMONG pedestrians killed in traffic accidents, approximately one-fourth had been drinking, according to reports from 21 states. In a 15-year study by Dr. S. R. Gerber, Coroner, Cuyahoga County, Ohio, autopsies of adult pedestrians killed in traffic accidents showed that, of 992 examined, 49 per cent had been drinking.

Alcohol and walking on the streets mix no better than alcohol and driving.

GOOD PEDESTRIAN HABITS

IT IS encouraging to find that most pedestrian accidents are caused by a very few unsafe practices.

Most pedestrians who get into accidents failed to follow a few sensible practices of *where, when,* and *how* to walk. In traffic, they are "jaywalkers," and no "jaywalker" has the right-of-way. Pedestrians need to form and consistently follow certain safe traffic habits. It will help to see these habits in summaries, as shown below.

Fig. 223. He was a jaywalker, Nurse.

Fig. 224. For a longer life, step out on the curb side!

THE following habits should always be followed by city pedestrians: **City Pedestrians**

1. Always look carefully in all directions before crossing. ◄
2. Never step out into the street from between parked cars.
3. Cross streets *only* at intersections.
4. Watch for cars that are turning, especially cars making left turns.
5. Obey traffic signals as rigidly as you expect drivers to obey them, crossing only with a green light or a pedestrian WALK signal.
6. Never cross a street by weaving in and out between stopped cars.

Pedestrians should take special care at times when walking in traffic is exceptionally hazardous, such as when:

It is dark, raining, or snowing ◄
You are in a hurry
You are carrying an umbrella or large bundles which obstruct your view or may slow you down
The streets are slippery
You are not well
You are worried or distracted

GOOD traffic habits are important when you are waiting for street cars and buses or alighting from them. Make it a firm habit always to: **Using Street Cars and Buses**

Wait on safety islands or in designated safety zones. ◄
Wait on sidewalks where there are no safety zones.
Face oncoming traffic if it is necessary to wait in unprotected zones.

349

Wait until traffic has moved on and you can be sure the
way is clear.

Never cross behind or in front of vehicles from which
you have stepped.

 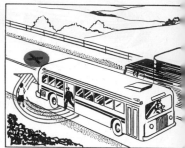

*Fig. 225. Danger
spots! Wait until
the bus moves on.*

*Walking Habits
on Rural High-
ways*

FOUR good habits for pedestrians on rural highways are:

1. Use highway sidewalks, where they are provided.
2. Walk on the *left* side of the highway, facing oncoming
   cars.
3. Step off the road if nearby cars are going to pass each
   other.
4. Wear or carry something white at night, or carry a
   light.

The habit of walking on the left is even more important
at night than in the daytime. A pedestrian can see the
headlights of an approaching car and safeguard himself
long before the driver can see him.

The habit of wearing something white or light-colored
at night, or of carrying a light, greatly increases the distance at which you can be seen. The white is seen at a
greater distance if worn low on your body. The lights of
a car are thrown low, and white shoes, light-colored
hosiery, or a white band tied around the ankle or leg is
seen more readily by a driver than white worn higher up.

*Fig. 226. This pedes-
trian is seen because
of light color worn
low. Her light-col-
ored blouse scarcely
shows.*

PEDESTRIAN PROTECTION PROGRAMS

THE pedestrian is such a frequent victim in today's rapid, heavy traffic that measures must be taken to protect him. An active pedestrian protection program can be carried out inexpensively by any state or local community. It should include:

1. Proper ordinances controlling drivers and pedestrians. ◄
2. Enforcement of the regulations where most needed.
3. Proper physical protective features—such as: sidewalks; well-marked crosswalks; WALK signals; pedestrian islands; pedestrian barriers where needed; adequate street lighting; fenced-in, off-street play places with proper supervision.
4. Elementary school traffic safety lessons and group activities.
5. Continuing public education on protective ordinances, pedestrian hazards, sound walking practices, and both driver and pedestrian responsibilities— through newspaper articles, radio and television programs, posters, and campaigns against jaywalking.

THE objective of any pedestrian protection program is to get good cooperation between drivers and pedestrians in sharing streets and roadways. *Driver and Pedestrian Cooperation*

If they stop to think about it, both drivers and pedestrians want to enjoy safe, convenient, and pleasant use of streets and highways. Traffic regulations, signs and signals, islands, barriers, and markings are set up to protect both. Dangerous conflicts between drivers and pedestrians are not necessary, except when either the driver or the pedestrian fails to do his duty.

Sometimes the pedestrian has a poor traffic attitude and forgets that he, as well as the driver, has traffic responsibilities.

Before the automobile, pedestrian responsibility was scarcely recognized. A judge once handed down the decision that: "According to the law, and when on the public highway, the pedestrian may walk anywhere, or how . . . and no constable may deny him progress, be that progress never so stupid."

351

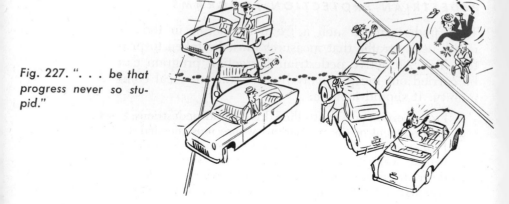

Fig. 227. ". . . be that progress never so stupid."

The automobile has changed this. No pedestrian can now afford a "progress" that is "stupid." The law no longer is willing to permit him such a "progress." The idea that the pedestrian has the right to walk where and when he pleases is out of date. Present attitude is more in line with a Connecticut law which states that:

"Any pedestrian who shall use any street or highway negligently or recklessly or shall wilfully fail to obey the signal of any traffic officer or shall recklessly disregard his own safety or the safety of any person by the manner of his use of any street or highway, shall be fined not less than two nor more than twenty-five dollars for each offense."

This kind of law is needed and should be observed by all pedestrians. Enforcement should be strict for all who do not voluntarily comply.

Play Yards and Playgrounds PROTECTION of children is important in any local pedestrian program.

The only satisfactory solution to child traffic accidents while at play is safe, fenced-in play yards away from streets. For toddlers and pre-school children, parents can provide this protection themselves by making attractive play yards at home.

Fig. 228. Happy play yards keep children off the street.

For older children, fenced-in community playground areas are equally important. They should be carefully selected, well-equipped, well-supervised, and made so attractive that older children will want to play there. Regulations forbidding play on streets should be passed for areas having off-street play places, and they should be strictly enforced. This combination of regulations plus adequate playground areas provides the best solution to the serious problem of child traffic accidents while at play.

Children are normally impulsive. They get an idea and act on it immediately. It is perfectly natural for playing children to act without caution. Unless playing children are kept off streets, drivers have to assume responsibility for their safety. When you drive, assume that every playing child is about to dart in front of your car. Children cannot be depended on to be cautious. You, the driver, must be cautious for them.

Fig. 229. Fenced-in playgrounds pay off in lives saved.

Pedestrian Education ALL pre-school children, under 5 or 6 years of age, should be kept off streets and roadways unless attended. The training and discipline of this pre-school group must come from parents, and older brothers and sisters. Example is important. Parents and older brothers and sisters must show little children how to use streets safely by *doing the right things in front of them.*

A child who is led across the street against the lights or between intersections is *learning* to cross in ways that are likely later to cause his death or injury. Any parent walking with his children, either of pre-school or school age, should always follow good traffic practices and point them out and talk about them with his child.

Fig. 230. Learning good traffic habits early.

Children of school age can be trained, both in school and by parents, to be good pedestrians. This is the age for forming good traffic habits. The understanding, skill, and caution of grade school children in traffic have been greatly improved in recent years by well-planned school programs in traffic safety education. Children are taught safe walking habits. They are taught to be safe pedestrians by means of stories, plays, discussions, posters, demonstrations, and games. They learn how to interpret traffic signals, when and where to cross streets, and how to use the help of school safety patrols.

The great value of early school training in sound pedestrian practices shows in the encouragingly sharp drop in child pedestrian deaths beginning at about the second year in school. Notice in Fig. 231 how this drop shows at about the seven-year age level.

Pedestrians over 15 years of age need to be so thoroughly impressed with the importance of sound pedestrian practices that they will follow them. A traffic safety educational program has reduced the traffic deaths of grade school children. Although a more difficult task, it can do the same for pedestrians over 15 years of age.

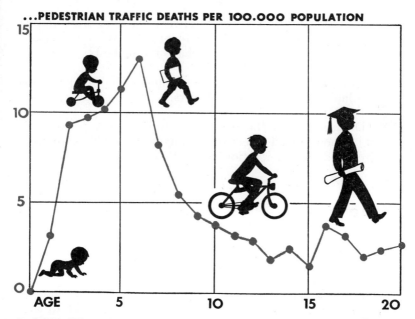

Fig. 231. There is a sharp drop in traffic fatality rate after the school-entering age.

TO TALK ABOUT:

1   Discuss the types of traffic accidents which pedestrians with non-cooperative attitudes can cause.

2   What seems to be the attitude of the average pedestrian in regard to traffic? Is he cooperative? Understanding? Reasonable? Does pedestrian attitude vary much with age? Illustrate.

3   How should experience as a driver help make you a better pedestrian? Or, experiences as a pedestrian make you a better driver?

4   Suggest ways of improving the pedestrian accident records of young people.

5   What setup in regard to illumination, road surface, car lighting, and pedestrian clothing would give the maximum visibility at night? The minimum?

6   Why do you think persons between the ages of 25 and 44 have the lowest pedestrian accident rate? Why do persons between 5 and 14 years of age have the highest?

7   How can non-drivers be made to understand the problems and limitations of cars and drivers?

8   Discuss, with blackboard diagrams, which is safer to cross: (1) a nonstopped street at an intersection with a stopped street; (2) an intersection where there is no stop sign.

TO DO:

1   Study the records of traffic injuries and deaths in your own community. In what percentage were pedestrians involved?

2   Examine the traffic records of your community to find the number of pedestrians between the ages of 15 and 19 that have been injured in traffic; below 15; between 18 and 39; 40 and 59; 60 and above. Are certain types of accidents

found more frequently in one age group than in others? Tabulate the pedestrian accidents according to their types.

Make observations at night, in both good and bad weather, **3** to get a better idea of the driver's limitations in seeing a pedestrian, particularly one in dark clothing. Write a 200-word statement, based on your observations, advising pedestrians how they should protect themselves in darkness.

Report all the things your community is doing for the **4** protection of the man on foot.

On a map of your community, spot the location of all **5** pedestrian fatalities and injuries in the past year. What conclusions can you draw from this study?

Get copies of last year's accident summaries for your city **6** and your state. Study the sections reporting pedestrian accidents. What were their ages? What were they doing when involved in accidents?

TO LOOK UP:

Accident Facts. National Safety Council, Chicago, Illinois. Annual Publication.

Here's How—To Combat Traffic Accidents with Safety Projects. National Association of Automotive Mutual Insurance Companies. Chicago, Illinois. 64 pp.

Let's Drive Right. Halsey, Maxwell. Scott, Foresman and Company. New York, New York. 1954. 465 pp.

Man and the Motor Car. The Center for Safety Education, New York University. Prentice-Hall Publishing Company, New York, New York. 1954. 367 pp.

Model Pedestrian Protection Program. American Automobile Association, Washington, D.C. 1954. 36 pp.

Pedestrian Traffic Accident Summary. American Automobile Association, Washington, D.C. 1954.

The Fundamental Principles of Driving. Tysor, James H. Banks Upshaw & Co., Dallas, Texas. 1953. 346 pp.

PART FIV

CITIZENS OF THE MOTOR AGE

IN OUR COUNTRY, the very face of the land has been changed by the Motor Age.

From the air, you can clearly see wide, crisscrossing highways, streams of vehicles, spread-out cities, mechanized farms, acres of oil fields, and outlying factories with broad parking areas.

In such a developing country, the advantages of citizens increase. So also do the obligations. For citizenship always has two sides, the *receiving* of privileges and opportunities and the *giving* of services and cooperation. Good citizens think of both.

Young people, soon to "come of age," find interest in the special opportunities and the special duties that have come with the automobile. Understanding and acting on them can help determine your success and enjoyment of life.

In time, you will no doubt need to manage family finances in purchasing, operating, and caring for a car. For, to most American families, a car is a major expenditure. Safeguarding so big an investment means much to your family pocketbook.

YOU AND THE MOTOR AGE

Since the automobile greatly influences the business life of the nation, here are questions to ask yourself about your future job: What does the Motor Age offer in occupations? Are there opportunities in driving as a job? What jobs require you to drive? May your driving skills, attitudes, and record mean you will get the job, keep the job, or lose the job? What kinds of businesses will increase as this Motor Age advances?

Soon your generation will assume the responsibilities of a motorized America. You will want clear ideas about what needs to be done and what improvement should be made. An amazing number involve highway transportation.

What are the needs for new fuels, metals, plastics, power? How can you help conserve human lives and our exhaustible national resources? What changes are needed in cities to solve problems of traffic flow and safety?

To continue the remarkable improvements now under way in cars, roads, city planning, and traffic safety, your generation faces endless opportunities.

CHAPTER 20

YOUR AUTOMOBILE ANC

AUTOMOBILES AND DOLLARS

THE automobile, either directly or indirectly, daily affects the pocketbook of every man, woman, and child in the United States. The whole economy of our country expands with the steady advance of the Motor Age.

Because of automobile production, hundreds of thousands of businesses employing millions of persons have come into being. The millions of motor vehicles produced and sold in the last half century have meant a staggering expenditure of American capital.

Salaries and wages paid in a single year to the huge army of workers in industries and businesses related to the automobile reach sums too large to grasp. The special taxes alone that are paid to government by motor vehicle users each year exceed three billion dollars.

Fig. 232. Will your car fit your pocket-book?

DO YOU KNOW:
What to consider when you purchase a car?
How to operate a car economically?
Where good care of your car can save you
dollars?
The relation between insurance and owning a
car?

YOUR POCKETBOOK

Large sums of money are involved in car ownership
and operation. The costs connected with owning and operating a car, like those of owning and operating a house,
are generally among the heaviest undertaken by the average family. Whether the family wastes or saves often depends on what is done with the car. The drag of the car
on the family pocketbook largely depends on the driver.

Part of the saving, when you use your car economically, is personal; part of it is of interest to the general
public. For the time has come when any waste of our
mineral resources, such as metals and petroleum fuels,
can no longer be passed over lightly. Some of the wastes
of the Motor Age are related, not only to a driver's personal pocketbook, but to the future welfare of this country and of the whole world.

THE CAR FOR YOUR MONEY

EVERYONE, of course, expects his pocketbook to enter
the picture when he purchases a car.

No one actually wants to pay more than a thing is
worth or more than he needs to pay. There is a lot to be
learned about how you can purchase, operate, maintain,
and insure your car intelligently and economically.

Whether a new or a used one, how should you go about
buying a car? What must be considered before you sign
on the dotted line?

361

A Bright New Car THERE are, of course, many advantages in buying a brand new car—one that no one has driven before.

The car is just out of the factory, where precision work has given smoothness and efficiency to engine parts. Its paint and chromium shine, not as a superficial cover over age, but with the honest brightness of newness. Its upholstery and finishings are spotless and handsome. It carries a new-car guarantee.

Even in purchasing a new car, however, you need to ask yourself a number of questions:

► Will this car fit your needs in weight, power, and design?
Has it been built with proper features for safety?
Has it riding comfort and design for convenience?
What will be its resale value?
Will service for it be readily available?
Is the financing plan for its purchase a good one?
Will its operating and repair costs be reasonable?
Can you afford to buy it?

For good budgeting, you must carefully consider every one of these questions.

Test the car on the open road and in traffic. Test its roadability, its ease in handling, and its fitness for your use. Try to think of all the needs you and your family will have in ordinary use of the car. Grade the car on its actual performance.

A Well-Conditioned Used Car IT MAY be necessary or wise for you to buy a used car. In that case, ask yourself all the questions and make all the tests you would make if buying a new car, and several others besides.

Fig. 233. Will it fit your family needs?

Fig. 234. A real "once over."

The greatest pitfall in purchasing a used car is the temptation to judge the car on sight. A glittering exterior can hide a multitude of future woes. You cannot trust exterior appearances. So you must be sure you are buying from an honest, reputable dealer who is as interested in keeping your future good will as in making a present sale.

The sad experiences of many used car purchasers point to an unfortunate truth. There are ways of "reconditioning" old, worn-out cars that are extremely deceiving. Cars can be so "doctored" by superficial and unreliable means that they look and sound and *temporarily* behave like bargains. That kind of "reconditioning," like "dope" to the human body, wears out in no time. The purchaser's bright hopes are rudely dashed to earth; his sad pocketbook pays and pays!

Anyone who buys a used car is properly cautious. Beware of the person who tries to rush the sale through, who belittles, or tries to block, careful check-ups and driving tests, or who drives the car himself instead of letting you test the car's performance.

Fortunately there is another side of the used-car picture. Some dealers actually recondition cars to a point of reliable performance. They give a used car a *future* as well as a past. They let you know the true condition of the car you are purchasing, and furnish a fair used-car guarantee.

If purchasing a used car, have a good mechanic whom you personally trust check the car over and drive it as if

363

he were going to buy it himself. You can well afford to pay him for his services. He will probably save you money in the end, whether you buy the car or not.

If you are mechanically inclined yourself, or unable to obtain the services of a competent mechanic, here are some of the general things to look into before you buy a used car:

▶ *1.* **Car History** Get the full history of the car, if possible. A reputable dealer will give you the name and address of the previous owner. Ask the former owner why he sold the car, what gasoline mileage he obtained, how much oil the car burned, whether it has been in any serious accidents. If so, what damage was done. Ask when the car was last overhauled, how many miles it has been driven since overhauling, how old the battery is, how many miles the tires have been used. Try to find out the total miles the car has been driven, for the speedometer reading of a used car has often been set back.

2. **Driving Test** Drive the car *yourself.* Drive far enough to warm the engine thoroughly and to loosen up the transmission and differential. Listen for unusual knocks and noises which may grow more serious. Note the steering wheel play. If it is a gearshift car, notice the clutch pedal clearance, which should be from ¾ to 1½ inches before the clutch is released. The steering wheel should have no more play than two inches at the outer rim, with the car standing still. Take note of how smoothly the gearshift lever and transmission operate *after* a few miles. Be sure the car does not slip out of any gear going up or down grade.

3. **Search for Leaks** Look under the car after you drive it and see if there are any oil, radiator, or gasoline leaks. Examine the wheel hubs—oil or grease around them may mean faulty packing. Tap the muffler with a screw driver to see if it has rusted almost through. Look over the exhaust and tail pipe with the engine running, to see if there are leaks in the system. Find out if the top, trunk, ventilators, or windows leak when it rains.

364

4. **The Following Test** Have a friend follow as you drive and notice whether the car "tracks" properly, the wheels wobble, the stop light and taillights work, and whether an excess of blue-gray smoke comes from the tail pipe when you accelerate in low or second gear. Such smoke could mean excessive burning of oil, and that the rings, pistons, and cylinder walls were probably badly worn. Or it could mean that the car has been driven more miles than you were led to believe. Improper "tracking" may mean a bent frame, or bent or broken front- or rear-end parts, which could have resulted from a serious accident.

"FOLLOWING" TEST

5. **Chassis Inspection** Does the car sag to one side? This could mean broken or damaged springs, faulty shock absorbers, a "sprung" frame, or a damaged front-end suspension. Even if the car shows no signs of sagging, make a good inspection of all chassis parts.

DO WHEELS TRACK?

6. **Tire Inspection** Examine the tires, including the spare. Front tires worn more on one side than the other indicate misalignment. "Cupped" tires may mean the brakes do not take hold evenly, the drums are badly and unevenly worn, or that the wheels wobble or are out of line. Look for bulges on tires. The side-walls may be broken; to prevent a blow-out, there may be only a "boot" between the tube and the outside of the tire.

SAG?

7. **Body and Finish** Look *under* the fenders. Use a knife or screw driver to scratch away the dirt and rust. Fenders may be nearly eaten through. Do the doors rattle? Do the windows roll up and down smoothly? Is the upholstery worn through, especially near the door handles? Is the paint worn off the door where the driver's arm rested with the window open? Are there "off-shade" patches of paint? Are the seat springs and upholstery in satisfactory condition? Look for clues to age and wear and tear.

8. **Car Inspection Record** If there is compulsory motor vehicle inspection in your state or city, find out when the car was last inspected and passed. Inspection stickers are

365

usually dated. If there is no sticker, insist that the car be inspected or have it done yourself before you buy.

RADIATOR?

9. **Radiator Inspection** Take the cap off and look into the radiator with the engine running and thoroughly warmed up. Gas bubbles may show up when the engine is accelerated, indicating the possibility of a cracked cylinder block, leaky head gasket, or cracked head. Oil on the water is another likely indication of these defective conditions.

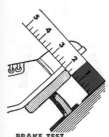

BRAKE TEST

10. **Safety Devices and Accessories** Check the accessories and safety devices. Try out lights, horn, windshield wipers, sun visors, ventilators, foot and parking brakes, heater, defroster, and radio, if any. The foot brake pedal should not go closer than 1½ inches from the floor. Apply the brakes hard and notice whether you get a smooth, even stop with no swerving or lurching.

Even when you can afford the cost of purchasing a used car, you may find that the operating costs of such a car are well beyond your budget. Be on the lookout for soundness of critical parts and for operating efficiency. A shiny exterior, clever salesmanship, and beauty of design must not attract your attention away from those parts that mean either economy in operation or serious expenses and loss.

ECONOMIES IN OPERATING YOUR CAR

ONCE you have purchased a car, know how to operate it to get a maximum return for your investment.

Your principal savings in operation come in connection with tires, fuel, and lubrication of moving parts.

Fig. 235. Your pocketbook is in this picture.

POOR MOTOR ADJUSTMENTS   SUDDEN STOPPING   IDLING

TIRE costs are a considerable item in motoring expenses. **Saving Your Tires**
Do everything you can to preserve them. Learn how to
operate your car at the minimum tire cost per mile.
Save money by following these rules:

1. **Drive at reasonable speeds** Tires will go twice as ◄
far at 30 as at 50 miles per hour. High speed is much
more harmful to tires in hot weather than in cold. Tire
tread wears out five times faster at 100 degrees temperature than at 40 degrees. Drive slowly on roads with sharp
projecting stones. *Take curves and turns slowly.* Speeding around curves can wear out tires ten times as fast as
moderate going.

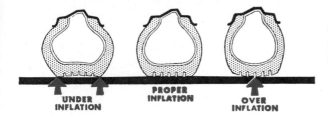

UNDER INFLATION   PROPER INFLATION   OVER INFLATION

**Fig. 236. Notice points of ex-
cessive wear with improper
inflation.**

2. **Keep correct tire pressure** Keep the pressure recommended by the tire manufacturer. Equalize the pressure *when the tires are cold* and before starting on a
trip. Pressure goes up and down with the heat of driving, but this does not harm the tires. So never "bleed"
tires when hot. The pressure would then fall as the tires
cooled and you would have under-inflated tires.

Even slight under-inflation increases rate of tire wear.
Six pounds under-inflation for a tire which should carry
30 pounds pressure can cut tire life by 20%. See that
each tire has its valve cap screwed on tightly.

3. **Never drive on a flat** This rule should be broken
only to drive the car entirely off the roadway for safety.

4. **Avoid striking sharp objects** Avoid curbs, holes,
rocks, etc. Any sudden, sharp bend in the tire casing—
as occurs when the tire fabric is crushed between the
rim and a hard object—is likely to snap cords within the

367

tire. Then other cords break around the weak spot and the tire fails. Cuts or bruises in the side-wall also greatly shorten tire life.

5. **Inspect tires weekly** Examine tires closely for blisters or bruises on the side-walls. Look for tacks, bits of glass, stone, or sharp pieces of metal imbedded in the tread or in weakened spots. Remove all such objects with pliers or screw driver, being careful not to damage the tire further. Have cuts sealed or vulcanized at once. Minor cuts tend to grow deeper. Water and grit work in and destroy the cord structure inside the tire.

A loss of as little as three pounds of pressure in one tire, in comparison to its running mates, means the tire should be removed at once and examined, or a flat may occur.

Notice the manner in which tires are wearing. A wavy wear on the outer edge of the front tires may mean a misalignment or improper adjustment in the steering system. This needs immediate correction to avoid further tire wear. Investigate the cause of any wearing condition, and have corrections made to prevent tire waste.

6. **Avoid jumping starts and screeching stops** Bad starts and stops scuff off tire tread. One ten-foot skid can take scores of miles off tire life.

7. **Keep brakes adjusted** No one tire should do more than its share of the braking. Keep the brakes so well adjusted that the braking force applies equally at front wheels and at back wheels.

Fig. 237. Check for causes when tires show exceptional wear.

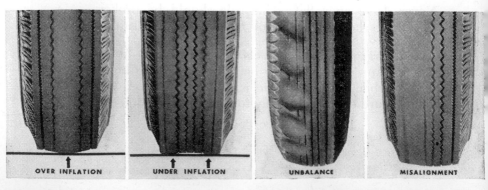

OVER INFLATION   UNDER INFLATION   UNBALANCE   MISALIGNMENT

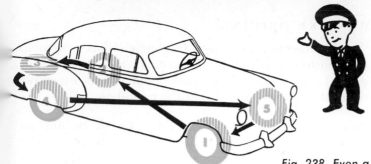

Fig. 238. Even a tire needs a vacation.

8. Switch wheels at regular intervals Have a regular tire switching plan. It is most important to get each tire used in each position. *Know your switching plan and stick to it.* Include your spare in the plan. This assures approximately even wear on all tires and increases tire life.

9. Check wheel alignment, "play," and balance Wheels out of line can shorten tire life one-quarter to one-half. Too much "play" in steering causes spotty wear of tires. The pounding or "shimmying" of a wheel out of balance wears the tire unevenly.

10. **Do not overload the car**

11. **Use tires of proper size**

12. **Keep oil and grease off tires** They deteriorate or rot the rubber, especially natural rubber.

Tire life can be greatly increased by following all of these rules. Perhaps the greatest single factor in prolonging tire life is choosing sensible speeds. Studies made at Iowa State College indicate that tire wear at 52 miles per hour is over 2½ times as great as it is at 33 miles per hour.

Every motorist wants to get as many miles as possible per gallon of gasoline. Several common-sense practices help improve gasoline mileage: *Saving Your Fuel*

1. Avoid racing the engine Racing a cold engine burns as much gasoline as speeding. ◄

2. **Avoid excessive choking** If your car has a manual choke button, push it in as soon as the engine runs evenly. Leaving the choke pulled out causes excessive raw gasoline to be sucked into the cylinders.

3. **Start, drive, and stop smoothly** Quick or uneven acceleration wastes gas. Maintain a steady pace. The "pedal pumper" throws away gas. Plan ahead so you won't have to make frequent screech-stops and waste gasoline. "Play the traffic signals" to "hit the green." Then you will not have to make repeated, unnecessary stops and starts at red lights. Drive in low gears only as long as necessary.

4. **Keep speed moderate** High speed uses much more gas per mile than moderate speed. Increasing speed for the average car from 40 miles per hour to 60 requires an extra gallon of gas for about every 86 miles. This means approximately 11½ extra gallons for every thousand miles of high speed driving.

5. **Shut off your engine during waits** In some cars, an idling motor can use a quart of gasoline in two ten-minute stops. For example, waiting with your engine running for a slow freight train to pass at a railroad grade crossing wastes gasoline.

6. **Keep tire pressure up** Learn the recommended pressure and check your tires, including the spare, once a week. Under-inflated tires make it harder for the engine to roll the car along, and that wastes fuel.

7. **Keep carburetor in proper order** Too rich a mixture, recognized by black smoke from the tail pipe, wastes gas. Keep the air filter clean.

Fig. 239. Fast driving costs extra gasoline.

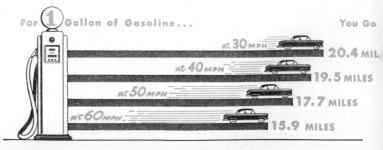

For 1 Gallon of Gasoline . . .   You Go

at 30 MPH   20.4 MILES
at 40 MPH   19.5 MILES
at 50 MPH   17.7 MILES
at 60 MPH   15.9 MILES

8. **Maintain proper engine temperature** When the engine is cold, more gasoline is used than when it is warm. If the engine runs cold, have the thermostat repaired or replaced. An overheated engine also wastes gasoline. If the engine runs hot, have a competent mechanic go over the cooling system.

9. **Have a hot spark always** You do not get the full power out of your gas with a weak spark. Fouled or improperly gapped plugs and worn distributor points are two common causes of a weak spark. Other causes are a weak battery, bad ignition coil, old or oily wiring, and loose connections.

10. **Keep ignition correctly timed** Incorrect timing means that the spark occurs at the wrong moment. The gas is not properly burned and fails to produce its full power.

11. **Avoid using heavy lubricants in winter** Using heavy lubricants in cold weather causes a drag which must be overcome by burning extra fuel.

12. **Have valves ground and carbon removed** Sticking valves reduce motor efficiency. Valves which are warped or do not seat properly cause loss of compression and waste fuel. Excessive carbon causes "pinging" and loss of power. This wastes gas.

13. **Replace worn piston rings** Worn piston rings cause loss of compression and excessive oil consumption.

YOUR car is such an important family investment that you want to preserve it from more than normal, gradual wear and tear. Your pocketbook will benefit from good car "housekeeping."

A suitable garage to prevent the destructive effects of weather is a good investment. Exposure, day after day, to rain, snow, ice, salt water, or salt air damages metals and finish. Avoid rust by good housing, proper washing

Keeping Wear and Tear at a Minimum

371

and polishing, and renewing paint and finish on chipped or damaged areas. Exposure to hot sunshine, week after week, wears out tires, windshield wiper blades, door-seal strips, and other rubber parts.

Smoothness in starting the engine, care in warming it up, correct shifting of gears, the habit of not "riding" the clutch, even acceleration, moderation in speed, and driving in accordance with conditions—all of these good driving practices help reduce the wear and tear on your car.

Keeping the clutch pedal pressed down while starting the engine, especially in cold weather, saves the starter by not making it work against the stiff grease in the transmission.

Warming your engine well before giving it the load of pulling the car avoids unnecessary wear on pistons, piston rings, bearings, and cylinder walls, by allowing the lubricants to become more fluid.

A car that is forced to work in the wrong gear for the driving conditions is under a strain. A clutch that is "ridden" is a clutch being needlessly worn out.

Engine life is prolonged with smooth, even acceleration. Moderation in speed reduces gasoline and oil consumption and increases the life of tires and brake linings. Indeed, all correct driving habits, whether for direct economy in car operation or for avoiding accidents, pay off to your pocketbook.

ECONOMIES IN MAINTENANCE

GOOD automobile husbandry means keeping all parts of your car working efficiently. This decreases operating costs and increases driving comfort and enjoyment.

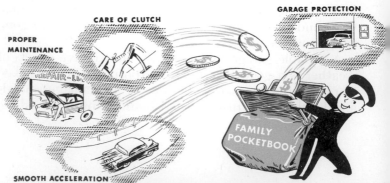

Fig. 240. Good car care pays off to the pocketbook.

Fig. 241. Watch out for a steaming radiator!

All working units require periodic servicing. The brake system, steering apparatus, and engine units should be inspected and kept in adjustment. Periodic servicing of the cooling, lubricating, and ignition systems is very important, if you want to keep your car in as near "new-car" condition and performance as possible.

HEATING beyond the normal temperature range causes strain on delicately adjusted parts and takes life out of an engine.

The Cooling System

Safeguard against overheating by checking the radiator water level every time you stop for gas. Keep the fan belt well adjusted. See that the radiator is not clogged with dirt, grease, or bugs.

If the temperature gauge shows near boiling, stop the car and engine promptly. Check the radiator water level. If you must add water, first let the engine cool off for a few minutes, because of the danger of cold water cracking the block or head. Then run the engine at idling speed while adding water.

Check the fan belt to see whether it is loose, off the pulley, or broken. Look for leaks around all hose connections, and tighten loose hose clamps.

If overheating persists, serious engine trouble may be the cause, and you should drive no farther than the nearest good garage.

Preparing the cooling system for winter weather is very important to your pocketbook. Look ahead, and winterize your car just before the average first freezing date in your part of the country.

Table XV gives a list of checks and adjustments to attend to.

PREPARING YOUR CAR
FOR WINTER WEATHER

1. Cooling System:

Flush radiator and cylinder block

Add antifreeze to radiator

Add rust inhibitor to radiator

Inspect and adjust fan belt

Check all hoses for leaks

2. Ignition System:

Clean and check spark plugs

Test conditions of battery and clean terminals

Check generator, condenser, distributor

Clean and adjust breaker points

Inspect starter motor

3. Lubrication:

Change oil and lubricants to winter grades

4. Fuel System:

Adjust carburetor

Check fuel line

5. Safety Features:

Equalize brakes

Check tires, rotate, or shift to winter tires

Check windshield wiper action and blades

Check operation of defroster and heater

TABLE XV

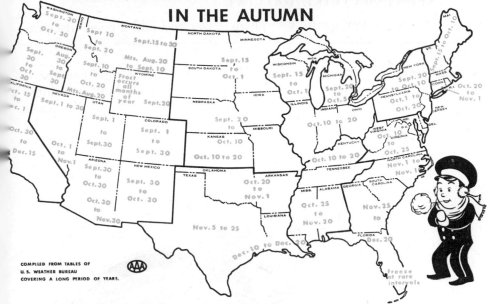

AVERAGE DATE OF FIRST FREEZING WEATHER
IN THE AUTUMN

COMPILED FROM TABLES OF
U. S. WEATHER BUREAU
COVERING A LONG PERIOD OF YEARS.

First, clean the cooling system thoroughly by flushing. Then add a good antifreeze solution. Satisfactory antifreeze solutions are of two types:

Fig. 242. Prepare your car for freezing weather.

1. High boiling point type, or "permanent."
   This is ethylene glycol sold under various trade names.
2. Low boiling point type, or "semi-permanent."
   This is ethanol (ethyl alcohol) or methanol (methyl alcohol), known as "radiator alcohol" and sold in bulk, or sometimes in containers under various trade names.

Use the manufacturer's installation instructions. Avoid harmful antifreezes, such as those made from calcium chloride or a petroleum distillate.

If you use a low boiling point solution, test it with a hydrometer now and then to keep the freezing point of the solution as low as the coldest temperature expected in your driving area.

If the car "freezes up" in winter, push it inside where it is warm. If this is not possible, nearly fill the radiator and run the engine slowly with the radiator covered.

After freezing weather is over, clean out the cooling

system again. Use clean water and add a good rust preventive.

Proper Lubrication LUBRICATE! Anyone who has had the sad and expensive experience of having to replace burned-out bearings, bushings, or other worn parts will emphatically warn you to *keep the car well lubricated.*

The manufacturer of your car has provided a lubrication chart. Watch the lubrication job when it is being done. Your presence and interest help assure a thorough lubrication.

Fig. 243. Be sure the lubrication job is thorough.

Take your car in for lubrication as directed on the manufacturer's schedule. Have it lubricated just before and during long trips, which always make special demands on lubrication.

Prepare your car for winter use with proper winter-weather lubrication. Use lighter oil and cold-test lubricants in the transmission, differential, and steering unit. When warm weather returns, be sure to change back to proper summer lubricants.

Take particular care when warming up an engine. *Never race a cold engine.* Slow warming up heats the oils and supplies an oil film to moving engine parts before they can be injured by heat expansion.

Check the oil level in the transmission of automatic transmission cars according to the instructions in the

Owner's Manual.

You can avoid exasperating "won't start" troubles by taking proper care of your car's ignition system. **Care of the Ignition System**

First, keep your battery charged. When starting the engine, always depress the clutch and have car lights turned off. These practices decrease the load on the starting motor and save the battery. Keep the battery plates covered with water. Unless the battery connections have rubber covers, keep them covered with grease to prevent corroding. If the battery is weak in turning over the starter motor, or if the lights are dim and grow dimmer when the starter motor is in use, have the battery recharged or replaced.

Spark plugs and distributor breaker points must be cleaned and properly "gapped" for good ignition performance. Wire connections in plugs and coils must be kept tightened and cleaned.

If your car pulls unevenly on hills, or the engine "skips," have a good mechanic check for improper carburetor adjustments, fuel-line breaks, a bad condenser, weak high tension coil, or other trouble.

During a severe rain storm, drive slowly. Or stop altogether and turn the front of the car away from the storm, if possible, to avoid getting water on the ignition parts and "drowning" the engine.

If, in a gearshift car, the battery is weak and the car must be pushed to start the engine, have the car in high gear, with the clutch depressed and the ignition turned on. When the car has considerable momentum, release the clutch gradually, and, at the same time, give the engine sufficient gas. See Chapter 9, p. 162, for suggestions about starting the engine by pushing if the car is equipped with an automatic transmission.

In winter weather, with a cold engine, the stiffened greases, lights used for longer hours, and the added load of a heater and defroster, the battery undergoes greater strain. It must then be kept well charged. If it is poorly charged, it is likely to freeze.

Care of all ignition parts is most important in winter weather. A strong battery and good strong sparks in cold combustion chambers certainly help make a car ready to venture out and operate efficiently on a zero morning!

INSURANCE PROTECTION AGAINST LOSSES

INTELLIGENT purchase, efficient operation, and sound maintenance of your car builds up a virtual wall of protection around the family pocketbook. Proper insurance against possible losses adds valuable bricks to such a wall.

The principle of protection by insurance is largely understood and appreciated by the American people. Carrying reliable insurance to cover a great variety of possible losses is a general practice. Responsible persons like the feeling of security against frightful, unforeseen losses that comes with proper insurance.

Anyone with property of value should have it insured. This is especially true of every owner and driver of an automobile. Many things can happen to cause losses in connection with driving and owning a car.

The car may be:

> Destroyed by fire
> Stolen
> Damaged by vandalism or accident other than collision
> In a collision

Accidents may:

> Cause damage to property belonging to someone else
> Injure or kill other street and highway users

From the point of view of a car owner, all these losses are serious. But from the point of view of his responsibility to others, the last two types of loss are by far the most serious. By carrying liability insurance, an owner provides himself with a means for meeting such social responsibility.

Fig. 244. Give the family pocketbook a sense of security.

A DRIVER's responsibility in case of accident is a very **Accident** serious matter. More and more states now recognize this **Responsibility** and are adopting stronger financial responsibility laws.

The power of the driver of a motor vehicle to do property damage and to injure and kill has made special legislation necessary. One of the obligations that society imposes by law on the owner and driver of an automobile is that he assume financial responsibility for his own actions and for those of anyone permitted to use his car. Both the driver and the owner may be held responsible for damages. Or, if you carry other people in your car, you may be held responsible for any injury which they suffer in an accident.

Accident responsibility begins immediately upon the happening of an accident, when drivers must stop, identify themselves and give aid if necessary.

Following an accident, you are required under the law of most states to demonstrate that you are financially responsible, that is, that you can take care of any accident damages for which you are held liable. Under the "security-type" financial responsibility laws, the security with which you show your ability to pay damages may be in any of three forms: (1) a pledge of money or property; (2) a surety bond; (3) liability insurance in certain amounts. The amounts of proof required run into several thousands of dollars. So most car owners prefer to use liability insurance to demonstrate their financial responsibility. The penalty for failing to furnish security is suspension of registration and license until security is given; and sometimes, proof of future ability to pay damages is also required.

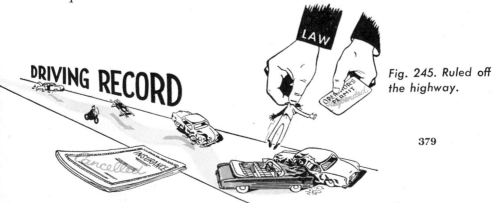

Fig. 245. Ruled off the highway.

379

As you learned in Chapter 12, motor vehicles must be registered and carry registration plates. Drivers must be licensed and carry cards which identify them with their licenses. If a car which you are driving or which you own is involved in an accident, these plates and cards identify you. You may then be charged with a traffic violation, and possibly be sued for damages in a civil action.

It is your personal duty to report an accident when required to do so by law. You may not "let the other fellow do it," or merely expect the policeman who is called to the scene to file a report.

Insurance You Can Carry STATE laws regulate the business of insurance companies in many ways. The company must be able to pay any claims or judgments for which the persons it insures become liable. For this protection, you pay the company a premium. The cost of the premium is based on:

▶ The type of insurance bought.
The amount of coverage.
The community's traffic record, and record for fair or excessive damage awards.
The driving record of the insured.
Whether or not, in many companies, a person under 25 will drive the car.

Sportsmanlike, accident-free driving can pay you real dividends by reducing the insurance premium you must pay. The cost of insurance premiums is determined, in part, by the accident experiences of all the persons insured by the company. If the number of costly accidents increases, the insurance company has to pay out increased sums of money. Then insurance costs go up.

Insurance companies suffer heavy losses if persons insured by them have serious and repeated accidents. Companies are very reluctant to insure such persons. Your accident record on a company's books is stacked against you for a lifetime. If it is bad, you may find yourself a risk that no company will want to take. This can make it difficult for you to keep a driver's license and may even rule you off the road.

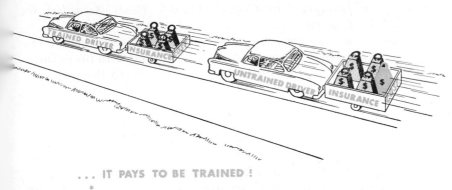

... IT PAYS TO BE TRAINED !

Fig. 246. This extra fourth added to insurance costs can be a heavy penalty on the pocketbook.

Even when you are accepted as a good risk and hold a policy, an insurance company reserves the right to cancel your policy if you have accidents and are no longer a good risk. Many insurance companies, because of the serious driving record of young people, refuse to issue policies where the car will be driven by persons under 25 unless a much higher premium is paid. Some companies, however, now recognize that young drivers who have taken good high school courses in Driver Education are safer, more competent drivers and do not charge this higher premium to cover cars driven by them.

Automobile insurance falls into two general classifications: (1) A policy protecting a car owner against losses to himself alone; (2) A policy covering losses for damages awarded to others because of an accident for which the owner is responsible.

1. *Insurance to Cover a Car Owner for Personal Loss:*
   a. FIRE INSURANCE—for damage to or destruction of a car by fire. ◄
   b. THEFT INSURANCE—for loss by theft, or damage done to the car in attempted theft, or while in the hands of the thief.
   c. COLLISION INSURANCE—for damage by collision or upset.

▶ 2. *Insurance to Cover Damage Costs Awarded to Others:*

a. PROPERTY DAMAGE LIABILITY INSURANCE. Protects the car owner, or person driving with his permission, against claims for damage to the property of others, up to the amount of the policy.

b. BODILY INJURY LIABILITY INSURANCE. Protects the insured, or person using his automobile with permission, against damages awarded because of injuries or death to others caused by use of his car.

Full collision coverage costs so much that many persons purchase a less expensive *deductible* policy. Under a $50 deductible policy, the insured owner must pay the first fifty dollars of a collision cost, and the insurance company pays for costs above that minimum. Under a $100 deductible policy, which is still less expensive, the insured pays the first hundred dollars of a collision cost, and the company pays the balance.

Many persons also hold accident and hospitalization insurance covering personal injury or death due to automobile accidents.

Very large assessments can be made against a driver or owner involved in an accident resulting in property damage or personal injury to others. Because of this, property damage and bodily injury liability *insurance*, to reimburse the insured for damages to others, is the most important automobile insurance to carry.

For such a variety of possible losses, insurance is the only sensible protection. A reliable insurance company handles your defense in damage suits, if you have liability insurance. It pays claims and judgments for which you are proved responsible. Whether or not you carry proper insurance is a matter of foresight. Do not wait until after the accident. The pocketbook of the uninsured motorist can get a knockout blow.

Liability of Drivers and Owners

A FAMILY without proper bodily injury and property damage insurance protection can be ruined with a heavy burden of indebtedness for years or lose the savings of a lifetime in a second. No wonder parents think twice before granting the privilege of the family car to new, young drivers who lack sound driver training.

The driver or the owner of one car may not be solely at fault in case of an accident. Accident causes can be very complicated. Liability is often very difficult to place. Several drivers and pedestrians may be involved, each contributing in different degrees to the accident.

Fig. 247. In this case, the whole family pays and pays.

Every effort should be made to determine to what extent each was negligent and contributed to the accident. The burden of damages can then be shared according to responsibility.

Business companies are held liable for damages resulting from accidents caused by drivers of their commercial vehicles. Taxi companies, trucking concerns, and owners of bus systems can be sued and found liable for the accidents of their drivers. No wonder they set up fleet training courses for their drivers and put on safe-driving contests. Commercial drivers make up a growing occupational group as the Motor Age advances. They play a big part in guarding the company pocketbook.

TO TALK ABOUT:

To what extent are the expenses connected with the own-   1
ing and driving of the family car among the heaviest family
expenses?

2   In what ways are economies in car operation and maintenance: (1) Personal economies? (2) Social economies?

3   What are the things a buyer should be careful about in the guarantee that goes with his car?

4   Before buying, what tests would you personally give a car?

5   What future trouble spots may not easily show up on first examination of a used car? How can you discover them?

6   What should you know about the past of a used car? Should descriptive labeling to show these things be required of dealers? Discuss.

7   Discuss the value, from the point of view of economy, of keeping the proper pressure in tires.

8   Can any owner of an automobile *afford* not to carry insurance? Discuss. What do you consider an absolute minimum insurance coverage for an automobile owner and driver?

9   Can you defend the proposition that every car owner should be required by state law to carry bodily injury liability insurance even *before* he has a traffic accident?

10   Explain and illustrate, by citing cases, what is meant by "contributory negligence" in traffic accidents.

11   Under what circumstances might an insurance company decide you are no longer a good risk and so refuse to give you a policy?

TO DO:

1   Find out the costs of the different kinds of insurance on your family car. Does your company charge a higher premium if a young driver is to use the car? How much does this cost your family? Will your company excuse this higher premium if you satisfactorily finish a good high school Driver Education course?

2   Examine and report on: (1) new car guarantees; (2) used-car guarantees.

3   Learn about and report on financing plans for the purchase of cars.

List in two columns: (1) the *direct;* (2) the *indirect,* costs 4
that can come with buying and operating a car.

Report on what you can find out about the practices of 5
dishonest used-car dealers in "reconditioning" cars.

Report on ways of honestly reconditioning a used car. 6

Make a list of practical ways of preserving the value of 7
your investment in a car. What would you include by way of
good car housekeeping?

Examine and report on the regulations of your state in 8
regard to insurance carried by motorists.

Set up a form on which to record the costs, on a weekly or 9
monthly basis, of operating the family car. Keep the record
for a definite time. What do you find is the cost per mile?

Compare the cost of gasoline and oil for a coast-to-coast 10
trip at an average speed of 40 miles per hour with the cost
of the same trip at an average speed of 50 miles per hour.

TO LOOK UP:

Automotive Antifreezes. Government Printing Office, Wash-
  ington, D.C.
Auto Repair Kinks. Toboldt, Bill. The Goodheart-Willcox
  Company, Inc., Chicago, Illinois. 1952. 224 pp.
Car Owner's Handbook. Green, Paul D. and Ritches, Ralph.
  Garden City Books, Garden City, New York.
Everyday Automobile Repairs. Crouse, William H., McGraw-
  Hill Book Company, New York, New York. 1952. 32 pp.
How to Cut Your Driving Costs. Williams, Frank. Harian
  Publications, Greenlawn, L.I., New York. 1953. 29 pp.
How to Get Your Money's Worth in a Car Deal. Williams,
  Frank. Harian Publications, Greenlawn, L.I., New York.
  1953.
Motor Services' New Automotive Encyclopedia. The Good-
  heart-Willcox Co., Chicago, Illinois. 896 pp.
You and Your Car Insurance. Coughlin, G. G. and Schneider,
  J. J. William Morrow and Co., New York. 1954. 192 pp.

CHAPTER 21

DRIVING

JOBS IN WHICH YOU MUST DRIVE

EVEN where driving is not actually your job, dependable driving ability is often important in holding your job.

Countless thousands of business and professional men and women, such as traveling salespeople, doctors, visiting nurses, inspectors, farmers, and business agents could not possibly carry out their work and make their incomes without driving skill. Business-trip miles make up more than half the annual automobile mileage.

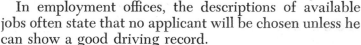

In employment offices, the descriptions of available jobs often state that no applicant will be chosen unless he can show a good driving record.

Employment on farms often depends on ability to operate motorized equipment. Automobiles, trucks, tractors, and all sorts of motorized equipment are used on modern farms. Many farms are operated without thought of a horse.

In vast numbers, factory workers and business employees go to work by driving their own cars. Look at the cars parked on streets outside offices, on city parking lots, and on the large parking areas at industrial plants. Such acres and acres covered with the parked cars of workers are unmatched in any other country. They are good evidence that young Americans need to be properly prepared drivers, to be ready to take part in the professional, business, and factory life of America.

DO YOU KNOW:

How important driving ability is to many jobs?
The opportunities in driving as an occupation?
What personal qualifications are needed by
   commercial drivers?
How they are selected and trained?
What driving practices their jobs require?

AS YOUR JOB

PROFESSIONAL DRIVERS FOR THE MOTOR AGE

IN THE United States today, there are millions of commercial driving jobs. With the steady advance of the Motor Age, driving as a profession offers an increasing number of occupational opportunities.

The truck, the bus, and the taxi add a flexibility to our American way of living that we could not have without them. From the Atlantic to the Pacific and from Texas to our northernmost states, the commercial life of our country owes much to great numbers of motor carriers.

Things we eat and wear, building materials, goods we produce, and the raw materials for industry are transported for long or short distances by motor trucks. Refrigerated truck loads of shrimp come into the north from New Orleans; consignments of livestock ride out from the ranches; heavy, newly-cut timber comes from our forests; thousands of automobiles move from assembly lines on motor carriers. Whether it is an egg for your breakfast table or an elephant for the zoo, it is likely to be moved all or part of the way on a truck driven by one of our millions of commercial drivers.

Bus transportation of people knits into American life and business thousands of communities which have no

Fig. 248. Professional driving offers many opportunities.

other means of mass transportation. Within local communities, the bus is used more and more. School buses daily carry about one out of every four children to school. Cities are served by taxis. Commercial driving is an important occupation.

America on wheels requires great numbers of responsible workers behind the wheel. "Responsible" is the best one-word description of a good professional driver. For, in addition to having sound driving knowledge and skills, a commercial driver must be dependable—whether he is entrusted with the lives of people going to work, perishable products from factories or farms, or the lives of children being taken to school.

Professional driving offers many interesting kinds of occupational possibilities. One can choose to be a private chauffeur, the driver of specialized equipment, of motorized fire apparatus, of an emergency unit, or of a taxi, bus, or truck.

Many commercial drivers prefer life behind the wheel to any other sort. They like action and find adventure in driving across country, through all kinds of weather, handling emergency runs, meeting the public, and stopping for coffee or meals along the route, with all the opportunities for friendship and exchange of experiences.

DRIVERS OF TRUCKS

ONLY a few decades ago the trucking industry was a rather unpromising infant! A story is told that, when the Federal Government bought its first three delivery trucks in 1899, each was equipped so that a mule could be hitched to it should it "refuse to run."

Fig. 249. In 1899, even Uncle Sam had to be reassured.

"YOU CAN HITCH THE MULE HERE"

At the beginning of World War I, America had only 325,000 trucks. Now there are in the neighborhood of 10 million registered trucks in the country, approximately 3 million of which are used on farms.

Such a huge number of trucks requires an army of trained drivers, maintenance and repair men, terminal workers, and supervisors. The Automobile Manufacturers Association estimates that jobs connected directly with truck transportation employ some six and three-quarter million persons.

Interesting facts prepared by the American Trucking Associations, Inc. help one grasp the huge size of the trucking industry:

Lined up, bumper to bumper, our trucks would reach ◄ more than around the world at the equator.

Each year, the ton-miles operated would make 200 trips to the sun with a ten-ton load.

Each year, enough gasoline is used to make five stacks of one-gallon cans to the moon.

Enough lumber is used each year in building trucks to build a boardwalk six feet wide from New York to San Francisco.

Enough glass is used annually in truck construction to enclose the ball parks of all major leagues in a glass cube as high as the Washington Monument.

With our enormous and growing volume of trucks, comes a growing demand for commercial drivers and special workers.

DIFFERENT kinds of trucking operations offer different kinds of jobs. **Kinds of Trucking**

You may drive a light delivery truck identical with a passenger car except in body. All of the operating parts may be the same as in the passenger car. Or you may drive a mammoth over-the-road power unit towing a huge semi-trailer. Then you may have two gearshift levers, ten to twelve forward speeds, and power-operated brakes for the tractor and semi-trailer, and you may need to learn brand-new techniques for starting, steering, backing, and parking.

389

Trucks vary greatly in design. Some are built for light, speedy work; others, for heavy duty. Some are for specialized uses and require handling by specially trained, high-salaried drivers. In fact, a truck driver practically always needs some specialized training, whether he drives a light truck, a moving van, a heavy-duty truck for lumbering or the transporting of automobiles, a tank truck for oil or milk, or a truck constructed especially to carry fruits or animals.

More than half of the trucks in the country are owned by people who have only one truck with which they carry on a small private business. On the other hand, there are large businesses which own and operate large numbers of trucks.

There are two main kinds of trucking businesses: (1) for-hire carriers; (2) private carriers.

The driver of a *for-hire* truck may work independently or for a trucking organization that carries loads wherever needed. Moving vans and pick-up and delivery trucks which you can call for special jobs are examples of for-hire trucks. Some for-hire truck lines operate on fixed schedules between regular terminals, just as railroads operate, and carry goods for different shippers. There are thousands of businesses set up to do for-hire trucking.

The driver of a *private carrier* truck works for a business concern that operates a fleet of trucks to serve its own needs.

Fig. 250. An early ancestor of today's truck. Built in 1900.

Fig. 251. Livestock is hauled from the ranches.

Fleets of this kind are often owned by department stores, oil companies, dairies, manufacturers, and other concerns that have businesses requiring long- or short-distance hauling. Some 44 thousand commercial fleets operate 10 or more trucks each.

State laws require for-hire trucking businesses to secure franchises before they can operate.

In some states, for-hire trucking within the state is controlled by a utility commission, in others, by a public service commission, a commerce commission, or a railroad commission.

Transportation of both property and passengers *between the states* is under the control of the Interstate Commerce Commission. So persons who wish to start interstate trucking businesses must apply to this Commission for permits.

Driving a commercial vehicle is a real job. It requires a high degree of physical and mental fitness. Driving must be done in all kinds of weather, over all types of roads, both day and night, and under constantly changing traffic conditions. Loads must be moved speedily, safely, without damage, and without loss.

Fig. 252. A driver is responsible for a well-secured load.

Studies indicate that a relatively small percentage of truck accidents are caused by mechanical reasons, such as failure of equipment or defects in the road. Most truck accidents are caused by human failures, such as inattention, carelessness, sleepiness, discourtesies, and slow reaction due to fatigue. So the Interstate Commerce Commission sets up physical and mental requirements for interstate truck drivers, in an attempt to reduce accidents due to such causes.

The Commission requires that a truck driver shall be free of all diseases, or physical defects, or limitations that might make him an unsafe driver. His vision and hearing must meet certain standards. He must know all regulations for commercial driving. He must be at least 21 years of age. He is prohibited from drinking on duty and from driving under the influence of alcohol or when ill or fatigued.

Most states have set up standards much the same as those of the Interstate Commerce Commission. Many trucking lines make even stricter demands on their drivers and use very rigid tests in selecting them.

Hiring the Driver FINDING the right man for the trucking job! That's what the employer is always trying to do. He hopes to select promising applicants and to screen out those who would prove unreliable, accident-prone, and costly to his business.

Fig. 253. The long-haul driver pulls off the road for "forty winks."

Fig. 254.
Heavy-duty
trucks bring
logs from the
forests.

He uses methods and tests such as the following:

A study of the job to determine what it will require ◄
An application blank, on which the applicant gives information about himself
A personal interview with the applicant
A test to show his knowledge about traffic and driving
Psychophysical tests of his physical, mental, and emotional make-up
A physical examination
Driving tests, to show how the applicant handles a car
The applicant's License Bureau record, showing any violations, accidents, arrests, license suspensions, etc.
References from former employers
Tests to show general intelligence, vocational interests, and hobbies
A personality analysis, to show how he will probably represent his company in public relations

One company with high employment standards gives an interesting report of what happened to 100 applicants for driving jobs. Written applications were accepted from 60. Only 40 of the 60 reached the personal interview stage. Physical examinations were finally given to 8. Only 7 of the original 100 applicants got jobs.

With such methods for screening applicants, followed by sound training methods, companies put the "gentleman of the highway," as good truck drivers are sometimes called, behind the wheel.

WELL-SELECTED, well-trained drivers are a good investment for a company. Only safe trucking operations are profitable ones.

Training the Driver

393

Fig. 255. Training truck drivers to precision maneuvers.

Safety means lower insurance costs, fewer claims for lost or damaged goods, less time lost by drivers because of injuries, time in court, or equipment tied up for repairs. It means lower costs for maintenance and repairs. Good drivers help a company run an efficient business.

As more and more businesses with fleets of trucks or buses see the value of trained drivers, they set up courses to train newly-hired drivers and also to retrain old drivers on the job. Many colleges and universities now offer courses to train fleet supervisors who, in turn, train commercial drivers. The driver learns to understand, operate, and care for his vehicle. He learns the rules of the road, regulations under which he will drive, and how to meet all kinds of driving conditions. He learns his responsibilities to his company and to the public.

A commercial driver is held responsible for checking the condition of his vehicle. He must know before he starts out that his vehicle is in road-worthy condition, with all control and safety devices in first-class order. He must learn proper loading, what improper loading can do to the performance of his truck equipment, and how

Fig. 256. Special skills are needed.

a shift of load can make truck units difficult to control and unsafe.

Drivers for small truck companies are often responsible for non-driving duties for which they need special training. They may have to load or supervise loading, prepare freight bills, keep books or records, make reports, make C.O.D. collections, and act as business salesmen for their organizations. They may have to keep the truck clean and make all minor repairs.

The driver of a huge over-the-road carrier may have to operate a two-way radio or handle communications by radiotelephone, to keep in touch with dispatchers and terminal managers. He is part of a mighty business. For his company, he is an important "front man."

The commercial drivers of tomorrow are the high school students of today. So the graduate with a sound foundation of driver education has a better background for a position in commercial driving.

DRIVERS OF BUSES

IN THE United States, there are some 200,000 drivers of buses, not including school buses. Most of them operate over short routes in cities; others drive from city to city or across many states.

The bus is a relatively new means of mass transportation. The earliest buses were little more than converted trucks. One of the first appeared about 1900 and was used for sightseeing in a Brooklyn park. Other early buses were simply lengthened touring cars, with very limited passenger capacity, and constructed with little or no consideration for comfort and safety.

Today, buses are no longer merely converted private passenger cars or trucks. They are built with structural soundness to meet special purposes. Billions of passenger trips are made each year, and passengers ride in comparative comfort and ease. Many buses have adjustable, well-cushioned, reclining seats, dual tires, air brakes, and modern heating and air conditioning equipment. Some have two-way radio and even radiotelephone service. **395**

Fig. 257. The first Mack
bus. Built in 1900.

From a small one-man business, bus operation has grown to a full-fledged industry. It is a well-financed and important addition to our means of transportation. The great majority of the bus drivers work on local routes. But many operate cross-country buses that link together all states and major cities throughout the nation. Others operate buses for factories, schools, sightseeing businesses, railroad companies, hotels, and various other groups.

The present bus industry offers job opportunities of several varieties. In addition to the drivers, large numbers of maintenance men, terminal workers, dispatchers, and supervisors are needed.

The Job of Driving a Bus PRIMARILY, the operator of a bus must be a safe and sound driver. But there are other duties that belong with his job. He is a public relations field man for his company. He is a conductor and a baggage-man. He must also be able to maintain his bus with minor repairs. Some of his duties are operational; others are clerical; and others have to do with dealing with the public as customers, and with the care of property belonging either to his passengers or his employers. His duties, depending on the type of run, are something like this:

> 1. Driving, public relations, and mechanical duties:

  a. Inspecting his vehicle as to fuel, oil, water, and condition of tires, brakes, motor, battery, and safety devices

  b. Making passengers comfortable and satisfied

    c. Driving in strict accordance with regulations
    d. Covering his route according to schedule or char-
    ter arrangements
    e. Making on-the-road check-ups and simple repairs

2. Clerical and reporting duties: ◀

    a. Making trip reports and filling out forms
    b. Reporting defective equipment
    c. Helping keep assignments in line with state and
    federal hours-of-service regulations
    d. Reporting accidents in the proper way

3. Financial duties and care of property: ◀

    a. Collecting fares, tickets, or passes
    b. Assuming responsibility for baggage—checking,
    storing, safeguarding, and delivering
    c. Delivering packages and securing receipts

The first consideration of a bus driver is the safety of his passengers. He also guards their comfort, and announces arrivals, departures, and rest and meal stops. He supplies information on routes and schedules on his own bus line and on affiliated or connecting bus or railroad lines.

ENTRUSTED with the lives of his passengers, the bus driver **What Makes a** carries responsibilities that are unmatched in the field of **Bus Driver** motor vehicle driving. So it is of greatest importance that a bus driver be most carefully selected. Trial-and-error screening would be too risky of lives. Applicants are selected by methods and tests that are much the same as those listed on page 393.

In addition to all the physical, skill, and intelligence tests described there, the personality of a person applying for a job as bus driver is considered with special care by progressive companies. The driver will be dealing constantly with people. So it is especially important to select applicants who are neat and well-groomed and who use good judgment and have good attitudes toward the public.

Unfortunately for the safety of the public, not all bus drivers are put through such a rigorous screening program. Carefully managed and operated companies, however, have such programs.

Training for the APPLICANTS who pass the screening tests and are hired,
Bus Driver receive specialized training.

A well-planned training course for bus drivers uses text materials, charts, lectures, films, discussions, inspections, projects, and supervised practice driving.

More and more companies put successful applicants through such a course of training. Their new employees study traffic safety, the responsibilities of drivers, federal and state regulations, and courteous attitudes toward company customers and the general public. They learn about the make-up of the company and the advantages available to employees. They analyze accidents and study various kinds of collisions—sideswipe, rear-end, head-on, and intersection—to understand their causes. They learn how to use safety devices, about sound speeds for various conditions, stopping distances, proper driving lanes, the value of keeping in good physical condition, and other safe driving practices.

In good training programs, new bus drivers learn how to handle the bus door, what to do at grade railroad crossings, what to do in case of an accident, how to be courteous and businesslike in conversations with passengers.
Fig. 258. School They learn how to manipulate the weight and length of
bus drivers the bus in varying road and traffic conditions. They
need special handle practice runs, and "get the feel" of bus driving.
training.

They are given a full sense of their responsibility to their passengers. Training of this sort puts competent bus drivers at the service of the traveling public.

TAXI DRIVERS AND CHAUFFEURS

THE taxicab business in general is not so well organized and controlled as truck and bus businesses, although some taxicab companies are.

The records as to the history, growth, size of the business, and the special requirements for drivers are not very complete. But it is perfectly clear that the streamlined city taxi of today, with its sky-top view and its radiotelephone, is a vastly different vehicle from the sensational, electric, "horseless cab" imported from France in 1897 for use in New York City.

Private individuals can go into the taxi business on a small scale, operating one car or just a few. Sometimes the owner-operators of single cars make up a loose-knit organization. The driver owns the car, but it looks as though it is company-owned, because the driver has joined an association and has paid for the privilege of painting his car with the colors and insignia of the organization.

On the other hand, there are large fleets of taxis owned and operated by big companies. In this country, thousands of such taxi businesses annually carry a couple of billion passengers, and give employment to something like 100 thousand drivers.

A taxi driver must pass tests to secure his special license. He has to meet the requirements of the city or state in which he drives and has to follow special local regulations controlling passenger carriers. He should be a driver of above-average driving experience and skill.

Very often you find that a taxi driver has been trained for another occupation or profession but has found taxi driving interesting. He likes the active, outdoor nature of the work, the fact that he is largely his own boss, has interesting contacts with the public, and good possibilities for income in fares and tips. As for his educational background, he may have had little training in school, or he may be a college graduate.

Another professional driver is the private car chauffeur. This driving occupation, while not open on so large a scale, is in some cases very well paid and offers special appeal.

Chauffeurs, like taxi drivers and all others who operate passenger vehicles for hire, must hold special licenses. The license requirements vary from state to state. Most states now have regulations that control the minimum age of chauffeurs.

A chauffeur has the education, appearance, responsibility, and driving skill at whatever level his employer demands.

States with strict regulations require all for-hire operators of passenger vehicles, such as chauffeurs and bus and taxi drivers, to supply recommendations, take special tests, and post identification photographs. The Interstate Commerce Commission requires the driver of a bus to be at least 21 years of age on runs over which it has control.

JOBS WITH A FUTURE

THE motorization of American life and of more and more areas of the world is certain to advance. Commercial driving will grow in importance as an occupation. Requirements will change; selection tests will become more rigid; training will be more complete.

There is every reason to believe that motor transportation will continue to grow. The number of vehicles, the number of passengers carried, the number of children riding buses to school, the ton-miles operated, the volume of freight handled—all these are on a rising curve. So the number of commercial operators needed to drive these vehicles will increase also. The future looks promising for driving occupations.

There are many opportunities to move from actual driving jobs to related jobs. Commercial driving experience is generally a requirement for men who act as dispatchers, terminal managers, personnel directors, and passenger agents.

Moreover, a truck business or a passenger-carrying business is a field for private enterprise. You can start a local operation with a single car. Sometimes you can buy the operating rights and equipment of established companies. Men with firsthand commercial driving backgrounds often take advantage of such sales to start businesses of their own. Commercial driving is a field that is definitely open at the top.

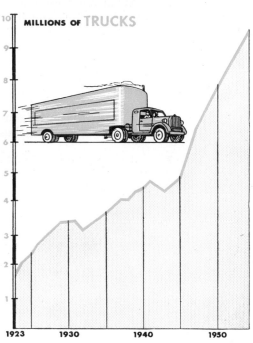

The future of any professional driver, like the future of any worker, depends, in large part, on his personal make-up. The worker with a high degree of responsibility and sportsmanlike qualities most frequently gets the advancement. Well-managed truck, bus, and taxi companies stress the importance of courtesy. Many com-

Fig. 259. Trucks have rapidly increased, creating more and more driving jobs.

pany safety directors believe that the most important safe-driving rule is the Golden Rule. They believe traffic safety results, almost as a matter of fact, with well-selected, well-trained, *courteous* drivers behind the wheel.

TO TALK ABOUT:

Discuss what your local community owes to motorized transportation. 1

What do commercial driving jobs offer by way of opportunity? Stability? Income? Advancement? 2

3   What kinds of applicants should by all means be screened out of commercial driving jobs?

4   What regulations would you set up to reduce the number of accidents caused by fatigue?

5   What regulations would you set up to control the use of alcohol: (1) By operators of trucks carrying merchandise belonging to you? (2) By operators of buses and taxis in which you or your family will ride?

6   Discuss the intelligence you would desire in a driver of: (1) your trucks; (2) buses in which you ride.

7   Do you think there should be more rigid regulations as to the physical condition of drivers of vehicles carrying passengers? Illustrate.

8   How well can truck and bus companies afford the costs of weeding out accident-prone persons from their applicants for jobs? Defend your statements with figures, if possible.

9   To what extent are other countries likely to follow the American pattern of a motorized working class?

10   Discuss jobs in which driving or experience in driving is essential.

TO DO:

1   Interview several drivers in well-managed trucking fleets. Ask them what training they received before making their first runs alone. Contrast their training with that of the usual private car driver. With that the airplane pilot.

2   Find out the average incomes for truck, bus, and taxi drivers. How do these average incomes compare with the income of the average worker?

3   Examine Interstate Commerce Commission regulations and report on some of the requirements as to: (1) qualifications of drivers; (2) driving practices; (3) safety devices; (4) reporting of accidents.

4   Report on tests used in selecting professional drivers.

Talk with truck, bus, and taxi operators and report on the 5
uses they find for radiotelephones and two-way radios as
part of their equipment.

Find out all you can about the safety devices on the most 6
modern trucks, and public buses, and discuss them in class.
What are the special safety requirements for school buses?

Look up statistics on the injuries and fatalities to bus 7
passengers in relation to: (1) the number of passengers carried; (2) the passenger miles covered; (3) other means of
passenger transportation.

Find out the licensing requirements of the various kinds of 8
professional drivers in your locality and state.

List several kinds of jobs and professions where the person 9
would be greatly handicapped without a high degree of
sound driving skill.

TO LOOK UP:

Bus Facts. National Association of Motor Bus Operators,
Washington, D.C. Annual Publication.
Getting into the Trucking Industry. American Trucking
Associations, Inc. Washington, D.C. Revised 1954. 18 pp.
Let's Drive Right. Halsey, Maxwell. Scott, Foresman and
Company, New York, New York. 1954. 465 pp.
*Motor Carrier Safety Regulations of the Interstate Commerce
Commission.* Interstate Commerce Commission, Wash-
ington, D.C. Government Printing Office. 1954.
Motor Truck Facts. Automobile Manufacturers Association,
Detroit, Michigan.
Trucks in 1975. American Trucking Associations, Inc. Wash-
ington, D.C. Revised 1954. 11 pp.
What Do You Know About Trucks? Automobile Manufac-
turers Association. Detroit, Michigan. 10 pp.

CHAPTER 22

IMPROVING

THE STORY OF THE MOTOR CAR

ALTHOUGH we live in an Automobile Age, our grandfathers did not. In 1895, there were four gasoline automobiles in the United States. People were shocked because these cars could be driven at "the ungodly speed of eleven miles an hour!"

In the United States today, some 60 million motor vehicles are driven on our streets and highways at speeds undreamed of by our grandparents. In a few decades, the automobile has had a phenomenal development.

The motorist in the early days of the automobile needed ingenuity, strength, and a sense of humor. Tires blew out with short use; springs were always breaking; axle shafts twisted in two; gas-burning headlights gave little light; engine trouble on the road was common. In 1913, "Get Out and Get Under" was the title of a popular song.

Today's automobiles are powerful and quiet. They ride smoothly and control easily. They are so dependable that drivers need not be amateur mechanics. Automotive engineering has made motoring comfortable, swift, reasonably inexpensive, and has developed important safety features in the car. The history of the automobile is a fascinating one, but only the highlights can be given here.

No one person invented the automobile. Charles F. Kettering, a leading automotive engineer responsible for numerous automotive inventions and improvements, once said, "The motor car is not the invention of any one

DO YOU KNOW:
What early automobiles were like?
What changes have taken place in the auto-
mobile?
The story of the development of motor fuel?

HE AUTOMOBILE

man—but a composite of many inventions. Although scarcely more than a generation old, the true beginning of the automobile antedates all recorded history." This is indeed true, for the automobile utilizes simple mechanical inventions like the wheel and the lever, and no one knows by whom or how long ago they were invented. The fundamental mechanical principles of the automobile were developed step by step by many inventors in many countries.

By 1776, James Watt had constructed a steam engine with commercial value. Engines with large boilers and steam-compressing cylinders and ponderous overhead walking beams slowly seesawing up and down followed. They had no method of obtaining rotary motion other than by use of a water wheel. They were the only source of machine-made power for nearly a hundred years.

Then Richard Trevithick produced in England the first practical high-pressure steam engine. People called his

Fig. 260. "Get Out and Get Under" was more than a popular song!

405

engines "the puffers." On Christmas Eve, in 1801, he tested the first self-propelled vehicle to transport passengers on a road. Use of the high-pressure steam engine rapidly spread and led to the famous steam locomotives of the early 1800's.

Fig. 261. Cugnot's "steam road carriage," 1784.

Small charges of gunpowder were used in the earliest attempts to operate a piston in a cylinder. This was the forerunner of the internal combustion engine, which was successfully made for the first time in France in 1860 by Etienne Lenoir. Lenoir's engine used illuminating gas for fuel and did not compress the gas-air mixture before firing. In 1876, Dr. Nicholas A. Otto designed in Germany the first four-stroke-cycle engine, using compressed gases before firing, as in the engine of today.

By 1889, Gottlieb Daimler had made a V-shaped, high-speed, two-cylinder internal combustion engine that started an intense rivalry with the steam engines that were then moving vehicles at speeds up to 25 miles per hour.

Fig. 262. America's "first." Built by Charles and Frank Duryea.

IMPROVING THE AUTOMOBILE

THE FIRST successfully-operated, American-built motor car was constructed by Charles and Frank Duryea in Springfield, Massachusetts, in 1893. It was designed like the horse-drawn buggies of those days, and so it was called a "horseless buggy." It can still be seen in the Smithsonian Institution in Washington. The Duryeas won the first road automobile race ever held in the United States, on Thanksgiving Day, 1895, covering the 54-mile course at a rate slightly over 7 miles per hour!

By 1900, there were 8,000 automotive vehicles in use in the United States. Most of them were steam or electric vehicles. Volume production of gasoline-burning vehicles had not yet been achieved. Cars were produced in tiny machine shops and backyard sheds. They were assembled one by one from parts roughly fashioned by inventive mechanics. This made them slow in manufacture and expensive in price. The next step was to learn how to manufacture them in quantity and at a price low enough so that many people could buy them. Mass production of cars was an American contribution.

The pioneer in mass production of automobiles was R. E. Olds, who organized his company in 1899. His famous, curved-dash "Olds Runabout" had a one-cylinder engine, weighed 700 pounds, and sold for $650. In 1904, the company produced 5,000 cars. In 1908, Henry Ford, another pioneer in mass production methods, who had built his first car in 1896, brought out the famous Model T, destined to number millions, and revolutionized the methods for producing cars.

Quantity production of cars depended, among other things, on the use of standardized parts. From carburetors to hub caps, the parts for a car of a given model had to be made identical and interchangeable. It then became easier to assemble a car and to replace lost or worn parts.

To speed up mass production, factories introduced wholly new manufacturing procedures. They set up conveyor systems, the "progressive assembly line," and specialized machines to make parts.

Fig. 263. Engine blocks move automatically on an assembly line.

This system uses continuously moving conveyors which carry parts and the developing car past groups of workmen. Each group adds a part or does one job for which it is specially trained, until finally, at the end of the assembly line, another new car rolls off. See Fig. 264.

Minor assembly lines feed into the general assembly line. Various parts, like the engine block, pass from one machine operation to another on their own production lines. There they are fitted in properly with other parts and then conveyed to the engine assembly line. Completely assembled, the engine arrives at the proper location in the general assembly line to be placed in the car. Other complex sections of the car are brought together in this same fashion. Mass production methods such as this have boosted production, greatly lowered costs, and given us our Motor Age.

FROM "HORSELESS BUGGIES" TO STREAMLINED CARS

SINCE the days of the "horseless buggy," many improvements have taken place in cars. Some have added to safety, some to performance, some to economy, and some to comfort. Many are indeed spectacular.

Closed Bodies   The first closed-body car appeared about 1910, but it was poorly adapted to general use. Squeaks developed rapidly; construction was flimsy. This early car was not a good match for the rough roads of the day.

For many years, the closed car was regarded as a luxury vehicle for occasional use on city pavements. But closed-body construction and design have been so vastly improved that open models are only a small part of the cars in use today. With the closed body, came greater year-round motoring comfort and safety, and motor transportation became adaptable to wide all-weather use.

Self-Starter Early cars had to be cranked by hand, sometimes at a painful expense of broken arms.

Fig. 264. Cars-in-the-making move down the assembly line.

Fig. 265. The self-starter brought "cranking" to a happy end.

In 1911, Cadillac installed an electric starting device invented by Charles F. Kettering, a very significant development which removed a serious motoring hazard and made general use of the automobile possible, especially by women, who for the most part had been unable to crank the earlier cars.

Improved Transmission In early cars, loud grating and grinding noises frequently accompanied the shifting of gears. With vastly better transmission systems, the driver of a gearshift car now shifts gears without clashing or grinding.

By giving the driver easier control of the car's power under changing road conditions and changing demands for power or speed, improved transmissions meant a valuable safety factor, especially on hills and slippery roads.

Further engineering improvements in the transmission of power are the fluid coupling, hydraulic torque converters, and planetary gear-type transmissions that shift automatically with changing needs for power and speed. The working principles of these transmissions are described in Chapter 7, on page 119. They so improve the ease and smoothness of driving that they are being produced and used at a rapidly increasing rate.

Multicylinder Engines The first American automobiles were "one-lung" cars. In time, four-cylinder engines became common. Today, six- and eight-cylinder engines predominate.

Four-wheel Brakes Today's speeds and complex traffic conditions require efficient brakes.

Early cars had mechanical brakes and on the back wheels only. The addition of brakes on the front wheels and the use of hydraulic control to give uniform braking were impressive brake developments.

SOLID RUBBER

Four-wheel brakes are now standard equipment on all passenger cars. They have materially reduced stopping distances. Better brake linings and drums, larger braking surface, more equal braking on wheels, and other improvements have tended to keep braking efficiency apace with increased driving speeds, and power braking has made braking easier for the driver.

Better Tires Fortunately for the motorist, improvement in the comfort, durability, and safety factors of tires has been steady.

HIGH PRESSURE

Improved cushioning quality in pneumatic tires lessens the jar from rough, uneven roads. Whereas passenger car tires once carried from 50 to 100 pounds of pressure, low-pressure tires with a larger cross-section now use only 24 to 30 pounds of pressure. The result is greatly improved riding comfort.

A few decades ago, a motorist was lucky if a tire ran 3,500 miles. Today, tires have become so dependable that we expect them to hold up for many times that distance. They give so little trouble, and the "spare" is so common that most motorists no longer carry a tire repair kit or even a pump, standard car equipment only a few years ago.

EARLY
LOW PRESSURE

Tire improvements give greater strength and durability; they also add to driving safety. New features help prevent blowouts; puncture-proof and tubeless, puncture-sealing tires are on the market; improved tread designs provide better traction on wet pavements; and the relation between the methods of curing rubber and the skid tendencies of tires is of increasing interest to manufacturers.

All-Steel Body Construction Because of the advantages of covering automobile tops with solid steel, large and

MODERN
LOW PRESSURE

powerful presses were built to make them possible. With modern construction methods, a dome-shaped top is pressed out by giant machines and electrically welded into place. A steel floor is then welded to the bottom edge of the body. The steel top is strengthened by rugged steel "beams." This makes a rigid, "one-piece" unit, shaped and reinforced to provide strength, durability, and protection in case of a rollover.

Lower Center of Gravity The tendency has been to lower the car's center of gravity by using smaller wheels and lowering engines, floors, gasoline tanks, and all driving units.

Lowering the center of gravity increases road stability, and in certain emergency situations decreases the likelihood of weaving and skidding. In some cases, this could mean the difference between safety and an accident, although a too-extensive lowering might mean the sacrifice of other important safety features.

Center of gravity may not be so important as the height of the driver's line of sight, which is the height of the driver's eyes above the road. If line of sight is too low, the

Fig. 266. Giant presses stamp out body parts.

driver's sight distance is shortened as his car approaches a hillcrest. A shortened sight distance could mean that an object just over the crest might be seen so late that the car could not be stopped before hitting it. Distances "Y" and "Z" on Fig. 31, pages 58–59, would be lengthened.

The driver's sight distance for objects on the road is determined by many factors: height of the seat from the road, condition of seat springs, slope of the hood, construction of the windshield, and the length of the driver's torso. All of these things should be considered in assuring a favorable sight distance.

Fig. 267. The center of gravity is lower in modern cars.

Many cars are now offering seats that are adjustable in height as well as in leg distance from controls, so that a short driver can raise the seat to permit seeing over, rather than through, the steering wheel, and, at the same time, lengthen his sight distance at hillcrests.

Sight distance is so important that it is well to remember it if you want to "customize," or rebuild, a car. Making the car look "smart," by putting the driver's seat practically on the floor, can make the owner look anything but smart if he is foolishly throwing away valuable sight distance.

Streamlining Research on "streamlining" airplanes probably speeded up the streamlining of cars and gave us simplified contours and fewer protruding parts. Other streamlining features are the airplane-type, V-shaped and curved windshields, modified fenders and wheel casings, enclosed spare wheels, "tailed out" rear ends, and inside "running boards."

Streamlining is relatively unimportant for lower speeds, but its importance increases rapidly at higher speeds. So streamlining is a very significant economy feature in any kind of high-speed transportation. 413

Other Improvements Many other features of modern cars increase the ease, economy, comfort, or safety of driving:

▶ Improved steering ratios
Power steering
Safety glass
Sealed beam headlights, with high and low beam patterns
Wider windshields, slanted to reduce glare and curved around to give better vision to the sides
Narrower frame supports to increase visibility
Power braking
Power-controlled windows
Larger rear windows
Seats, power-adjustable—both up and down and forward and backward
Better ventilation, and air conditioning
More easily read speedometers and gauges
Sway stabilizers
Automatic transmissions
Improved trunk capacity
Built-in windshield defrosters
Designs and devices to improve riding and roadability

Highly technical research goes on to improve still further the construction features of motor cars of the future. Important crash injury research studies are conducted in attempts to learn the causes of injuries in accidents of various kinds and ways of reducing injuries. In safety, economy, and ease in operation, additional important changes will no doubt come to the automobile in the lifetime of each of us.

THE STORY OF "DRAKE'S FOLLY"

THE story of improving the fuel for the car is as interesting as that of the development of the car.

In 1859, Colonel E. L. Drake drilled the first oil well at Titusville, a little lumber town in northwestern Pennsylvania. The only drilling machinery he had available was makeshift. Indeed, drilling a well for oil was such a novel idea that the enterprise was called "Drake's Folly." On

414

August 27, 1859, oil was discovered in the 70-foot well. Few discoveries have had a more profound effect upon society.

With his 70-foot well, Drake probably never dreamed of our present wells drilled to depths of miles. He could not have foreseen the time when millions of barrels of crude oil would be produced daily in the United States.

In Drake's time, petroleum, or "crude oil," was considered valuable primarily for medicinal purposes and for obtaining kerosene for use in lamps. Then, as the automobile developed, it provided an almost limitless use for the petroleum product, *gasoline.* As demand increased, chemists developed the "cracking" method of refining oil, doubling the gasoline available from crude oil. Further research produced the gasoline of today, with higher octane ratings and a chemical make-up to reduce engine knocking and give greater power and fuel economy.

As with our other natural resources, we need to conserve natural gas and petroleum. If natural gas escapes unused into the air, or if oil is overproduced, an important natural wealth is wasted. The government and the petroleum industry now jointly determine policies and regulations in the interest of both the industry and the country. For, as a nation, we need careful conservation of petroleum, so vitally useful both in peace and war.

Methods of transporting petroleum have kept pace with the growth of the industry. Crude oil was first shipped in barrels, then in tank cars and tank vessels.

Fig. 268. "Drake's Folly" introduced a gigantic industry.

Later came the pipe lines, such as the Big Inch and Little Inch lines connecting the Texas fields with the Atlantic seaboard some 1,500 miles away.

At present, gasoline is the principal motor car fuel. A less-expensive diesel oil is increasingly used in large trucks and railroad locomotives. The possibility of exhaustion of our oil supply sometime in the future has stimulated research for the development and production of new kinds of fuel and new types of motors.

Petroleum research is an expanding new frontier of science. Developing new products and new uses is a challenge to petroleum technologists. Motor fuels and lubricants can be "tailored" to fit the engines in which they perform. In our lifetime, new miracles of fuel development and motor efficiency can be expected to result.

Just ahead lies the development and application of atomic power to peacetime industrial use. Who knows what this may mean to the future of transportation?

TO TALK ABOUT:

1   What are some of the advantages of conveyor systems and assembly lines?

2   Discuss the evolution in the general appearance and design of automobiles.

3   How are such features as smoothness, quietness, ease of operation, comfort, power, and convenience important to safety of operation?

Fig. 269. Oil refining has become a mighty business.

Discuss the importance of petroleum in our economic life.   4

Discuss the personal qualities of "pioneers" like Col. E. L.   5
Drake. In what fields are persons with such qualities most
needed today?

Discuss the importance to car owners of dependability,   6
economy, comfort, and safety, attractiveness, power, and
length of car life.

What special features add to the safety of cars?   7

TO DO:

Compare, point by point, an early model with a present-   1
day automobile. Arrange the items in parallel columns. Discuss the advances in automobile design.

Make a scrapbook of: (a) various makes and models of   2
passenger cars; (b) various types of commercial vehicles.

Look up and report on what is meant by "cracking" oil?   3

Find out more about "streamlining" and its relative im-   4
portance at various speeds. What would the front of a car
look like if the streamlining idea were fully applied?

Learn as much as you can about the research being car-   5
ried out on the nature of crash injuries. Discuss in class the
aims and methods of the studies.

TO LOOK UP:

A Chronicle of the Automotive Industry in America. Auto-
  mobile Manufacturers Association, Detroit, Michigan. Re-
  vised edition 1953. 68 pp.
Fill 'er Up! The Story of Fifty Years of Motoring. Partridge,
  Bellamy. McGraw-Hill Book Company, Inc., New York,
  New York. 1952. 235 pp.
Those Wonderful Old Automobiles. Clymer, Floyd. McGraw-
  Hill Book Company, Inc., New York, New York. 1953. 220
  pp.
What It Takes to Make Your Car. Automobile Manufacturers
  Association, Detroit, Michigan. 1950. 48 pp.   417

Fig. 270. Today's needs require modern roads.

MODERN ROADS ARE INDISPENSABLE

OUR motorized civilization requires well-built, modern roads. Good roads are necessary for business, public service, and defense activities, as well as for personal trips for pleasure and recreation.

We use highway transportation for many important purposes, such as:

▶ Business transactions
Movement of produce and all kinds of merchandise
Mass transportation of people
Delivery and pickup of mail
Protective services of physicians and police and fire departments
Governmental and military activities

Each highway should be planned and built to meet future traffic needs. Different uses require different kinds of roads. Some roads must be built to carry large volumes of traffic; others can be built for lighter traffic. Some need much heavier construction than others, because they serve large numbers of heavy, commercial

DO YOU KNOW:
How important roads are in American life?
What are the features of the best modern roads?
How seriously we need new and improved roads?
What problems face the highway engineer?
What we can expect in the highways of the future?

CHAPTER

23

HIGHWAYS FOR THE MOTOR AGE

vehicles. Some roads are important main arteries connecting cities, states, and regions. They must carry large volumes of through traffic and also serve local needs. Most roads, on the other hand, have the single job of serving local purposes.

ROADS have to be widened, straightened, paved, and improved in different ways. As funds permit, road engineers rebuild old, worn-out roads and build new ones designed to meet the needs of our time. Sometimes old two-lane roads cannot carry increased volumes of traffic without redesigning and widening into four-lane or even six-lane arteries. Sometimes it is more practical and less expensive to choose a new location and build an entirely new modern highway.

Roads Must Be Changed with Needs

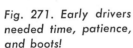
Fig. 271. Early drivers needed time, patience, and boots!

Before the automobile, people generally traveled only short distances and were mainly concerned with local roads. The automobile created demands for good roads for long trips. Congress made available Federal Aid grants to states for important roads; the Federal Government organized the Bureau of Public Roads; and state highway departments were formed. The few decades of the automobile have brought about very great changes in road design and construction to meet changing needs.

BUILDING BETTER ROADS

MAN has long known how to build roads that remain hard and reasonably smooth even in bad weather.

Two thousand years ago the Romans needed durable highways to bind their conquered territories together and to make possible the movement of military forces without delay. They built sturdy roads with strong foundations in which great blocks of stone were closely fitted together. Many were so well built that they have weathered the centuries. Some are used today. Tourists still drive along the historic Appian Way.

Foundations NEW modern methods are now used in building solid foundations and hard, water-tight surfaces.

In building a road over a new route, tree stumps, roots, large rocks, vegetation, and top soil are removed. Hillocks and high spots are cut away. Low places are filled in. The roadway is properly graded and planned for adequate drainage. Then a good, durable foundation is laid, many inches thick for better-type roads. Finally, surfacing is added.

Fig. 272. Model of the Appian Way, by the Bureau of Public Roads.

Fig. 273. Pouring and spreading concrete and finishing the surface.

MODERN road surfacing differs greatly, depending on the **Surfacing** importance of the road and on the traffic for which it is designed. Surfaces on minor roads may be of gravel or gravel topped with a mixture of sand and clay. More important minor roads may have layers of crushed stone, with large stones at the bottom, smaller ones above, and then be topped with chips of screenings. All layers are rolled solid. Oil is generally sprayed on the surface to keep down dust, help water run off, and hold the surface together. Asphalt or bituminous material is frequently used to bind the surface together.

A heavily-used road must have both a strong foundation and a well-built surface, in order to bear heavy loads, keep out water, and wear well. The surface may be of concrete, bituminous material, sheet asphalt, or stone block laid in cement. Experiments are now being made in which rubber is included in bituminous surfaces. And there is increasing interest in producing surfaces on which skidding will be greatly reduced. With today's

Fig. 274. A 3-lane highway violation such as this causes serious accidents.

traffic and speeds, no highway engineer wants to see signs reading "slippery when wet," especially on new or reconstructed roads.

Wider Pavements FASTER speeds and wider vehicles have made it necessary to increase lane widths. Twelve-foot lanes are now recommended for all important roads, with even greater widths on curves.

On busy highways, traffic volumes make two-lane roads inadequate. Passing with only one lane in each direction is difficult and dangerous. A third, or middle, lane has sometimes been added to be used exclusively for passing. But, with traffic heavy in both directions, there is too much competition for that middle lane, and where hillcrests, curves, and "dips" prevent seeing far enough ahead to pass with safety, the three-lane highway proves very dangerous. So most traffic specialists and highway engineers regard the three-lane road as an unsound design. Most widening is now done with from two to four lanes. And, happily, more and more four-lane divided highways are now built to assure separation between traffic in the two directions.

Longer Sight Distances THE FASTER you drive, the farther ahead you must see in order to stop safely, or to overtake and pass safely. Higher speeds make it dangerous to try to pass where hillcrests, curves, and "dips" can hide approaching cars. "Blind corners" are also dangerous at the speeds now traveled. Good highway design provides sufficiently long sight distances.

The American Association of State Highway Officials

finds that the minimum sight distance for passing should be 1,600 feet for a speed of 50 miles per hour and 2,300 feet for 60 mph. Even where passing is not permitted, you need long sight distances to stop safely in your own lane after seeing an obstacle blocking it. In building new roads and in bringing older ones up-to-date, plans have to be made for adequate sight distances.

Road Crowns

MOST older paved roads were crowned considerably higher in the middle than at the edges, as illustrated in Fig. 114, b, page 196. It was thought necessary to build them this way so that water would run off promptly. The lower crowns used in modern road design are much safer. Roads are now banked on curves according to the sharpness of the curve. This makes them safer and also easier to negotiate.

Divided Highways

A CENTER or median strip, separating the highway into two one-way roadways helps prevent head-on collisions, cutting-in crashes, and crashes caused by headlight glare. Accident studies show that separator strips are very valuable safety features.

For overtaking and passing, divided highways must have at least two lanes on each side of the center strip. Some divided highways have three, four, or even more, lanes on each side. Traffic volumes are becoming so much greater that many more divided highways must be constructed in the future.

Fig. 275. Divided highways need wide separator strips.

Other Road Improvements   OTHER improvements in modern roads include:

> Wider bridges
> Elimination of deep side ditches
> Gentle side slopes, making guard rails unnecessary, and reducing "ran-off-the-road" accidents
> Wider, firmer shoulders
> Better guard rails where needed
> Elimination of culvert headwalls near the paved surface
> Continuation of road "shoulders" under overhead bridges
> An extra paved lane on bridges
> An extra lane on steep upgrades for slow-moving vehicles
> Special stopping spaces or turnouts, for loading or unloading buses
> Widened and improved intersections
> Channelized intersections
> Underpasses and overpasses
> Grade separations at intersections

IMPROVEMENT OF INTERSECTIONS

IN CITIES, approximately one-half of all accidents occur at intersections. Even on rural roads, a great many accidents occur at road crossings.

To take care of heavy traffic, improvements such as the following are used at intersections:

> Traffic control devices, such as signals and stop signs
> Broader and less sharp curb lines, to make turns easier
> Isles of refuge for pedestrians, and channelizing islands to separate vehicles
> Longer sight distances
> Special lanes for right-turning traffic
> Long, wide approaches and exits, so that:
>> Drivers can get into proper positions for turns
>> Cars need not line up far behind the intersection, and can enter and leave intersections two or more abreast.

Two types of intersection design are especially important in modern highway engineering—the *traffic circle* and the *grade separation*.

Fig. 276. Traffic sorts itself out on a traffic circle.

TRAFFIC circles are intersections where all vehicles move counterclockwise around a large central island or circle. See Fig. 276. Drivers move around the circle until they come to the street they want and then turn right to leave the circle.

Well-designed traffic circles help reduce stopping and waiting at intersections. Unless circles become over-loaded, there is generally a "steady flow" instead of a stop-and-go. Properly-designed circles compel drivers to slow down. They eliminate right-angle conflicts. This re-duces intersection crashes in number or severity. Traffic circles are an improvement over the usual street inter-section, but they are not suitable for roads with very heavy traffic, where the only adequate solution is to separate traffic completely at intersections.

Many factors such as cost, grades, and available land have to be considered before a traffic circle is decided upon. Circles require considerable land and pavement, and this makes them much more costly than the usual type of intersection. Furthermore, if there are pedestrian crossings at the circle, the vehicular traffic is often de-layed or interrupted. Like any other traffic aid, circles must be properly designed and used only where they are appropriate.

Traffic Circles

425

Grade Separations WHERE busy traffic arteries cross, a type of intersection is needed that completely separates the traffic on the intersecting roads. This type is called a *grade separation.*

Fig. 277. A unique 4-level grade separation.

Traffic is kept moving by carrying one road over the other, just as a grade separation lifts a highway over a railway. This eliminates intersection collisions. At such an intersection, turns have to be made possible, and this sometimes makes the intersection seem complicated. The complete *cloverleaf* design and the *directional interchange* design eliminate all right-angle conflicts. Another design, the *diamond grade separation,* has its place also but does not eliminate left-turn conflicts. Study Figs. 278, 279, 280. Trace out, over the roads of each figure, the paths that cars would use in making right and left turns. Notice how conflicts that frequently cause delays and accidents are eliminated.

When traffic is heavy, over twice as much traffic can flow, without interruption, at a crossing when one road is carried over the other than through an ordinary intersection.

A *diamond grade separation,* as shown in Fig. 278, is a good design where a main artery crosses a lesser road and where left turns are not heavy. The connecting roads or ramps roughly form a diamond, although obstacles

426

such as streams or hills may somewhat change the shape. Left-turn conflicts remain, but they are moved from the main express artery to the cross road.

Fig. 278. A "diamond" grade separation.

The *cloverleaf intersection* shown in Fig. 279 makes turns possible in all directions without conflict. To turn left you go straight past the cross road and then make a right-turn loop.

Fig. 279. The cloverleaf makes a left turn possible by turns to the right.

Fig. 280. Making a left turn at a directional interchange.

A *directional interchange,* as shown in Fig. 280, is generally thought best for heavy turning traffic and at very important intersections. You change to another route merely by moving into the proper lane or ramp. This design is generally more costly than the other grade separation designs, because of the numerous bridges and the amount of land needed.

ENGINEERING THE HIGHWAY

HIGHWAY construction is costly. The location of the road is decided after careful study by engineers. Then the highway, bridges, intersections, and roadsides are designed and laid out on drawings. Complete specifications are written out, as a basis for competitive bidding and to make sure that the successful bidder builds exactly what is wanted.

Even before surveyors begin their work, the engineer must have many FACTS and make many decisions. How important is the road going to be during its road life? How much traffic must it be designed to carry? How much bus and heavy truck traffic will there be? How many lanes wide should it be? For what speed should it be designed? What type of pavement is needed? Should it be a divided highway? For what minimum sight dis-

428

tances should it be designed? What special intersections should there be? How much money should be spent for it? What will be the maintenance cost?

Challenging problems like these show why highway engineers must be highly trained and experienced. The public loses money unless it insists that highway planning, design, and construction be done and supervised only by experts.

Large sums must be spent for a good foundation, a well-constructed and paved surface, drainage needs, shoulders, guard rails, bridges, highway sidewalks where needed, and roadside grading and planting to avoid erosion and to make highway and roadside more attractive.

A mile of new, high-type, concrete-surfaced highway, two lanes wide, with grading, and built in average, open country, costs about $80,000. Divided expressways cost much more. The purchase price for land on which a road is built can vary from a moderate amount in undeveloped rural areas to hundreds of thousands of dollars per mile in built-up areas.

After a highway is completed, it must be well kept up to protect the investment. Bad shoulders, worn or broken surfaces, and eroding side slopes must be kept in repair. Administration and maintenance add to the heavy costs of modern highways.

Construction of city streets requires additional expenses for curbs, sewers, and sidewalks, and to make way for water and gas pipes, lighting cables, and other utilities under the surface.

ROAD RESEARCH

GROUPS like the state highway departments, the United States Bureau of Public Roads, and the Highway Research Board collect facts, conduct researches, and develop improved road-building methods. Sometimes they make use of university research centers. Research helps highway administrators get the most for the highway dollar. New facts and better methods are constantly being sought on all road and traffic subjects.

In recent years, some states have been making thorough studies of their own highway needs. They study their total road systems. They try to learn what roads are needed to take care of present and estimated future needs. These studies are called State Highway Planning Surveys and are made with the cooperation of the United States Bureau of Public Roads. States also study the way their highways are now financed, and how they should be financed in the future to be fair to all. Some states study their own highway laws, and decide what changes should be made to bring them up-to-date. Such surveys and studies are important in helping decide what roads are needed, what governmental agency should be responsible for them, and how much money should be spent on them.

State and federal officials have developed origin-destination traffic surveys for city areas. Home owners throughout a city are interviewed to find out where and how they traveled on a certain day. Engineers use the findings to help them select route locations for city arteries so they will best serve the largest number of people.

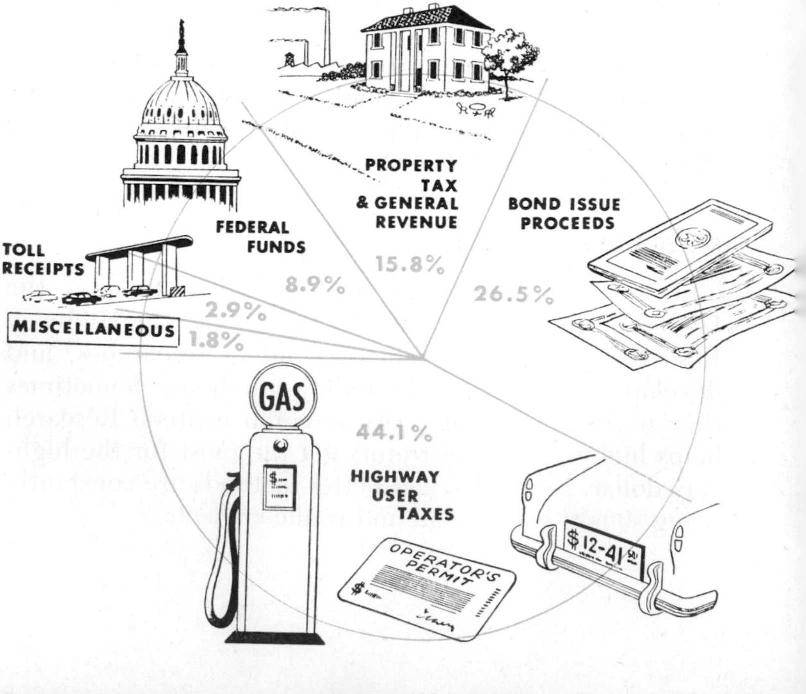

Fig. 281. Sources of funds for highways.

PROPERTY
TAX
& GENERAL
REVENUE

BOND ISSUE
PROCEEDS

FEDERAL
FUNDS

15.8%

TOLL
RECEIPTS

8.9%

2.9%

26.5%

MISCELLANEOUS 1.8%

GAS

44.1%

HIGHWAY
USER
TAXES

OPERATOR'S
PERMIT

$12-41

430

HIGHWAY FINANCING

EACH STATE administers and has the chief responsibility for financing its major highway systems. Counties and cities generally finance their lesser rural roads and city streets. In some cases, state grants are made to help in the road work of counties and cities. For a long time, the U.S. Congress has appropriated considerable funds to aid states in building important highways. The state, counties, and cities which benefit must agree to maintain all such roads in proper condition.

In the early days, when traffic was almost entirely local in nature, road building was financed mainly by taxes on real estate. As motor traffic became less local, states started taxing highway users for part of the cost of highways. The gasoline tax, started by Oregon in 1919, proved a popular means of getting motorists to share road costs. Motorists themselves suggested this tax in order to get better roads. It is unusual for a tax to be suggested by those who must pay it.

Today, motor fuel taxes, vehicle registration tag fees, and driver license fees amount annually to billions of dollars and are the principal sources of funds for building and maintaining roads. But some of these special taxes paid by motorists have been used for non-highway purposes.

The taxes paid by motorists are badly needed for highway improvements. During World War II, materials and labor needed for roads had to be used largely for war purposes. At the end of the war, thousands of miles of highway were, therefore, urgently in need of reconstruction and improvement. After this long neglect and with increasing traffic volumes, improved highways are sorely needed in many places. The entire country now faces a tremendous job of catching up in providing highways fitted to modern needs. It is, therefore, urgent that all special motorist taxes be used for road purposes.

Motorist taxes should be used chiefly on roads of general use and those which carry considerable traffic, such as major rural highways and principal through-arteries

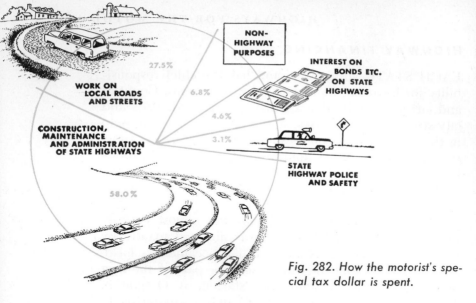

Fig. 282. How the motorist's special tax dollar is spent.

in cities. When determining how tax funds should be distributed, it should be remembered that half or more of gasoline tax funds result from city driving, since half or more of all road traffic is in cities or their suburbs. Lesser roads and streets, which are built chiefly to serve the properties along them, should be paid for principally by general taxation, rather than by special motorist taxes.

A LOOK TO THE FUTURE

HIGHWAY engineers must continue to find ways, through research, of making the highway dollar do more in providing good, modern roads and streets. They also need public support in overcoming the efforts sometimes made by special interest groups to have highway money spent in places and on roads where studies show the expenditure is not justified.

Expressways EXPRESSWAYS, or "controlled-access highways," will be used much more in the future. They are, however, so costly to construct and maintain that they can be built only on routes where traffic volumes are very heavy.

Expressways eliminate interruption from cross traffic

or entering vehicles. You can enter and leave express-ways only at locations selected and planned by highway authorities. These access points, usually known as "inter-changes," use grade separations and other special fea-tures. All cross traffic goes over or under the express lanes.

On expressways, many hazards of the ordinary high-way are eliminated. No vehicles enter the road at unex-pected places. Restaurants, garages, and filling stations are limited in number and their locations carefully planned and controlled. So cars are not turning into or out of the fast traffic lanes just anywhere and every-where along the way. There are no intersecting private driveways. No local traffic interferes, because private property owners along expressways are provided, where warranted, with service roads which lead to inter-changes.

Expressways are built with central dividing strips, wide lanes, long sight distances, easy curves and grades, and high-quality paving.

Modern expressways should produce very low acci-dent rates. On one major parkway, which is an express-way not open to commercial vehicles, the traffic death rate, in its first four years of operation, was only one-third as high as the rate for the nation as a whole during the same period. A city expressway had only one-fourth as many accidents as streets with similar traffic volumes in the same city.

Expressways have some hazards of their own. Speeds tend to become excessive. When accidents do occur, cars tend to pile up fast, and many may be injured in the same accident. Driving on an expressway is so easy on

Fig. 283. Hollywood Freeway.

the driver that sometimes it becomes monotonous. Then drivers may become inattentive or even fall asleep. Also, driving at fast, even speeds for long distances tends to make some drivers become "velocitized." That is, they grow less aware of the speed at which they are driving. Then, when they come to situations where they need reduced speed, they may think they are slowing down a lot and still be driving much too fast for changed conditions.

Know what the special driving dangers are on expressways; keep them in mind; avoid the typical expressway accidents.

National System of Interstate Highways AFTER Congress passed the Federal Aid Highway Act of 1944, the state highway departments, the United States Bureau of Public Roads, and the Defense Department complied with a provision of the Act and worked together to select a limited network of the most important, most used routes in the nation. These routes were designated as the National System of Interstate Highways.

When completed, this system will connect most of our principal cities. It is estimated that, while making up only a little over one per cent of our highway mileage, this system will carry over 20 per cent of our traffic. It

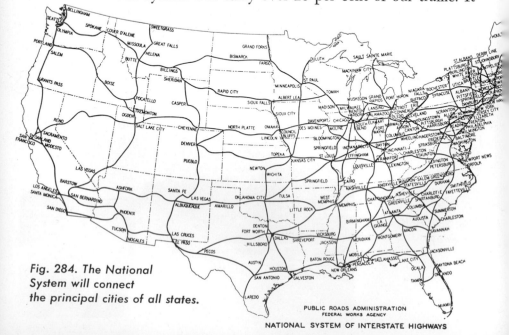

Fig. 284. The National System will connect the principal cities of all states.

PUBLIC ROADS ADMINISTRATION
FEDERAL WORKS AGENCY

NATIONAL SYSTEM OF INTERSTATE HIGHWAYS

will form a basic national network of highways of greatest value to the nation both in peacetime and in case of war.

The roads in this system are being built differently in different sections of the country to take care of varying needs. But they will all have easy grades, long sight distances, easy curves, and wide lane widths. In heavily-populated areas and over heavily-used routes, there will be divided expressways, some with extra lanes.

Costs of some of the roads in the system will be very high. This is especially true in heavily-populated areas. It is very important to find adequate funds for this national interstate system. It is needed for the economic development of our nation, and should war come, it would be of greatest importance for defense. The Federal Aid Highway Act of 1954 fortunately earmarked for this network $175,000,000 a year for the following two years. But much larger amounts will have to be spent on this network if it is to be completed even by such a distant target date as 1970.

National Defense

FOR national defense, a special priority system of highways must be assured for military use. Expressways and other special highways in and through city areas and between key defense areas would be critically needed for defense.

Highways linking the countries of the entire Western Hemisphere are also highly important. They would not only bind together the peoples of the Americas, but they would prove highly valuable in both the economic development of the countries and in their military security.

Future Research

OUR country has led the world in road research. This research has saved millions of dollars and countless lives.

No longer can any old road be improved and used. For the future, we need more accurate knowledge about how roads should be built for increased speeds and heavier traffic loads. We can secure this knowledge only by extensive, thorough, and continuous research.

Groups like the United States Bureau of Public Roads,

435

the Highway Research Board, the states, and other interested organizations must continue their research on the many problems of the modern highway. For this research work, as well as for other highway work, many more well-trained engineers are needed, with technical knowledge on highways and broad vision for the needs of the future. Here are good vocational fields for young people to consider.

TO TALK ABOUT:

1 Why are many present roads unsuited to today's traffic needs? How critical is this situation? Select some road your group knows and discuss what might be done to modernize it.

2 Debate: "We can't afford the great amount of money required to correct road hazards. Instead, drivers should suit their driving to road conditions."

3 Debate: "Special motorist taxes should be used only for highway purposes."

4 Discuss the interest of the Federal Government in developing a highway system. Can you justify Federal Aid for highways? If so, how, and for what classes of roads.

5 Discuss the part played by toll roads in the early development of our highways. Why has the toll method of financing roads again come into prominent use? Explain why you think tolls for expressways are or are not justified.

6 What are some of the most urgent needs for the roads of the future?

TO DO:

1 Collect pictures of traffic circles, cloverleafs, diamond grade separations, and "directional interchange" intersections. Make diagrams of these intersections, sketching in the route to be followed in making every possible kind of turn.

2 Using Fig. 282 as a pattern, make and discuss a similar "tax dollar" distribution chart for your state.

On a map of your county, indicate with blue pencil the **3** well-paved roads of ten years ago. With a red pencil, show roads which have since been well paved. Discuss the map in class, deciding what roads seem to need special attention.

Find the cost of construction for improved highways in **4** your vicinity. Calculate the cost per mile and per foot. Make a chart showing name of highway, length of highway, type of construction, average cost per mile, average cost per foot. Discuss this chart in class.

Find how some concrete highway in your area was con- **5** structed. What kind of foundation has it? How thick is the concrete layer? Are steel reinforcing rods used?

Construct a model or make a large drawing showing the **6** steps in the construction of a modern concrete highway.

Find what has been done in your state with the Highway **7** Planning Survey. Discuss its value in class.

Find, if possible, a road in your vicinity that originated as **8** an Indian trail, pioneer pathway, or early connecting link between important points. Investigate the history of this road. Write out its "life-story" as a script for radio or television.

TO LOOK UP:

Highway Practice in the United States. Bureau of Public Roads. Purchase from Government Printing Office, Washington, D.C. 1949. 230 pp.

Highways for Our National Life. A symposium, edited by Jean Labatut and Wheaton J. Lane, Princeton University Press, New York, New York. 1950. 475 pp.

Highways in the United States. Bureau of Public Roads. Purchase from Government Printing Office, Washington, D.C. 1954. 22 pp.

Toll Roads and the Problem of Highway Modernization. Owen, Wilfred and Dearing, Charles L. The Brookings Institution, Washington, D.C. 1951. 204 pp.

CHAPTER 24

MANAGING

TRAFFIC ENGINEERING FOR THE MOTOR AGE

WHEN sound traffic engineering is applied to traffic problems, guesswork is out. Improvements are made only after FACTS are gathered to point the way.

Good traffic engineering gives us orderly and efficient traffic flow. It increases safety and convenience for all of us.

Here is an example of a traffic regulation based on guesswork, before a careful study of the local situation was made. Parking in the central district of a large city was causing serious traffic delay and congestion. What should be done? The City Council passed an ordinance eliminating daytime parking in an area of nearly two square miles. See A in Fig. 285. This regulation did not work. It was so unreasonable that, before long, folks were violating it. The police realized that such a wide no-parking area was unnecessary. Furthermore, they were "short-handed" for officers to enforce the regulation. So they tagged cars on some streets but not on others. Confusion and complaints resulted.

Fig. 285. A. Unnecessary parking restrictions made before the study. B. Suitable restrictions made after the study.

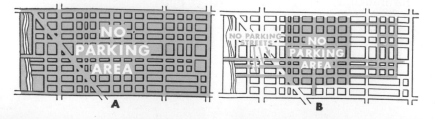

DO YOU KNOW:
Why traffic engineering is needed?
How traffic engineers improve traffic situations?
What traffic engineers need to know?

MODERN TRAFFIC

The city then employed a traffic engineer. One of his first jobs was to straighten out the downtown parking situation. First he gathered FACTS. He considered such things as: street widths, traffic volume, speeds of cars on various streets during both light-traffic and "peak" hours, the demand for parking, loading needs for commercial vehicles, the number of streetcars or buses using various streets, and many other facts that an engineer must have. He then recommended no parking in a much smaller area and on certain major streets. See B in Fig. 285. As a result, confusion and discrimination ended, and a good, logical solution was found for a bad traffic condition. This time the parking regulation was based on FACTS.

Traffic engineering means far more than mounting signs and signals and marking streets. It means planning the safest and most efficient use of streets and highways and of parking and loading facilities. It means applying knowledge of traffic and of the way drivers and pedestrians act. The traffic engineer determines how much traffic a street or intersection can carry at peak hours. He makes studies of the origins and destinations of vehicles, and plots most favorable routes. He spends much effort on preventing accidents. He redesigns intersections and highways so they will meet modern traffic needs. He helps plan the streets and highways of the future. 439

Fig. 286. We must find ways to eliminate delay and congestion.

Railroads and transit companies operate their transportation systems with the help of engineers to work out routings, schedules, stopping and loading points, terminal facilities, and accident prevention measures. Cities and states also need engineers to help operate their vast street and highway transportation systems.

The value of traffic engineering has been proved in many localities. A properly installed signal system and improved parking regulations in the Chicago Loop district reduced accidents about one-fifth and speeded up traffic about 50 per cent. Marked traffic lanes on a major artery in Philadelphia increased the number of vehicles which could use the street in peak hours by about one-third. The first year's operation of the signal system on North Broad Street in Philadelphia reduced fatalities from twenty-three to eleven. At a rural junction of two important highways in Michigan, accidents were reduced 65 per cent after proper signs were installed. In Los Angeles, proper channelizing islands and signals greatly reduced fatalities. In Baltimore, traffic accidents were reduced from 10 to 15 per cent through the proper use of one-way streets. In another city, retail sales increased 27 per cent after a one-way street plan was installed. We get good results when we approach traffic problems after learning FACTS.

Fig. 287. Accident reports help the traffic engineer correct conditions.

THE CITY TRAFFIC ENGINEER AT WORK

TRAFFIC engineers make much use of accident records. Let's see how they use them.

ONE job of the traffic engineer is to correct conditions that cause repeated accidents at the same locations. He first finds out where the worst accident locations are. Accident *spot maps* help him do this. Clusters of spots on such a map as you see in Fig. 288 indicate places where accidents are frequent. Accident records also help. They are filed by the location of each crash, and after a time a "worst corner" list is prepared, as shown in Fig. 289.

Accident Prevention

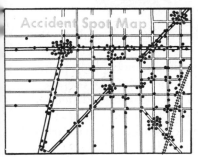

Fig. 288. An accident spot map and a collision diagram.

After a "worst corner" has been located, the question is: "*Why* does this or that intersection have so many crashes?" Clues to the answer must be found. A "collision diagram" is made, showing the directions of movement of vehicles and pedestrians involved in the accidents, the times of day or night, the times of year, and other helpful facts. See Fig. 288. All these *facts* are then analyzed for clues to the trouble.

After the trouble at "worst corners" is spotted, the traffic engineer works out remedies. This may mean removal of a sight obstruction at a corner, such as a high fence, shrubbery, or billboard. It may be necessary to install one or more stop signs or islands to cause vehicles to move in a more orderly way and to aid pedestrians. In other places, stop-and-go signals may be needed. The best remedy is the one which corrects the situation with

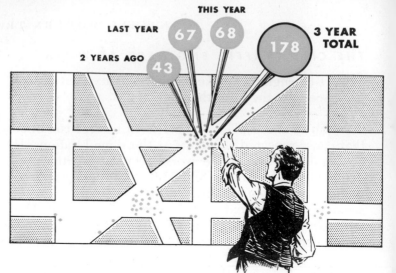

LAST YEAR 67 68 THIS YEAR

2 YEARS AGO 43

178 3 YEAR TOTAL

Fig. 289. "Worst corners" for accidents are spotted and remedies found.

the least interference to traffic movement and at the least cost.

Again using accident facts, traffic engineers help police officials assign their men where they can do the most good in preventing accidents. They recommend needed regulations. They supply material for traffic education. Drivers and pedestrians who are careful to prepare complete and accurate reports when they are involved in traffic accidents help traffic engineers in this accident prevention work.

Traffic Signs and Signals TRAFFIC engineers determine the need for signs and signals. They decide what types should be used, how they should guide or control traffic, and then install them.

Signs cause confusion if they are not standardized or if they are set up in the wrong places. Standard signs should be used; those that apply to hours of darkness should be fully visible at night; they should be placed only where *facts* show they are really needed; they should be installed in standard positions. If they are too high, hidden by branches, or not properly installed, they can actually be "crash-breeders."

Traffic control or "stop-and-go" signals can help conditions at intersections, or they can cause needless delay, irritation, and accidents. If installed by guesswork, they may fail to reduce accidents or to improve traffic flow.

Three studies have shown that signals installed at intersections without the services of competent engineers and without proper study of facts actually *increased* accidents in about 30 per cent of the cases and made *no improvement* in about 15 per cent.

The method by which the signal is controlled should also be decided by an engineer. There are two main types of signals: (1) those operated by electric clockwork; (2) those operated by the traffic itself. Most signals are of the first type. The length of the complete cycle of green, yellow, and red lights is determined by a clock. There are ingenious ways by which the length of the "stop" and "go" periods can be caused to change automatically for traffic needs at different times of day.

Some signals, called "traffic actuated," are controlled by the passage of vehicles over devices in the pavement. Such signals regulate "go" intervals according to vehicular traffic demands. At some locations, pedestrians can request a "go" interval by pressing a push button.

Properly engineered traffic signals are a great help to drivers. Have you ever driven along an "artery" with so many signals on it that you have to stop constantly for red lights? On the other hand, have you driven through a "progressive" signal system and been pleased by the way each signal changed to green as you approached, provided you drove at the speed for which the system was timed, as described on p. 289? What makes the difference? In the first case, no adequate study had been made of how to get the best movement along the artery. The signals at each intersection operated independently. They were not "tied together" into a signal system. In the second case, traffic engineering had been used.

TRAFFIC control signals should fit the needs of pedestrians as well as drivers. Signals which apply to pedestrians should be placed directly in the pedestrians' line of vision. Both the order of signal indications and the length of time each signal in the cycle shows should fit the pedestrians' needs.

Pedestrian Signals

443

Fig. 290. WALK and DONT WALK signals give the pedestrian a safe time for crossing.

Pedestrians are more likely to obey signals when the time allowed for a complete change of signals is fairly short. If the cycle of changes is too long and motor traffic is not continuously using the intersection, pedestrians may grow impatient and cross against the signal. However, if the cycle is too short, pedestrians have too little time for crossing, and also vehicular traffic gets tied up. The timing of the cycle is very important.

Many cities have WAIT and WALK signals for pedestrians at busy intersections. The WALK signal usually shows during only the earlier part of the green GO signal for cars, so that pedestrians will not start to cross too late and be caught in the roadway when the light changes. At busy pedestrian crossings, the WALK signal may show only when all vehicular signals are red. Such an "exclusive pedestrian interval" assures pedestrians time to cross with no interference from turning cars. However, this kind of signal cycle gives less time to vehicles. So it is used only where careful study shows it should be used. For complete protection, the WALK signal should be followed by a WAIT or DON'T WALK signal.

444

Fig. 291. A "traffic flow" map shows which streets carry heavy traffic.

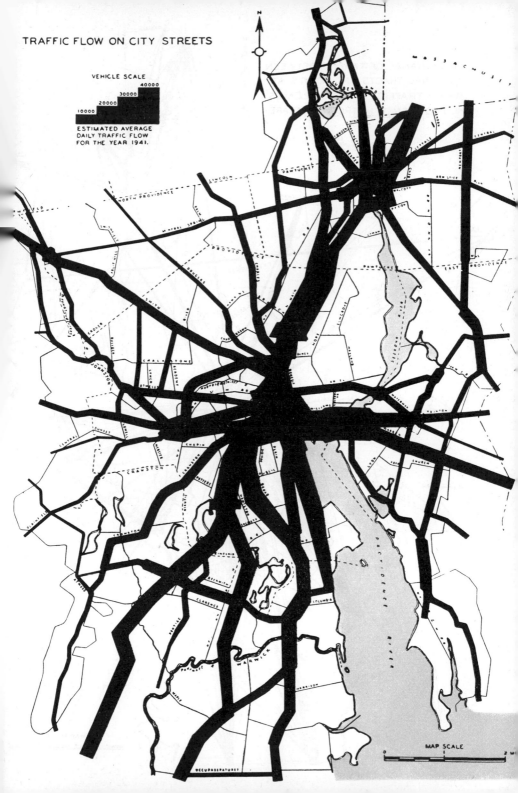

TRAFFIC FLOW ON CITY STREETS

VEHICLE SCALE

40000
30000
20000
10000

ESTIMATED AVERAGE
DAILY TRAFFIC FLOW
FOR THE YEAR 1941.

MAP SCALE

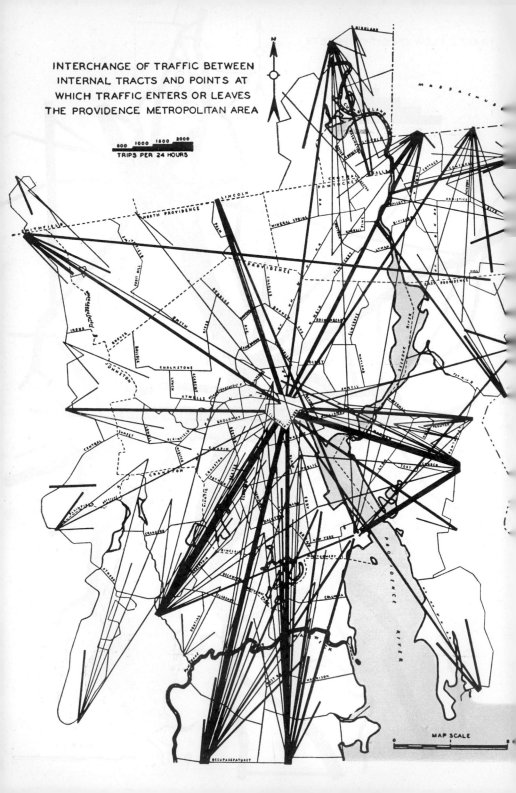

INTERCHANGE OF TRAFFIC BETWEEN
INTERNAL TRACTS AND POINTS AT
WHICH TRAFFIC ENTERS OR LEAVES
THE PROVIDENCE METROPOLITAN AREA

800 1000 1500 2000
TRIPS PER 24 HOURS

MAP SCALE

At places where there are schools, factories, or sports centers and pedestrian traffic is heavy only at certain times, pedestrian WALK signals that can be "demanded" by a push button are sometimes used. When a pedestrian pushes a button on a post at the curb, the signal changes in his favor after a pre-determined interval for vehicles. After an interval during which pedestrians are to cross the street, the signal automatically changes back in favor of motor traffic.

Routing Traffic

DID you ever drive in a city that seemed to have stop signs everywhere? The trouble may be that an untrained official assumed that the way to reduce accidents was to install stop signs wherever there was complaint of danger. Or he may have set up entirely too many "through streets" with stop signs at all cross streets.

Studies prove that excessive "through streets" set up by guesswork often increase accidents. Some drivers decide there is no need for so many stops and violate the signs.

A sound "through street" plan requires careful study. A vehicular flow map is made to show which streets carry the most vehicles. On such a map, as shown in Fig. 291, the wider the black band, the more vehicles use the street.

In planning a sound "through street" system, traffic engineers consider such things as traffic volumes, mass transportation routes, street widths, road surface conditions, cross traffic, vehicle speeds, and how to help through traffic by-pass congested sections. Out-of-town drivers, who want to get through a city quickly and conveniently, appreciate good "through street" planning. Carefully routing such traffic also helps reduce congestion in busy areas. Most traffic approaching all but very small cities, however, has its destination in the city and this also must be taken into consideration. Planning a "through street" system is a job that can be adequately handled only by a trained traffic engineer.

447

Fig. 292. A chart showing principal origins and destinations of traffic helps engineers plan for traffic needs.

Fig. 293. Channelizing islands help both pedestrians and drivers.

Good Engineering at Intersections TRAFFIC engineering is needed in designing and redesigning intersections. The best solution for a particular location can be found only after an engineering study.

Have you ever entered an unfamiliar, irregularly-shaped intersection that had so much roadway area that you were puzzled about where to drive? Badly designed intersections such as that can cause confusion, delay, and accidents. Good traffic engineering avoids or corrects bad intersection design.

Fig. 294. Before and after installation of channelizing islands.

"Channelizing islands" often help at intersections. In Fig. 294, notice that left turns cannot be made except around islands. When such islands are properly located the correct way is the natural and safe way to turn. Well-planned channels reduce the number of points where turning cars could come into conflict with other vehicles and pedestrians.

Raised islands, such as you see in Fig. 293, are much better than painted lines.

PROPERLY-designed loading islands give pedestrians protection while entering, leaving, or waiting for a streetcar or bus. Various types are used. Sometimes the loading island, or safety zone, is simply outlined with steel posts and chains. Raised loading islands, constructed of concrete, wood, or steel, give the best protection to pedestrians. *Loading Islands and Safety Zones*

The length of safety zones is determined by the number of streetcars or buses which must load and unload at the same time. The zones are usually about 4 feet wide and 5 to 7 inches high. Some of them have barriers to separate the platform from vehicle lanes. Then pedestrians have to enter and leave at the crosswalk end. This type of loading island protects pedestrians, keeps the traffic pattern orderly, permits drivers to proceed without unnecessary interruption, and reduces loading and unloading time for streetcars and buses.

PEDESTRIAN crosswalks are provided and maintained to encourage the pedestrian to cross only at carefully selected locations. They are marked by paint, buttons, or other pavement inserts. Crosswalks are generally about as wide as the sidewalks of which they are extensions. At busy crossings, they may be somewhat wider. *Crosswalks*

At some places, traffic engineers find it necessary to mark off mid-block crosswalks. Such crosswalks, where used at night, must be marked especially clearly and be well illuminated, so they will be clearly recognized in advance by drivers who do not ordinarily expect them in

449

mid-block. Such special crosswalk lines should be 24 to 30 inches wide.

England and other European countries mark crosswalks by the more conspicuous "zebra" design shown in Fig. 295.

Fig. 295. "Zebra" pedestrian walks in Rotterdam, Holland.

Barriers of chain, pipe, or rope are sometimes erected along the curb adjacent to crosswalks at exceptionally dangerous places to assure use of crosswalks and to prevent "jay walking." Notice the barriers in Fig. 296.

Pedestrian Tunnels and Overpasses HEAVY pedestrian traffic frequently conflicts with heavy vehicular traffic at or near sports areas, schools, factories, beaches, parks, and business centers. At such a location, traffic engineers sometimes advise a pedestrian tunnel or overpass. Either one completely removes the danger of traffic accidents, if pedestrians cooperate by using it. Approaches to tunnels or overpasses built with ramps rather than stairs are more popular with pedestrians and bicyclists. However, ramps require more space because grades of ramps must be gradual.

450

Fig. 296. Chain barriers help protect pedestrians.

Pedestrian tunnels and overpasses are costly, but the expenditure at certain locations can be justified by the saving of lives, the prevention of pedestrian injuries, and the elimination of traffic delay. Unfortunately, it is often necessary for police to enforce their use, or fences or other barriers are needed to prevent pedestrians from crossing at the roadway level. See Fig. 297.

OLD residential districts were usually laid out in rectangular, "checkerboard" design with no protection against through traffic. With this kind of street plan, as traffic becomes too heavy for one street, some of it moves over to a parallel street which motorists find will take them straight through toward their destination. More and more motorists find this less-used route and decide to use it to avoid heavy traffic. In this way, what was once

Safeguarding Residential Areas

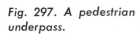

Fig. 297. A pedestrian underpass.

a quiet residential street becomes another busy, noisy, secondary artery.

The street then loses its attractiveness to residence owners. Hazards to both drivers and pedestrians are increased. Children must cross more busy streets to go to schools and playgrounds. Residents get tired of noise, fumes, dirt, and heavy traffic. Many sell their homes, even at a loss, and move to a quieter, more pleasant location. Corner stores and gasoline filling stations often appear, attracted by the heavier traffic. The value of residential properties drops.

The old checkerboard layout of residential districts was all right for horse-and-buggy days. But something quite different is needed for the motor age.

Fig. 298 shows part of the plan of a residential community designed for the motor age. The wide, central general-traffic artery serves through traffic. Secondary arteries serve traffic to and from the residences. In some cases, small "turn-around" circles serve traffic to residences. Narrow, dead-end roadways lead from the secondary arteries to parking courts at the backs of residences. Delivery trucks use these service roadways, and family garages are entered from them. All through traffic by-passes the residential areas.

Good community engineering such as this means safety, convenience, and beauty. It preserves property

Fig. 298. A residential area designed for the Motor Age.

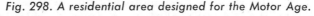

values in residential areas. Houses front on private park-like areas with foot paths conveniently located. No vehicular traffic roars by. Children go to school or playgrounds without crossing a vehicular roadway because the plan includes underpasses and overpasses for pedestrians. This is the kind of modern planning in residential areas that appeals to citizens of this Motor Age.

WITH today's traffic conditions, street play is extremely **Play Places** dangerous. Most child pedestrian deaths and injuries occur to children playing in streets or entering the roadway while at play. The remedy is suitable play places, to *keep children off the streets.*

Children under six need play yards in their own block. Older children need larger play areas, such as playgrounds and parks.

Progressive traffic engineers encourage community playgrounds, with sandboxes, teeters, swings, and other equipment. They use accident facts and other data to determine where playgrounds are most needed. They locate play areas where they can be reached with a minimum of danger, and design barriers in front of exits to prevent children from running carelessly from playgrounds into streets.

Where separate play places are not available, "play streets" can be blocked off, during play hours, to all traffic except that going to places within the block.

TRAFFIC engineers encourage and often help design **Street Lighting** proper street lighting which has a close relationship to night traffic accidents to both pedestrians and motorists, as many studies show.

Standards are now available for safe, effective traffic lighting. Scientific methods can be used to determine how efficient the lighting is on any street and how nearly it approaches correct standards. Greatly improved street lighting units are available. When they are properly spaced and mounted high, they give much better uniformity of illumination and a lighting efficiency not possible a few years ago.

453

Fig. 299. Before and after efficient street lighting.

All too few city streets now measure up to satisfactory standards of lighting. Streets, especially those carrying heavy traffic, need modern lighting, properly installed under the supervision of trained engineers.

Where Shall We Park? WHERE to park is a major question in most communities today. Vehicular traffic grows heavier and heavier, and street space available for parking becomes smaller and smaller. More street space is needed for loading and unloading, and for the movement of vehicles. Even where curb parking is still permitted, parking time has to be limited to enable more drivers to use the space.

Most cities have numerous parking lots, but usually they do not supply enough space. More and more cities are providing for storage of vehicles *off the streets*. Multi-level parking structures are increasing. Two such parking garages are shown in Fig. 300. Such buildings provide car storage space on several floors.

454

City traffic engineers study parking needs and help develop sound plans for off-street parking facilities. They recommend location, size, and type of parking areas. They study the locations of entrances and exits, which can cause serious congestion if poorly located. Property owners who want to develop off-street parking facilities make valuable use of such engineering studies.

Fig. 300. Urban off-street parking.

Traffic engineers working with the city planning agency, the city engineer, and property owners, can provide the facts and forecasts needed in developing good parking plans and programs.

City Parking Boards are often set up. They consider proposed plans and programs, decide which to adopt, sponsor helpful state laws and city ordinances, and consider how the financing should be done. Sometimes such Boards merely advise. Sometimes they carry out the plans and programs.

Adequate parking facilities are of great value to merchants, property owners, and the general public. They stimulate business and add to downtown property values. This, in turn, pays off to the city in good tax revenues. City parking is such an important matter that it should not be allowed to drift along without expert attention.

455

Fig. 301. Highway sidewalks help protect pedestrians.

TRAFFIC ENGINEERING IN RURAL AREAS

TRAFFIC engineers are needed in rural areas as well as in cities. They take care of such matters as collecting facts, determining how accidents can be reduced, erecting warning and guide signs, installing signals and pavement marking, determining no-passing zones and speed zones, and providing advice on highway design problems related to traffic.

Thousands of pedestrians are killed and injured on suburban and rural roadways. Well-engineered highway sidewalks safeguard pedestrians. Such walkways are needed in the outer sections of cities and towns, near schools located at the edges of towns, and wherever pedestrian traffic is heavy. Highway sidewalks should have hard, smooth surfaces, should be carried across side roads which become muddy or rutted in bad weather, and should be kept clear of snow, mud, leaves, or trash.

Fig. 302. Lengthening the sight distance reduces the hazard.

Yet only a very small mileage of highway sidewalks exists today. In six months after Massachusetts constructed 500 miles of walks along main highways, pedestrian fatalities in the areas dropped 31 per cent. This is an example of the value of good engineering.

Rural no-passing zones need to be clearly determined and marked. After speed zoning is worked out scientifically, speed signs that are clearly visible both day and night should be put up. Rural danger points where accidents occur, or are likely to occur, should be hunted out and remedied to reduce rural accidents. Rural intersections should be designed on the basis of traffic engineering studies. Such rural road improvements are problems for the engineer.

TRAFFIC ENGINEERING AS A VOCATION

TODAY, many cities, states, and counties employ engineers who devote full time to traffic matters. The future will see the number increase. Opportunities will grow for men who are especially prepared for this profession.

Every city of over 50,000 population needs full-time traffic engineering. The Federal Government employs traffic engineers. So also do safety organizations and semi-private and private organizations, such as transit companies, insurance groups, automobile associations, and consulting engineering firms. As traffic volumes grow and speeds increase, there are more demands for trained engineers to reduce congestion, improve traffic flow, and cut down accidents.

Opportunities increase for the special training of traffic engineers. Several universities now offer special courses dealing with traffic problems. Yale University, in its Bureau of Highway Traffic, offers a nine-month graduate course in traffic engineering. The Institute of Transportation and Traffic Engineering at the University of California provides under-graduate and graduate training. Other universities and colleges offer short courses to give specialized traffic engineering training for engineers already employed. Here is a good occupation for interested and trained young men.

TO TALK ABOUT:

1   Does your city have traffic engineering service? Your state? If so, what results do you see in your community? Along your state highways?

2   Under what conditions is automatic traffic-signal control better than police officer control? Find out and discuss the advantages and disadvantages of each type.

3   Discuss various ways of managing traffic at intersections to reduce congestion and accidents.

4   Discuss the advantages and disadvantages of "through streets" in cities.

5   What things that a traffic engineer would attend to should be done in your community to safeguard pedestrians? Discuss what your state has done or should do regarding sidewalks along rural highways.

6   What has to be considered before deciding whether a pedestrian island is needed at a certain location?

7   Are the school children in your community properly protected when going to and from schools? When at play? Discuss the need for better protection and control at certain actual locations. How can faster progress be made in protecting the children in your community?

8   Do your local engineering facilities encourage sound pedestrian practices? Explain.

TO DO:

1   Find out what important traffic studies your community has made in the last few years. What are the findings and recommendations? What has been done about them?

Obtain or make an accident spot map of your community **2** showing all accidents that occurred during the past year or six months. The type of accident should be shown by the size, shape, or color of the spot. Visit points where repeated accidents occurred. Can your group suggest remedies?

Study intersections in your neighborhood where there have **3** been repeated accidents or where brakes are always screeching. Discuss at which ones the accident situation might be improved by cutting down a hedge, trimming low branches of a tree, installing channelizing islands, or some other means.

Secure or make a street diagram of a business area of **4** your city. Indicate in red the no-parking zones along these streets. Indicate in blue the restricted parking zones. Ask your traffic engineer or a traffic officer for comments on the parking problems in these areas. What off-street parking facilities are there in the downtown area? Are they adequate?

Secure or prepare a map of the main highways near and **5** entering your community. Show how through traffic could by-pass the city. Find out what proportion of the traffic wishes to by-pass.

Make a survey of traffic signs and signals in your town or **6** city or along major highways in your community. Prepare a report on how well they are designed, installed, standardized, operated, and maintained.

What has your city, county, or state done towards providing highway sidewalks? As a group, plan some action on this **7** subject that you think might be taken and ask an appropriate official to come and discuss it.

Build a model or make drawings of an irregular street **8** intersection in your community to show: (1) dangers to both motorists and pedestrians; (2) the way in which these dangers have been, or could be, lessened, as, for example, by installing islands. Invite an appropriate city official to come and discuss this with your group.

9   Design and draw a plan for adapting some undeveloped area of your city to suit the motor age. Reduce pedestrian and vehicular conflict as much as possible. Plan for adequate playgrounds and traffic control devices.

TO LOOK UP:

How to Get the Most Out of Our Streets. Chamber of Commerce of the United States, Washington, D.C. 1954. 51 pp.

Let's Drive Right. Halsey, Maxwell. Scott, Foresman and Company, New York, New York. 1954. 465 pp.

Man and the Motor Car. The Center for Safety Education, New York University. Prentice-Hall Publishing Company, New York, New York. 1954. 367 pp.

Manual on Uniform Traffic Control Devices for Streets and Highways. U.S. Bureau of Public Roads. Purchase from Government Printing Office, Washington, D.C. 1948. 214 pp.

Parking—How It Is Financed. Automotive Safety Foundation, Washington, D.C. 1952. 46 pp.

Parking Manual. American Automobile Association, Washington, D.C. 1946. 181 pp.

Parking Programs. American Automobile Association, Washington, D.C. 1954. 194 pp.

Traffic Engineering as a Profession. Holmes, Robert S. Eno Foundation for Highway Traffic Control, Saugatuck, Connecticut. Reprint, Oct. 1949 Traffic Quarterly.

Traffic Engineering Functions and Administration. Public Administration Service, Chicago, Illinois. 1948. 136 pp.

Traffic Tune Up. American Automobile Association, Washington, D.C. 1948. 19 pp.

INDEX

A

Acceleration
and car wear, 372
and getting out of a skid, 307
and skidding, 304–5
Accelerator Pedal, 103, 105, 112,
134
Accident(s)
and following distance, 269–70
and highway design, 423, 424–
8, 432–4, 456–7
and nature's laws, 190
and street lighting, 453–4
and traffic engineering, 440–42
and violations, 229, 260
at railroad crossings, 278–9
caused by alcohol, 45, 48
city and rural, 264
collision type, 201–3
costs, 14–15
day and night, 32, 43, 312
driver responsibility for, 253–6
driver responsibility in case of,
217–18, 379
effect of driver failures on, 255
in agricultural areas, 319–20
in winter months, 301
insurance against, 378–83
number of, 14
on deserts and plains, 318–19
railroad, 15
to pedestrians, 338–48, 453,
456–7
truck, 392
what to do in case of, 379, 380
Accident-Investigation Squad,
238, 239
Accident-Prone Driver, 75–6
Accident-Repeaters
re-examining, 221
Acuity, 22–4

Advancing Age
see Physical Condition of
Driver
Air
see Cooling System
Air Temperature
effect of on skidding, 305–6
Alcohol, 44–9
and cooling system, 375
and pedestrians, 348
and reaction time, 69–70
see also Physical Condition
of Driver, intoxication
American Association of State
Highway Officials, 422–3
American Automobile Association
Pedestrian Protection Contest
(table), 344
service calls, 330
American Bar Association, 48
American Medical Association, 48
Council on Pharmacy and
Chemistry, 70
American Trucking Associations,
Inc., 389
Ammeter, 98–9, 103
Angle Parking, 176–7
Animals and Animal Crossings,
321
Antifreeze Solution, 375
see also Cooling System
Appian Way, 420
Attention, 84–5, 264–5, 318–19,
433–4
Attitudes, 75–6
and car condition, 335
pedestrian, 351
social, 76
sportsmanlike, 87
toward pedestrians, 341
see also Driver(s)
Automatic Choke
see Choke